In Palamedes' Shadow

IN PALAMEDES' SHADOW

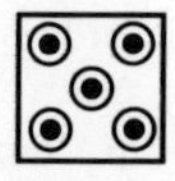

Explorations in Play, Game, & Narrative Theory

R. RAWDON WILSON

Northeastern University Press
BOSTON

Northeastern University Press 1990

Library of Congress Cataloging in Publication Data

Wilson, R. Rawdon.
In Palamedes' Shadow : explorations in play, game, and narrative theory / R. Rawdon Wilson.
p. cm.
Includes bibliographical references.
ISBN 1-55553-070-2 (alk. paper)
1. Literature—History and criticism—Theory, etc. 2. Play in literature. 3. Games in literature. 4. Narration (Rhetoric). I. Title.
PN81.W483 1990 89-48693
801-dc20 CIP

Designed by Ann Twombly. The ornamental devices were drawn by computer and based on the designs found on the playing board and pieces of the Royal Game of Ur, in the British Museum.

Composed in Trump by Graphic Composition, Inc., Athens, Georgia. Printed and bound by Princeton University Press, Lawrenceville, New Jersey. The paper is Heritage Book, an acid-free sheet.

MANUFACTURED IN THE UNITED STATES OF AMERICA
94 93 92 91 90 5 4 3 2 1

To
PACO
Artifex Ludorum

the rules of the game stipulate you may only pass through where you have not yet passed previously
mind hero
maze only a topological idiot begins at the middle but there he would start at the minotaur king
ways mirrored seek
wind clearest supercalifragilisticexpialidocious the initiation into absolute realities lost
into drear and winding can tricks mute
form muddy always miscomprehensions internal despair many win myriad trials awry
amid murky as labyrinthine tortures ways the errors misery path
word foggy situational inclinations grace counterproductivity big abound memory gone
play angry if stress but as one misted spaces agee
with alone it blackens now honorificibilitudinitatibus at but in the gloomy dire
wise as be for led out from an not silent abject sand
wits misapprehensive any low way sesquepedalian what oh tie enigma terror lead
also all dim for him septuagenarian will we the around losing away
amusements yet for way you for transmogrifies be do end puzzle string from
atrocities who any far who web fear not so bend middle wall
perturbing may shy out did and into o for of in inoperative mischief catacombs
involution bay sly bet net bull a him no a nearer
disturbing buy particularities her minotaur but inconsequanciality often page danger
intimation cry perhaps let id for as nor lame darker
omnivorous out wayward Ariadne's magic thread the if reappearances one weak vaster
dismayings woe mishaps one it so how nor face deeper
amazements all apprenticeship for the neophytes who be be if all two is always
heed day being to can in it it can but by confused
need lamenting paths an amplification of be win an be pan ten us dismayed
want gnashings found fun dry in his ambidextrous out for as diffused
loss tormented along yet Theseus wry it way tauromachian ill the we huddle
fail innerness route not old as out yet man hide wonder
fall hint angle new misanthropist in ambivalently in the last who bump wander
lame that mythifying but or in an eschatological had hunt pander
lose near miraculous old by can it incorrigible Shakespeherian set miss simper
limb here intramural age an one entrancement venerabilities out muse dodder
slip were meddlement can id outsmart with no exit overwhelmingly the fade weep
slop some try be Daedalus of map bended sift
mere gravel blind blunderers on antidisestablishmentarianist overambitiously waning flop
atom an architectonic to as away
floccipaucinihilipilifications anomic bewilderments misunderstand phantasmagoria if slip
find vagary underhandedly mystery in hope
flay the loss of the spirit as an illusion in the act of creation history honeycomb near
slay concealedly ends
or like its maker and his son make wings of feathers with wax and fly toward the sun and escape thus

Jon Whyte

Contents

Acknowledgments

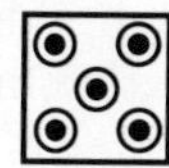

THIS BOOK springs from a longstanding interest in narrative entrapment. John Fowles's notion of a godgame, a narrative situation in which one character exercises its superior cunning to entrap other characters, interested me, but I had never thought to seize upon the game element in the word to prompt an expanded investigation. The conceptual shift from an interest in Fowlesesque godgames to games in literature generally came rather abruptly a number of years ago when I observed my son, Paco, to whom this book is dedicated, working on a ninth-grade English project. He was studiously transforming Thornton Wilder's *Bridge of San Luis Rey* into a board game. His English teacher did not care much for the finished game (preferring, it seemed, posters and collages), but I was struck by the clarity of its oblique claim: symbolic structures can be, as every narratologist should know, transposed into other, even radically different, structures. A spark flying from that ninth-grade project fired my fascination with games, both as symbolic structures in themselves and as models for those other symbolic structures we call literature.

I owe many people, friends, colleagues, and students, a great deal for their help in the development of my ideas about play, game, and narrative. Helena Fracchia gave me useful advice in the early stages concerning Classical literature and Latin grammar. In particular, she introduced me to Mary Grant's translation of Hyginus's fables. My colleague Shirley Neuman gave invaluable intellectual help in the formulation of ideas when I was first beginning to think about this project. I must thank the English Department of the University of Alberta, which, in inviting me to give the annual Edmund Kemper Broadus Lectures, allowed me a public forum in which I could tease my ideas into tentative formal shapes. I wish also to thank Pauline Carroll, who arranged for me to be a visiting scholar at the State College of Victoria (Toorak) in Australia so that I could present a series of public lectures on the topic of play and game theories in literature. This second opportunity to shape formally the ideas behind this book was extremely stimulating and helpful. The administration and staff of the college, and especially its head at that time, Norman Currie, made my extended visit both profitable and pleasant. Above all, I want to thank my former colleagues at the University of Melbourne, who crossed Melbourne's rush-hour traffic (through a drizzling Victorian winter) to attend my lectures and offer combative interventions. I owe intellectual debts to Howard Felperin, Peter Steele, Brian Edwards (who drove the nearly one hundred miles from Deakin University to be there), and the late, profoundly missed, Vincent Buckley, all of whom came to each of the lectures. From each I learned important lessons. Vincent Buckley hammered insistently at my formal distinction between play and game, urging me always, when I seemed most charmed by an abstraction, not to trust wholly even my sharpest formulations. Howard Felperin continually reminded me to stick closely to what I knew best (literature) and not to wander uncertainly in the discourse of the social sciences. He also advised me, fruitfully as it turned out, to pay more attention to Derrida and the significance of free play in the effort to get things straight. Peter Steele reminded me, as he continues to do, that play is an essential and recursive aspect of all human existence. Shirley Neuman, who was also present, criticized my thinking with her customary, and always rewarding, tenacity. No single event was as important to the early formation of the discussion of play/game theory in this book as that series of public lectures at Toorak. I should like to thank Edward Milowicki and his colleagues at Mills College who have made it possible, more than once, for me to visit that idyllic campus to present papers on the aspects of the argument of this book to the students and faculty.

I owe a great deal to several individuals who aided me in the analysis of specific problems. Aritha van Herk introduced me to the exciting scope of ficto-criticism and, by extension, ficto-theory. Suzette A. Henke, in conversation as well as through her book *Joyce's Moraculous Sindbook: A Study of "Ulysses,"* corrected my normal inclination towards literary formalism and made me aware that an attention to the interiority of literary texts, the dimension of consciousness, should be inescapable. Doreen Maitre, who wrote *Literature and Possible Worlds,* introduced me to the possibilities of possible-world theory. My colleague Uri Margolin, whose varied interests in literary analysis seem repeatedly to parallel my own, has been constantly a reminder that I should strive for the clarity and precision that all applications of narratology and textual semiotics demand. MaryLynn Scott helped me immensely in the evocation of Parisian street scenes. Brian Edwards, from halfway around the world, has contributed greatly to my thinking on all aspects of play/game theory, criticizing (even reviewing occasionally) my writings and sending me his own (which I have taken as an important intellectual resource). A number of students have also helped me in providing information and in making constructive suggestions. I should like to thank especially Diane Chisholm (now a colleague), Gerald Wandio, Alan Knight, Don Perkins, Robert Einarsson, Elizabeth Hollis Berry, and Brad Bucknell. I also owe a particular debt of thanks to Aischa Gaboune, who read the first typescript version of this book and corrected many infelicities in both English and French. Jon Whyte has generously allowed me to reprint his labyrinth poem from *Open Spaces* as the epigraph to this book.

Several parts of this book appeared first, often in very different form (even sometimes drawing rather different conclusions), in scholarly journals. I should like to thank the editors of all the journals in which an early version of a part of this book appeared.

The *Canadian Review of Comparative Literature/Revue Canadienne de Littérature Comparée* published early versions of Chapter 1 and a section of Chapter 4.

boundary 2 published "Ludopolites," now section IV of Chapter 2, in volume 15 (Fall 1986–Winter 1987): 323–42.

Open Letter published some of the material that now makes up Chapters 2 and 4.

The *South Central Review* published an early effort to work through the argument of Chapter 3.

An early version of Chapter 6 appeared in *English Studies in Canada* 12 (June 1986): 138–62. Copyright © 1986 by the Association of Canadian University Teachers of English. Reprinted by permission of the Association.

A part of Chapter 4 originally appeared in *Mosaic* 14 (December 1982): 1–22.

A part of Chapter 2 originally appeared in *Mosaic* 19 (Winter 1986): 73–89.

In Palamedes' Shadow

CHAPTER 1

Palamedes' Discourse

There is a story which I have used before and shall use again: A man wanted to know about mind, not in nature, but in his private large computer. He asked it (no doubt in his best Fortran), "Do you compute that you will ever think like a human being?" The machine then set to work to analyze its own computational habits. Finally, the machine printed its answer on a piece of paper, as such machines do. The man ran to get the answer and found, neatly typed, the words:

THAT REMINDS ME OF A STORY

A story is a little knot or complex of that species of connectedness that we call relevance.

—*Gregory Bateson,*
Mind and Nature: A Necessary Unity

THE FIGURE OF THE HERO Palamedes looms over anyone who invents, plays, or discusses games. Within the compass of his shadow, elongated but obscure, stand all the human activities that can be called games or gamelike. (For the Western mind, all human productivity may be seen, as metaphor or as archetypal resonance, to stand within the shadow of some archaic figure: Dionysus casts his shadow over freedom and carnival as well as drunkenness; Hermes, over theft and literary interpretation.) Consider the following anecdote.

A few years ago a scholar returning from a conference in Australia found himself stranded in Fiji. The plane in which he had been traveling had lost an engine and, after a relatively smooth landing, was forced to wait on the tarmac at Nadi until a new engine could be flown from Sydney. The passengers were lodged in a hotel near the airport, but (since they were not told how long they might have to wait) they were confronted with an acute problem of how to occupy themselves. Restless, filled with anxiety, knowing that at any moment they might be called to board the plane, they wondered how to pass their time. One of the passengers observed that they were in the situation of sailors aboard a becalmed sailing ship waiting for the wind to blow. The scholar reflected that, odd as it might seem, passengers aboard a 747 and sailors of a former time can have much in common and, as well, that a lost engine and an absence of wind both result in the need to occupy oneself while all activities are open to instant truncation.

The scholar realized that there is a class of games which seems especially suited for stranded passengers and becalmed sailors: simple games that, demanding some skill and some concentration (but only *some*), are played with shells, pebbles, sticks, holes, and words. Since he knew a few of these games (relics of previous becalmed conditions), he found himself, almost inadvertently, teaching them to his fellow passengers. A group sat around the bar of the Dominion International Hotel and played, following his instructions, games of acrostics, anagrams, charades, crambo, mancala, nim, palindromes, puzzles, riddles, and many varieties of simple wordplay. When, more than two days after they had been forced to land, they received a brusque summons to leave for the airport, one of the passengers observed to the scholarly gamewright that he had been very resourceful—as resourceful, he reflected, as Palamedes must have been.

With his minimalist games, the scholar had done for some stranded travelers on Fiji (filled time, cut through restlessness, busied them all toward a fresh wind) much as Palamedes had done for the Achaeans when their war fleet was becalmed at Aulis. Palamedes seems a fittingly elusive figure to have lent his shadow to a minor gamewright: he is said to have added four letters to the Greek alphabet and to have invented lighthouses, measures, the discus, and dice games. He possesses, in his cleverness, an important qualification for any gamewright, but he is destroyed by the greater cleverness of another hero, Odysseus. Like play and game concepts, Palamedes eludes a fully exhaustive account.

In his study of Attic black-figure vases, J. D. Beazley comments on a vase by Exekias that shows the heroes Achilles and Ajax playing a kind of backgammon (a game of both skill and chance): "The ingenious hero Palamedes . . . invented various games to while away the long hours at Aulis; one day at Troy the two chief champions of the Greeks, Achilles and Ajax, became so absorbed in their board-game that they did not hear the alarm, and before they looked up the Trojans were in the Achaean camp."[1] This tale points directly toward two important ideas.

First, games may be invented by one person but played by others; that is, a structure in the mind of one person can be absorbed, digested, and become the temporary structure of another's mind. (Hence as logically primitive modes of textuality, games pose the problem of intertextuality with paradigmatic clarity: each game exists in a field of other games of which some, like Ashtapada or the Royal Game of Ur, are forgotten except for their surviving boards and pieces—museum stuff—but many possess fully known rule structures and histories of their playing. Every move, every roll of dice, every strategy and tactic in a game calls to mind others, replicating or modifying them. Games define themselves, much as literary texts do, through a containing, though never fully visible, field of echoes and resonances.) The analysis of games, like the analysis of textuality, never entirely escapes the dual problem of structure and field. There are few constitutive rules and many permutations. Yet the permutations of play within a particular game never exhaust the possibilities of the rules. Like texts, games invisibly recall other games, replicate them (often unconsciously), and build upon them in such matters as improving skills, developing better strategies, and creating more sophisticated play.

Second, games are, or can be, absorbing; that is, they pull the minds of the players into them and function preemptively and exclusively. In the scene depicted on Exekias's vase, Achilles and Ajax, to borrow Bernard Suits's exemplary phrase, are locked into a "lusory attitude": they have accepted the rules of backgammon in an exclusionary manner. It might be said, playing somewhat loosely with Suits's definition, that the lusory attitude of players "formulates the playfulness of game-playing . . . it is the player's state of mind that makes the rules of a given game acceptable and allows him to engage in an activity that has been made, by the rules that have established it, a purposefully inefficient manner of obtaining certain ends. When a lusory attitude has taken over, the mind might be said to have shaped itself parasitically upon the body of the rules."[2] The disparate problems of intertextuality and intersubjectivity, apparently mutually displacing though actually inextricable, cling tenaciously to any analysis of game and play concepts.

Not only must a considered discussion of game and play take into account the problems of structure, field, intertextuality, and the psychology of play (the attitudes of gamewrights, players, and kibitzers alike), but it must note the paradoxical relationship of Palamedes to the two greater heroes whose play he makes possible: he serves others, but he also masters them. Achilles and Ajax have taken into their minds an aspect of his, something of his making, and have abandoned something of their ordinary poise, their habitual alertness to reality. (As Johan Huizinga remarks, "The arena, the card-table, the magic circle, the temple, the stage, the screen, the tennis court, the court of justice, etc., are all in form and functions play-grounds, i.e., forbidden spots, isolated, hedged round, hallowed, within which special rules obtain."[3]) Games constitute blocks of conceptual space within which skills, and hence mastery, are exercised and tested. Palamedes, as a gamewright, may claim a dominant, if merely contingent, superiority over the players whom his intention serves. Structure, field, intertextuality, play psychology (brilliantly, if fleetingly, caught in the self-absorption of play), and mastery are among the recursive problems around which all discussion of play/game theory must thread itself.

Palamedes is not merely clever, an inventor and a gamewright, he is also a trickster. In the *Republic*, Plato has Socrates comment, "Palamedes, whenever he appears in a tragedy, proves Agamemnon ridiculously unfit to be a general. Did you never remark how he declares that he had invented number, and had numbered the ships and set in array the ranks of the army at Troy: which implies that they had never been numbered before, and Agamemnon must be supposed literally to have been incapable of counting his own feet—how could he if he was ignorant of number."[4] Such arrogance bodes an abrupt end. And, indeed, Palamedes' end, brutal and unfair, stems directly from one of the triumphs of his cleverness. The story is told in two of the fables of the late Roman fabulist Caius Julius Hyginus.[5] In the first, Hyginus recounts how Agamemnon and Menelaus traveled to Ithaca to persuade Odysseus to join the Achaeans in the war against Troy. Odysseus has been warned by an oracle that (as did occur) he would return home only after twenty years, alone, needy, and having lost all his comrades. To avoid having to join the Achaean host, he pretends madness. He yokes a horse and an ox to a plow and pretends to work a field before the visiting heroes. Palamedes guesses that Odysseus is feigning madness, however, and takes Telemachus from his cradle and throws him in front of the plow. Odysseus swerves and as a consequence is constrained to join the other Achaeans in the conquest of Troy. From that time, Hyginus observes, Odysseus was hostile to Palamedes. In the second fable, Hyginus shows Odysseus besting Palamedes through his superior cleverness. He tricks Agamemnon into moving the Greek camp for one day, uses the interval to bury gold under the floor of Palamedes' tent, and then arranges for a Phrygian captive to be killed while carrying a forged letter purporting to be from Priam to Palamedes and offering, if Palamedes will betray his comrades, the precise sum of gold that had been secretly buried beneath his tent.

Cunningly entrapped, Palamedes is accused of treason, the damning gold is discovered, and he is put to death before the entire army.

These rather spare indications of Palamedes' accomplishments and end tell a plain tale: inventiveness can be outinvented; every player can be outplayed. The typical arrogance of gamewrights and players should be viewed ironically: anyone can be beaten, for, in the world of games, invincibility is impossible. Palamedes is beaten by a superior trickster, himself a gamewright (who creates, for example, the game of "no one" for Polyphemus to play), who, to bring about Palamedes' downfall, constructs a godgame of deep strategy. In Odysseus's godgame, Palamedes becomes a mere player and a losing one.[6] The shadow that Palamedes casts forward upon all subsequent games, their players and theorists, contains some obscurities that are darker than others. The subject is both illusive and elusive: it opens to many different modes of analysis, toward countless subordinate problems, after mare's nests, up *faux fuyants*, occasionally into genuine discovery.

The concepts of play and game (separable in English but always twinned) have come to play important roles in contemporary literary discourse. It sometimes seems as if George Steiner's dictum "All literature is play"[7] has been widely (if not universally) accepted and all that remains for criticism to do is to derive, or wring out, the consequences. The problem of critical discourse might be seen as a series of questions about play asked on the empirical level of particular texts: who is playing? with what? by what (or whose) rules? to what ends? with what degree of skill? Alternatively, the critical questions may be transformed into queries concerning games: what game is this? where did the author find it? did he invent it? who else plays this game? what is its goal? what are its constitutive rules? what patterns, modes of order and disorder, does it manifest? in what does winning consist? must someone always win? Questions about play and game (applications, definitions, analyses, models—an entire alternative discourse in its own right) can always assert themselves, often as if nothing else obtained. In some critical discourse play and game concepts seem to behave like magic motifs in traditional folk literature in that, like an endless sausage, an unstinting goose, or an unemptiable bowl, they not only dominate the other elements in the scene but are ontologically inexhaustible, swallowing, like black holes, all other analytic lexica. Once one has the concepts of play and game firmly in hand, it might appear unnecessary to talk about anything else and, for that matter, anything else may be talked of in precisely those terms. Play and game can fill the conceptual horizon.

Although typologies of play and game concepts have been constructed (most significantly, perhaps, the one that Roger Caillois provides[8]), the history of these concepts has not been written. Such a history, if written, would prove to be virtually coextensive with Western thought. At least since Heraclitus philosophers have brought play and game concepts into their discourse. If play has normally been underesteemed as a human activity (devalued by the doubtful antithesis between it and seriousness and by the narrow assumption that it is, at best, "merely" play), it may have been overesteemed in the past two centuries. The unwritten history of play and game concepts would probably reveal that, since Immanuel Kant, nearly every thinker who has thought seriously about human life and its institutions has made some contribution to making the subject more complex. Individually or in its historical collectivity, as a cultural or a psychological phenomenon, as an irrational motion from the unconscious, or as an abstract expression of conscious ratiocination, there does not seem to be any aspect of human existence untouched by play and game. The interest in play/game theory, cutting across the boundaries of several disciplines, can be viewed as a confluence of distinct lines of analysis and of dissimilar preoccupations.

In any contemporary discussion, a number of ways of formulating the problems of play/game theory are likely to have run (or flowed) together from ordinarily remote sources. This study will attempt only a partial disentangling. The chief burden of the discussion will be to identify and analyze some phases of the analogy between games and literary texts and (a somewhat different matter) between play and both textual production and reception. Even though this study will not exhaustively examine all eight categories of game and play models that follow, it is important to identify them and to indicate the ways they direct distinct formulations of game and play. Aspects of each of these models will play recursively through the subsequent discussion, helping to focus conceptual difficulties.

First, there is a philosophical tradition, dating back to classical times, that treats play as an important, or as an exclusive, mode of education, as *paideia*. In particular, games can be seen as educative. Children learn the values of their culture through games. The constitutive rules of children's games transpose the goals and norms of their culture into a parallel, alternative, or (even) "golden" world of simulation, make-believe, and playfulness. Children may be said to rehearse the social roles that, outside of games, they will someday play in total seriousness. Roles, toys, playthings, even the patterns of games, can be regarded as practice for adult life or as stages in the indoctrination of cultural values. Erik Erikson, for example, observes that if "childhood play seems extraterritorial to the verifiable facts and responsible acts of adult reality, it is only that playing and learning are the child's business."[9] Similarly, George Herbert Mead argues that in games children learn social responsibility (that is, their "business"), to relate to others, and to integrate themselves within social collectives. The child who plays in a game, Mead writes, "must be ready to take the attitude of everyone else involved in that game." Mead goes on to remark that in games there are sets of responses among players "so organized that the attitude of one calls out the appropriate attitudes of the other," the child player's nonself.[10] (Mead's model of educative play has not, clearly, appealed to everyone: Christopher Lasch writes that games "quickly lose their charm when forced into the service of education, character development, or social improvement."[11]) Not only is it possible to see play and game concepts within the perspective of education, socialization, and cultural indoctrination, but, as a simple converse function, it is also possible to judge social institutions, or particular cultures, by the kind and degree of play they permit. Thus Oswald Spengler insists that "genuine play" is no longer possible in a "worldcity" (of whatever civilization) but only degenerate games that "strain" after pleasure.[12] In *Homo Ludens*, Huizinga argues that play is a measure of civilization and that, in Europe at least, the range and scope of the play element have diminished as civilization has advanced. Lasch, too, follows a Spenglerian line of analysis both in claiming the importance of games and sports as indexes of a culture's well-being and in finding contemporary North American play trivialized by "a breakdown in the conventions surrounding" sports and other public games.[13] Play, in this perspective, is inherently serious.

Second, another philosophical tradition, reaching back at least as far as Friedrich Schiller, holds that play is both central and fundamental to human experience because it is in play that human beings manage to realize themselves or, put somewhat differently, to make real their highest ideals. This seems to be what Schiller means when he argues, in *On the Aesthetic Education of Man in a Series of Letters*, that only in play is man fully himself (fifteenth letter).[14] The drive to play mediates between two other basic "drives," toward the material and the formal, or the empirical and the ideational (as Kant formulated the opposition) and allows the actualization of human thought. Play is, thus, the vehicle of human expression and the foundation of all aesthetics. Schiller's insistence upon the centricity of play, or the play drive (*Spieltrieb*), has had a continuous line of succession: psychologists, philosophers, and historians, such as Huizinga, have argued that play is fundamental, or that it represents the zenith of human potential, or that human culture is based on play. In all versions of Schiller's argument, play is conceived of as spontaneous, exploratory, constructive, and creative. "Man's playing," Kurt Riezler writes, "is his greatest victory over his dependence and finiteness, his servitude to things."[15]

Third, psychoanalysis has deepened and complicated all literary theory, but it has had its greatest impact in making available a generalized psychic model that posits an unconscious as a powerful (even scheming and cunning) agent that influences and may even control totally all conscious surface manifestations. In this sense, the unconscious may be said to play through its surface manifestations or, in a somewhat stronger formulation, to make a game out of the conscious mind. In a postpsychoanalytic context, critics have taken the obscurity of motivations for granted as well as the authentic intelligibility of apparently (on the surface) nonmotivated behavior such as laughter, dreams, hysteria, or madness. If human language is the playground of the unconscious, each literary text will be particularly so. Surface wordplay, for example, will reveal unconscious connections, displacements, and condensations of meaning that are invisible from the opaque surface of consciousness. Thus Sigmund Freud seeks the origins of art in the artist's daydreams and private fantasies. These are, he observes, "the raw material of poetic production, for the creative writer uses his daydreams, with certain remodelings, disguises and omissions, to construct the situation which he introduces into his short stories, his novels or his plays. The hero of the day-dream is always the subject himself, either directly or by an obvious identification with someone else."[16] One may take other psychological positions or replay Freud through reinterpretations (Jacques Lacan's, for instance), but the chief point will remain: the surface is a gamelike, rule-derived manifestation of the unconscious. In this visible game constituted by invisible rules, the illusive surface manifests the results of exploratory and creative activity played out in the dark latency of a hidden mind.[17]

Fourth, a great deal of the current fascination with play and game concepts centers around the idea of role-playing (or role-simulation) games. The "actions that a man might play" turn out to be diverse. The most extended sense of role-playing, make-believe, is what Schiller had in mind when he described human beings as most fully realizing themselves in play. In the Schillerian view, play is a sublime form of sour grapes. Children make believe in their play, but the fictions they create and impose upon themselves are to them true. The play of make-believe (alternative, compelling, self-enclosed) takes the place of reality. And in this model of play, it probably amounts to a more than fair exchange. Art, the most extreme development of make-believe, is also a believed and accepted alternative to nature. It does not merely improve on nature, detailing its potential idealities, as Renaissance literary theorists such as Philip Sidney frequently argued, but actually replaces it, in an act of psychological displacement, with a better and more acceptable world. Play is both idealistic and sour grapes. This idea is open to strong formulations. A single instance illustrates the point: Eugen Fink writes that play "can be experienced as a pinnacle of human sovereignty. Man enjoys here an almost limitless creativity, he is productive and uninhibited because he is not creating within the sphere of reality. The player experiences himself as the lord of the products of his imagination—because it is virtually unlimited, play is an eminent manifestation of human freedom."[18]

Analogous, if less forceful, versions of the Schillerian argument can be found throughout European philosophy and psychology. Even when the category of role-playing is assimilated to the category of *paideia*, of learning, directed or undirected, it retains Schillerian undertones. For instance, Jean Piaget writes, "Practically every form of psychological activity is initially enacted in play. . . . Cognitive activity thus initiates play, and play in turn reinforces cognitive activity."[19] Piaget is still Schillerian (though rather Rumpelstiltskin in appearance) in his insistence on the cognitive and constructive side of play and its really-the-case status. But it is possible to separate the concept of role-playing from Schillerian associations so as to examine it as a number of specific activities, carried on at all stages in human life, that are context-dependent. Thus social institutions (education, marriage, work, leisure, and so forth) may be analyzed into the particular roles that constitute them. The role is not the actual person, who may be conceived of as either hiding behind the role or being composed of many different roles that are brought into play in discrete contexts, but the mode of the person's existence. It is even possible to create role-simulation games in which trained behavioral psychologists observe individual actions in artificial situations and draw practical conclusions concerning employment, job assignments, and promotion. Role-simulation games such as Dungeons and Dragons have been, for several years, among the most popular games being played in North America. They allow players to experience an open, ongoing, narrative situation in which a variety of roles may be lived from within an invented character's imagined experience with maximal openness and intensity, including at the level of advanced play the vast possibilities of cross-world identities (characters who cross from one game to another much as literary characters are sometimes thought to cross textual boundaries). It might be argued that all games permit this living-from-within experience, as in chess one may feel that one "is" a Knight or a Queen, say, but the charm of highly complex role-simulation games lies in the combination of openness and imaginative detail that massively promotes the free, exploratory, and creative dimension of play.

Role-playing may be both a mode of education and a vehicle for self-expression. Either model of what role-playing entails can provide a basis for literary analysis, but the latter, since one of the most typical situations of traditional realism has been to show characters struggling against the restrictions of society and socially imposed roles toward greater self-realization and expression, seems to be most fruitful. Furthermore, role-playing often hides the secret advantage of master illusionists: characters who, like Shakespeare's villains, bamboozle their victims by the impenetrable roles they gracefully assume. Role-playing is a necessary element in literary godgames.

In literary criticism, the concept of role-playing can lead to a global analysis of texts based entirely on one or more distinct premises: (1) that characters play roles; (2) that characterization is nothing but complexes of roles; (3) that characters are latent aspects of the author's self now being played out indirectly but publicly; and (4) that characters are unfilled roles waiting on the reader's exploratory playfulness. The distinction between an apparent, but merely surface, identity and an inapparent, but real, unconscious seeking its own (coded and disguised) manifestation can be reformulated as the active compulsion, driving up from inaccessible depths, to try on roles, to hide behind pretense, to define and redefine oneself differently, or to expose more of the actual human reality than could be captured in any single role. This reformulation of the generalized psychoanalytic model reflects the impact of Jungian analytic psychology on characterization in modern literature. Characters in novels by Hermann Hesse, Patrick White, Doris Lessing, Robertson Davies, and many others display this wholly positive, metamorphic play of the unconscious in conscious life.[20]

Fifth, since Ludwig Wittgenstein's *Philosophical Investigations* (1952), the significance of which it would difficult to overestimate, there has been a widespread tendency to subject all human activity, including language, to an atomistic analysis in which the discrete parts may be called games. A game, in this sense, is a logically primitive activity that possesses its particular rule. Larger, more complex activities may be considered as composites of primitive games or as being themselves games. (A sentence might be a game in a particular context, but it presupposes the game of language.) What counts is that the activity can be isolated, that a rule can be identified which makes sense out of the activity (the absence of which would leave the activity either inexplicable or incoherent), and that some description, or formal account, of the activity can be given. A rule, then, would be particular and expressed by the activity it shapes. In such an atomistic analysis, rules derive their significance from the actual game in which they function (as, in general, meaning must be taken as a function of use). It is easy to see why this conception of game and rule should have proved so attractive to literary critics: atomistic analysis is close to the heart of literary formalism, it allows textual examination on the level of specific linguistic exchanges between characters, and it assimilates the discourse of the literary text to that of ordinary language. Thus it both fulfills the desire for mimesis that appears so often in literary criticism and tugs a forelock toward those academic philosophers who have, for the purposes of *their* discourse, privileged that mythical entity known as "ordinary language."[21] This limited, if powerful, model of game has reached its current apotheosis in various appropriations of speech act theory (the close analysis of language uses, particularly exchanges, between persons or, by analogy, characters) in literary criticism.[22]

Sixth, the invention of mathematical game theory has prompted application of its specialized terminology to a variety of activities. It may also promote the sense that games and, hence, all other semiotic activities, including literary texts, are essentially sequences of decisions (which can be mapped as "trees" of decisions taken or declined). Thomas Pavel's *Poetics of Plot: The Case of English Renaissance Drama*, for example, develops an extensive analytic mechanism, based on game theory, for the mapping and interpretation of dramatic plots. Pavel's analysis suggests that "plots as strategic clashes cannot be reduced to sequences of anonymous actions; a proper understanding of plot includes knowledge of the person or group who performs an action, the reason for it, and its effect on the overall strategic configuration."[23] That is, the plots of Renaissance dramas may be mapped as trees of decisions, but the decision also must be interpreted as an action taken by a character based on its knowledge of options and understanding of both alternatives and consequences. In many cases, the application of game theory to the analysis of choice, sequences of action, and plots may seem like an inaccurate extrapolation because game theory is based on the rationality of the decisions to be taken and assumes the knowability, or the total availability, of possible options. Neither games nor texts strike everyone as always so lucid, open, and available. Pavel may be seen as having constructed a provocative but overextended model for the analysis of dramatic plots or as having worked with unusually responsive materials. To the extent that literary criticism merely borrows the terminology of game theory (which is, in sum, the logico-mathematical analysis of rational strategies for decision making in certain restricted contexts) little seems to be gained other than a highly abstract jargon in which, for example, "zero-sum conflict" may displace a recognizable category such as Caillois's "agon," or many looser formulations of antagonism, as a descriptive phrase.[24]

The invention of game theory, however, does seem to have alerted critics to the possibilities of viewing literature as, in itself, a game to be played between an author and a reader. If it is thought of as a cooperative game (*not*, that is, a "zero-sum conflict") involving coordination rather than conflict, or a "mixed motive" game, then a line of analysis is opened on the side of textual reception, or reader theory. It is possible, as Elizabeth Bruss argues, to see literature as a form of game played, for the stakes of meaning, between author and reader on either a cooperative, mixed motive, or competitive order.[25] Many authors (Shakespeare, Cervantes, Sterne, Joyce, or Nabokov, say) seem characteristically playful in the creation of word games, allusiveness, parody, and the metafictional foregrounding of literary and rhetorical conventions: the essence of their seriousness, as Robert Alter writes of Laurence Sterne, is playfulness.[26] For this reason their writing seems to challenge the reader, for the "stakes of meaning," within a gamelike situation. Nonetheless, it does not seem possible to predict either the author's or the reader's moves. The rational strategy behind their "moves" remains intractably inaccessible, but that accessibility, precisely, is the rationale for game theory: its central purpose is to provide the basis for predictive models. Perhaps one might say that game theory has given literary criticism and theory an amount of jargon (of narrow utility) and a few suggestive metaphors.[27]

Seventh, the concepts of play and game appeal to writers and students of literature who argue that literary texts are both reflexive (or self-referential) and self-contained, always governed by their own distinctive rules. In this sense, literary texts are taken to be games because they follow from certain assumptions (which, with more or less precision, one may call "rules" or "axioms") that are not necessarily those of the world outside the text. The assumptions of a fictional, or "possible," world may be said to correspond to those of a game in that they restrict what may happen, delimit action, and make certain other things (character, incident, description, events, and existents) possible with a high disregard for what may be the case outside the text. Perhaps more exactly, text-specific assumptions are conventions that may be said to equal the rules of a game. Having granted the assumptions of literary texts, it may be argued that, as rigorously as the theorems of a geometry or the conclusions of any axiomatic system, a number of consequences are enabled. The conviction that literary texts follow from specific assumptions and that such rulelike assumptions may be changed freely, enabling strange literary potentialities, underlies the OULIPO: the collective project, cofounded by Raymond Queneau, to explore the potential of literariness by imposing gamelike conditions, in constructing specific rules prior to writing, upon its production.[28] The worlds of fantasy, in legends, romances, or science fictions, may be called games, or gamelike, simply because they begin with specific assumptions concerning what is possible (a flying horse, for instance, or a faster-than-light spaceship) and then draw out the narrative consequences. One scholar writing on the subject of fantasy notes the paradox at the heart of all fantasy: "To create an imaginative and imaginary world it is necessary to observe faithfully the rules of logic and inner consistency which, although they may differ from those operating in our own world, must nevertheless be as true to themselves as their parallel operations are in the normal world."[29] Such assumptions may be counterfactual, counterintuitive, unsupported by any body of knowledge extrinsic to the text, yet they will work, in observing "the rules of logic and inner consistency," adequately to establish the "world" of the text in which, as in a game, anything conceivable becomes possible. Fictional worlds are, as Félix Martínez-Bonati succinctly puts it, the "sphere of imaginary representation"[30] and, as such, limited by, and constructed within, the assumptions that imagination admits and grasps. Though one may call these worlds "possible," in deference to the lexicon of semiotics, it seems evident that many, if not most, are inherently impossible, unenactable, except in the imagination. Moreover, if fantasy is a game, it will not be difficult to show that *all* literature (because all literature will depend on its assumptions, and these will be both specific and selective, however ordinary, commonsensical, or "realistic" they may appear to be) is, in this sense, either a game or gamelike. The golden world of Renaissance literary theory and the playworld of Schillerian philosophy merge.

Eighth, it could be argued that the single most significant conception of play to have emerged in Western thought during the past half-century (since, say, Wittgenstein or Freud) has been delineated within poststructural textual analysis and, in particular, within deconstruction. Here the central play concept is Jacques Derrida's sweeping formulation of *jeu libre* (free play): both indefinitely capacious and a tool for clearing discourse, as neatly as a tabletop, of enclosing, restrictive concepts. Paradoxically, it may be said that *jeu libre* is so wide a concept that it is not a concept at all. If it is ontologically unbound[31] or as general as being itself (which it effectively replaces in Derrida's discourse), then it may be impossible adequately to formulate it. In reviewing *Of Grammatol-*

ogy James S. Hans writes that the concept (or nonconcept) of free play resists formulation: it is "precisely the continual working out of the relationship between various 'non-centers' and complete randomness."[32] Nonetheless, even if one were limited to the *via negativa* of absence in discussing free play, it should still be possible to indicate how the term functions, what claims are made for it in deconstructionist arguments, and how the model of textuality behind criticism undergoes transformations once free play has been postulated.

Although inclusive and recalcitrant to all formulation, free play has played a persistent, if anamorphic, role in Derrida's writing and in that of other deconstructionists. In "Structure, Sign and Play in the Discourse of the Human Sciences," Derrida argues that the field of free play excludes totalization: "Nontotalization can also be determined in another way: no longer from the standpoint of a concept of finitude as relegation to the empirical, but from the standpoint of *play*. . . . This field is in effect that of *play*, that is to say, a field of infinite substitutions only because it is finite, that is to say, because instead of being an inexhaustible field, as in the classical hypothesis, instead of being too large, there is something missing from it: a center which arrests and grounds the play of substitutions."[33] In *Of Grammatology*, he writes that one "could call *play* the absence of the transcendental signified as limitlessness of play, that is to say as the destruction of onto-theology and the metaphysics of presence."[34] Thus, though it may not be possible adequately to define the concept, Derrida seems to make it clear that free play is limitless, unlimited by any irreducible signified or transcendental concept that cannot be further decomposed, and that it manifests itself in the process of indefinite substitution. Play, considered as free play, lies beyond stable, centered structures, makes them untenable, decenters them, and deprivileges them. To say that it "lies beyond" falsely spatializes the problem. Even to say that free play precedes, or is logically prior to, must also falsify what appears to be an incompletely conceivable relationship. It is as a condition of its complex modalities that all signification (each signifier, every chain of signifiers, any supposable complex of signifiers, in whatever shifting relations to whatever signifieds) can be made to decompose, to decenter.

That signifiers exist in a field of substitution (an unbounded metonymy) is an idea that recurs persistently in Derrida: in his interview with Julia Kristeva, in *Positions*, he observes with great emphasis, in attempting to clarify the concept of *différance*, that there are only, in whatever direction, differences and the traces of traces.[35] This "open play of signification"[36] must be seen as both a universal condition of language and a universal effect: it is both an endless semiological linkage, a fabric of traces entailing other traces, and that which makes signification possible. In a deconstructive perspective, a writer (*scriptor ludens*, say) may be said to play only because the game of language plays through him. He plays because the system of language, which he seems to manipulate and perhaps actually believes that he masters, plays through him, both inevitably and as a matter of course. It seems much like saying that chess, or any game, plays through the players who play: the play system precedes the play, as the condition of *its* modality, and merely manifests itself in play.

Derridean free play has been very attractive as a conceptual tool for literary analysis. Free play has tended toward displacing all other play concepts in literary discourse, *as if* all play were free play and there were no other analytic task than to trace the play of substitutions from one signifier, or chain of signifiers, to another. The concept's appeal seems to lie in its protean applicability (*ex vi termini*, all texts must manifest free play and respond to a deconstructive analysis), in the awareness of mastery, of power over the text, that it gives the critic, and in the way it corresponds to the postmodern sensibility that sees literary texts as highly artificial constructs always already verging on dissolution and, in their pervasive reflexivity, mocking, parodying, and *playing with* their own conventions. It is certainly possible for a critic either to assume or to explore this presumed correspondence between the deconstructionist notion of free play and the postmodern commitment to reflexive self-parody.[37] Derrida (or his laughing absence) may be perceived everywhere both in contemporary critical writing and, more inevitably, in literary theory. Above all, it is free play, often alienated from its normal discursive context, that displays an irresistible charisma. Under the pressure that deconstruction exerts, it is possible for critics to achieve a "ludic recognition" of the critical models within which they work: deconstruction is "nothing other than language scepticism in the mode of play, an exacting and rigorous form of play, but play all the same."[38]

The eight models of play and game introduced in this chapter, at once distinct formulations of human playfulness and confluent lines of analysis, do not exhaust the current discursive complexity of the subject. They do suggest the intricate, perplexed, and attractive nature of play/game theory. Not only do play and game concepts slip in and out of many distinct perspectives, but (in their conceptual swirl) these perspectives are framed within uncertain boundaries. Education and role-playing, for example, though clearly separable, must often become interlaced since so much educative play is actually role-playing. (In role-playing, furthermore, the Schillerian claim is most precisely visible.)

Beyond the attempt to distinguish the models in which play and game have been considered, other complexities appear. The twinned terms possess an inordinate diversity and range in ordinary language as well as a large number of technical meanings.

The twinning of the terms in English does nothing to ease the burden of complexity. Consider the word *play*. We play musical instruments, odds, hunches, markets, hands, and roles as well as games. We habitually play not only with words but also with toys, fantasies, notions, ideas, possibilities, signs, signification, other people, and playmates. In the froth or exigencies of the moment, *anything* might become a plaything, played for high stakes, or for low, or simply for the fun of it. And (briefly to play a prepositional game) we play with, we play by, we play up, we play down, we play both beyond and within (the possibilities, the rules, what is permitted, one's expectations, the limits), we play on, we play back, we play through, we play over, we play under (the cover of, or simply the covers), we play at, we play for and from, we observe watchfully how "things" will play, and we commonly (alas) play out. Any activity or object can be playful; anything, even a game, can be transformed into a plaything; and anything can be either the subject or the object of play. It is possible, Bernard Suits writes, "to make a game out of virtually any other activity or practice, from driving to work in the morning to explaining a logical principle."[39] Someone else's game may become the object of our play as we playfully hypothesize absurd rules, obscure intentions, ludicrous goals, or (most seriously) place bets on the outcome. On long trips, children and reluctant parents often escape boredom by playing perceptual games watching for cows, horses, or cars of certain colors. Similarly, the dullest moments in an adult's life may be enlivened by inventing a rule that will promise a reward or transform mere tedium into the observation of possibilities. Clearly, many transformations of the ordinary into play are conceivable but not actually playable. A person driving to work in the morning through the predictably dense snarl of freeway traffic might decide to relieve his boredom by inventing a game of dodge-'em in which he rules that he will change lanes without looking and without signaling, and that, if he manages to do this five times without killing himself, he may declare himself "king of the freeway" and award himself an extra cold beer for lunch. Readers, within the comparative safety of the mind's eye, may transform texts into private games, reading in hopscotch fashion or inventing alternative fictional worlds, and there would seem to be nothing, either in the author's expectations or in the text itself, to prevent their doing so. (Frank Kermode speaks of the literary text as being "playful."[40]) What can so many diverse senses have in common? (No doubt there are those who would cry, "plenty!" or "everything!" or like benighted Cratylus in Plato's dialogue, they might answer quickly, "Why, they have 'play' in common!") Play is making and it is teasing: it is both a constructive and a deconstructive activity; it is purposeful and also random, pointed in opposite ways yet interbound.

Works of literature may contain games as, for example, Alexander Pope's *The Rape of the Lock* contains a game of *ombre*, and Lewis Carroll's *Through the Looking-Glass and What Alice Found There* and Vladimir Nabokov's *Bend Sinister* and *The Defense* contain chess problems. Julio Cortázar's *Hopscotch* exemplifies, as well as metaphorizes, the children's game of hopscotch that it encodes. Italo Calvino's *The Castle of Crossed Destinies* builds on the signifying possibilities of Tarot cards. Indeed, many works of literature, in many languages, contain actual games, versions of games, invented games, or extend the ordinary sense of an empirical game, as Cortázar does, toward metaphorical and metaphysical play without becoming that game. It is a simple requirement of empirical literary history to understand certain games.[41] Literary texts may contain all kinds of wordplay (or even, in Nabokov's term, mirrorplay), all of which need to be, at some level, explicated. In what is, perhaps, the widest sense of all, "any *playful*, self-conscious and extended means by which an author stimulates his reader to deduce or to speculate, by which he encourages him to see a relationship between different parts of the text, or between the text and something extraneous to it" may be called a "literary game."[42] These difficulties, all of which demand that the critic as well as the literary historian possess some understanding of games, cut through the various perspectives from which play/game theory has emerged.

The mere fact that literary texts may contain games does not imply that they must, in themselves, be games. A text might be constructed entirely out of games and not be a game, much as a philosophy (or a theology) might be built out of jokes and yet not be a joke. A writer might adopt the generative rule, for example, that, in true OULIPO fashion, every sentence in a short story will have to be a question: the resulting narrative, entirely in questions, would not itself be a question.[43] The claim that a literary text (any or all) is a game, or is a certain kind of play, or represents playfulness, is different from the assertion that literary texts may contain empirical games that require explication. There are a number of ways in which a text might be a game, and that it is a game in one sense will not mean that it is in any other sense. Hence all the problems inherent in the discussion of play return, distributed on several levels, hedged around by innumerable qualifications, and made more difficult by literature's distinctive elusiveness, when one asks, "Is literature a game?" (Is it only, or more than, a language game? Under what conditions is it a game? Can it be created, or received, as a game without being itself, *eo ipso*, a game? Can a text be *invented* as games are? Is it inevitably playful? Inevitably a game? Could it be one and not the other? If it is a game, does it have rules? Are rules different from conventions? How does one discover them? and so forth.) Clearly, when Palamedes invented games at Aulis, he solved one problem (idleness) by creating a category of problems that, tenaciously unyielding to solutions, continues to expand. His games, like nets, have been widely flung.

The purpose of this book is to explore the uses and the usefulness of game and play concepts to the study of literature and to the understanding of narrative in particular. Palamedes' fiefdom (or, perhaps, his playground) has been traveled before: since the watershed issue of *Yale French Studies* on "game, play, literature," the concepts of game and play have been invoked in many ways and have been turned to the analysis of all literary forms.[44] On the practical level, play and game often seem like incantations (or particularly bright feathers in the witch doctor's professional outfit), and even on the levels of metacriticism and literary theory a great deal of confusion between models is evident. Since 1968, when "Game, Play, Literature" was published, new approaches to the concepts have been suggested and at least one striking reformulation of the concept of play, that of *jeu libre*, has been introduced. (Derrida had given his paper "La structure, le signe et le jeu," at John Hopkins University in 1966, but the reverberations had not reached Jacques Ehrmann and the contributors to *Yale French Studies* in 1968.) Three other important global models of play that have appeared since 1968 are M. M. Bakhtin's theory of dialogism, and in particular the concept of carnival, which first reached English-speaking critics through the translation of his *Rabelais and His World* in 1968; Hans-Georg Gadamer's investigations of play as the fundamental mode of being in works of art, particularly in *Truth and Method*; and Bernard Suits's *The Grasshopper: Games, Life and Utopia*, which argues for a simple, lucid, and universal definition of "game."[45] The argument of this book will attempt to keep the ideas of Derrida, Bakhtin, Gadamer, and Suits closely in focus. Furthermore, the analytic concepts of textual theory (which is not exclusively Derrida's production) have a direct bearing on any contemporary discussion of play and game.[46] The concept of intertextuality, for example, first formulated by Julia Kristeva, postulates a discursive space between literary texts in which multiple texts coexist, collusively inscribing congruent and overlapping paths of signification.[47] This has become possible only because the concept of intertextuality follows upon, and reflects, the textual revolution in which literature has come to be seen as an indefinite body, related necessarily but invisibly, of systematic linguistic and rhetorical phenomena. Fundamental notions of traditional literary analysis such as citation, allusion, and parody lose their orthodox clarity once they have been transposed to subsets within the inclusive concept of intertextuality. It is possible to consider extended intertextual relations as modes of play or as being, in some inescapable manner, the "game" of literature itself. In the discursive space constituted by the concept of intertextuality, texts jostle each other, echo and reinscribe each other, even mutually create each other, in a complex process, not necessarily deliberate and conscious, that reaches either way on a linear time scale. To many students of literature, this has sounded like a mode of playfulness.

The argument of this book will accept the obligation to confront the implications of poststructuralist textual theory, but it will consistently uphold the position that, in recent years, the most important contributions to thinking about play and game have been those advanced by Bakhtin and Suits. *In Palamedes' Shadow* pursues several kinds of discussions. All are pointed toward clarifying the key terms, *play* and *game*, and all examine aspects of the analogy between literary texts and games, but they are unequally concerned with the theory of game and play as such. The analysis turns frequently upon the examination of specific literary texts. Some of these are drawn from the period of the Renaissance, some from the contemporary (or postmodern) period. This bracketing of modern literature between early and late phases tells no story. Texts from both periods, for whatever contextual reasons, are characterized by their rhetorical exuberance and intricacies. They are often narratively complex, involving time shifts, *mise en abyme* embeddings, abrupt shifts in focalization (and/or point of view), and they are rich in discontinuities and short circuits. Frequently, they are overtly metafictional. In other words, these texts provide a wide range of evidence for a discussion of how, and in how many ways, literary texts may be played, be playful, or be games. (The discussion will neither write a history of play and game concepts nor attempt to exhaust the topic's labyrinthine complexities: neither history nor exhaustion is intended.) The argument will return to many of the concepts identified in this chapter as making up the confluence of distinct preoccupations in the construction of play and game models. Role-simulation games, for example, and Schilleresque notions of play, as in Mead or Piaget, are never far from the topic being analyzed. Literary texts seem inevitably to be related to concepts about the workings of the imagination: make-believe, pretense, role, and fictional worldhood. Whenever the imagination operates in these modes, play must be present; when they are sustained, given a narrative structure, organized over a definite duration, a game may be present as well.

In Palamedes' Shadow analyzes a limited number of interconnected aspects of play and game insofar as these bear on the understanding of literary texts. The movement of the discussion is often oblique, breaking away from conceptual analysis to the intimations of parables and other illustrative tales, but the apparent discontinuities do not, one hopes, cloud the intellectual unity of the book. The discontinuities, abrupt shifts, or allegorical intercalations are intended to enhance the argument by showing, in concrete ways, both the elusive qualities of the topic and the close correspondences between play/game and narrative theory. The problems raised in narrative theory often appear to parallel those raised in play/game theory. The understanding of one can only be enhanced by an understanding of the other.

Chapter 2 examines two current notions of play, Derrida's free play and Bakhtin's carnival. The discussion focuses particularly on the usefulness of carnival as an analytic tool for textual analysis. Chapter 3 looks specifically at the analogy that has often been claimed to obtain between game and text. It discovers three crucial paradoxes in the analogy, at least to the extent that it insists on the equivalence of "rules" in games and "conventions" in literary texts. Conventions, it is argued, because they are flexible and open to great variation, can neither be rules nor, *a fortiori*, axioms. The assumption that they are essentially rigid and inflexible, as rules and axioms are (by definition), entails embracing a high degree of unnecessary paradoxicality. Chapter 4 investigates the notion of a "godgame" in terms of an underlying conceptual structure: the labyrinth. The chapter argues that godgames are transhistorical (Cervantes and Shakespeare create them as well as Jorge Luis Borges and Thomas Pynchon) but, even so, peculiarly attractive to late modernist and postmodernist writing. The discussion thus turns largely on the concept of a labyrinth, but also, since a transhistorical phenomenon (the godgame) seems to belong so closely to certain historical periods, it examines the notion of period and genre, sharing equally in the fundamental instability of all categories, and brings into the foreground an analysis of collections, particularly museums, and *their* distinctive illusions. Chapter 5 returns to the notions of rules and axioms discussed in Chapter 2. Here the argument examines the interiority of both the game and the reading situations. Both involve an inside to their experience: a capacity to feel oneself exclusively within the activity and to accept it, for the time being, as reality. The argument looks closely at such notions as fantasy, magical realism, fictional space, and fictional worlds. Conventions are argued to function *as if* they were axioms from within the interiority of reading literary texts (or playing games). Chapter 6 returns to the idea of play as a pervasive textual mode. The dominant concept is that of intertexuality. The chapter investigates modes of textual interplay: the ways in which text may be said to play with, off, or against each other. In an effort to show their interconnectedness, the final chapter reprises the main concepts of the book's discussion, returning specifically to the stories and other narrative embeddings that have built a structural pattern of shifting, oblique movements from one conceptual area to another.

The view of play and games from the Dominion International Hotel in Fiji is strange but fruitful. Play is seen to be at once fundamental to human activity and absolutely metamorphic; game, at once atomistic and total, voluntary but inevitable. The gamewright's task (to busy others toward fresh winds, to kill idleness, to invent rules to structure play) turns out to be simple. What game, after all, could be more ideally simple than "nim"? Yet the task is also complex. What game could function more complexly than does "nim" in Alain Robbe-Grillet's *L'Année dernière à Marienbad*? The gamewright's task seems always to be a fusion of elementary strategies and global models. When the crafty Palamedes flung the concept of "game" forward into Western intellectual history, he created an area of (and for) ludic exploration that has not yet been exhausted.[48] Reflection on the roles played by Bakhtin, Derrida, Gadamer, and Suits in play/game theory should indicate that good arguments ("contributions") only widen the ludic field further. The concepts of play and game are so fascinating, and so potentially useful, that it is worth the effort to think them through.

CHAPTER 2

The Play of Carnival and the Carnival of Play

To be is to do. —Aristotle
To do is to be. —Sartre
Do be do be do.
—Sinatra [Californian Graffito]

IN "THE LIBRARY OF BABEL," Borges conceives an infinite library: a boundless repository of all possible utterances. This elegant fiction imagines utterances to be organized according to an incomprehensible plan and an unknowable order. The order is presumed to exist: it may be sought, but it cannot be found. Physically, the library "is composed of an indefinite and perhaps infinite number of hexagonal galleries, with vast air shafts between, surrounded by very low railings. From any of the hexagons one can see, interminably, the upper and lower floors."[1] Borges's narrator continues with great emphasis, *"The Library is a sphere whose exact center is any one of its hexagons and whose circumference is inaccessible."*[2] The narrator is a librarian (who, indeed, has been born in the library), and his concern to understand the library seems natural: what *could be* the relationship of a librarian to the infinite respository of which he is one (of an unknown number) custodian? If there is an infinite number of utterances, what relationship could a mere custodian, a librarian, bear to this total universe of discourse? Faced with that question, one might feel much like Borges's narrator: puzzled, exploratory, haunted by futility, lost, baffled.

Students of literature confront a situation analogous to that in which Borges's narrator finds himself. Even if the sum of written utterances is not infinite (assuming for the moment the traditional logocentric distinction between speaking and writing), it is certainly indefinitely vast, inconceivably and immeasurably numerous. One's relationship to this totality must be always in doubt. Of course, a student may close himself within one of the available hexagons, inventing an order and a rationale for it, brightening it a bit with pleasant assertions that the other hexagons either do not exist or do not matter. Or, like Borges's narrator, he may make an attempt at exploration, try to puzzle it all out. The second student finds himself outside his hexagon, outside any of them perhaps, in the windy, cold, and comfortless spaces between the hexagons. This windy space is the necessary domain of literary theory. Unlike criticism, which may be conducted comfortably enough from within any hexagon, literary theory concerns the scope of the totality of utterances, the connections between them, the paths between the hexagons, and the unknowable order itself. Literary theory seems normally to be pursued in emptiness, in the realm of paradox and aporia, upon "the slippery groundlessness of discourse."[3] It is always a bit baffling. The problems of literary theory belong to the "vast air shafts," the empty spaces between hexagons.

Literary theory, it has been argued, is both "arbitrary and inescapable."[4] As anyone who has read in the subject over the past twenty years knows, it undertakes many tasks: providing metaphors (often startling) for the common activities of literary study, composing cross-references, and creating baroque networks of allusiveness. Above all, it creates models of how things might work, how texts might make sense, what might be the case. Literary theory seems always to coast a world of analogies that waits exploitation. It does its work of exploration in the spaces between the established, and carefully plotted, activities of literary studies. Searching for theory, one will discover it between the known hexagons.

If literary theory is an exciting undertaking, as so many contemporary students of literature believe, it is also an entirely normal aspect of literary studies. Everything has its theory or its theoretical dimensions: even as these words are being read, there are probably serious men and women discussing the theory of hangnails. In the study of literature, theory takes the shape of problems, of questions to be asked. It does not follow that these problems must be solved or that anyone could, except conditionally, solve them. Literary theory constitutes an optional investigation. The questions that theorists like to ask often strike one as being reasonable enough, even fairly ordinary, but not strictly necessary.

One can do a fairly good job in the study of literature simply sticking close to a familiar hexagon. Literary theory comprises a number of tough questions, as dry, and as interminable in discussion, as they may be conceptually exciting. Still, even if it is no more than a number of difficult questions that are askable, it would be difficult, though not quite unthinkable, to live one's life entirely on the level of theory. (Still, one might also reflect that Parisians have done precisely that for generations and that they do not seem any the worse for it. As Claude Lévi-Strauss might have said: Let them think cake.) It seems best to think of theory as an optional activity, though not necessarily marginal, to be carried on by those people who find literary texts interesting enough to interrogate.

On this humble level, prior to the theorist's ambition to formulate total views, global strategies, or tactical models, the concerns of literary theory are easy to identify. They appear as questions, certain exemplary problems or paradigmatic difficulties that can be isolated from their possible contexts in larger schemes and discussed for their own sake. What is a riddle? What relation does it bear to a puzzle? to an aporia? a paradox? a parable? Is there such a thing as paradoxicality? Should we pay attention to it if there is? How shall we recognize it? What is play? (Each one of the questions raised in the first chapter now returns as an instance of theoretical interrogation.) Are puzzles, aporia, paradoxes, and parables *play*? How does one play with a paradox? with a parable? The ordinary problems of literary theory often seem to come in elusive shapes. In the Borgesian metaphor of the air shafts, the pursuit of literary theory is rather like collecting vials of dust, small tapes of noise, slivers of random light: microsemes that fall through the interstices of utterance.

I

> The model has a considerable currency nowadays, though I should say that much of the play exhibited amongst the commentators is either elephantine or lugubrious.
>
> —Peter Steele, *The Autobiographical Passion: Studies in the Self on Show*

Like Maypoles amid their ribbons, certain concepts constellate others into cognitive networks based on affinity and kinship. The concept that creates the constellation (a family or, in a different metaphor, a network) becomes central, apparently originary, dominating and extending its influence over the subordinate concepts, holding them, however loosely, within its rule. To grasp any one of the concepts within the family, it will be necessary first to have grasped the ruling concept, yet the subordinate concepts in the extended family are also important for a better understanding. The paradox of the hermeneutic circle is evident: the whole cannot be understood without first understanding the parts; the parts, without first understanding the whole. Conceptual networks are instable and (as families) come together and drift apart. The process of constellation and reconstellation takes place over and over again. A ribbon may itself become, within a discourse that has undergone a paradigm shift, a Maypole. Families of concepts often extend and contract, by marriage and remarriage as well as by birth and death, and in so doing they acquire (or lose) cognitive affinities. That cognitive families periodically require new maps, or call for fresh cartographical expression, should not appear unduly surprising.

Play suggests an illustrative case. Drawing with it a number of subordinate concepts such as self-representation, make-believe, role, rule, move, strategy, tactics, aleatory combinations, and so forth, play has shifted from a descriptive vocabulary appropriate to the activities of children and the leisure of adults. It may be used as a model to describe and explain all kinds of human activity: learning procedures, social interaction, personal expressivity, cultural formation and transformation, as well as a wide range of activities that involve the creation and reception of works of art, simulation, dissimulation, risk-taking, strategic thinking, tactical decision making, structural experimentation, the testing or trying out of ideas.

The importance that play has assumed in recent literary criticism parallels the importance that it currently possesses in several of the social sciences, including psychology, sociology, and anthropology. The questions that one may ask concerning play correspond, roughly at least, to the different disciplines of the social sciences. Why do human beings play? Does the play of animals tell us anything significant about ourselves? What social gains are achieved through play? Can conflict be played? (What does conflict amount to when it is considered as play?) How are social roles played? Do roles actually constitute the human individual? What can we learn about other peoples and their cultures by investigating their distinctive forms of play? Mihai Spariosu accurately describes the radical exfoliation of play concepts: "While play has always had an important, if sometimes unthematized, role in art, its modern revival in science started with philosophy, at the end of the eighteenth century, and, after a short set-back with Hegel and Marx, it reached a new peak with Nietzsche and the neo-Kantians, gradually spreading, in the twentieth century, to the 'new', and not so new, sciences, such as biology, anthropology, psychology, education, sociology, economics, political science, modern warfare, cybernetics, statistics, philosophy of science, theology, etc."[5] Furthermore, under the reign of play concepts old questions may be asked in new ways. In any paradigm shift the questions to be asked undergo metamorphosis. For literary theory, the relevant questions about play are somewhat different from those in the social sciences (though for the pursuit of literary theory, *all* questions about play bear some relevance): Are texts playful? Is play important to, or even the foundation of, human creativity? Do authors play? Does (for example) Cervantes play with textual potential? with the allusive resonances of his text? with other texts? with narrative techniques? with his characters? with his readers?

Within the cognitive family now constellated by the concept of play, the subconcepts of transgression and carnival (sometimes, it seems, taken as synonyms) provide a narrowed field for investigation. Their apparent ordinariness hides perplexities of definition. They flow together in current usage from diverse sources: transgression from the discourses of law and morality; carnival from European social history, festivals and local fairs, playgrounds and holidays. Both have undergone significant deformations and both capture a surprising range of diverse phenomena in their current manifestations. In Derrida's theory of textuality, for instance, transgression is the mode of language itself. For Bakhtin, it amounts to no more than a move in the social transaction through which meaning is created, whereas carnival, always a privileged concept in Bakhtin, stands out as the preeminent expression, both historically and textually, of the dialogic (mutually transgressive) exchange. For Gadamer, transgression, if it had any precisely textual sense, would merely describe the ordinary to-and-fro movement that inheres in all playful activities ("we say that something is 'playing' somewhere or at some time, that something is going on"). Carnival, for Gadamer, would fall into perspective as a festival whose most important aspect would be neither its dialogic potential nor its momentary transgressiveness, but the way that each festival, in its playfulness, reveals the truth of its being, its present time experience as celebration, its repetitive human temporality.[6] The notions of play in the theories of Derrida, Bakhtin, and Gadamer will provide the boundaries for the discussion that follows.

As a constellating concept, play inevitably brings together a strange family: at the very least it implicates all the members of its family in the paracursive concepts of creativity, self-representation, make-believe, and paradoxicality. Since play is an older and more broadly reaching concept, both transgression and carnival fall within it (whether as family members or as parts of a network) rather as specialized subdivisions or as synecdoches. Nonetheless, as subconcepts of play, both transgression and carnival are available for cognitive tasks that have only recently become thinkable. Although it is not certain at what point *transgression* metamorphosed into a positive term within literary criticism (and theory), it is clear that as long as it remained a legal and moral concept only, it must have been essentially negative and, hence, normally a disapprobative term. As it approaches the concept of play, however, transgression begins to appear in a positive light. Brief reflection should indicate that play normally works important changes upon borrowed, or subsumed, vocabularies: the lethal terms of destruction, for instance, are not merely neutralized in play but become positively transformed into descriptions and predictions of skill and mastery as when, in chess or in football, one notes that certain moves are "crushing," "deadly," or that they will "wipe out," "destroy," or "kill" the opponent (in some languages, such as French or Spanish, one "eats" the opponent's pieces during boardplay, fiercely consuming them into nonexistence). One may suppose that critics of a neoclassical age would have considered a transgression to be a violation of decorum, or correct literary behavior, or the goodwill of the audience and, for all these reasons, legitimately open to chastisement and reprehension. After all, Horace begins the epistle to the Pisos with the advice not to transgress either convention or the audience's expectation. Derrida observes cunningly that transgression "is not thinkable within the terms of classical logic."[7] From the perspective of classical literary criticism, transgression, if its existence could be admitted, must seem to be violation, error, fallacy, crime, or madness.

In recent literary discourse transgression might be said to signify what is most valuable (that is, most literary) in literature. At the least, since dada, surrealism, and, in many of its ramifications, modernism, transgression has come to seem constructive: a way to upend, even (paradoxically) to kill, what is dead in literature. As a mode of literary experimentation, exploration, and mastery, play transforms transgression. Lubomír Doležel gives the current valorization of transgression a lapidary formulation when he writes that "in the domain of literature no norm is safe." There is, he continues, "a permanent process of norm modification, creation and destruction." One thread in the argument that runs through the essays in Alain Robbe-Grillet's *For a New Novel* holds that dull readerly audiences need to be shaken up and that conventions, at least those that have been handed down, are a form of bondage to be broken. Contemporary writers, Robbe-Grillet argues, know that "the systematic repetition of the forms of the past is not only absurd and futile, but that it can even become harmful: by blinding us to our real situation in the world today, it keeps us, ultimately, from constructing the world and man of tomorrow." Echoes of this dictum resound from many quarters. Transgression can—perhaps must—become the criterion by which to distinguish postmodern literature from its precursors. David Lodge, writing in a similar vein to Doležel, has defined postmodernism as "an essentially rule-breaking activity."[8] If a student of literature believes that the literature he likes best, or values most, or reads most readily, should be defined by its willingness to break rules, to be transgressive, then it is only a quick move to the stance that transgressivity, in its most plural and diverse potential, may be both positive and desirable: it breaks, frees, opens, makes possible both construction and reconstruction, and guarantees literariness.

To understand the concept that transgression has become in its escape from the rule of law and morality and concurrent subordination to play, consider four distinctions.

First, a transgression may be no more than a plot move, a device to free the action. As such, a transgression is simply an aspect of narrativity, a convention that shapes content in a certain way, and, as a conventional plot move, makes possible specific narremes. For example, in fairy tales and in many romances, an injunction or prohibition precedes a transgression, but the latter is narratively desirable because it frees the action. Without a transgression there could be no narrative, only a static world of prohibition. "Bluebeard," whether in Charles Perrault's version or Angela Carter's, does not simply turn upon the young wife's transgression of an (apparently) arbitrary prohibition; rather, it *is* transgression. There is nothing else wholly fundamental, narratively ineradicable, to the story. This is how transgression appears in Vladimir Propp's study *Morphology of the Russian Folktale* and in most structuralist analyses of narrative.[9] Obviously, transgressive plot moves function analogously in more complex narratives. In its narrative development, *Great Expectations* depends on Pip's willingness to transgress domestic rules so he can steal a pie for the terrifying stranger in the graveyard. Transgression can possess positive value on the level of narrative functions.

Second, transgression has been used to describe the force of certain narrative strategies with regard to the expectations of their readership. If readers are predisposed (and this seems likely) to recognize conventional treatments of known themes and to react strongly when they do not find them, then it is possible for an author to play against these predispositions. This is an evident mode of narrative playfulness, but it can also be vastly complex. For example, Marcel Proust's play with readerly expectations with regard to characterization (that it should be stable and supported by the principle of continuous identity), James Joyce's and Pynchon's with regard to narrative voice, or John Barth's with the notion of referentiality, all take their force from the premise that readers have expectations that may be baffled. To grasp this sense of transgression, one needs only to recall how Borges plays transgressively with such fundamental expectations of empirical experience as the size of libraries in "The Library of Babel," the linearity of time in "The Garden of Forking Paths," or the mere fictionality of fiction in "Tlön, Uqbar, *Orbis Tertius*." Similarly, to cite a central example for this discussion, Cervantes may be said to play transgressively with his readers' expectations with regard to the reliability of narrators not merely to exceed the bounds of their patience but to do so in a salutary manner since a reader can never be overinformed concerning the duplicities of narrators. In this second sense, the problem of transgression may be adequately expressed by a concept that Doležel employs in his analysis of Franz Kafka's "fictional world": that world is, Doležel argues, "hybrid" in that it allows for bizarre creatures and events. This hybridness in Kafka's narratives cuts against expectations concerning both the natural world and the supernatural world since it is, simply but following its own laws, both a space of visibility and invisibility.[10] Bizarreness, a function of the dual inscription of contradictory literary codes within a single discursive space, also marks, as will be seen in a later chapter, what has become known as "magic realism."

Third, transgression may describe an author's exploratory play with the body of conventions available at the time he begins to write. This is precisely how Christine Brooke-Rose uses the term in her *Rhetoric of the Unreal* when she analyzes Robbe-Grillet's novels. Rules are necessarily the matrix of transgression (anything can be made into a plaything, but only a rule structure can be transgressed) and, to the extent that textuality may be brought under the tempting analogy of game, literary conventions have sometimes seemed to behave much like rules. This point will be discussed more fully in the next chapter. Gérard Genette writes admiringly of Proust's "decisive transgression" in making so much of his narrative turn upon (what, relative to the norms of "mimetic theory," Genette calls) the paradox of "mediated intensity." Elsewhere, bearing in mind Proust's general transgressiveness, Genette writes that Proust inaugurates "the limitless and indefinite space of modern literature."[11] In this third sense, transgression actually constitutes the freedom to write: it is the essential aspect of the literary text's openness, its dialogism, and its creativity.

If one accepts the basic distinction between story and discourse (or *fabula* and *sjužet*), then any deviation from chronological time in the disposition of an actual narrative will seem, inevitably, transgressive.[12] Though never full, story time is sequential and follows the event-by-event sweep of human clocks; discourse time perturbs this neutral ongoingness. The force of this distinction, which Brooke-Rose grasps with great enthusiasm, seems unmistakable. It requires that *all* instances of narrative depart from chronological time. Considered in temporal terms, to tell is to transgress. A short step further along this line of argument, which Brooke-Rose explicitly takes, one confronts the position that any manner of avoiding, turning, ignoring, or subverting conventional narrative modes must be seen as both transgressive and positive. At that point one would have reached the playfulness, the striking ludism, of postmodern narrative.

Fourth, from the perspective of poststructuralist textualism, transgression must be seen as the inevitable play of language. All language may be said to transgress itself: it always subverts, through its inherent abstractness and arbitrariness, the conventions of its use. Transgressiveness in this sense exceeds what Linda Hutcheon has aptly called "generative word play" as the totality of any system exceeds the particular acts, or any collection of acts, within that system. What holds for *langue* not only exceeds all that may hold for *parole*, however numerous its instances, but actually transcends it. Particular puns, though they may be many-sided and frequent, do not add up the indeterminacy of the system of language itself: the "use of the pun as a structural linguistic model" in (say) *Ulysses* or *Finnegans Wake* does not equal, or perhaps even approximate, the openness, the indeterminate plurisignificance, of language itself.[13] The Saussurian model of language, which more or less pervades contemporary literary theory, emphasizes the arbitrary connection between the two components of a sign, the acoustical/graphic signifier and the conceptual signified, and the necessary distance that separates them. That distance is radically unbridgeable. The signified decomposes into further signifiers, by a process of substitution and *enchaînment*, so that ultimately what one thinks of as a signified is only another signifier, a chain of them perhaps, or a bundle. Thus a kind of play opens up within language. The intrinsic distance between signifier and signified, and between signified and any presumptive referent, constitutes a subversive, transgressive, ludic field. Individual puns bear a relationship to this total ludism rather like that a particular bean might be said to bear to the cosmos as a whole: something of the whole survives in the part and one might come to believe that, by straining one's attention upon the part, the whole might be seen therein. Both Derrida and Gadamer agree that the fundamental sense of play lies in the possibilities of enchained movement, the to-and-fro of object to object, though Gadamer conceives this play within the terms of spatiotemporally limited arenas whereas Derrida seems to suppose an always already illimitable boundlessness. In any case, it is play as movement, "not tied to any goal which would bring it to an end," that explains the linguistic play at the heart of transgressive ludism.[14] In this fourth sense, transgressiveness is no longer a move (conscious or unconscious) that the writer makes. It becomes the condition of significance.

A discussion of transgression raises several problems: how these four levels of transgression relate to one another; the presumed history of the term (a question of empirical literary history, but also one that belongs to theory because the term has been used within the peculiar discourse of different systems and models); whether there can be transgressions that are not both positive and desirable; what practical courses one might take, as a writer or critic, in the face of so much inevitable transgressiveness. These good questions and any others, fall within the scope of some other discussion. The problems of formulating the concept of play may be seen most clearly by examining one common synonym for transgression: carnival. As a sociocultural term describing certain classes of periodic events in European history, carnival indicates a form of transgression. (Looked at from a different perspective, it becomes an instance of festival and thus, as Gadamer argues, important because it exemplifies temporal reiteration.) It must be apparent that carnival does not function in literary discourse as straightforwardly as it does in the language of social and cultural history.

II

> Carnival laughter, the intrusion of everything forbidden or slanderous or joyfully blasphemous into the purified domains of officialdom, expressed a complex sense that the material body was not unequivocally base: every death contains within it the meaning of rebirth, every birth comes from the same region of the body as does the excremental. And the excremental is itself a source of regeneration—it manures life just as the dogs' urine in Panurge's trick becomes the source of a well-known "modern" creek.
>
> —Wayne Booth,
> *The Company We Keep: An Ethics of Fiction*

Carnival belongs to the history of European culture, but it also belongs to a system of linguistic and literary analysis developed by the Russian thinker Mikhail Bakhtin. Before the translation of his *Rabelais and His World,* Bakhtin was virtually unknown in English criticism and theory.

Now, he might even be called, to use Michel Foucault's phrase, a "founder of discourse" because many writers, most of whom have no knowledge of Russian, have borrowed his theoretical model, in part if not in the whole, and appropriated the key concepts of his technical vocabulary.[15] Tzetvan Todorov calls him one of the most important Soviet thinkers in the human sciences and the greatest literary theorist of this century.[16] Bakhtin's ideas about literature, about the formation of meaning, and about the incorporation into literature of nonliterary modes of signification have proven to be compelling.

In English, Bakhtin's theory of language (which precedes, and upon which depends, his literary theory) has come to be called "translinguistics."[17] That label more or less indicates his central and recurring preoccupation: meaning is created by the exchange of voices, by collaboration, willing or unwilling, in particular social contexts. As Michael Holquist puts it, if "we" do not make meaning, then "we may at least *rent* meaning."[18] Holquist places Bakhtin's translinguistics between (that is, in between) personalism and deconstruction. Bakhtin occupies the space between the opposed views that meaning is the property of the speaker, necessarily determined by an intention, and that meaning is the unowned function of language, a tentative resident of language systems that must inevitably decay. Still, Bakhtin's model has not been absorbed as widely as his name has been invoked. One finds bits and pieces of it scattered about and used casually. Of all the pieces of Bakhtin's body of theory that have been picked up and given fresh employment, none has shown as glowingly, if only like fox fire, as carnival.

Bakhtin's translinguistics stresses the multiplicity of voices, of different languages, of separate dialects, sociolects, patois, and jargons (of all manner of language codes) within a single utterance. This heteroglossia within language both creates meaning and makes it difficult to isolate: we may "rent" it, but it may prove slippery to hold. One human voice can borrow, beg, or steal the words of another human voice, though this is not at all like taking physical objects such as marbles or coins from someone else, but rather more like appropriating another person's dreams or slivers of his mind. One speaks necessarily from within a fluid social context in which multiple linguistic codes play back and forth. One speaker picks up another's words, but the other concurrently picks up his: meaning, then, resides temporarily in the fluid, unique space of social exchange that exists between them. Bakhtin rejects the formal implications of the Saussurian linguistic model that meaning is a product of the textual properties only, such that they may be analyzed in abstraction from any possible social context, of an utterance. From the point of view of the speaker, "his words are not only 'always already there'; they are also 'never ever before' because those words must be spoken in contexts that are utterly unique and novel to the speaker."[19]

Discourse may be likened to a game of voices in which words are tokens that are played back and forth and the final state of play is the sum of the words' use (the totality of the ways they have been played) in a particular exchange. Utterance is essentially dual; at its utmost, polyphonic. For this reason Bakhtin valorizes the novel as a literary genre because, in a deep sense, it is not a genre at all but, always redefining itself in each new instance, a genre-in-the-making. No scholar could satisfactorily formulate the conventions that constitute novel writing, or even exhaustively list them; no single novel wholly exemplifies the possibilities of novel writing. Although a similar argument might be made for other literary genres, even such seemingly stable and "rule-governed" genres as the detective story or the pastoral, the novel stands out as almost self-evidently "rule-ungoverned" and indeterminate in the face of whatever inventory of conventions one might collect. The novel allows for the greatest amount of diversity in utterance, the greatest scope to the play of voices. In a fully polyphonic novel, the effect of linguistic diversity, in which separate utterances manifest the distinct "worlds" behind them within a single context, must be intense. Thus Bakhtin writes of "the plurality of independent and unmerged voices and consciousnesses" in Dostoevsky's polyphonic novels: "What unfolds in his works is not a multitude of characters and fates in a single objective world, illuminated by a single authorial consciousness; rather a plurality of consciousnesses, with equal rights and each with its own world, combine but are not merged in the unity of the event." Similarly, such forms of discourse as parody, travesty, mockery, Menippean satire, "dark bodily grotesque," and linguistic upendings are all potentially novelistic and, considered separately, belong to the prehistory of the novel. The importance of "parodic-travestying forms in world literature is enormous."[20] They are important because, in incorporating a duality of voice, an inherent dialogism, they point ahead toward the novel. No one parodies another without borrowing the other's voice for that purpose.

It should now be possible to see how the concept of carnival works in Bakhtin's theory. Carnival marks a stage in the history of laughter. It belongs to the same category of activity as the classical saturnalia and the modern comedy show. The pantomime and, above all, the circus clown also belong to this category of mocking laughter, but no other mode of human laughter quite approaches the carnival, in its medieval and early Renaissance forms, for the power and thoroughness of its upendings. For Bakhtin the carnival seems like an especially glorious moment in the history of human laughter because so many ordinary people whose voices normally would not have been clearly heard participated in it. The force in which carnival found "its true origin and extra-systemic sanction is," Holquist writes, "folk laughter."[21] Carnival worked against the power and compulsion of authoritative discourse: the voices of rulers, of the clergy, of the law. (Even if one can imagine no more than the attenuated colors of surviving carnivals in Europe and South America, it should be apparent how minimal and colorless a comedy show or a sitcom is by comparison.) Carnival is a ritual social event, collective and egalitarian, that plays the unofficial voices of the people against the official voices of authority. It is a festival, though it is not for Bakhtin, as it is for Gadamer, its reiteration over time that counts. It possesses no essence in itself, but only its social function, its peculiar mode of exchange in mockery and laughter. Medieval and Renaissance carnivals were social, paralegal, cultural, and historical phenomena, but it is not their historicity as such, their human temporality, that concerns Bakhtin.[22]

As a sociocultural phenomenon, carnival is "*syncretic pageantry* of a ritualistic sort." Nonetheless, it is possible for writers to borrow carnival humor (all the rude jokes, the billingsgate, the travesties, the mocking violence, the dark bodily grotesqueries) and to incorporate them into written discourse. Bakhtin calls this process of incorporation and reinscription "carnivalization," and it is this, not carnival as such, that lies at the heart of his literary analysis. For example, it is Rabelais's mastery of the process by which the images and symbols of carnival life could be transposed into literary images that makes him not only the founder of the novel but the high point of carnivalesque usage in written discourse. The Renaissance writers whom Bakhtin most admires, Rabelais, Grimmelshausen, and Cervantes, found ways to transpose into their narratives aspects of popular carnival and popular language, but Rabelais brought to perfection the medieval conventions of carnivalized humor, which, as Bakhtin writes, constituted a "vast and manifold literature of parody." Yet, as Andrew McKenna argues, after Rabelais it "all seems to go downhill . . . the festive, ambivalent laughter, both gay and mocking, assertive and denying, suffers a progressive 'degeneration', with a few circumscribed exceptions." Bakhtin himself calls the Renaissance the "high point of carnival life," after which it begins to decline.[23] Thus it is carnivalization, not carnival as such, that is the specifically literary concept. In a paradox not always observed by Bakhtin's commentators, carnivalization is the wider concept: classical writers understood the process and may be said to have carnivalized popular materials, the saturnalia or the days of laughter, but they did not draw upon carnivals (which are medieval) any more than do modern stand-up comedians when they carnivalize popular, mocking humor.

As does everything else in Bakhtin's theoretical model, carnival turns upon doubleness. It is dialogic (never monologically impersonal) and many-voiced. Everything serious, Bakhtin writes, "had to have and indeed did have, its comic double." Carnival laughter is "the laughter of all the people . . . it is universal in scope; it is directed at all and everyone, including the carnival's participants. The entire world in its droll aspects, in its gay relativity. . . . This laughter is ambivalent: it is gay, triumphant, and at the same time mocking, deriding. It asserts and denies, it buries and revives."[24] Carnival is a second voice, an unofficial one, that mocks, derides, and upends (even the laughing speaker's own voice), but it is also, and this seems essential to formulating it clearly, a double voice: authority calls it forth and gives it being. For, indeed, as Prince Hal reflects, "If all the year were playing holidays, / To sport would be as tedious as to work" (*1 Henry IV*, 1.2.192–93). Carnival always plays against an official discourse. It is the mask, the overt doubleness, of the official discourse that it mocks and travesties.

As in the case of sociocultural carnival phenomena, carnivalized literature displays ambivalence, duality, and relativity: there is no unofficial discourse without a prior official discourse to call it forth. The popular comedy that pervades *Don Quijote* (the dialectical variants, the homespun games, the folk sayings, or the many vulgarities) and that floods Sancho Panza's voice, requires for its effect the prior existence of the labyrinthinely elegant discourse of chivalric romance that, both in stylistic echoes and in basic structure, brims overflowingly in Don Quijote's own voice. In carnival, the official and the unofficial are locked together, joined in a discursive dance to make a complete, whole utterance. Carnivalesque speech neither destroys nor replaces the official voice of authority, it merely completes it, bringing it forward to reveal its hidden features. One might say that no one has ever known his or her face until seeing it in caricature. No one knows his or her own discourse until hearing it mocked in parody or lampoon.

Even this cursory account of Bakhtin's analysis of carnival and carnivalization should indicate clearly how far these concepts, as he employs them, stand from a simple synonymy with transgression. Even if all carnivalesque gestures (acts, masks, and words) are, in some sense, transgressive, it does not follow that all transgression is carnivalesque. There are interesting implications to removing Bakhtin's concept of carnivalization from its place in his discourse and transforming it into the hircine embodiment of linguistic playfulness and ludism. The problem that this conceptual transformation raises is brittle: *scriptor ludens*, as

Rabelais, Cervantes, and Shakespeare make plain, can be genuinely carnivalesque in his play, but if all linguistic play, all ludism in writing, is carnivalesque, then Bakhtin's categories will be swallowed, their force absorbed and diffused. As seems often to have been the case in discussions of play/game theory, a precise concept will have been swallowed by a larger, less precise one.

There is a distinction between the completion of an utterance and its depletion. On one hand, Bakhtin's concept of carnival and carnivalization argues for a specific human situation, social and dialogic, in which utterances are made more meaningful, completed; on the other, the textualist use of *carnival* as a synonym for transgression indicates a generalized linguistic condition, even automatic and inescapable, in which utterances are stripped of their contextual meaning, depleted. Once carnival is abstracted from its context (as a mode of heteroglossia, dialogism, and polyphony), a number of consequences follow. It becomes a more generalized term that loses its connotations of social involvement and wholeness. It becomes a rubric for underscoring a wide range of linguistic playfulness. Carnival can even become (and this is very common) thematized as merely one more thing to look for in a literary text: an anagram in Nabokov, a bewilderingly deformed narrative convention in Robbe-Grillet, a paradox in Borges, a mocking personification in Robert Coover, or any number of feasts, parties, and rodeos, any and all of which may be called *carnivalesque*. The appropriation of the "specifically Bakhtinian notion of carnival" into other systems may seem at first to be "quite satisfyingly polyphonic," but actually it displays a powerful tendency toward monologism.[25]

III

> Now this last named element, the *fun* of playing, resists all analysis, all logical interpretation. As a concept, it cannot be reduced to any other mental category. No other modern language known to me has the exact equivalent of the English "fun." . . . it is precisely this fun-element that characterizes the essence of play. Here we have to do with an absolutely primary category of life.
>
> —Johan Huizinga,
> *Homo Ludens: A Study of the Play-Element in Culture*

The vigorous lifeworld of carnival, filled always by its vulgarities and its enthusiasm, contrasts all contemporary forms of commercialized fun. Modern social structures for laughter (to borrow Huizinga's tone), such as professional sports, amusement, and "theme" parks or mass audience films and television, seem washed out, largely passive in their possibilities for expression and subject to massive external regulation. The North American megamalls, for example, are designed as technobowers: they must be seen not merely as convenient places to shop but as places for pleasure, even excitement and delight. A technobower may contain innumerable shops, department stores, restaurants, motion picture theaters, amusement parks with rides as large as roller coasters, video game arcades, museums, small zoos, even artificial lakes with equally artificial waves. The assemblage of pleasure-giving machines is unspontaneous and highly controlled. One suspects that even singing might result in expulsion. The technobower is an illusion of fun but essentially funless. (It might remind the disinterested ethnographer of those frighteningly funless casinos at Las Vegas, Reno, or Atlantic City, where unlaughing gamblers pursue unplayful play, while clowns or circus acts perform just beyond the edges of their vision, in an ambience as funless as a torture chamber.) What carnival was, or might have been, can be partially gauged by the antithetical technobower. Carnival survives its Renaissance exuberance only in dim shadows and stale imitations. But it also survives in the literature of the time. A reader can still experience carnivalized humor in Rabelais, Shakespeare, and Cervantes, among others. A reader can also find the literary techniques of carnivalization in many modern writers.

Although social historians such as Natalie Zemon Davis and intellectual historians such as Dominic La Capra have made use of Bakhtin's concept of carnival, it seems more commonly to have been directed to the uses of literary analysis.[26] Thus one encounters carnival, and its related terms, performing fairly ordinary tasks. (It is sometimes used, even by those who should know better, to designate social savagery, mere brutal insult.) When this happens, it is often difficult to perceive what remains of Bakhtin's concept: a dialogic act that completes an utterance, that creates a whole out of internal differences. Yet one can scarcely overestimate the current popularity of Bakhtin's vocabulary for social and linguistic analysis among literary scholars.[27] In this sense the first major discussion of Bakhtin's literary theory remains not merely instructive but exemplary as well: in *Séméiotikē*: *Recherches pour une sémanalyse*, the book that first brought Bakhtin to the attention of French literary theorists and, indirectly, critics writing in English, Julia Kristeva argues that carnival is a transgression, both linguistic and logical, that establishes its own law. That is, the carnivalesque act imposes a law and does so against, and upon, that to which it is a response: in effect, it replaces its antinomical object. Kristeva writes, "Carnival struggles against God, authority and social laws; it is rebellious in the measure that it is dialogic: it is not astonishing that in the service of a subversive discourse, this word 'carnival' should have acquired a signification in our society that is extremely pejorative and uniquely distorted." She calls attention to the dialogic nature of carnival as well as to the "structural dyads" that it creates, but she also stresses its subversive and transgressive role in combating authority.[28] In Kristeva's analysis of carnival, as well as in all subsequent textualist appropriations, the importance of the social context in understanding the carnivalesque act (or the carnivalized utterance) is made marginal. In textualist analyses, carnival normally becomes a synonym for transgression, *and only transgression*: as its own law it becomes no longer a complement, a replacement that stands in place of that against which it has transgressed. The true carnivalesque then becomes, in Christine Brooke-Rose's words, the unthroning of authority by "wild and happy" crowds of transgressors.[29] Carnival has been transformed into a synonym for undoing, for transgression, for destruction, and for *re*placement. Nothing counts except the "wild and happy" carnivalians and whatever they represent.

Textualist models of literary analysis are more or less extreme. Any student of literature should be able to construct easily a working scale of textualist extremity. (Such a scale might range, for example, from New Criticism, as less extreme than Russian formalism, to deconstruction.) If one takes carnival as a mode of play, as equivalent to ludism, say, or as a synecdoche for ludic acts generally, then its meaning will shift from one textualist model to another. Carnival will occupy a somewhat different space in each. In deconstruction, *scriptor ludens* plays, necessarily and ceaselessly, because the game (of language) plays through him. The point made in the first chapter, that the play system precedes acts of play and only manifests itself in play, comes into focus. One might borrow Heidegger's dictum about language to say that (for instance) chess plays José Raúl Capablanca or Garry Kasparov. Indeed, Gadamer does borrow this dictum to account for the loss of subjectivity that occurs when the player becomes absorbed in the structure of play: "Play itself is . . . transformation of such a kind that the identity of the player does not continue to exist for anybody. Everybody asks instead what it is supposed to be, what is 'meant.' The players (or poets) no longer exist, but only what of theirs is played."[30] The game, or work of art, is "what is played by the players it plays."[31] Writing writes *scriptor ludens* whose transgressiveness manifests the extent to which he has been himself transgressed.

Once one has defined carnival as transgression, or more complexly as revolution or as war, a law that replaces another law against which it has transgressed, it is logical to assimilate the concept to any extreme version of ludism, including deconstruction. When Vicki Mistacco, in a formulation that Barthes's *S/Z* permeates, defines *ludisme* as "the open play of signification," she evidently has in mind the boundless movement, the endless *touching upon,* of signifiers as they lead to one another, briefly simulating the role of signifieds but without ever reaching a final, ultimate signified. The play of signification (all that the human mind possesses and, paradoxically, that which keeps it from ever having more) mirrors the play of the world, all ongoingness and dissolving boundaries.[32] If carnival could be transcribed into a model of textual analysis within which Mistacco's definition functioned axiomatically, it would become both a multiform element in an unending linguistic process and an involuntary linguistic act. And, of course, carnival *could be* so transcribed.

This possibility points directly toward the textualist assumptions of poststructuralism and, in particular, deconstruction. The "play of signification" appears both as a universal effect and as a necessary condition of language: a view of language that, whatever intellectual bliss it promises, places all linguistic concepts a vast distance from Bakhtin's translinguistic model. In *Of Grammatology,* Derrida makes the point that the absence of any transcendental signified means that there is a play of signification that has no limits, a play that "shakes" both onto-theology and the metaphysics of presence. Hence, he continues, there is a play of the world that necessarily precedes particular play within the world: "It is therefore *the play of the world* that must be first thought; before attempting to understand all the forms of play in the world."[33] Conceived of as free play, play makes all structures untenable, decenters them and deprivileges them. Derrida also argues, famously in "Structure, Sign, and Play," that the field of free play excludes totalization: the substitutions that occur within the field of free play are infinite, but the field itself is finite and lacks "a center which arrests and grounds the play of substitutions."[34] The permutations of this formula are numerous. In "Living On: Border Lines," Derrida writes that there is no "core" or "edge" to discourse but only continuous deferral, and hence a text must be taken as a "differential network, a fabric of traces referring endlessly to something other than itself, to other differential traces." Or, as he argues in "Structure, Sign, and Play," since concepts are taken from a given syntax and system, "each particular borrowing brings along with it the whole of metaphysics." Similarly, in his interview with Kristeva in *Positions,* referring to the concept of *gramme* or *différance,* Derrida argues that the interweaving of semiological traces constitutes the text (or, one might say, textuality itself) such that each text is the transformation of other texts. Thus, "This interweaving, this textile, is the *text* produced only in the transformation of another text. Nothing, neither among the elements nor within the system, is anywhere ever simply present or absent. There are only, everywhere, differences and traces of traces." Commenting on this passage, Jonathan Culler writes that the force of Derrida's argument, through all the metamorphic formulations of free play, is to undermine "the attempt to found a theory of language on positive entities either in the speech event or in the system." The "open play of signification" (as *différance*, as the endless semiological linkage, as the fabric of traces entailing traces) must bring to mind that "ludic advantage" and the "galaxy of signifiers" of which Barthes speaks so lovingly.[35] It is both endless and unbreakably linked (*une enchaînment*): that which makes signification possible, but itself monological, monistic, and mute.

One could multiply versions of Derrida's formula: it has been, for good reasons, not merely persistent, though metamorphic, within his writing but pervasive as well. (Free play, considered within the strict terms of Derrida's theory, cannot be described accurately as having formulations any more than it can be called a concept.) Two propositions follow: first, play is involuntary and impersonal, a condition as well as an effect; second, play is universal. Carnival is neither. It remains to inquire how carnival belongs to the conceptual family ruled by the concept of play. It is there because contemporary usage has put it there; it also belongs there as an intuitively evident manifestation of human playfulness. Even if carnival is not (properly or validly) a synonym for transgression, one may still ask what relationship it bears to the latter within the family of play concepts. How should one think of carnival? How does it fit into the more general category of festive celebration? As a play concept, how does it relate to transgression, ludism, and deconstructive free play?

IV

> *French Deck.* Solitary stoker of cards. He
> dealt himself a hand. Turn stills of the past in
> unending permutations, shuffle and begin. Sort
> the images again. And sort them again. This
> game reveals germs of truth, and death.
>
> The world becomes an apparently infinite, yet
> possibly finite, card game. Image combinations,
> permutations, comprise the world game.
>
> —Jim Morrison, *The Lords and the New Creatures*

Consider the following allegory

If likelihoods always bore fruit, then Ainslie Wellfleet would have become the prime minister of Canada. He came from the right family, an extended, rentier-dominated conglomerate of the kind that rules central

Canada, and thus the nation. He had the right education. He graduated from Upper Canada College, then from the University of Toronto with a first-class honors degree in economics and political science. After that he took an M.A. in philosophy before reading law. He lacked only one ingredient for success in Canadian political life: a fluent command of French. His family had paid lip service to the principle of bilingualism, but no one in his family actually spoke French and most were notorious Francophobes. Duncan, his older brother, whom I have long known from brokerage circles, never misses an opportunity to pour contempt on Francophonism. I remember once sitting with Duncan and some commodity brokers in a small restaurant in Montreal when he called the waiter over to our table just as we were getting up to leave. A short, squarely trimmed old man with thick gray hair, a bristling mustache of an outmoded type, he might easily have been a *poilu* of 1918. The old man came up and stood beside Duncan. "Here," Duncan said, warmly and smiling, "this is for you." The old man put out his hand discreetly and Duncan slipped him a lighted firecracker. As he ran from the restaurant laughing, his friends hooting and yammering, I stayed to apologize. I left a tip with the old man, but the damage was irreparable, both to his self-esteem and to a tiny corner of French/English relations in Canada. With such attitudes widespread in his family, it is no wonder that Ainslie did not learn to speak French.

Yet during the long command of Prime Minister Pierre Trudeau, it had more and more come to seem that only a man with genuine pretension to fluency in both official languages could hope to lead a major party and, eventually, the government. Canada's status as a bilingual nation had solidified into official myth just in time to consign Ainslie, and anyone like him, to the sidelines of public life. More than twenty years of his family's indoctrination appeared to have been wasted. It was for this reason, as an act of self-preservation, a desperate move to enable him to cling to the illusory promises of power, that Ainslie decided to apply for a government scholarship to study philosophy at the Sorbonne. It was true that he did not need public funds to pursue an education. He might have studied any subject in comfort anywhere in the world. Yet he perceived, correctly, that the cachet of having had such a scholarship would contribute to his aura. He had always bitterly resented having been passed over for a Rhodes Scholarship. Hence he seemed disproportionately overjoyed when he received the award. A glowing letter form Ottawa informed him that it was young people like himself in whom the future of Canada resided. He withdrew from the study of law and left for Paris late in August of 1979.

I think that it is clear that Ainslie Wellfleet did not seriously intend to study philosophy at the Sorbonne. He discussed his plans with me on two occasions during that summer, and I had no doubts that his only purpose was to prepare himself for public life, either in politics or, failing that, in the mandarinate of the public service. As a secondary benefit, he hoped to learn enough French not only to achieve his political goals but also to enjoy dining in the better restaurants in Montreal. He looked ahead to the possibility of a stint as minister of external affairs or as an ambassador. These roles would have required him to possess a working bilingualism, to be sure, but nonetheless he consistently viewed learning French as a matter of appearances, a necessary but inessential acquisition. I remember distinctly how he laughed at the thought that the government of Canada had given him the scholarship when there were probably hundreds of studious, Francophile students in the universities across Canada any one of whom deserved official support more than he did and would have gained more fruitful knowledge from it. That, he said, smiling in the chill, flinty manner that all the members of his family possess, was merely the chief rule of Canadian life: to support the establishment of Central Canada, to which he belonged by birth, habit, and intent. I once heard Duncan's smile compared unfavorably to a hangman's, and when issues arose such as the scholarship, Ainslie made his family resemblance evident. I am sure that when he left for Paris his dominant sentiments were Francophobic. At the party that was given for him by friends from the university and Osgoode Hall, he made a jocular speech in which he treated his departure as a painful exile to a land of poor hygiene, extravagant mores, and cerebral obfuscation.

Hence it was something of a surprise when I received a short note from Ainslie in February of 1980 indicating that he was having a wonderful time and enjoying his lectures at the Sorbonne. He had taken a marvelous flat on the rue de Babylone in the seventh arrondissement with three rooms and a view looking over the Hôtel des Invalides. He walked along the Bd. St.-Germain each day, stopping in bookstores on his way to lectures, and then later having coffee with friends from the university. It certainly did not sound like the Ainslie Wellfleet whom I knew, nor like the one who had made the comic speech the night before his departure. The Ainslie I knew had no intention of studying philosophy, and indeed, despite his M.A., had no deep interest in the subject. His note baffled me. I realized that something must have happened and that a change so basic and so contrary to his long-standing dispositions could not have taken place without sufficient cause. I supposed at first that he must have met a beautiful Parisienne whose presence had lured him to lectures that otherwise he would not have attended. In any event, I was alerted to an inexplicable change.

During the subsequent two years, Ainslie wrote to a number of friends as well as to members of his family. I knew his sister Rowena and occasionally spoke to her when our paths crossed. From her I gathered a great deal of corroborating evidence. Ainslie had become a serious student of French philosophy, loved Paris, and had flatly declined to pay any visits home for the first two years of his scholarship. He spoke glowingly of the distinguished French intellectuals whom he had met and conversed with. The latter comment, which was reported from several sources, particularly astounded me, for it implied that Ainslie had already learned how to speak French well enough to hold discussions with the leading figures of French intellectual life. In a rather snarling manner, Duncan remarked that Ainslie's brain must have turned soft from eating too much French cheese. He wrote Rowena that he now intended to remain in Paris until he had completed a book on contemporary philosophical issues. His father was thought to be considering ordering him to resume the law or to manage family property in Edmonton or Vancouver. But nothing came of this and Ainslie remained in Paris. His presence there gradually became an established mystery. At dinners, or meeting casually at the Royal Yacht Club, people would inquire after him, exchange witticisms at his expense, laugh, and go on to more interesting matters. But I never lost my astonishment at Ainslie's change of intention, and I began collecting the comments, suppositions, and theories that his friends and family put forward to explain his absence.

After Ainslie abruptly vanished in early 1983, I attempted to discover everything that reflected upon his paradoxical immersion in French intellectual life. I asked to see letters that he had written, begged anecdotes, and turned every conversation away from the tragedy itself to the question of the unexpected fascination that Paris had exercised over his mind. At the time, I did not surmise that my investigations into the mystery of his intellectual metamorphosis might eventually provide an explanation for his sudden and distressing disappearance.

Quite rapidly I began to put together a picture of life in Paris that was wholly unexpected. Repeatedly, Ainslie had written of his Parisian existence in words that must have, as I felt then, described the margins, the fringes, the accidents, but not the essence, of intellectual life. Nearly everyone to whom he had written reported that Ainslie had stressed the odd, the bizarre, the eccentric. He had consistently given accounts of intractable yet trivial problems that he had heard discussed, problems that seemed rooted in the most ordinary experience, or in the pratfalls of ordinary language, but, once isolated in analysis, wore the masks of clowns: distorted, grotesque, funny, but disturbing. Ainslie had been attracted to the experience of play and paradox. This conclusion did not actually emerge from any individual letter, but once I had begun to collate all of his comments on life in Paris, a larger obsession became evident. He seldom mentioned restaurants, museums only when they led him on to a paradoxical commentary, and the ordinary aspects of social existence in a great city not at all.

From Ainslie's letters I was able to cull a number of significant anecdotes. They are all linked by his obsession with play and paradox, but they go beyond these abstract games. Taken together they present a conceptually coherent narrative in which a limited number of highly colorful issues recur and in which a cast of *dramatis personae*, as bizarrely colorful as the ideas they discuss, create the stage they walk on. The problems that recur have in common that they are intractable, open to endless discussion, but closed to definitive solutions, while being always marginal to human life as people live it. I have been told that these problems constitute the common playground of certain philosophers and many literary critics. I can only say that they were entirely new to me: I read Ainslie's letters with an increasing sense of amazement and bewilderment.

In his letters Ainslie reports discussions in which leading French intellectuals discuss such problems as signification, play, games, carnival, masks, codes, absence, presence, and the nature of systems or, as Ainslie once put it, systematicality. Some of these, at least, would strike almost anyone as legitimate difficulties that intelligent men and women might discuss. In Ainslie's accounts they invariably take on such odd shapes, follow such outrageous twists, that the context of the discussion seems almost to destroy the validity of the problem itself. Certain names assume an immense presence in Ainslie's anecdotes: Roland Barthes, who died soon after Ainslie arrived in Paris but whose ghost, as it were, continues to haunt all discussion, Jacques Derrida, Gérard Genette, Tzetvan Todorov, and Michael Bakhtin. The latter appears to have been a dead Russian who, though always absent, makes himself present. Furthermore, there seems to be a secondary group of people, followers and disciples, who participate in the discussions but do so on the level of punctuation. The names of Red Gallagher, Bernard Galazzo, Lysiana Medine, Marie-Hélène Cahuzac, Michel Tasd'homme, Colette Tourbillon, Georgina Hiboux, and Yves Zagli give a sense of narrative depth to Ainslie's anecdotes. I came to know them as his familiars, as students dedicated to essentially opaque problems, if not to their clarification. They are the devoted admirers of the great *maîtres de penser* themselves.

Having made these preliminary remarks, I wish now to record some of Ainslie's philosophical anecdotes. I believe that the narrative coherence that binds them will become evident. They do present, to be sure, a distorted and perhaps unappealing view of intellectual life in Paris, but it may be a view that carries a significant measure of truth. In any event, they reveal Ainslie in a perspective that makes plain the gulf that separated him in Paris from himself in Toronto. I think they may also suggest why he crossed this gulf so soon after arriving in Paris and why he stubbornly refused to cross back over. It may prove to be a more difficult point to make, but I also believe that these anecdotes, culled from his letters, will cast light on his disappearance. They may even contain the seeds of an acceptable hypothesis to explain it.

[THE following anecdote has been taken from a letter that Ainslie wrote to his sister Rowena in March 1980. Versions of this anecdote, or fragments from it, appear in letters that he wrote to his friends after that date. This, however, is the first and most complete version. I am recording it here as he wrote it for Rowena except that I have taken the phrase "semic raw material" from a substantially shorter version that appears in a letter he wrote to a university friend, Elizabeth Scott, and placed it in apposition to the phrase "texture of semes."]

One day Roland Barthes strolled up the Champs Elysées toward l'Etoile and met an outside-insider. There are many outside-outsiders and a few inside-insiders, he would say, and there are even a very few inside-outsiders, like Todorov and Kristeva, but the authentic outside-insider is rare. *Bien sûr* it is difficult to catch him in motion for he is, etymologically speaking, elusive.

Barthes encountered a large man, evidently a foreigner, wearing a dirty turtleneck and desert boots. He had glasses and an unkempt beard with considerable gray in it. Over one shoulder he carried (a pure gesture of style) an elegant leather purse. Barthes stopped to stare, and the man returned the stare. Quite rapidly, the man's costume disappeared and his flesh began to melt. A human being is a system of signs, a nexus of semes, cooperative and combative, that illude him. This foreigner (*un vrai type*, Barthes would say) had garbed himself in semes. He wore them like a thick encrustation: a shell, an armor, an enchanted cloak woven with emblems and spells. His semes proclaimed him even as they attempted to protect him. One lives in a sleeve (*un manchon*) of semes. Across the fabric of this foreigner's cloak, all the texture of semes, the semic raw material, had been perverted, twisted into an abyss by contrary, even random, signification. Travel makes us speak strange languages without knowing it. One may suppose that he is unswervingly monoglot, but travel imposes the gift of an unconscious polyglossia. The texture of semes begins to speak within the foreign culture and to generate novel signification.

It is possible to overrule the inside semiotic systems that govern the particular semes that one carries with him. The man appeared to say (in his own system) that he was confident, indifferent to opinion, an intellectual, someone serious. Had he been within his native semiotic system, the signification of his encrusted semes would have worked as he intended. He would have proclaimed that he was an intellectual and resided within the tiny segment of culture where things most count because it is there that norms are set, judgments made, opinions established. He would have proclaimed that he was an inside-insider who belonged to the avant-garde, to the ruling class. In Paris (which contains the intellectual world), however, his semes had been compelled to function within a different semiotic system. Now they proclaimed him to be poor, untidy, gauche, *jaune sale*, painfully an outsider. In the Parisian context, his cloak of semes worked against him (though, of course, he could not have perceived this) and demonstrated his outsideness. Thus he was an insider (somewhere) who had become, solely by virtue of traveling to Paris, an outsider.

This story (which I first heard from Colette Tourbillon) does not report whether the man stopped collusively, staring first, or what he thought of Barthes. [It is important to note the relatively plain style that Ainslie employed in his early letters. Later he came to write from somewhere within the conventions of the philosophers whom he so admired. Subsequent anecdotes are less accessible.]

[I HAVE established the following anecdote from collated versions of letters that Ainslie wrote to Elizabeth Scott, Rowena, and his mother between August and the end of November 1980. I have been struck by how often Ainslie's *contes philosophiques* take place in museums and galleries. One must suppose that the Parisian *maîtres* spend an inordinate amount of time visiting museums. Although this would seem odd by North American standards, where philosophers normally appear to do nothing at all, it may not be odd by the standards of Paris. I should think that a museum would be a very stimulating place to carry on intellectual argument. After all, a museum is a kind of ocular syllabus of human knowledge.]

One Sunday at the Beaubourg, Genette and Derrida paused in front of Picasso's *La femme en bleu*. "Read this," Derrida exclaimed, and thrust the plastic card with annotations into Genette's hands. The museum's annotations claimed, he observed, that the creation before them, with one breast, no hands, a neck like a pyramid, one eyebrow, two dissimilar eyes, and a face decomposed into six planes, was *un personnage*, a character. (When Lysiana Medine told me this story I at once secretly recalled the painting by Henri Hayden in the Art Gallery of Ontario, which is provocatively called *Personnage* and of which similar questions might be raised.) Genette replied that *La femme en bleu* was an explicable consequence of the artist having employed certain necessary conventions for the formation of character in painting.

Marie-Hélène Cahuzac, who had come to the Beaubourg with them, then asked if it was not the case that a character was simply a proper name. If so, then *La femme en bleu* could not be a character because she did not have a proper name. "Unhappily, no," Derrida answered, "if only it were so simple. That is a falsification of formalist doctrine for which we are, I believe, indebted to Roland Barthes." He went on to point out that the proper name united the semes, as Barthes liked to call them, and invested them with an identity. Nonetheless, the character was composed of the semes, was constituted by their recurrence, and the name merely capped the heap. The name marked a momentary (that is, illusory) solidification.

"Do you then accept the formalist doctrine concerning characterization?" Genette asked. "Is a character, for you, merely the inventory of its semes, as Barthes seemed to hold in certain moments, or the totality of its traits as Tomashevsky and the other Russians maintained? That is a surprisingly weak position for you to hold. A character is more ungraspable than that, more incoherent than that doctrine will allow: a character is always a creature in flight." Derrida laughed and responded that if such were the case, then *La femme en bleu* could be a character as much as Odette de Crécy or M. de Charlus, for certainly they are all equally in flight and ungraspable. He then added that an American neoformalist had asserted that literary characters were mostly empty canvas (which, no doubt, applies as well to painted characters) and that was, perhaps, the furthest position into which formalism could advance.

Red Gallagher, who was also along, then asked what could constitute a character, in literature or in any other art that was capable of generating characters, beyond the semes, recurring or otherwise. Genette replied that three linguistic functions constituted a character in literature (and their equivalents, if there were any, in painting): the conventions that brought it forth, the idiolectic properties of its discourse, and the focalization in which it appeared, either through the narrator's voice or through that of some other character. He went on to claim that the idiolectic properties of the character's discourse were, in themselves, varieties of semes so that, in the end, it was the combination of semes and conventions. To this Derrida smirked rather insultingly and replied that if M. Genette were correct, if that were a sufficient account of the problem, then *La femmme en bleu* could easily appear in a narrative since the physical aspects of her body, which the museum's plastic card partially enumerated, could be easily transcoded into linguistic signifiers and incorporated into the discourse of narrative. And conventions, he added, are notoriously polymorphic, open (like Cartesian wax) to metamorphosis. Red Gallagher and Marie-Hélène Cahuzac agreed that this seemed so. But Red Gallagher reminded everyone that Barthes had said that discourse itself was a character and he wondered how, in a reverse process of transcoding semes, one would paint discourse. Everyone then turned to observe Genette phrase his reply.

"Yes, that may be so," Genette responded, ignoring Red Gallagher's final question, "and I suspect that, with a knowledge of narrative conventions, one could, indeed, create a discourse in which *La femme en bleu* could be constituted as a character." Derrida laughed at this, having already placed his secret response in readiness. But before Derrida could intervene, Red Gallagher challenged Genette to write such a narrative. To everyone's surprise, he agreed to do this, and it was decided that in two weeks they would all meet at L'Auberge Basque to hear Genette read his narrative. Before they went on to another painting and different problems, Marie-Hélène Cahuzac asked Derrida what he thought might pass for a sufficient definition of character. Derrida laughed once again and replied that M. Genette had fallen into a trap, a typical, perhaps inevitable, trap of formalism. "There are no characters," he exclaimed, with the vivacity of a player exposing a hidden check in chess, "there is only characterization." He went on to explain that a character, if constituted by anything, must be made from signifiers, but these, to make sense, depended on a principle of structuration, a hidden artifice which was, no doubt, what M. Genette had in mind when he spoke of conventions. The hidden artifice could only be known through the signifiers and hence, paradoxically, it must change as the play of signification shifts (as it will inevitably) with each reading. Change invariably becomes exchange. A character is no more stable than the discourse that constitutes it (the textuality that contains it) and that, he concluded triumphantly, is indefinitely unstable.

Two weeks later, at L'Auberge Basque, Genette read his narrative. In it a man becomes obsessed by a beautiful woman with long black hair and classic features. Whenever he sees her, she wears blue. In his obsession, the man begins to dream about the woman. The dream continues and each night he dreams once again about the beloved. In each dream the woman is subtly different. Features shift, change their location minutely, in an endless play of mutability. Some night, in some dream, Genette proclaimed victoriously, the man will dream *La femme en bleu*, for at some point that particular combination of traits must be reached.

Derrida admitted that Genette had solved the conundrum brilliantly. There is only characterization, he observed, and never character, only the play of difference between the semes. "M. Genette has hit upon the solution to the problem of character: in the free play of characterization, which is no more than an aspect of that which constitutes the text, its shadow, and its synecdoche, it is not necessary to have been played, to be played, or to come to be played. It is only necessary that the play be open." Marie-Hélène Cahuzac giggled and remarked that she believed that Picasso had known this before Genette had learned it.

[I HAVE collated the following anecdote from several versions written between February and March 1981. The most important version appears in a letter written, within a context of affectionate reminiscences, to Elizabeth Scott. Duncan has informed me that, in a letter to him, Ainslie once referred to the Beaubourg as the omphalos of Paris.]

Another afternoon at the Beaubourg, Derrida stood with Genette looking down from the acrylic tubeway on the fifth level. The Place Georges Pompidou was, as always, crowded with hawkers, buskers, spielers, acrobats, artisans, confidence men, and (one must suppose) every variety of human *escamotage*. Both Genette and Derrida were drawn to the efforts of a Houdini-type escape artist who was struggling to free himself from a series of ropes and knots that his audience had loaded upon him. The escape artist had been tightly bound, and his efforts to break loose seemed to be in vain. There, Genette exclaimed, is the struggling icon of this museum! Art fights against immense odds to free itself from its official interment. Even in its failure to break free, it mocks the mighty success of its captors, its bounds, its official status.

Michel Tasd'homme, who usually makes a point of accompanying the philosophers when they visit museums, then asked if art did not on occasion, as every Houdini, succeed in struggling free. Genette suggested that the unsuccessful Houdini could only be an icon for art captured within the walls of a museum, as the modern art collection was bound, on movable walls and plastic cards with simplistic annotations, like Beauty in the castle of the Beast, there within the Beaubourg. Derrida laughed at this. (I have been repeatedly struck since I arrived in Paris by how often Derrida is reported to have laughed. Many of the stories about him begin with him laughing. He seems to be, in this respect, the incarnation of Democritus. Perhaps philosophers who believe in the void must laugh. Certainly a concept of void, not to say voiding and voidance, seems to put things into perspective.) He then remarked to Michael Tasd'homme that, as usual, M. Genette, had played a losing hand.

Anything may be twisted into an icon of anything else, but it gains only the bare illusion of substance from this honor. The audience has bound the escape artist to see him free himself: that is similar to the way readers bind the text, with conventions of order, priority, and expectations, to fix the meaning they wish to know. The ropes are like the text itself, binding, holding, but always capable of being slipped, of giving way, of slipping free, of being free, of freeing. The man, who reminds us so forcefully of Houdini, is significance: bound, struggling, but infinitely resilient. He doubles textuality.

Georgina Hiboux recalled that Julia Kristeva has once observed that the process of semiosis, the mind's unconscious *chora*, resembled a circus. The acts were like the spontaneous outpourings of signification. Kristeva had once seen Martine Gruss at the Cirque à l'Ancienne leaping the garters in a voltige act and it had reminded her of the mind's, the unconscious language's, spontaneous domination of form. The slippered feet high above a horse's back indicated, Georgina Hiboux argued, that art can slip free much as unconscious semiosis does despite the bounds of syntax and usage. But Michel Tasd'homme saw in the Kristevian anecdote only the illustration of binding, not freeing. Gruss's feet had been trained, he pointed out, bound in a way nearly Chinese. It might have been that her feet, before binding, had been spontaneous, capable of spontaneous play before play loses itself in the specious salvation of games.

Then Derrida invited Michel Tasd'homme to drink a beer with him. The only icon, he observed, is the movement itself. But M. Genette, like every other binder and unbinder, wishes to freeze this movement at some congenial point. In reality, if there is a true literary Absolute (*l'Absolu littéraire*), it is movement itself, the irreducible play of signification. Genette writes as he does so as not to become bound himself and thus, in unbinding, becomes bound. He is always a bound binder of the unbound, unbindable bound.

[OF all the philosophers who play the dominant roles in Ainslie's anecdotes, none is more appealing than Todorov. He appears to possess a genuine humanity. Ainslie records him lovingly, unlike the way he describes Derrida or Genette. Derrida seldom appears physically in the anecdotes other than as a laughing holder of the last word. Of course, he is said to wear a leather jacket and to have, like a fugitive character from a Malraux novel, the cold glance of a terrorist. Todorov, however, is often described as thin or angular and as having a lion's mane of tousled, unkempt hair. Ainslie several times records his odd habit of speaking with his hand inside his trousers, as if he were unaware of his own body when he spoke and needed to remind himself of its essentiality. The following anecdote is mentioned a number of times in letters written between the end of 1981 and June 1982. The event it recounts must have occurred some time earlier.]

Todorov loves to ride bicycles. He can often be observed riding along the streets and boulevards of the fifth and sixth arrodissements. He rides to and from his home in the eleventh arrondissement over the Pont de Sully sometimes more than once a day. He rides with an insouciance that has become legendary. Once, after he had begun writing his study of M. M. Bakhtin, he fell from his bike in the midst of traffic at the intersection of rue Jacob and rue Bonaparte. Evidently he caused a minor traffic jam (that is, a block, a knotting up, of free-flowing traffic, bound from one point to another, all of the intentions of which are directed beyond the space that has been corked or knotted up).

He was probably fortunate that he had not been immediately run over. (Considered separately, each vehicle, insofar as it embodied an intention to go beyond, might have stated that Todorov was an unworthy cause, too insignificant to be allowed to jam traffic.) As the traffic piled up and horns began to beep, Todorov reflected upon what constituted an official flow of traffic. He had fallen in front of it, almost under it, had (in fact) impeded it, turned it back, blocked, jammed, corked, knotted, and perplexed it. (Bent, he would say, a straight line in upon itself: created a knot and a labyrinth, both perplexities of straightness.) What, then, was his relation to it? Was he like a jester? or a revolutionary? If the traffic flow was official (legitimized by the laws of Paris, the conventions of driving, a community of intention), then simply in falling he must have become, *tout court*, unofficial.

Lysiana Medine, who joined a waiter from a restaurant on the corner in helping Todorov from the center of the intersection, says that he asked her as soon as she reached him whether he had become carnivalesque merely in falling. Had he mocked the official flow of Parisian traffic from Montparnasse to the Seine by falling? Certainly in falling he had been under (become a member of a fallen, underclass) and had thwarted the official flow. He had been, if only momentarily, to the official flow of traffic what the unofficial is to the official in general: mocking, parodic, disruptive, and unwelcome (Derrida later pointed out to him that, taking the uncertain romance origins of *traffic* into account, a term for exchange, negotiations, commerce, and trade, for the flow of human artifacts, he might just as well wonder whether he had become a pirate. Yves Zagli is reported to have offered the compromise that Todorov describe himself as a *filibustero*.)

Alas, questions of carnival and the unofficial are never so simple. Todorov was forced to conclude that all traffic is unofficial, carnivalesque in relation to itself and to the only truly official manifestation of Parisian traffic: the rules, laws, and conventions (and the police) who regulate, or try to regulate, the people's joy in flowing. In Paris, he remarked, the carnivalesque is ubiquitous (it is the Parisian mode): traffic is its emblem.

[IN first culling, and then editing, these anecdotes, I have been struck by the central position that the dead Russian thinker M. M. Bakhtin occupies in Parisian intellectual life. The philosophers, normally so arrogant and xenophobic, appear to have opened their minds to this most un-Parisian, one-legged Russian linguist. The following anecdote can be found most fully expressed in a letter that Ainslie wrote on July 14, 1982, to his old friend from varsity days, Dr. Woods Drumm, now a professor of linguistics at the University of Lethbridge. I have modified it slightly by reference to fragmentary versions of the anecdote in other letters.]

After Kristeva had introduced Bakhtin to Parisian intellectuals in her *Séméiotikē* certain Bakhtinian concepts became widely discussed. Both Red Gallagher and Abel Trigo-Cabral have been loud in their appreciation of Bakhtin's insistence upon the concept of dialogue, of duality in human utterance. Structuralism, Red Gallagher likes to argue, is essentially (he draws that word out, underlining it with his lips) monological. It has always been an act of theoretical terrorism. Lévi-Strauss, A. J. Greimas, or Claude Bremond might be seen to have the same relationship to human thought as terrorists to human society. (In another incarnation, Red Gallagher would say, they might have been *thugs*, slipping up behind unwary victims: practicing the sudden garrote with an elegant waxed cord.) This had been a minority position throughout the seventies (*Séméiotikē* had been published in 1967), but it was still argued, with great (if intermittent) ferocity, by the Bakhtinians when I arrived in Paris in 1979.

Todorov has always insisted upon viewing Bakhtin whole. He dismisses discussion of dialogue or carnival outside of their place within the onion-layered (and -domed) edifice of Bakhtin's global strategy for linguistic analysis. Even after Todorov had published his book on Bakhtin, however [This must be *Mikhail Bakhtine: Le principe dialogique*, which was published in 1981 by Editions du Seuil. It is a study of Bakhtin's thought followed by four essays by Bakhtin and translated from Russian by Todorov himself. Ainslie does not refer directly to Bakhtin but always limits himself to what has been said about him in the circles he frequented. That is, he limits himself to the role that Bakhtin played in the discussions of the philosophers.] the situation did not change: intellectuals still discuss the notion of carnival or of dialogism but not much else. (One did, occasionally hear, even before Todorov, if I can believe Abel Trigo-Cabral, about polyphonic discourse and even heteroglossia, but these were distinctly minor chords in the labyrinthine fugue of Parisian discourse.) In particular, *carnival* (a charismatic word if there ever was one!) tends to be assimilated to play or to game (*jeu*, of course, so one can never be quite certain), which transforms the Bakhtinian term into a net of wide applicability (having large holes) ideally suited for seining. Hence *carnival*, as it is commonly used, becomes a mere synonym (though quite picturesque) for *ludisme*, the playful transgression of official rules.

After Todorov fell from his bicycle, one heard the question of official as against unofficial discourse occur more frequently. Todorov had been struck by his own suddenly unofficial role and continued his meditations out loud even after he had regained his official status as semiotician and intellectual. Followers of Todorov in the matter of Bakhtin began (adopting the masks of urban ethnologists) to observe the authentic expressions of carnivalesque spirit in Paris. They actively sought out instances of collective play, spontaneous or ritualistic (it didn't seem to matter: although Todorov himself thought that it did), in crowds and flowing throngs.

The steps in front of Sacré-Coeur and La Place des Poètes beneath the Montparnasse Tower are cited as fruitful vortices of the carnivalesque. Indeed, most of the well-known squares, places, parvis, and concourses of the city seem normally (or can become) carnivalesque. On the other hand, such crowded places as the Bd. Saint-Germain-des-Pres or the rue Saint-André-des-Arts do not seem genuinely carnivalesque since they are thronged by tourists, semiological outsiders. (They are also linear and this makes a difference with respect to carnival: authentic carnival is both spontaneous and synchronic, an exploration of the available paradigms for action, and hence metaphoric, but tourism is planned and diachronic, a run-through of the possibilities for combination, and hence metonymic. Carnival, as the Bakhtinians define it, is a metaphor, but tourism is just another metonymy.) It is impossible to have carnival at the Opéra, even if they are singing *La Bohème*, Red Gallagher likes to say, but one can always have a bit of carnival in the concourse of the

Métro at l'Etoile. How can you have ludic transgressions of rules where the rules are not understood? Wherever one can observe readers of tarot cards, singers of folksongs, fire-eaters, mimes, buskers, clowns, African strongmen, Houdinis, or what have you, there is a good chance to observe authentic carnival.

The place in front of the Beaubourg (the spot where Derrida and Genette had remarked an escape artist fail, and, from this *échec*, drew both semiological and aesthetic conclusions) has become the favorite vantage from which to observe the unflowing of carnival. And in one sense it would be difficult to find a more spontaneously carnivalesque spot in Paris (being every day what the steps in front of Sacré-Coeur are on the night of July 14). Derrida has been heard to remark that the kaleidoscope of acts (all extremities of human prowess, hence "acts") mocked the glacial congealing of modern art that takes place within the Beaubourg. He is said to have looked down once from the fifth-level pedestrian tubeway and watched a Cameroon strongman press his chest against the tines of a pitchfork as three men attempted to drive him from within a circle he had drawn on the concrete. There stands, Derrida laughed, modern art resisting the official impulses of French government to humiliate it, to defeat it, to push it away out of its spontaneous signification.

Todorov, the lessons of his bicycle fall always fresh in his mind, refuses to allow the assimilation of carnival to a concept as generalized as *ludisme*. Carnival is essentially unofficial, he likes to say, but it cannot exist other than in a dialogue with the official. The mocker must always borrow (or steal) the utterance he intends to mock. To parody one must speak in the voice of the parodied: together, locked in a discursive embrace, mocker and mocked (screwer and screwee) perform a semiotic dance. Todorov often cites Propp that "theft cannot take place before the door is forced." Abel Trigo-Cabral, his admiring follower, declares that Paris is a city engaged in a carnival that fills the space between the exuberance of the people and the inflexible weight of the official rules. The one cannot exist without the other. Their coduration constitutes Paris.

[IN editing Ainslie Wellfleet's anecdotes, I have been repeatedly struck by how central a role is played by the concept of play. In all my studies at the University of Toronto, I do not remember that play was ever discussed. I should have thought, before reading through Ainslie's letters, that play was something that children did until they grew up and that there was little more to be said about it. But it appears that earnest philosophers can take play seriously and that it can pervade the most astringent arguments. I suppose that I should confess that I had never taken carnival to be an important concept, and yet, within the milieu in which Ainslie lived, it was clearly important. In Canada we have many winter carnivals, of which we are justly proud, but I doubt that anyone has thought about the word itself or attempted to define it. Duncan surprised me when he reported that Ainslie had called the Beaubourg the omphalos of Paris by adding that Ainslie must have lost his dictionary since, clearly, he should have called it the *aisselle*. Now that is a good example of Torontonian wordplay, if rather unusually bilingual. Our play is dry and precise. Hence I think it is evident that Ainslie's interest in play indicates, more than any other single factor, the distance he had crossed. The following anecdote comes from a letter written to me in November 1982.]

Paris is a city at play. The unofficial voices are heard in all the gardens, on all the parvis, in every place. I attempted this definition (and its poor English pun) the other night in conversation. Yves Zagli thought that it was improper for me, who has lived a bare three years here, to offer definitions of a city so many-leveled, so labyrinthine, as Paris. Bernard Galazzo was more encouraging. He suggested that the first act of a mind confronting a phenomenon it cannot understand is to define it. There then arose a dispute as to whether I had offered a definition or a classification (some cities are at work, others, like Paris, at play), an analogy or only an impression. Yves Zagli reminded everyone that Walter Benjamin had called Paris the "capital of the nineteenth century," but this rubric (whether definition or impression) would have made sense neither to the Parisians of the last century (obsessed by Baron Haussmann's urban renewals, the consequences of revolution, and the implications of alien ideologies) nor to those of this century. I might call Paris a city at play, if I chose, but it only reflected my outside-not-yet-inside condition. It was no more than an interpretive, not a genuinely hermeneutic, move.

Then Bernard Galazzo remembered that Derrida had once suggested that Paris should be considered a ludopolis (certainly not, as Maurice Roche had claimed, a mnemopolis) in recognition of the levels, the varieties, and the conceptually distinct modes of play that can be observed here. A philosopher's paradise (he said) and hence a ludopolis. Genette had replied that M. Derrida must not mean that Paris can be defined in terms of its free play (*jeu libre*) since that, as everyone who had ever tried to read M. Derrida's writing knew, was simply the condition of signification, of everything, *tout court*. No doubt he must mean that Paris can be defined by its modes of transgressive play, its mere *ludisme*. Like any text, Paris is constructed upon diverse codes. To play one must understand these codes (just as in playing a game one must understand the rules: if one didn't understand the rules of chess, he might play with the pieces and board, he might make them into playthings, but he could not play chess): for they are the matrix of transgression. Hence the play of Paris (Genette had continued) is full of knowledge. It is like M. Derrida's writing, like *Glas*, say, but not like his concept of play. The play of Paris is a game of initiates, of code users and code violators. It invaginates an external system of repression into an internal ludic space. Parisian play is not (as M. Derrida appears to believe) merely a random mutability. It is not something so prior in necessity that it must be ontologically unbound.

Bernard Galazzo further remembered that Todorov, who had been listening intently but silently up to that point, interjected to remark (in his Bakhtinian mode) that Paris was an infinite utterance (*un énoncé infini*) in which the unofficial voices speak to the official, undercutting but also enhancing them. Derrida, who (for obvious reasons) does not highly regard the Bakhtinian concepts that have attracted so much attention, then proclaimed that *if* Paris were a text, then it would contain its opposite, its *obversus*, hidden within its shadows. One must then read it (if M. Todorov's assertion were correct) according to the conventions of semiological construction, and one must expect to encounter all the semiological bogies that, like a Spanish *sacamantecas*, lurk along the dark interstices of sigification. For that reason, he added laughing, the play of Paris is perhaps most evident at night. But it is, in any case, the condition of all its meanings and not simply (as M. Genette has claimed) the ludic acts of transgression, however many of these there are.

Todorov then interjected (inconsequentially, Bernard Galazzo thought) that, as Bakhtin had remarked, realism is only one of the possibilities of reality. Derrida responded (in the high spirit of philosophical laughter) that if this were so, then one must maintain that reality is merely a possibility of realism. It is then no more than one possibility of its own textuality. A single street, a single action, a word lost in passing, becomes immediately (even as, and only because, they exist) another, touch upon some other, make intentionless networks. There the semiological bogey lurks, the one (a true *sacamantecas*) who drains the fat from healthy constructions: there is where the playful find their play. The infinite text of Paris is incessantly being inscribed merely as the condition (and the consequence) of its own textuality.

[THE following anecdote appears in its most complete form in a letter written to Rowena on January 10, 1983. Sometime not long afterward Ainslie Wellfleet disappeared. Fragmentary versions of this anecdote occur in letters written as early as September 1982. The meal to which Ainslie refers must, then, have taken place during the summer of 1982. I have collated all the available versions of the anecdote. Oddly, the only significant discrepancy regards the exhibition of paintings by Vlaminck to which Ainslie refers only in a letter to Elizabeth Scott.]

Colette Tourbillon likes to cite Barthes to the effect that "we live in a sleeve [*un manchon*?] of semes" or, as she occasionally remembers the phrase, in a semiotic envelope. Once sitting with Georgina Hiboux and Michel Tasd'homme in a restaurant across from l'Ecole Militaire (avenue Duquesne), she was asked when (since it appears nowhere in his writings) Barthes had used this phrase. Michel Tasd'homme broke in immediately to deny its authenticity. Barthes, he argued, could not have used such a phrase since he believed that we (humankind, I suppose) generate and construct signification in our cognitive activities. To live in a sleeve of semes would make one too passive for authentic Barthesque analysis. Then, just before Colette Tourbillon could make an angry rejoinder, Lysiana Medine remembered the amazement Barthes had experienced when he discovered that there was a science known as "moulinologie." Barthes had traveled to Chartres in the company of Genette, Red Gallagher, and Marie-Hélène Cahuzac. Their intention had been to study clownage in the stained glass (that is, faces, gestures, and costumes that indicated clownage). Barthes had always enjoyed reiterating the fourteenth-century monk who had observed that "images are the literature of the layman." During the afternoon they had made a brief visit to the small museum behind the cathedral particularly to see an exhibition of Vlaminck's paintings. While they were in the museum they stumbled upon a display dedicated to windmills: their purposes, history, construction, and distribution. Barthes was delighted to hear that there were Frenchmen who chased windmills, worked (like amateur archaeologists) to discover the sites of vanished windmills, collected parts and surviving bits, and generally spent all their disposable time studying and collecting information (and bits) about windmills. A large *affiche* under a wooden model announced that the study of windmills was known as "moulinologie." Barthes was especially happy in this wonderful neologism since Jean Moulin had once lived in Chartres and had, indeed, been the prefect of Eure-et-Loir. Moulinologie would be the scientific study both of windmills and of Jean Moulin.

It thus appeared, Barthes noted, that moulinologie is a subdivision of hagiography. It is the archaeology not only of a certain type of edifice but also of a certain type of human spirit. It will take its practitioners (even if they decline to travel together) from the fields of Normandy to the Pantheon. Then Red Gallagher reminded Barthes that the study of windmills must also be a subdivision of literary history since one of the seminal narratives concerned, at least in one striking passage, the shapes, movements, and significance of windmills. Genette evidently liked this codicil to Barthes's discourse since he then began to argue that *Don Quichotte* had been the central (the inescapable) narrative in the history of narrative. Red Gallagher then quoted Marthe Robert to the effect that *Don Quichotte* had given the modern novel the work it had to do (*sa tâche*): everything that later had come to seem so massively significant was, like a germ (a sprouting seminary, I thought) already contained in that novel. Genette liked that idea and expanded it, in returning to his initial proposition, to claim that the significance of *Don Quichotte,* as a narrative, as semiotic system, as a text to be read, and as a manifestation of textuality itself, was already contained, encoded, within the early encounter with the windmills. For this reason moulinologie could be seen as the prototype of literary archaeology.

Barthes was even more delighted by this proposition. Moulinologie became, not an obscure and aberrant pursuit (akin to stalking mare's nests or tilting up *faux-fuyants*), but an essential exploration of the human spirit. It was at once the disciplined study of Jean Moulin, of Don Quichotte, the character, and of *Don Quichotte,* the text. Perhaps all semiotic investigation should be renamed moulinologie, Barthes suggested. Would it then be the case, Genette inquired, that they had all become by the inadvertency of discovery moulinologists? Or perhaps if we believe Julia Kristeva (and he nodded, smiling precisely, toward Georgina Hiboux), they must all, in the full flowing of semiosis, ride unendingly the mill's sails, like Don Quichotte at the exact moment when his lance catches the illusive fabric.

Lysiana Medine reported that they all returned to Paris in good spirits and ate a meal of goat cheese to honor their arcadian discovery and to invoke the memory of the archetypal subject of moulinologie, Don Quichotte, who had once eaten goat cheese and, in so doing, had himself been reminded of the Golden Age. We all enjoyed a good laugh at this anecdote. The hostility between Michel Tasd'homme and Colette Tourbillon that had been brewing over Barthes's imputed use of the term *sleeve* [*un manchon*?] now calmed. In a spirit of empathetic reiteration we all called for baguettes and goat cheese. And laughing, perhaps just slightly carnivalesque (though if Todorov had been there he would surely have denied it), we bent our minds to the furthering of moulinological analysis.

[Ainslie's final anecdote indicates that he had adjusted fully to the life of a philosophical disciple. He appears to be at ease, confident, and fluent in French. I infer that last point from his careless use of the English word *sleeve.* It makes quite a difference in French whether one says *une manche* or *un manchon,* but in English there is, of course, only the single word. I believe that someone less than fluent in French would have attempted to translate the term exactly as, for example, a "shirtsleeve" or a "cylinder sleeve." Although there is some comic potential in saying that we live in a shirtsleeve, there is, I think, more philosophical sense in saying that we live in a surrounding cover of semiotic signification in which, like pistons, we slide up and down. Anecdotes such as this one make Ainslie's disappearance all the more unbearable for we can see clearly what, in time, he might have contributed to philosophy as well as to the understanding of French in Ontario.]

AFTER I had several times read through Ainslie Wellfleet's letters to his friends and family, I culled from them a number of anecdotes that suggest the style of life he had elected after arriving in Paris. These that I have published here are typical, but they are not exhaustive. I soon realized that Ainslie had done little else in Paris than listen to talk. He had been fortunate, it seemed, though perhaps it had been natural enough for a young man who had always known the most important people in Toronto, in making the acquaintance of certain important *maîtres de penser* and their followers. If one's purpose is to learn French and study philosophy, what better way could be found? To that extent, it seemed self-evident that Ainslie had simply taken his usual intent, purposeful, highly efficient way of going about things.

After a time, it became apparent that Ainslie had derived more than a casual pleasure from these conversations. His French must have improved rapidly for it did not seem likely that his new friends would have admitted him into their company if he had continued to *balbutier* as he had always done in the past. What began to emerge was a picture of a young man who had taken himself in hand, so to speak, and changed himself in very significant ways. He had undergone a massive transformation of character. Ainslie Wellfleet had allowed himself to become Frenchified with a will. He must have set himself the goal, with the true determination of the Ontario Establishment, of becoming a full member of the circles he attended. Perhaps he even longed to become an insider or, as he quotes Roland Barthes, of becoming an inside-outsider. Considerations such as these tend to explain why he steadfastly refused to return to Toronto. It would not have been like him to run against the wishes of his father and older brother except for something extremely important. I submit that the attraction that kept him in Paris was not a Parisienne but Paris itself or, to speak more exactly, the scintillations of Parisian intellectuality.

Of course, this does not explain his tragic disappearance. It is commonly assumed that he has been murdered. Perhaps, indeed, he was robbed and then dumped in the Seine or in a convenient sewer. Those of us who knew Ainslie can only feel deep sorrow and chagrin at the thought. Canada's loss, if this is true, has been great. My close reading of his letters, however, suggested another explanation, one not less stunning but less appalling to contemplate.

Several cognitive attitudes are evident in Ainslie's letters. If one read them casually, or read them in the context of an emotional involvement, as gossip or familial reportage, say, it might be easy to miss these qualities. Needless to say, I read his papers with an eye to discovering how his mind worked and I tended to blot out mere family gossip and to concentrate on the anecdotes that indicate Ainslie's relationship to the intellectual life of Paris. Looking with such narrow eyes, I could see that all his accounts of life in Paris reflected intense pleasure, even joy, in the discussion that took place and a deep commitment to making himself a part of the milieu. It is not difficult to surmise that Ainslie found his life in Paris so enchanting that he had no wish to return to the wintry grayness of Toronto. In itself, this does not provide a hypothesis to explain his disappearance.

In rereading the anecdotes that I had culled from Ainslie's letters, I observed a striking fact. In all of his accounts Ainslie assigns names to the participants in the conversations. The great philosophers are indicated by their last names alone, and their disciples are designated invariably by the combination of their first and last names. Thus we encounter Derrida and Genette but also Red Gallagher and Lysiana Medine. Ainslie's practice in reporting the discussions in which he participated or, in some cases, heard about after they had occurred is to give a precise indication of who said what in order to characterize explicitly the transsubjective dynamics. He needed no supernumeraries in his accounts. Nor, given what seem clearly to be his methods of writing, should one expect there to be any. Yet there is one.

Throughout Ainslie's reportage there is one supernumerical character. He is never said to speak. He makes no comments. He does not participate. He seems only to observe. Significantly, the longer Ainslie remained in Paris and the more detailed his reporting became, the more commonly this silent, observing character appears. Thus one reads such notations as the following: "Farkhondé Sabi was present" or "Farkhondé Sabi sat in a chair near the window" or "Among the group Farkhondé Sabi took his usual place." Ainslie gives this character a bare notation, simply acknowledging that he was present, that he sat, or ate, or stood. He alone of the characterizations that Ainslie works so hard to develop remains always silent. It is my hypothesis that Farkhondé Sabi is, in reality, Ainslie Wellfleet himself. Why else would Ainslie make a point of noting his minimally discursive presence?

If, for the sake of the hypothesis, we assume that I am right, that Ainslie Wellfleet referred to himself as Farkhondé Sabi, we have both to answer the question, why, and to show how this explains his disappearance. The first problem is, I think, dealt with easily enough. Ainslie was shy. Initially his French must have been shockingly weak. Yet he was accustomed to being at the center of discussion, to being taken seriously at all times. It would have rubbed deeply against his grain to record that he had remained silent, cut out of the dialectical passion that inhabits discursiveness. By adopting the mask of Farkhondé Sabi, he could record the conversation that he witnessed, and that so fascinated him, without calling attention to his own silence. Farkhondé Sabi was silent, not Ainslie Wellfleet.

I believe that Ainslie first adopted the mask of Farkhondé Sabi and then dissolved into this assumed identity. It became his *nom de guerre*. It would have been easy to accomplish, easy at any time, perhaps, but superbly easy in that ludopolis, that city of play, of carnival and masks. It may even be that some of his friends in Paris knew of his metamorphosis but have kept their silence about it. That would explain why Ainslie's father and his brother Duncan were unable to locate him or even to find anyone who remembered having seen him in the recent past. These same people might well have known where to find Farkhondé Sabi. Thus Ainslie may have found the means by which he could make himself, more readily at least, an insider to the circles he admired and by which, furthermore, he could break completely those ties to Ontario that he had come to find irksome, if not odious. Farkhondé Sabi would not need to leave Paris. Neither imperious father nor condescending brother could ever make claims upon his obligations.

This much I think we may confidently assume. Ainslie Wellfleet has disappeared, but only as one identity flows into another. His disappearance has been that of metamorphosis, not extinction. I also suspect, though I admit this is neither easy to support nor to believe, that Ainslie may have chosen this metamorphosis so he could undertake certain acts of anonymous terrorism. French intellectual life is, after all, terroristic in its deep grain. Its spirit is that of thuggee: determination, laughter, and a waxed cord. It destroys all cognitive stability. The soundest models are twisted and hurled, askew and broken, into the dustheaps. It is something to be feared as well as admired. My own very personal conviction is that Derrida chose Ainslie for acts of terrorism outside of France and that his *nom de guerre* is precisely that, a warrior's name, a war cry to be shouted and to spread terror in the minds of traditionalist thinkers.

In my mind's eye, I can see Farkhondé Sabi walking the streets of Vancouver, Melbourne, Dublin, or Atlanta, wherever contemporary French philosophy is unregarded. He walks, his face suffused by an oblique leer, wearing a cap with a raffish tilt, in the pursuit of intellectual combat, seeking conversations to enter, arguments to explode. He masters discussions: a slanting finger jab, a quick mind trained to grasp analogies, an opaque but glistening lexicon, all bringing intimidation, breeding fear. In each gathering, each pub, tavern, or café, he drives the disputants to surrender, to admit defeat or to give up thinking. People who have been confident in their assumptions, who have never needed to examine the bases of their discourse, are driven, perhaps in tears, certainly in anger, to concede the doubleness, the plurality, the undecidability of their arguments. Perhaps even today Farkhondé Sabi is driving a taxi in Atlanta. Perhaps he has enrolled as a student at the University of Melbourne, pulling the cloak of rationality over his tutors like a sheepskin hood.

V

> I like this word [play] for two reasons. Because it evokes a properly ludic activity, and also the play of an apparatus, a machine, that tiny extra movement possible in the fitting together of its various elements.
>
> —Roland Barthes,
> *The Grain of the Voice: Interviews 1962–1980*

Derrida's writing invokes at least three distinct concepts of play. For this reason, carnival bears an instable, or shifting, relationship to Derrida's use of play depending on which sense of the concept is in focus. Derrida discusses play as it has been understood elsewhere in philosophical discourse. In *Dissemination*, for instance, he analyzes Plato's understanding of play, its relation to the more diffuse concept of the *pharmakon*, and, in particular, the way, in Plato's discourse, the "*singularity* of play" becomes neutralized by its subsumption to the concept of game ("Play is always lost when it seeks salvation in games"[36]). Derrida also often plays in a fairly ordinary sense of the term. Wordplay, glittering paronomasia, bewildering textual strategies, seemingly a Mad Hatter's delight in combination and permutation, compile an anthology (or, perhaps, a pharmacy) of scribal moves that suggest writers as diverse as Joyce, Nabokov, Sanguineti, Calvino, Borges, or many practitioners of *le nouveau roman* and *le nouveau nouveau roman*. Geoffrey Hartman has suggested that *Glas* is, in its "beautiful strangeness," something like a philosophical *Finnegans Wake*. Hartman further develops the analogy when he writes that in *Glas* the reader seems "to skirt Joyce's words within words, his 'echoland'."[37] These diverse uses of, and allusions to, play are overmastered, however, perhaps even swallowed, by the ruling concept of free play. It is on this level that the contrast with the concept of carnival (and carnivalization) seems both sharpest and most instructive. As a term already appropriated by a textualist model such as Kristeva's, carnival might well describe Derrida's own wordplay, but as a dialogic term, indicating how meaning can be created out of the agon between distinct monologic and incomplete utterances, carnival opposes free play. It does so in an essential, deeply contrastive, manner.

Play possesses two irreducible senses: it may be conceived as free, voluntary action or as random motion. The two may be seen as interlocked such that the possibilities of random motion underlie, as Gadamer argues, all free, uncompelled action. But the two core senses of play lead to irreconcilable accounts of play and the play element in human life. The dichotomy constitutes a fundamental opposition, though one that readily opens to conflation. Indeed, all discussion of play appears vulnerable on this point: merely as phenomena, play-acts from either category may seem to be similar and may be given similar descriptive accounts. Whether movement, give-and-take, or plain bouncingness express freedom or random motion may not be discernible from the outside. The most extravagant to-and-fro motion, however loud, brightly colored, or startling, can only be opaque from the outside. One must penetrate the phenomena to obtain a grasp of its intention or intentionlessness. The opposition turns upon the presence or absence of purpose. A hidden differentia (that is, one that can only be known on extrinsic grounds, by inference and hypothesis) may be actual enough, but its occult status prompts both misapprehension and deception.

Play is a philosophically charged term. Though the history of philosophy contains various accounts of play, stretching back as far as Heraclitus and including both Plato and Aristotle, the modern importance of the concept springs from Kant and develops complexly throughout the nineteenth century and the early twentieth century. Spariosu writes that "Kant and German idealism in general begin the long uneven, reverse process of restoring literature/play to its pre-Platonic privileged position; this process will culminate in the middle of the twentieth century in the work of Heidegger and Fink. From a suppressed epistemological prop of philosophy, play becomes in our age, an indispensable cognitive tool, indeed a fundamental way of understanding Being which is again seen as disclosing itself only as and in play."[38] Though Kant begins the modern history of play, the central instance of its use, and that from which most modern thinking on the subject stems, can be found in Friedrich Schiller's *On the Aesthetic Education of Man*. In this series of letters Schiller argues that play constitutes one of three distinctive drives (*trieb*) that urge human beings toward the abstract, in one direction, and toward the sensual, in the other. The play drive (*spieltrieb*) provides a principle of mediation. According to Schiller, play is the means by which humankind expresses the voluntary and creative dimension of will. One becomes exteriorized in play and realizes, in unrestricted creativity, the possibilities of imagination. (In a post-Jungian age, one might even say, still in true Schillerian phrase, that the potentialities of selfhood are realized in play, especially in make-believe and role simulation.) In play one is no longer bound by external limitations: though, of course, one does not become infinite in play, merely untrammeled. Schiller puts his point forcefully when he remarks that man "only plays when he is in the fullest sense of the word a human being, and he is only fully a human being when he plays."[39] Play, then, is distinctively human, the source of freedom and self-realization: that which is most valuable in human nature.

Once again, the illusions of the modern technobower suggest an instructive contrast. The pleasures may be numerous, but they are neither spontaneous nor voluntary. The freedom of the technobower, whether to choose (lines of action or mere commodities) or to play is largely illusory. The chill, commercial system directs choice, limiting and channeling, and prohibits anything that might become genuine play. Much the same can be said about professional sports. Spectators who lack skills in the games being played, who do not play themselves, cheer or boo teams for reasons that have little to do with either the recognition of skills or the spirit of play. (One thinks of those spectators of professional hockey who attend for the violence or to see the blood glistening on the background of white ice.) There is no true self-realization in either case. These funless experiences mask themselves as fun, but no one who has ever played, who has ever felt "inside" a game, is likely to be fooled. Even from Gadamer's fairly narrow perspective on play, in which both skills and the subjectivity of the players are discounted, the technobower would still fail to correspond to the concept of play. It does not allow anyone to "be" anyone else, to be the play itself, or to see this (as a genuine spectator) in others. From a Schilleresque perspective, both technobowers and professional sports would seem inauthentic and stultifying.

Eugen Fink's *Play as World Symbol* makes a Schillerian argument in absolute world terms: in play man actually jumps out of himself and realizes otherwise unrealizable potentialities (though, since this is what being is doing through the world, man is also a plaything as well as a player).[40] In Fink the sour grapes principle ("the world is inadequate, I don't like it, but I don't care because I have something better") inherent in Schiller's discussion is brought to a maximal point. Fink's analysis of play also illustrates what Spariosu means when he speaks of play as having become an "indispensable cognitive tool" since it is through play that man learns about, and comes to understand, being. Similarly, though perhaps on a lesser level, all play is exploration, a trying out (or on) of possibilities, a touching upon the imaginable, and in this manner also a cognitive tool. When one encounters the concept of play, from psychoanalysis to children's folklore, the chances are that one has met a Schillerian idea, or at least the vestige of one.[41]

In contrast, it is possible to define play as random movement, impersonal and wholly inevitable. One speaks of the play of fountains, of waves, of light, of rain, of energy, of molecules, of ideas, of possibilities, and of signification. Play is random, a ceaseless give-and-take, an inevitable mutability. The relationship between these two evidently opposed concepts of play can be illustrated by invoking the familiar structuralist opposition between synchrony and diachrony, between paradigm and syntagm, or, to advance Roman Jacobson's formulation, between metaphor and metonymy.[42] These oppositions are often visualized as the lines of intersecting vertical and horizontal axes. In this simple model, the vertical axis represents the synchronic availability of choice (hence it stands for the paradigmatic possibilities of language) while the horizontal axis represents the diachronic choices of combination, the linear sequence of a sentence (hence it stands for the syntagmatic possibilities of language). The Schillerian sense of play points to the human potential to explore, to play up and through the possibilities of a given paradigm, to create metaphors. The other sense of play points to the potential to combine, to form endless series of permutations, to create metonymies. The first sense of play might be taken as the basis for, and as the fullest expression of, metaphor; the second, as both the basis for, and the fullest expression of, metonymy.

In the Schillerian perspective, play is always purposeful. Its purpose is internal (expressable by Kant's dictum: purposeless purpose), but nonetheless actual. The internal purposes of play are unlike the compulsive, external purposes imparted by an injunction, a prohibition, or a command. The Schillerian definition of play strikes an equation between freedom and creativity. Children in play really are, in some valid fashion, what they play at being, as is the artist, who, in his creativity, actualizes possibility. (Hence this freedom may appear to be *either* a sublime form of sour grapes *or* the pinnacle of human achievement.) This is most evident in make-believe games, but it will fit into the account of all games. In Gadamer's revision of the idealistic position, though it accepts both the self-enclosed nature of play and the "really the case" psychology of players, it is always the game, the nature of the play itself, that is revealed, not, in self-revelation, the players. The opposed sense of play (which may be associated, mnemonically, with Derrida), since it postulates only random permutations, makes play into a mode of bondage; it confers no special privilege of self-expression, fulfillment, and creativity. As post-Nietzschean commentators observe, in being understood for what it is, free play makes possible the gaiety, the joy, of following clear-mindedly the paths of inevitability. Free play describes a necessary condition and an inescapable effect, not a willed, free, or purposeful act. Play may be followed, understood, and enjoyed, but not willed. A suitable metaphor for the Schillerian concept of play could be drawn from any human activity of shaping, molding, or forming; within the discourse of deconstruction, an appropriate metaphor for play, or for the transgressive free play of signification, might be a kaleidoscope: an endless linear series of permutations, each spectacular in itself, each different, with no potential for correction, enhancement, or culmination.[43]

The metaphor of a kaleidoscope would apply weakly to Bakhtin's concept of carnival. There can be no kaleidoscopism because there is neither randomness nor endlessness. Conversely, there must be correction, enhancement, and, above all, culmination. There will not be an endless (or even an open) play of difference but a wholeness composed of differences within a single utterance. Discourse is an action, as Holquist writes, and language is an "ecosystem."[44] If one *were* to seek an accurately expressive metaphor for Bakhtin's concept of carnival, one would have to invoke images from the experience of music, dance, copulation, or the bivalvular movement of lips: images that suggest union, responsiveness, creativity, completion, and wholeness.

Speaking of Bakhtin's discussion of death in carnival dress, Dominic La Capra writes that "with an alacrity that sometimes seems precipitate, Bakhtin underplays the role of anxiety in order to stress the relationship between death and renewal in carnivalesque forms."[45] Carnival, through mocking, undercutting, and upending, always a travesty, is also positive. Its positive force arises from the negative act that is its necessary first move. The mocking, carnivalesque mask calls into question an official discourse and, in so doing, enhances and completes it.

Carnival is a mode of the human double voice. A discourse in which one monologic level of speech (any single voice, say) is mocked *and* replaced, destroyed in play but not completed, cannot be carnivalesque as Bakhtin appears to understand the concept. If travesty and derision create their own laws, as Kristeva argues, and in so doing outlaw the discourse that is the butt of the mockery, then they are not carnivalesque. They may well be ludic.

Abstracting the concept of carnival from Bakhtin's discourse and compelling it to labor in a textualist model of literary analysis seems both to do an injustice to the complexity of his thinking and to impoverish the concept. Carnival and carnivalization are, La Capra argues, "critical dimensions of life that must coexist and interact with other dimensions." The ceaseless flitting of ludic transgressiveness (always the knife's edge of infinite negatability), each momentarily stabilized position, whether of law or thought, giving way to the next, is another, and essentially irreconcilable, concept. Milan Kundera speaks in an authentically Bakhtinian voice when he comments that the "synthetic power of the novel is capable of combining everything into a unified whole like the voices of polyphonic music."[46]

Where, then, does carnival belong in the family of play concepts? Or, what node in the cognitive network of play concepts does it fill? This may seem like a superfluous question, one that has been sufficiently answered by the opposition between Schiller's and Derrida's concepts of play. Carnival *must be* a Schillerian concept. But the small problems of literary theory are seldom resolved effortlessly. In the family of concepts that play rules not only are there distances but surprising proximities.[47]

If the differentia dividing the two senses of play can be expressed as the presence or absence of a purpose, then it would seem that Bakhtin's concept of carnival must belong to the Schillerian celebration of human play, always both free and intentional. It stresses the dialogic exchange between people, the mocking carnivalians, not, as Gadamer argues, the essential structure of a recurring festival. Among other things, carnival is free, voluntary, creative, a manifestation of the human double voice, and whole-making. Yet in being double and whole-making, a discursive dance between at least two voices, it must also participate in the seriality of all combinations. (Much the same can be said, in Bakhtinian terms, about any other semiologically coherent systems: gestures, fashion, manners, architecture, cuisine, and so forth.) Bakhtin's concept of carnival might be said, in effect, to occupy the angle between the vertical, paradigmatic axis of metaphor and the horizontal, syntagmatic axis of metonymy. There is something ongoing about carnival, though it is limited by the finite spatio-temporal boundaries of particular utterances.

In a genuinely carnivalesque narrative such as *Don Quijote* (which Bakhtin calls "the classic and purest model of the novel"[48]), the carnivalized folk humor, the dialectical variants, Sancho's proverbs, the jokes, the crude games that are played on both Knight and Squire, the many instances of bodily grotesque, all contribute, through a short series of permutations, to the completeness of the Knight's character and to that of the distinctive courtly idiolect that he has chosen to speak.[49] Although the Knight might have written a continuation of the adventures of Don Belianis, so thoroughly has he mastered the discourse of chivalric romance, still his elected idiolect requires the completive thrust of mockery. The Knight, "emaciated, tall, ascetic, mad, and grandiloquent," and the peasant, "corpulent, gluttonous, sane, and colloquial," as Borges calls them,[50] not only need each other for the symmetrical disharmonies of comedy but also to establish the nature of the language each speaks. The moments of carnivalized humor that punctuate the narrative make clear the authentic properties of the discourse of the chivalaric romances that speak, from the first page, through the Knight's voice. Mocked by Sancho's ironic materialism, confronted by the picaresque inelegancies of Ginés de Pasamonte, humiliated by the Knight's failures though never exalted by his successes, reconstituted freshly in each of the Knight's adventures, reflexively expanded in each of his narrative accounts, the discourse of chivalric romance had never been clearer, or more clearly seen, than in the *Quijote*.

Bakhtin's concept of carnival holds an unusual position in the family of play concepts. It appears to belong to (or to occupy the angle between) both opposed definitions of play. Carnival cannot be reduced to either extreme formulation of play. It is a social act, an exchange, and can be explained neither entirely as a free or voluntary action nor as the involuntary byplay, the to-and-fro, of systemic movement. Furthermore, though it is certainly a festival (of sorts), it does not exist only to display itself through its celebrants. It exists, at least as Bakhtin sees it, to offer a critique of a particular sociocultural situation and its corresponding discourse. A transgression in Bakhtin's theory, neither destructive nor a replacing law to itself, would be completive. Its transgressiveness would create a fresh, much richer situation. One might say that carnival must always enhance the context in which it occurs as well as the antagonist against which it plays. Bakhtin's contemporary L. S. Vygotsky puts the principle of duality succinctly when he writes that freedom in play (the aspect of play that Schiller stresses above all others) is "an illusory freedom for [the child's] actions are in fact subordinated to the meaning of things."[51] Carnival is "subordinated to the meaning of things," but it is also ongoing and completive. The "meaning of things" keeps its original, if etiolated, clarity and straightforwardness in the play of carnival while gaining much besides. Carnival's essential duality and metonymical ongoingness characterize the concept as much as do its spontaneous and free travesties. Hence carnival is, in the family of play concepts, both a distinctive and a powerful idea. As a reading of *Don Quijote* makes plain, carnival is always a difference contained within, and helping to make, a whole utterance.

The conceptual complexity of play, constellating a family of previously unrelated or barely related subordinate concepts, is remarkable. Play is free, creative, metaphoric; it is also involuntary, bound, and metonymic. It has been used to describe the highest and fullest human achievements and to measure human potential; it is used to designate a universal and inescapable human condition. It is also, as Gadamer argues, the mode of being of a work of art: to understand art, including literary texts, one begins with play. Play is constructive; it is also destructive (and deconstructive). A concept such as carnival seems torn between these opposite definitions. Bakhtin's linguistic model, of which carnival is a significant part, occupies a position between the two opposed views of play, but it suggests the possibility of mediation as well. It seems evident that an account of play, leading in opposite directions, must bear several senses of the concept in mind.

The remaining chapters of this book, insofar as they return to the question of play, will examine Bakhtin's model as a possible mediative path between the two directions that play takes. The most important problem to be solved, however, concerns the distinction between play and game. English seems fortunate in possessing the twin terms *play* and *game* since their copresence promotes a wide range of distinctions. These may, of course, be illusory distinctions, as instable and shifting as most propositions connected with the analysis of play, but their availability, resting on the intuitive separateness of the twinned (if not necessarily entwined) terms in English, has always run through criticism written in English, giving discussions of play/game a snappiness not always found in Continental writing. The distinction between an author's playfulness and his gamefulness, replicating that between an exuberant activity and a cunningly constructed structure, projects a fundamental opposition within the pathways of human thinking.

The argument of this book threads itself among the polarities of play/game theory. The cunningly constructed structures of games are a test case for all human artifacts since a rule structure exteriorizes a cognitive model. (If, for example, one *did* know the rules for the Royal Game of Ur, then significantly more would be known generally concerning the history of human thinking.) All artifacts, from junk to technobowers, machines or artworks, occupy the shifting shadow world that games delimit: products of one mind, received and played by others, displaying an invented (or borrowed) structure, but open to the imposition of other, newer, or more efficient structures, always to be seen from the outside, experienced from the inside. Inescapably, the analysis of games, analogues to all other cunning artifacts, returns one to the problem of play. Experiencing a game from within, feeling oneself inside the game, caught up in the play, points to a general paradox of artificial structures. The rules (conventions, directives, or axioms) that make them possible, that give them their distinctive shapes and allow them to make their claims upon our intelligence, are seen from the outside as arbitrary, reflecting only one choice from a paradigm of choices, but are experienced as rigid and exclusive.

In the discussion that follows this paradox will be investigated in terms of the analogy between games and texts. In Chapter 3 the argument will distinguish between the rules of games and the conventions of texts to the extent that the former can be analyzed as rigid and difficult to modify while the latter are flexible and open to constant modification. Beginning in Chapter 4 and continuing into Chapter 5, the discussion explores the inwardness of both playing and reading in which conventions, the flexible directives of textual structures, are analyzed as being, when experienced from the inside, both exclusive and axiomatic. Textual conventions are experienced ("from within") as pseudo-axioms. The intricacies of play/game theory reveal something important about all symbolic structures, but literary texts in particular: descriptive analyses, based on accurately observing the parameters of use and the matrix of directives, whether rules or conventions, that make symbolic structures possible, fail to account for the experience of use. Play seems significantly different from the games that are played: from within the game, nothing ever looks or feels quite the same.

CHAPTER 3

The Game/Text Analogy

three paradoxes

Is it true that the common root of madness and mania is, at least in certain cases, the will not to participate in the great tournament (or comedy) of social existence? This is a perilous game, a game where the rules change quite often, become complicated or are improvised before the match is over, a game full of cheaters, of counterfeiters, of rogues, of assassins.
—Paolo Santarcangeli,
"The Jester and the Madman, Heralds of Liberty and Truth"

ONCE ONE RECOGNIZES the complex sociocultural phenomena that are gathered together by the concept of play, it becomes possible to distinguish between the many different senses in which play is used as a term of literary analysis. Within the boundaries of literary texts, the byplay of culture reappears in attenuated, deformed shapes, but textual play, the fundamental mode of being of any artwork, as Gadamer argues, also reaches out into culture. The human sense of play, of its possibilities, its potential forms, reflects what has already been imagined. Carnival, a highly specific form of playfulness, reflects in a sociocultural arena a wide range of imaginative shapes (the masks, grotesqueries, mocking language), but it also reappears in the language of literary texts as popular humor, as literary travesty, as an alternative voice. Play is voluntary, creative, and exploratory; it is movement in the random permutations generated by a system (a set of conditions, a field or a ground); it is the semiotic transaction between distinct individuals, who, without negotiating in advance a covenant or any plan for mutual exchange, create meaning by borrowing, masquerading within, or mocking each other's words. It is clear that, in the analysis of literary texts, one might describe the author as playing in the first sense, the text as playing in the second, and the author and reader as playing between themselves in the third. Thus it is possible to argue that there are significant ways in which Schiller, Bakhtin, Gadamer, and Derrida all provide models that explain textuality and do so in ways that are congruent with aspects of the play concept's normal diversity.

One may make even more complex claims, of course: that (say) the playfulness of the text lies in its traps, snares, puzzles, aporia, paradoxicality, wordplay of every conceivable sort, allusiveness (whether deliberate or systematic), vast openness to intertextual citation, and inherent ambiguity, as well as in its play of signification. Presumably, Frank Kermode has this complexity in mind, and not the poststructuralist notion of free play, when he speaks of the text as being playful.[1] Furthermore, it seems evident that any and all of these aspects of textual playfulness might be attributed, not merely to the labyrinthine motions of textuality but, equally to the author, to the reader, or to the interplay between them.[2] The play concept's multiple formulations and pervasive applicability exceed, *elude* one might say, the boundaries of any single model of literary analysis.

Considerations such as these lead directly to the problem of the distinction between play and game. One might suppose that play must be the more general concept and that though all games presuppose playfulness, not all play leads to gamefulness. As Huizinga insists, however, many games are played without the spirit of play, without playfulness.[3] Modern professional sports are largely technical exercises, the competent execution of which does not require that the players enjoy what they are doing, that they wish to do it, or that they are having fun. (*Fun* is a word that Huizinga thinks to be unique to English and to describe superbly what goes on in genuine play.[4]) One can imagine games in which players are compelled, perform joylessly, or in which the play element of the activity (insofar as this involves freedom, self-absorption, joy, or fun) is unequally distributed between the organizers, the players, and the audience. This, in fact, more or less describes the degree of playfulness to be found in a godgame (the topic of the next chapter). In a godgame, the players experience a singularly intense but funless situation. An attempt to isolate the gamefulness of games and to distinguish games from play, however, begins most reasonably from an analysis of rules. If any single thing distinguishes games from mere (or pure, or informal) play, it will be the presence of at least one constitutive rule, a piece of enabling legislation that makes possible precise directions, objectives, and even modes in play.

The distinction between unstructured play and a game, even an extremely simple one, can easily be observed on any playground. Children play (run, chase, whirl), and they also play games. The line between the two is often fuzzy, a boundary that it is perhaps not entirely possible to preserve and which dissolves abruptly as intentions shift, but which nonetheless proclaims itself. In the absence of a convenient playground, Istvan Szabó's short film *Square* illustrates wonderfully the point being made.[5] Szabó's film depicts one of his favorite parts of his native Budapest and makes a kind of diptych with another film of his, *City Map*. In *Square*, Szabó presents a formally varied montage of children at play. It is rather like a modern version of Pieter Brueghel's *Children's Games* in which the activity (and energy) of play are placed in the foreground of the film rather than, as in Brueghel, the rule-specific characteristics of a playground's diverse movements.

Square provides evidence that a great deal of play takes place with maximal energy, the activities constantly changing and shifting into new movements. There is, for example, considerable whirling, activities characterized by speed and dizziness. (This play corresponds to what Roger Caillois calls "ilenx": activities that cause vertigo, with all of its risks and pleasures. Caillois, of course, thinks that ilenx constitutes a game and, if dizziness is sought as an objective, or if it is measured in its effect between different players, this claim seems reasonable.) Szabó's main point seems to be the ephemeral nature of such play, its kaleidoscopic swirl. But informal play turns into game with startling rapidity. Children who have been running, jumping, or whirling abruptly begin complex role-simulation games (in which a constitutive rule is borrowed from the sociocultural context of the adult world) playing at being soldiers, doctors, married couples, and so forth. Two children play at being dentist and patient by using a crude plumber's wrench as a medical implement. Szabó isolates one game, in itself eye-catchingly static in contrast to the normally frenetic activity of the playground, as the essence of gameful simplicity: a boy hangs from a branch of a tree, apparently to see how long he can hang. The camera periodically returns to him, punctuating the fluid sequence of informal play. In mere play, a child might hang from a branch because it is fun to do so (the sensation of gravity, the feeling of swinging, or sensing muscles work; the fun of such play might come in many shapes); in a game, the rule of hanging *until* it is necessary to let go supplements, and thus transforms, the activity.

The rule of "hanging until" actually constitutes the game: in its absence there will be no game (or a different one) or simply play in its unstructured, unconstituted form of pure activity or (say) ilenx. Two serious objections confront this distinction. First, it might be objected that play is *never* "merely" or "simply" and that, in Schillerian phrase, it is always doing something: expressing and (hence) creating. Second, the scorn that Wittgenstein pours upon the notion that concepts can be adequately defined (or become more real in proportion to the exactitude of their definitions) outside of their contextual use takes as its primary instance the case of games. "Don't say: 'There *must* be something in common, or they would not be called "games"'—but *look and see* whether there is anything common to all.—For if you look at them you will not see something that is common to *all*, but similarities, relationships, and a whole series of them at that."[6] No doubt it is impossible to answer the first objection satisfactorily. The boundaries *are* both shifting and fuzzy, the interior contours difficult to map, the topology obscure. Yet one can claim that distinctions, even if only methodological, are possible. Aristotle observes that the convexity and concavity of a curved line are inseparable, but geometricians separate them routinely. Play and game may be separated (even if, in existential situations, all play led to games and all games were playful) because it makes sense to do so since the two concepts, when applied to literary texts, point in opposite directions and gather together dissimilar aspects of textuality. Talk about games in literary texts does not always invoke the concept of play but rather such factors as pattern, form, and structure.

Wittgenstein's well-known comment on the impossibility of defining games raises more intransigent difficulties. One would not wish to pursue mare's nests or to be caught playing a fool's game. But if one sidesteps the difficult requirement of seeking a common essence or of saying what *form* or *objective* games share and rather seeks to locate the necessary conditions of their being, the problem, recast in that open-ended manner, will not seem so foolish. In his *The Grasshopper: Games, Life and Utopia*, Bernard Suits follows this procedure: a game, after several reformulations, turns out to be an activity constituted by rules (at least one, e.g., "hanging until") and engaged in with a "lusory attitude." These are necessary, though not sufficient, conditions. In their absence, no activity, even if one might wish to call it playful, could be a game. Constitutive rules establish the game activity and make it possible: "To play a game is to engage in activity directed towards bringing about a specific state of affairs, using only means permitted by rules, where the rules prohibit more efficient in favour of less efficient means, and where such rules are accepted just because they make possible such activity."[7] Constitutive rules correspond to what are often called, in philosophical discourse, "rules of practice" (as ethical codes make possible, or enable, specifically prescribed moral actions, say).[8]

Constitutive rules are invariably limited, and the game situations they generate are enormous, yet all are equally dependent on the logically prior rule or rules. The rules of chess, for example, are few while the possibilities of play are inconceivably vast. The lusory attitude, on the other hand, formulates the playfulness of game playing and might be described as the inwardness, the reflexivity, of gamefulness. It is the player's state of mind that makes the rules of a given game acceptable and allows him to engage in an activity that has been made, by the rules that have constituted it, a purposefully inefficient manner of obtaining certain ends. If, for example, one's only objective were to place a small ball in a hole or place chess pieces in a position that gives mate, then it would be unacceptably inefficient, indeed absurd, to *obey* the rules of golf or of chess. Suits calls the mental state in which one merely desires to achieve a certain objective "prelusory" to distinguish it from the lusory attitude that makes actual game playing possible, even desirable in itself. Suits's analysis of games and the necessary conditions that games must meet (and in the absence of which they are flatly impossible or transformed into something else, such as technical exercises or mere work) provides the general model for the discussion of games in this book. When set against this model, most of the uses of "game" in recent literary discourse seem sadly invertebrate.

This definitional flaccidity in literary discourse stems from a normal disinclination to take the problem of definition seriously and a corresponding willingness to rest with ludicrously inadequate definitions, but in the specific case of games and the use of game concepts, it also seems to reflect poor observation. It is sometimes difficult to say whether the fault lies more in the poor theory (or in the critic's assertion of the humpty-dumptyesque maxim that words will mean what they are made to mean) or in the poor observation. On one hand, many inadequate definitions of *game* obviously derive from the simplified, artificial definitions of game theory, the situations of which bear little resemblance, in their rationality and open accessibility of options, to actual games. On the other hand, the ideas of games advanced by some literary scholars should convince readers that they could never have played even a very simple game.[9]

Most critical uses of the terminology of game concepts have been descriptive only (new ways to reclassify familiar evidence), and that is surely a partial argument for wariness, if not downright skepticism. In *The Grasshopper,* Suits's protagonist puts the issue succinctly: there has been, the grasshopper remarks, "a great deal of loose talk about games these days."[10] Not proceeding from a precise definition of *game,* most critical uses of the concept simply assume its translucence. Thus, for example, Susan Sontag (capturing in the elegance of a conditional proposition the true casualness of game analogies in literary discourse) argues, "If art is the supreme game which the will plays with itself, 'style' consists in the set of rules by which this game is played." Sontag conflates, with dazzling *sprezzatura,* the concept of game with that of play, postulates a hierarchy among games, personifies "will" into a separate psychic entity capable of playing games, and introduces the additional concept of "rule" as the logical justification for the analogy. Ordinarily, the analogy is made more flatly, though not less sweepingly. Gabriel Josipovici, for instance, asserts categorically that "modern art moves between two poles, silence and game" (that is, on one hand, the anguish of interior trauma; on the other, the complexity of tightly wound structures). Similarly, George Steiner observes, almost in passing, "To the extent that it is language in a condition of autonomy, that it operates within conventional, non-utilitarian rules, all literature is play." Elsewhere, Steiner remarks that "much of the modern genius can be understood from the point of view of a sufficiently comprehensive, sophisticated theory of games." An even stronger (and starkly uncompromising) formulation of the game analogy occurs in Arthur Koestler's *Act of Creation,* when he states, "All coherent thinking is equivalent to playing a game according to a set of rules."[11]

The potential list of similar statements would be long. The few cited here should suffice to indicate the reason for the edge in the Grasshopper's voice when he comments on the "loose talk about games." The enthusiastic applications of the game analogy share a conceptual nonchalance: if one merely uses a new word (the assumption seems to be), then surely one will discover something new or, at least, significantly reorder old understandings. More important, such applications also commonly assume that the chief properties of games (and thus of literature insofar as it is game) are arbitrariness, complexity of structure, and dependence on rules. The last may suggest Bernard Suits's analysis of constitutive rules in game playing, but it is important to remember that Suits distinguishes between constitutive rules and all other kinds, that the constitutive rules of games transform activity into game by limiting and regulating options, and that they make possible the transition from prelusory attitudes to lusory ones. It is not the number of rules that determine gamefulness but the presence (or absence) of a particular kind of rule.

Reducing games to complexity, or even to the possession of complex structures, is a fallacy. Consider the analogously mistaken process of viewing a game of chess from above during a single state of play and then supposing that a description of the board at that single moment could provide an adequate account of the game. Such a procedure would confuse an accidental configuration with structure, freezing the momentary patterns of games into static, even concrete, aesthetic objects. In a kind of critical handy-dandy, the normally sought-for complexity in literature becomes attributed to games (as if all games were games of strategy), the presumed qualities of the tenor (literary text) warping the vehicle (game) in the analogy. To the extent that *game* can be defined, or the properties of any given game expressed in an adequate formula, it will have nothing to do with the momentary configurations that games take in the unfolding embodiments of their rules through states of play. Every chess player knows that the board and pieces are irrelevant and that even a merely cerebral system of notation is a contingent materialization of the rules.

In his novel *The Defense* Nabokov precisely captures the immateriality of games. His chief character, the chess master Luzhin, feels chess to be combinations of possibilities composed of "invisible chess forces" and is disturbed by their actual "wooden materiality" in pieces ("the Knight's carved mane . . . the glossy hands of the Pawns"). An instructive lesson on this point occurs in *Alice in Wonderland* when Alice plays a game of croquet with live flamingos and hedgehogs on a ridged and furrowed surface that is, no matter how incongruously, a game of croquet.[12] Rules, in general, do not specify the physical manifestations of games. Thus in Satyajit Ray's film *The Chess Players* (1977), the two obsessed players find that they can play chess with vegetables after the disgruntled wife of one steals their usual ivory pieces. A chili can be a rook, a lemon a knight, nuts can be pawns as functionally as bits of wood or ivory (just as a live flamingo could be a mallet in a game of croquet), if they are used as the rules prescribe. For that matter, a rook in chess ceases to be a rook the instant it is moved diagonally or in the corkscrew manner of the knight.

The structures of games may be rigid or they may be nearly as flexible as children's informal play. These structures may be "out there" on the field, the turf, the board (wherever), or solely "in here," in the players' minds or in the rules, a cognitive map for structuration, that potential players may absorb, as Achilles and Ajax do the rule structure (or map) for backgammon that Palamedes has created, and transform into the ordered, rational play of games. Games may be, as the writers of books on how to play suppose, objective phenomena, or, as Paul Valéry so well expresses it, perhaps "the reality of games is in man alone."[13] The experience of games, as the argument of this book maintains, suggests that games, rather like literary texts, are both. They have both an exterior and an interior dimension; both playing and reading are objective, building on physical objects, operations, and within prescribed limitations, but both are also subjective, incorporating feelings, moods, thinking, and imagination. Although both dimensions are essential to the experiences of playing, they are radically different in their formulations. Concentration on one dimension only, in theoretical analysis, seems to lead to the exclusion of the other. Thus a complete account of either games or texts will require a method for descriptive analysis, a means for determining and describing rule structures, say, or a convention matrix, but also one for describing the player's, or reader's, interior state of mind while engaged in the activity.

Although games may seem to be either extremely simple (a single constitutive rule such as "hanging until," for instance) or vastly complex (as the intricate rule books of such role-simulation games as Dungeons and Dragons or Chivalry and Sorcery demonstrate), it is clearly complexity as such that has attracted critics writing on literary texts with the game analogy in mind. Steiner's remark about the "sufficiently comprehensive, sophisticated theory of games" that will (perhaps) explain modern art entails this view that games are, in essence, complex. It is also the sense behind Frank Kermode's casual mention of "plot-games" in his *Genesis of Secrecy*. It is the meaning that William H. Gass gives to *game* when he writes, with a comparable nonchalance, of the "rigorous gamelike structures" in Borges's fiction.[14] But complexity as such will not serve either as a definition of *game* or as a model for the ludic analysis of literary texts: many things are complex, and even to assert that games are implies a mistaken act of classification since not all games are complex, nor are all complex games necessarily so. A very poorly played game of chess, for example, may be far more complex, in the sense of being involved, or of having a momentarily paradoxical configuration, than a strongly played game. The potential usefulness of game concepts in literary analysis, or of analytic models derived from reflection on games and game playing, must owe little or nothing to the prior concept of complexity.

Rather than complexity, the usefulness of game concepts probably turns upon achieving some clarity concerning the meaning of rules as they may be said to manifest themselves in both games and literary texts. For this reason Bernard Suits's analysis of constitutive rules in game playing seems to point toward an adequate basis for textual analysis.[15] It is important to determine the extent to which rules, even defined as narrowly as Suits defines them, operate within literary texts. There is, of course, another term often employed in literary discourse: *convention. Rule* and *convention* are often, perhaps normally, conflated in the discourse of literary analysis, but it is far from clear that this is a fruitful procedure. The analysis of game and play concepts in literature requires that an effort be made to distinguish between the two.

I

> In this world we must either institute conventional forms of expression or else pretend that we have nothing to express: the choice lies between a mask and a fig-leaf.
> —George Santayana, "Carnival," in *Soliloquies in England*

On a beautiful summer afternoon some years ago, a scholar stood on the little pier that juts into Lake Louise. The high backdrop of the Canadian Rockies (fissured glaciers and forest) surrounded the water, green-blue with glacial melt, like an up-curving palm. Abruptly, loud laughter and unintelligible shouts broke his contemplation of the scene. He looked toward the end of the pier where the noise came from and saw, beyond a knot of gesticulating and laughing people, a young couple in a canoe about one hundred yards out on the lake. They were both energetically occupied in paddling, furiously dipping and thrusting against the water. The reason for the crowd's hilarity was immediately obvious: the two were facing each other in the canoe and thus all their vigorous effort to move forward resulted only in a circular movement. They were spinning in tight circles and spinning more quickly the more determinedly they attempted to paddle forward. One has only to imagine the scene to perceive that the young man and woman have done something wrong. Clearly, two people do not face each other in a canoe if they wish to paddle together, cooperatively, in a forward direction. Of course, they have acted correctly if they *want* to move in circles, but since one assumes that circular motion is not the normal objective of two-handed canoe paddling, one is justified in inferring that they have done something wrong. One might even mentally join that little knot of gesticulating and jeering people on the end of the pier at Lake Louise.

But what *have* they done wrong? Have they broken a rule that governs the activity of two-handed paddling? Is there a constitutive rule that makes possible and delimits that activity? Or have they merely violated, through ignorance or neglect, a simpler, less exacting stipulation than a rule? If there is such a rule, how could they have known about it? What rule book should they have read or what lessons might they have taken to make two-handed paddling possible? or even to allow them to paddle? The foolishness of the young couple at Lake Louise, once visualized in the mind's eye, raises an issue of great generality but of particular significance to anyone who likes to believe that the game/text analogy provides a fruitful equation: do the artificial activities of human culture possess other bounds, limitations, prescriptions, restrictions, and enabling legislation than rules? It may be that distinctions will prove more helpful than equations.

In *A Treatise of Human Nature*, David Hume remarks that "two men who pull the oars of a boat, do it by an agreement or convention, tho' they have never given promises to each other."[16] Without having entered into a formal undertaking (one reinforced by sanctions), the two men have been brought together in an agreement that will allow them to collaborate. In an important sense, their understanding must have preceded their conventions, their coming together to pull the oars. Hume's argument leads to a conclusion that there are implicit agreements between human beings that allow for collaboration, mutual action, exchange, and reciprocal benefit. These agreements are not formalized (no promises have been given), but, as Hume's example makes plain, they make possible such activities as boat rowing or canoe paddling and, in so doing, create reciprocal benefits. Hume's argument embodies a historical perspective: rules, such as those that regulate the "stability of possession," or even those that regulate language, arise gradually out of, or on the basis of, conventions. In Hume's argument, convention is an older and looser basis for reciprocity than rule but one that logically precedes the latter. One might say that conventions are the genetic materials out of which rules emerge, over a period of time. If conventions precede rules but presuppose understanding (as the two men in the boat must have understood what they intended before convening their activity), then the concept of rule, at least in the kind of analysis that Hume suggests, seems to describe a relatively small area of human exchange: a tight, highly aware, extremely deliberate subset of assumptions that constitutes certain human activities (rules them, in effect) and may be precisely formulated.[17]

Although Hume's argument offers a basis for distinguishing between rule and convention in terms of historical precedence and logical priority, the analysis of the game/text analogy requires an even more capacious set of distinctions. Such complex phenomena, even considered independently of each other and not only in terms of the intricate relationships at which the analogy seductively hints, demand multiple distinctions between assumptions, or enabling legislation, as well as a model that will allow the distinctions to be made synchronically as well as diachronically. (The different assumptions must be capable of copresence, substitution, and interpenetration and not merely historical replacement.) What goes on in a game or in a literary text can perhaps best be approached through a model that permits plural assumptions, of differing degrees of flexibility, in a continuously complex state of interaction.

The enthusiasm that one sometimes encounters for the equational potential of the game/text analogy obscures a large number of possible distinctions. The fact that literary texts are self-enclosed, separable from other activities, possess their identifiable text-specific assumptions (which are their enabling legislation), and are, or seem to be, autotelic has promoted the analogy with games. It has been developed widely by many critics and theorists and has been frequently transformed into an equation ("All literature is play," "literary texts are always games," "the game of literature," "the gamelike structure," and many other similar proclamations), but whether this leads to clarity or to obscurity remains an open question. One may distinguish between constitutive assumptions that are more or less inflexible and may or may not be ignored. Certain assumptions, such as the axioms that constitute geometries and logical systems are so inflexible, closed to substitution and transformation, that not to follow them must either destroy the system or instantly place the nonfollower outside the system, making him effectively nonexistent. Other assumptions such as the directions that constitute recipes may be substituted almost at will with no consequences other than to vary the taste of the dish and perhaps to give the nonfollower (who may be either ignorant or an innovative *bricoleur* in a tight corner) a reputation for culinary genius. The distance between a geometry and a recipe, between an axiomatic system and a directional system, may be greater than that between a game and a literary text, a gap that suggests no fruitful analogies. Still, the common factor of specific assumptions, or enabling legislation, makes the distance conceptually bridgeable.

The argument here will be that conventions are looser, less abstract, more resistant to formulation, and altogether more flexible than rules. They are learned differently from the way rules are normally learned: not deductively, as tightly construed prescriptions to be applied, but inductively, as a matter of experience and through practice. Thomas Pavel, who likes the analogy between texts and games but only insofar as *game* signifies social games of coordination (games that require cooperative solutions between players), writes that "literary games enhance the pleasure of taking risks, of feeling oneself more and more in control . . .

the practising reader senses the growing of his power and dexterity; he enjoys his progress and loves to continue the practice."[18] The absorption into the text in reading and the progressive mastery of textual strategies seems, in important respects, quite different from the absorption and mastery of players in games. Like playing, reading does appear to improve with practice, but the rereading of the same text does not necessarily lead to greater excitement and pleasure. One's technical grasp may become stronger, but it does not seem evident that one will have more fun in rereading. In games, so long as one is playing the same game (for example, chess), the technical grasp increases and so does the capacity for pleasure.

Unlike rules, conventions are neither descriptive nor predictive; they are difficult to formulate, and there is no particular sanction if they are ignored. With conventions, it is hard to imagine cheats, triflers, and spoilsports.[19] One may ignore a convention, or simply get it wrong, without entirely destroying the activity in question. Even if one adopted the strong form of the conventionalist position, which states that *all* human activities are conventional in that they are nonnatural, arbitrary, and learned, it would still be necessary to distinguish between types of conventions and their dissimilar scopes.[20] What are being called conventions in this argument might then require another term, but it would still be important, even within a discourse of radical conventionalism, to distinguish flexible from inflexible, necessary from possible, assumptions. Unlike rules, other assumptions (call them conventions) cannot be broken; they can only be ignored or neglected. The young man and woman who were observed that summer's afternoon at Lake Louise did not break any rules that constitute the activity of two-handed paddling. After all, they might have done many things that would still have been canoeing: they might have alternated paddle sweeps or even have continued facing each other and paddled in turn with a resulting motion rather like that of a horizontal pendulum, nor is there anything in the activity of canoeing that proscribes circular motion (it is merely unconventional, perhaps abnormal). What the couple did was to neglect a convention, a loose and implicit agreement between canoe paddlers that they will move ahead in a collaborative manner. Indeed, it is not even quite correct to say that they neglected such a convention: they only failed to enter into it. Though they were together in the canoe, nothing relevant to canoe paddling had brought them there.

It is commonplace to confuse rule and convention or to use them interchangeably. Claudio Guillén speaks of "those prescriptive conventions called rules." Jonathan Culler, in *Structuralist Poetics*, consistently employs the two terms as synonyms and speaks evenhandedly of both "constitutive rules" and "constitutive conventions" that lie behind and make possible all human culture.[21] This conflation of terms, though opaque in that it denies that cultural activities may be constituted differently, is possible and in certain critical practices might even be desirable. Jay Schleusener refers to the "conventional" meanings of literature as being "determined by a body of more or less invariant rules," but he does so within an argument to distinguish conventions from context.[22] Compared to a third item not itself actually constitutive of an activity, the distinction between convention and rule may seem to fade. Nonetheless, it is an important distinction. No to have it blunts critical language: its absence leaves one with a homogenization of conceptual orders and a leveling of all cultural activity into the capacious boundaries of a single formulation. If rule and convention are synonymous, if they do point to the same cultural phenomena, it will be necessary to grant that *axiom* is equivalent to *rule* and thus to *convention.* Literary criticism could then inherit, joyfully or tearfully, an entire series of interchangeable terms, *axiom, law, rule, convention, direction,* and *supposition,* each indicating the range of diverse assumptions that constitute semiotic and cultural acts. Doing geometry, playing chess, writing a narrative, baking a casserole, paddling a canoe, or merely supposing, as in a daydream, a possible state of affairs would all appear to be equivalent because they would all imply similar constitutive demands.

There are different activities (or essentially different semiotic systems) some of which, such as games, can best be accounted for as having rules and others, such as literary texts, as having conventions. No doubt they do have something in common: both must be members, or subsets, of a larger set that is the set of all cultural activity or of all semiotic systems. One could pursue a formulation that might encompass them all: when Federico Fregosso, in Baldesar Castiglione's *Courtier*, remarks that language is an "invention bounded by certain rules," he indicates the scope of such a formulation.[23] The voracity of Fregosso's formulation swallows up distinctions. Not merely language but all human culture, every activity involving semiosis, might be seen as an invention bounded by certain rules. How do rules work that allow one to distinguish them from other semiotic legislation? The constitutive rules of games not only make the activity possible, but in their absence the activity ceases to be possible or becomes transformed into something else. Take one rule away from chess (the Knight's move, say) and what remains of the game? or what name should be given to the new game?

The assumptions that constitute games, which one normally calls rules, are invariable and prescriptive. Their formulations are tightly inflexible (though in many games, including all athletic games, one must distinguish between the constitutive rules and what are sometimes called rules of skill, which state, informally, only what one ought to do if one wants to play the activity well) and can be used to describe the game or even to recapitulate, or replay, a previously played game. If one accepts Bernard Suits's analysis of games as rule-constituted activities that establish goals, prescribe artificially inefficient means, and demand a lusory attitude on the part of the player (that is, his willingness to play with the rule-determined inefficient means), then it is possible to state that rules mark off a certain kind of semiotic activity, including all games and the mere gamelike, in accordance with the invariable nature of their constitutive assumptions. No doubt, rules can be changed (and have been, as Indian chess becomes European by the addition of the optional two-square first move for pawns or rugby becomes North American football by the addition of the forward pass), but to do so always entails, radically or somewhat, a different game. Yet there remains a vast area of semiotic activity that seems constituted by assumptions more flexible, more open to transformation, than a rule. One variable assumption may be called *convention* (without inquiring whether the directions that constitute recipes or the suppositions of daydreams are also conventions) to distinguish it from *rule*. It is necessary to show, first, that *convention* is a distinct concept from *rule* and, second, that literature, though it may contain rules (because it may contain descriptions of empirical games or games that, as in "The Rape of the Lock," characters play), and though it may approach closely the condition of a game, is essentially a convention-governed, not a rule-governed, activity.

II

> Whence two systems of reading: one goes straight to the articulations of the anecdote, it considers the extent of the text, ignores the play of language (if I read Jules Verne, I go fast: I lose discourse, yet my reading is not hampered by any verbal *loss*—in the speleological sense of that word); the other reading skips nothing; it weighs, it sticks to the text, it reads, so to speak, with application and transport, grasps at every point in the text the asyndeton which cuts the various languages—and not the anecdote: it is not (logical) extension that captivates it, the winnowing out of truths, but the layering of significance; as in the children's game of topping hands, the excitement comes not from a processive haste but from a kind of vertical din (the verticality of language and of its destruction); it is at the

> moment when each (different) hand skips over the next (and not *after* the other) that the hole, the gap, is created and carries off the subject of the game—the subject of the text.
>
> —Roland Barthes, *The Pleasure of the Text*

Certain literary texts have normally struck readers as more rule-governed, more gamelike, than others. Highly codified genres, such as the sonnet or the detective story, may seem unmistakably to be activities constituted by inflexible rules rather than by flexible conventions. Pastoral literature, to take an example with more historical range, normally is considered to be highly codified. It is, Paul Alpers writes, a "'kind' notoriously conscious of rules, precedents and usages." But these terms, as Alpers also writes, are "more elusive than their frequent and confident deployment suggests."[24] In chapter 67 of the Second Part of *Don Quijote*, the Knight, having been defeated in Barcelona by the Knight of the White Moon and bound to a promise to return to his village, proposes to his Squire that they should both become shepherds and lead the life of a pastoral Arcadia. This is not a new theme in the *Quijote*: the notion actually occurs to the Knight because they have passed a spot in the road where earlier they had seen a number of young women and men, "gay shepherdesses and gallant shepherds," seriously (or lusorily) engaged in trying to revive just such an Arcadia.[25] As early as the sixth chapter of the First Part, during the inquisition in the Knight's library, the niece had urged that the priest burn certain volumes of pastoral poetry found among the huge collection of chivalric romances that her uncle had acquired: "For once my uncle is cured of his disease of chivalry, he might very likely read those books and take it into his head to turn shepherd and roam about the woods and fields, singing and piping and even worse, turn poet, for that disease is incurable and catching, so they say."[26] There then follows a list of sixteenth-century pastoral texts, including *La Galatea*, by an author named Miguel de Cervantes, that is saved from the fire though banished from the shelves of the library.

In the *Quijote* there are other allusions to pastoral literature, to the ideal of the Arcadian life, and to the common postulate of pastoral that there had once been a Golden Age of human ease and cooperation. In chapter 11 of the First Part, when he and Sancho accept the hospitality of the goatherds, the Knight is moved to proclaim, "Happy the age and happy the times on which the ancients bestowed the name of golden, not because gold, which in this iron age of ours is rated so highly, was attainable without labour in those fortunate times, but rather because the people of those days did not know those two words *thine* and *mine*.

In that blessed age all things were held in common. No man, to gain his common sustenance, needed to make any greater effort than to reach up his hand and pluck it from strong oaks, which literally invited him to taste their sweet and savoury fruit."[27] Readers of the *Quijote* perceive early that pastoral and romance have something in common and that the Knight's chivalric vocation does not exclude a pastoral calling and may actually invoke it.

The niece's fears are well grounded because the conversion to the shepherd's life is always a possibility within the world of a chivalric romance. Edmund Spenser illustrates this conversion in the Sixth Book of *The Faerie Queene*, when Sir Calidore accepts the rude existence of the shepherds willingly and without feeling humiliation. Sir Calidore even has a model to imitate in the character of Meliboe, who has given up a courtly existence to return to the pastoral life. Pastoral literature makes many assumptions, and, as Alpers argues, it normally seems highly conscious of "rules, precedents and usages," yet it is difficult to state explicitly which, and only which, assumptions it necessarily accepts. An inventory of pastoral conventions, of all the text-specific assumptions that texts of pastoral literature have made, from Theocritus to Robert Coover, would be extensive.

Many critics, from Walter W. Greg on, have observed how flexibly the conventions of literary pastoral have made available a number of textual contrasts (claiming to be essential) such as that between city (or court) and country, or between nature and art, or nature and society, or the real and the ideal.[28] In Greg's view, for example, the invariant pastoral convention is "the recognition of a contrast, implicit or expressed, between pastoral life and some more complex type of civilization." He adds that a contrast between "town and country was essential to the development of a distinctively pastoral literature." Harold Toliver provides a chart of such contrasts in which he lays out oppositions between nature and society, nature and art, idyllic nature and antipastoral (or realistic) nature, nature and celestial paradise. Alpers, eschewing both invariant oppositions and structural paradigms of oppositions, argues that the convening force of pastoral is fundamental both in the sense that characters come together to lead a pastoral existence (in which, typically, they sing eclogues: collaborative and conventional songs) and in the sense that a pastoral poem, in its ordinary allusiveness, convenes other pastoral writers, invoking the power of resonance and echo.[29] Yet even if this is the case (and it does seem to be so in the *Quijote*), it is possible to think of many other assumptions made by pastoral texts and to remember other, nonpastoral Renaissance texts, such as all of Shakespeare's plays, that make similar assumptions. (Nothing so essential to all literary texts, to literarity itself, as allusiveness, as the inevitable play within the intertextual field of literary production, can serve as a differentia for a specific kind.) What can one conclude concerning the pastoral assumptions that, embedded within the discourse of romance and antiromance, display themselves infrequently, though strikingly, within the *Quijote*?

The pastoral life in literature is an expression of disdain and contempt for worldly success; it is often critical of social forms and values since beneath its cheerful surface there can lie, and may always lie, a corrosive negativity. Pastoral holds the ordinary modes of existence within the human polis (society, marketplace, and court: all the complex arena of human transaction and exchange) to a mirror and finds them worthless. It is a literature of rejection, even of defeat and despair. It is also a literary expression of the idealization of human experience: it suggests, as Don Quijote so plainly sees when he is with the goatherds, what once may have been, what might have been, and what still might be, momentarily and in a little space, given enough goodwill. Pastoral, then, is double-edged. As the literary image of human innocence and ease, it is the vehicle of radical idealization and of social criticism. Citizens scorn society when it is no longer desirable, that is, when it has refused to offer the rewards they desire or when the object of desire has fled them. At that point the pastoral world becomes a refuge for society's excluded and self-excluding. The literary shepherd's song, the eclogue, is characteristically an exaltation of love and a lament on love's biting pains. It is at once an expression of hope and of hopelessness.

When Don Quijote suggests becoming a shepherd, he is, momentarily at least, fully serious. His proposals, like his devotion to knight-errantry, show that he is extremely well informed concerning the nature of pastoral literature. Evidently, he has read and understood those books that his niece wants burned. He has absorbed two modes of textuality, both pastoral and chivalric romance. Thus he proposes to Sancho the conversion of a pastoral existence with a scholar's attention both to detail and to necessary conditions:

> I will buy some sheep and everything needful for the pastoral vocation. I will call myself the shepherd Quixotiz and you the shepherd Panzino, and we will wander through the mountains, woods and meadows, singing here, lamenting there, drinking of the liquid crystals of the springs, or of the limpid streams, or the mighty rivers. The oaks shall give us of their sweetest fruit with generous hands; the trunks of the hard cork-trees shall offer us seats; the willows, shade; the roses, perfume; the broad meadows, carpets of a thousand blended colours; the clear, pure air

> shall grant us breath; the moon and the stars their light, despite the darkness of the night; song shall afford us delight, and tears gladness; Apollo verses, and love a theme, whereby we shall be able to win eternal fame, not only in the present age but in those to come.[30]

They will, he continues, invite their friends, the priest and the barber, who can change their names, too, and they will invent typical pastoral names for the women they love, though the Knight quickly points out that the name of the woman he loves, Dulcinea, is so beautiful that it will serve for pastoral as well as it has for romance. They will sing and play instruments, he adds, and he even names the instruments they will play. Among these are some called *alboques*. Sancho asks what these are because he has never seen one or even heard the name before. The Knight answers that it is a Moorish instrument, describes it, and goes on to give an account of Moorish words in Spanish, and suddenly they have slipped out of pastoral and into the familiar paroemiological discourse concerning Sancho's linguistic habits. It is a relatively brief discussion as these things go in *Don Quijote*, but it reveals that, beyond doubt, the Knight knows a great deal about pastoral literature. Yet, as the digression on Moorish words indicates, he also knows too much. In the web of pastoral conventions that the Knight has expounded (the idealized landscape, the Italianate names, Apollo giving verses but Love, themes), philology is beside the point, even, rather like a knowledge of hydrodynamics in canoeing, altogether impractical and even irrelevant.

What *does* the Knight know about pastoral literature? Certainly, he knows how things are often done in pastoral writing and what the surrounding physical aspects of life are like, or at least how they might be. That qualification marks the uncertainty in the answer: the Knight does not know anything that is strictly necessary to pastoral, anything that, being absent, would preclude a narrative from being pastoral; nor does he know anything that, being present, would suffice to justify the label *pastoral.* Even if one cannot readily recall an instance of pastoral without sheep (and they are, indeed, the first items that the Knight mentions in his excursus upon a future Arcadia), it is surely possible to imagine one: bring together a number of the common pastoral motifs and, if they are skillfully handled, who will miss the presence of sheep? Could there not be a pastoral written entirely from inside the shepherd's hut? or, as happens in the fourth act of *The Winter's Tale*, from within the sheepshearing feast? (But take the Knight's move out of chess and what will remain of the game?) Nor is it strictly necessary for a pastoral narrative to be placed in a pastoral setting, though (of course) not to do so would play with the reader's conventional expectations.

Urban pastoral might sound contradictory, even Polonian, but it is eminently conceivable and actually occurs in Robert Coover's pastoral short story "Morris in Chains," which recounts the adventures of a shepherd (with real sheep) urged on by a conventional pastoral motive, escape from ordinary human society, but who exists within a very solid, futuristic city.[31] In other words, nothing that the Knight knows about pastoral literature is rigorously demanded by any particular work, but none of what he knows is beside the point. One can easily recognize pastoral literature in his excursus, but it does not seem that he has enumerated the rules of a game, or that he has cited conventions that are constitutive of pastoral as rules are of games. He has merely alluded to some of the motifs (some aspects of setting, some features of characterization, some common themes, some examples of nomenclature, some mythic citations) that often come together in pastoral literature. Not even the beguiling Italinate names that he suggests for himself, Sancho, and their friends are necessary to pastoral, though names such as the ones he suggests seem pastorally commonplace. Every reader of Milton knows that pastoral can concern characters with names far simpler than Lycidas, names as simple as Adam and Eve. And Coover's shepherd, unforgettably, is named Morris.

What Don Quijote understands about pastoral literature are conventions. He knows some of the assumptions that may be made in order to breathe life into a certain kind of narrative. Yet he does not know what others, who also know a great deal about pastoral, know. He seems to know only half of what Alpers knows (he knows that pastoral brings characters together but not that eclogues, in their intertextual allusiveness, bring poets together), though that is assuredly significant. He does not seem to know, as Hallett Smith does, that the "central meaning of pastoral is the rejection of the aspiring mind" or that pastoral is "essentially a celebration" of the idea of "content, of *otium*."[32] One can infer that he does not know these essential pastoral conventions because in the passage cited he gives as a reason for seeking the pastoral existence that he and his Squire will win eternal fame as shepherds. There is no evidence that the Knight knows, for all of his deep learning in literature, what the shepherd Meliboe knows in *The Faerie Queene*. Sir Calidore has just commented on the apparent happiness of pastoral existence because it is free (as far as Sir Calidore can see at that point in the narrative) of "all the tempests of these worldly seas" as well as of "warres, and wreckes, and wicked enmetie." Then Meliboe responds by saying that the pastoral life depends upon being content with what one has, not envying others what they have, avoiding both pride and ambition, and doing what one wants to do (*Faerie Queene* 6:19–23). Nowhere in the Knight's version of pastoral do the first three of these objectives appear, and yet it seems that he does understand pastoral, perhaps as well as, though differently than, Meliboe. Spenser also knows a great deal about pastoral. After all, he wrote not only the Sixth Book of *The Faerie Queene* but *The Shepheardes Calender, Astrophell,* and *Colin Clouts Come Home Again* as well. What Spenser knows about pastoral is quite different from Don Quijote's knowledge, but it is also different from Meliboe's. Spenser knows, as Meliboe comes to know but Don Quijote does not (and neither Alpers nor Smith admits), that the pastoral existence is fragile, that it is never entirely safe from intruders, that the wolf's fang of greed is always just outside, that violence and death cannot be left behind, however much a weary knight, such as Sir Calidore, might wish, and that ravening brigands can always break into, and even break up, any pastoral setting.

Pastoral literature involves something much more flexible than a rule, something less abstract and far more difficult to formulate. It is a set of conventions that, almost like the shifting bits of a kaleidoscope, fit together in an astounding range of permutations. Yet no single aspect of pastoral, neither sheep nor flutes nor beguiling names, is demanded by a rule. It is not a necessary condition of pastoral that characters reject society and seek *otium*, as Smith argues, or that they convene an interplay of generic allusiveness, as Alpers insists. The play of conventions is more open, more free, than that of rules.

III

Tenuous king, slant bishop, bitter queen,
straightforward castle and the crafty pawn—
over the checkered black and white terrain
they seek out and enjoin their armed campaign.

They do not realize the dominant
hand of the player rules their destiny.
They do not know an adamantine fate
governs their choices and controls their journey.

—Jorge Luis Borges, "Chess"

If rules are, as this argument holds, abstract, easy to formulate, descriptive as well prescriptive, predictive, and inflexible, then it is difficult to see where they are to be found in literature and how they would work. (For the purposes of the immediate argument, some of the easier senses in which a literary text might be a game may be excluded: that writers play games when they adopt certain conventions, that they play games with themselves when they set goals or impose limitations upon themselves, that they play games with readers who must discover the conventions that writers have chosen and avoid the snares they frequently set, that readers play games with texts by imposing interpretive rules on them, that readers play games with writers by outsmarting them and by making of their texts what they had never imagined, are all notions, neither indefensible nor unreasonable, that have had many theoretical defenders in recent years.) A scholar may formulate a convention so that it appears to be a rule (for example, "Pastoral literature is the embodiment of an ideal setting in poetic language with the supplement of sheep"). This is only intellectual sleight of hand. Even if one did formulate pastoral conventions in the guise of rules, or as a single maxi-rule, it would be impossible to demonstrate their invariability. Take away the flutes, the idealized setting, even the sheep, and there may still be a pastoral effect. Nor would one be able to use the newly formulated pastoral rules to describe what is going on in a given text or use them to predict what may happen next, either in the text one is reading or in some subsequent text using the same rules. Further, since rules in games are both descriptive and predictive, they are also recapitulative: they can be used to reconstruct, or replay, past games. For example, most serious chess players have recapitulated the "Immortal" (a game played in London in 1851 between Adolf Anderssen and Lionel Kieseritzky) at least once. The formulations of literary conventions, however, will not allow anyone to rewrite the literary text.

If one had (and the supposition is astounding) a complete inventory of all the conventions employed in a given work, *Don Quijote* or *The Faerie Queene*, say, it would still not be possible to reconstruct the text. That blank impossibility rings with ironic force through Borges's fiction, "Pierre Menard, Author of the *Quijote*." To pursue his "solitary game," Menard binds himself by two self-imposed "polar laws" (to admit variations in the original text and to sacrifice them to the original), but these two rulelike laws have nothing to do with the novel he wishes to recreate.[33] The actual process of writing someone else's narrative turns out to be wholly empirical: a labyrinthine exercise in making choices, the determinate reasons for which have been lost. Thus "Pierre Menard" may exemplify the proposition that readers play games with literary texts, devise and impose personal rules, or it may exemplify the converse proposition that writers impose binding regulations upon themselves, but it does not illustrate the dissimilar proposition that texts are games. There is an abyssal uncertainty in literature whenever critics try to formulate what takes place (what textual events occur) in writing. The "slippery groundlessness of discourse," to borrow Howard Felperin's phrase, yawns openly at one's feet.[34] If rules are not present in the text, and do not serve as the foundation of its construction, then what does make textuality possible? What constitutes, or has constituted, that which one so clearly, and so unclearly, reads?

The answer that there are semiotic systems, among them literature, that do not depend on assumptions as definite as axioms, or even on rules, but on assumptions that are looser, more flexible, and less amenable to formulation, which one may call conventions, may not please everyone. The distinction between rules and conventions may be defended further, but first it makes sense to examine a test case: the literary text that has been deliberately founded on the abstract pattern of an empirical game. The history of literature records a few instances of texts that absorb a known game for the sake of an underforming structure. Cortázar's *Hopscotch* and Calvino's *Castle of Crossed Destinies*, one using a common child's game, the other the cards of the tarot pack, come immediately to mind. Because of its comparatively greater familiarity among English readers, the best example for this argument seems to be Carroll's *Through the Looking-Glass and What Alice Found There.*

Carroll's second *Alice* is patterned on a chess game. The sequential steps in the narrative correspond, in some sense, to the moves in a chess game at a certain stage of play. More precisely, the underforming pattern of the narrative is that of a chess problem. Carroll himself refers to the pattern as that of a chess problem and appends a diagram of the problem to the preface of the 1896 edition. A chess problem is distinct from a game in that, though bound by constitutive rules, it accepts certain unorthodox conventions. (Games, too, may be said to possess conventions as well as constitutive rules and rules of skill: looser and more flexible agreements about such matters as modes of play or arrangements of the board or field. For example, the use of chalk to mark baselines or yardlines is conventional, not determined by constitutive rules but commonly agreed upon; certain designs for the pieces in chess are conventional in this sense. Conventions do not constitute the play of games, but they do modify their physical embodiments.[35]) Conventions in the play of chess problems are peculiar. They are always, it has been remarked, unfair to the Black King because each chess problem begins, "White to move and mate in X number of moves." Modern chess problems invoke the convention of no superfluous pieces, whereas in an actual game, when mate is given, the board may be cluttered with pieces whose value and utility have suddenly deserted them. In a chess problem, as W. K. Wimsatt eloquently observes, the "only real contest . . . is that between the composer and the solver—and the solver, though there may be hope that he will be interestingly delayed, is not really expected to lose."[36]

The underforming chess problem of *Through the Looking-Glass* ("White pawn [Alice] to play, and win in eleven moves") is certainly unorthodox but, nonetheless, comes within the conventions of a special variety of chess problem known as "fairy chess," which make possible the addition or subtraction of regular pieces, squares, and moves.[37] Carroll subtracts certain moves from the Red (or Black) side: the "alternation of Red and White is perhaps not so strictly observed as it might be," as Carroll puts it. Beyond that it can be argued that the chess problem makes sense. It has even been possible for a student of chess, in the *British Chess Magazine* (1910), to construct an entire game for which Carroll's problem would be the actual endgame. Martin Gardner writes that at "no time . . . does Alice exchange words with a piece that is not then on a square alongside her own. Queens bustle about doing things while their husbands remain relatively fixed and impotent, just as in actual chess games. The White Knight's oddities fit admirably the eccentric way in which Knights move; even the tendency of the Knights to fall off their horses, on one side or the other, suggests the Knight's move."[38] Further, Alice's rapid passage by train through the third square neatly evokes the pawn's meteoric crossing of that square when one plays the optional two-square first move of European chess.

Yet even though the underforming chess problem makes sense on its own terms and can be transposed into particular situations and "moves" in the narrative, *Through the Looking-Glass* is not a chess problem. It is not necessary to understand anything about chess to grasp the narrative. Perhaps one's insight into the narrative will be enhanced by that specialized knowledge, as it is so often in reading (whatever the specialized knowledge), but this does not indicate a necessary condition of understanding. Millions of children, and many university students, have read and understood *Through the Looking-Glass* without knowing more about chess than a dim perception that it is played with pretty pieces (and that, of course, is a false perception). From this, two propositions follow. First, a knowledge of the rules of a game will not create an understanding of a text founded (in any sense) on that game. Second, an understanding of the text does not need, but may incorporate, a knowledge of the rules of a game. The first proposition seems virtually self-evident. The second requires some commentary: what is necessary for an understanding of the text is a function of an actual interpretation.

Some understandings of *Through the Looking-Glass* might hold that a knowledge of Victorian society is necessary, others that a knowledge of language games and wordplay, or that a knowledge of Carroll's scholarly studies in logic, or that a psychobiographical knowledge of Carroll's unusual interest in prepubescent girls, or that a knowledge of fantasy as a literary genre or of narrative methods in general are necessary preconditions for an understanding of the text. What is necessary, and the position that it is given in the order of importance which any interpretation may ascribe to the elements that it claims to understand, is a function of the interpretive model itself. The point may be made quite starkly: whether the underforming chess problem matters for an understanding of *Through the Looking-Glass* depends on how one has understood the narrative. The chess problem is an abstract pattern that Carroll employs, but, once embedded in the narrative, it cannot be formulated as a series of chess rules particularly actualized in time (which would be the case if one were only talking about a chess problem or situation on the board) but only incorporated into the total apprehension of the text.

IV

> Even when experimental epistemologists, in their centuries-long quest for artificial intelligence, have at last made a machine that thinks, its common sense will probably be just just as instinctive and fallible as ours. Thus at its core, rationality will always depend on inscrutibles: the simple, the elegant, the intuitive. This weird paradox has existed throughout intellectual history.
>
> —Douglas R. Hofstadter,
> *Metamagical Themas: Questing for the Essence of Mind and Pattern*

If the game/text analogy is taken as an equation (or to the extent that it is so taken), three paradoxes emerge. First, on the basis of an equation between game and text, it will be necessary to take literary conventions as rules, and this will entail that they must be learned as rules, as preconditions of the activity. Second, whether that of an actual game or of some other mode (for example, any code, set of protocols, or secret knowledge) of abstraction employed to structure plot, an underforming pattern cannot be recovered by direct inference from the literary text. Third, if literature is game, then its rules will be acquired in an inverse order, after rather than before the activity of playing the game. Thus the gamefulness of literary texts, if this is thought of as an aspect of formal structure or of the text's ontological status, manifests itself in markedly paradoxical ways. Furthermore, it is evident that the first and the third paradoxes are contradictory: the first states what no reader of literature could admit; the third, what no player of games would grant. Hence the game/text analogy, if it is taken as asserting the *formal* game nature of literary texts, proves to be complexly double-sided.

The fullest experience of the game occurs when the player's minds, like those of Achilles and Ajax during the moment depicted on the vase by Exekias or those of the two chess players in Satyajit Ray's film, have been absorbed into the exact scope of the game's rules, the delimitation they impose and the structures they generate. The more one knows about a game, about its theory and its special strategies, the more likely one is to understand it, enjoy it, and, to use Huizinga's phrase, be "run away with."[39] Absorption into a game stems from knowledge or, at the very least, demands a knowledge of the rules as a necessary condition. The "lusory attitude" that Bernard Suits proposes as one of the necessary conditions of all game thinking might even be said to be the internalization of the rules: the moments in play when the mind shapes itself parasitically upon the body of the rules. Yet in literature nothing comparable takes place.

Reading also makes absorption possible. The mind takes various words, arranged in certain ways, internalizes them, takes them as clues, as indications, as rather indefinite clusters of signification perhaps, and recreates an experience or creates a new one. (This is a minimalist phenomenological position adopted for the purposes of this argument: everyone may give an alternative account from within a chosen interpretive framework.) In this process, no actual knowledge of the relevant conventions is strictly necessary. Still less does the mind need those abstract formulations that scholars can give to conventions in the expectation that they will thereby become rules. Indeed, to have that knowledge of the conventions probably frustrates the absorption into the text that makes reading enjoyable and appear to be identical with playing a game. None of the many pastoral conventions seems actually to be a precondition for reading pastoral literature. It does not seem necessary to understand that, as Alpers formulates its conventionality, pastoral *convenes*, both shepherds and allusiveness. Nor does it seem necessary to know, in another of Alpers's formulations, that it is "the essence of pastoral to apprehend the naive in a sophisticated way." The perception of that textual gap does not appear to be a precondition for reading either the pastoral enclaves of *Don Quijote* or the Sixth Book of *The Faerie Queene*. The more the reader knows (in the cold, formulaic sense of understanding the rules), the less likely he is to be "run away with."

There is a division between knowledge and experience in reading literature that runs counter to the fusion of the two in game playing. In games, commentary (decoding) is the direct application of known rules to describe and predict; in literature, commentary (interpretation) is the movement away from the experience to a model of signification. In literature the interpretive model succeeds the act of reading; in games, the model is an extrapolation of a known code that precedes the act of playing. If literary texts are games, they are paradoxical ones, to be accounted for in terms the inverse of those normally apposite to games.

Consider the way in which feelings enter into the activities of game playing and reading. The procedures of commentary in the two activities (decoding, on one hand, interpretation, on the other) are in inverse order. In games, the feelings that players have during the course of play are beside the point; they are irrelevant to the game and to the definition of *game,* though on the subjective level, they may not be irrelevant to the players. One may feel that a certain game, or a certain state of play, is beautiful or ugly, but that does not matter insofar as it is a game. There are chess games, such as the "Immortal," that are remembered for their elegance and beauty and are often recapitulated (or replayed) for these reasons. Nabokov, looking back on his novel *The Defense,* remarks that "replaying the moves of its plot, I feel rather like Anderssen fondly recalling his sacrifice of both rooks to the unfortunate and noble Kieseritsky—who is doomed to accept it over and over again through an infinity of textbooks, with a question mark for monument."[40] This aesthetic tradition has nothing to do with games as games. The Anderssen/Kieseritsky game, the "Immortal," is neither more nor less a game of chess because it is elegant, beautiful, and haunting. One's feelings that the "Immortal" possesses these qualities have no more to do with its essential gamefulness than if one were to sneeze while recapitulating it. Yet literature clearly entails feelings, and certain kinds of literature entail an explicit range of feeling. Todorov defines an entire genre, the "fantastic," on the quality of feeling that it engenders (a hesitation between natural and supernatural explanations),[41] and more than a hundred generations of Aristotle's followers have made the feelings of pity and fear a part of the definition of tragedy. What is a suspense tale without the feeling of suspense? a love story without the feelings of love? a pastoral without the evoked desire to be there, to share it, to live pastorally?

The second paradox is as starkly simple, and as central to the concerns of literary analysis, as is the first. No doubt a game's pattern, a particular situation (as in the case of a chess problem), or even the code of rules itself may be transposed into the plot steps of a narrative. Carroll's *Through the Looking-Glass* demonstrates that this is not merely possible but narratively effective. Yet once this has happened, the game ceases to be a game and becomes something else; the game rules that are mimicked by the plot steps metamorphose into aspects of the text's conventionality. In this way, something (a game) that is fundamentally inflexible and abstract becomes something else that is flexible and concrete. This metamorphosis leads directly to the second paradox. Whatever the abstract game pattern that may have underformed a narrative, it cannot be seen immediately and directly within the text that (perhaps) it has shaped. Just as given conclusions may have a plurality of possible premises or any actual event a plurality of causes, so a particular text may be seen to have a number of structural, apparently originary, patterns. Furthermore, texts seem to swallow their assumptions, and the more abstract these are, the more deeply swallowed they become. Perhaps a critic could, given a highly precise and analytic method (not, alas, currently available), recover an underforming game pattern from a literary text. The paradoxicality of the game/text equation requires only that this is neither evidentially simple (as it would be to find the presupposed rules in any actual game) nor intuitively easy. To demonstrate this, one would have only to ask a good chess player to retrieve the chess problem that Carroll gave in his 1896 Preface from a close reading of *Through the Looking-Glass*. Carroll's use of a chess problem to inspire a narrative structure that, the problem having dissolved into the structure, obscures its imaginative origins exemplifies a common authorial technique. In this sense, the author plays a game with himself, setting up an intellectual challenge that must be overcome. Raymond Roussel proposed phrases, syntagmatic chains invented for their resonance, that would stimulate other, quite different, phrases. No reader would be able to infer Roussel's private games from the text. Similar generative games characterize the textual procedures of the OULIPO, the French textual laboratory organized to stimulate "potential" literature.[42]

The text-specific assumptions of literature cannot be adequately formulated and perhaps not even fully enumerated. Conversely, the game-specific assumptions of play, rules, are formulations. One may know that a text incorporates and even rises upon certain conventions, but one can formulate them so diversely that the result will be a series of alternatives each differently indicating the conventions that have been in use and differently assigning value to them. Textually embedded, conventions become protean and difficult to grasp. In activities that are rule-governed, an observer can easily make successful rule formulations. In literature the range of interpretations shows that this is not the case. One may argue that conventions are present and possess important functions in literary texts but still find it difficult to formulate them, either immediately or easily, as the rules of a game might be formulated. From what text of pastoral literature shall one descend to those pastoral conventions that Don Quijote understands so well? Unlike the transitive relationship between a game and its rules, that between a text and its conventions is intransitive.

The third paradox states that if literature is a game, in the structural sense, then its rules must be learned in an inverse order. What is necessary to a literary text is determined by something outside of it; what is necessary to a game is internal, an absolute function of what its rules prescribe and proscribe. Whether the chess problem in *Through the Looking-Glass* is necessary to an understanding of Alice's adventures hinges on the interpretation. If it is necessary, that claim reflects the (ec)centricities of the interpretive model. The rules of the model determine the chess problem's necessity. A reader must have understood the text before identifying its necessary constituents. If literary texts were games, one could state their rules only after having played. The strong paradoxicality of a game that keeps its rules secret until after it has been played (perhaps more than once) should be evident. The White Queen could scarcely have devised a game more appropriate to the asymmetrical world of the looking glass. If literature is game, readers must always find themselves in the role of being able to say whether the rules have been kept, or significantly deviated from, only to the extent that they have already played (by, with, or through) these rules.

Cervantes does not allow his Knight and Squire to turn shepherd and wander about the mountains and fields "singing here, lamenting there." That fascinating possibility remains suspended in the limbo of untold stories, of forever unactualized texts. Still, for argument's sake, one may suppose that Don Quijote and Sancho do create their new pastoral Arcadia: so one may imagine them now, their names beguilingly Italianized, leaning on shepherds' crooks and singing eclogues to Dulcinea and Teresona, their beloved ladies. Whether the Knight sings a correct eclogue to Dulcinea must depend on how one has understood the eclogue and its conventions. Its textual "correctness" turns entirely on how one interprets it within the narrative as a whole, within the allusive field created by the other poems the Knight has written (such as that, carved into the bark of a tree, allusively evoking Ariosto's Orlando, a knight maddened by love and, in a sense, temporarily pastoralized, that figures significantly in chapter 26 of the First Part), within the unfolding of the Knight's characterization (itself a perplexing problem in literary analysis), within the context of the new Arcadia itself, and within the context of the history of pastoral eclogues. The example of the eclogue in *Don Quijote* illustrates the paradox that the rules of literary texts, if texts were games, must be posterior to understanding, even contingent on interpretive models that have been created according to a distinct set of rules of their own. No game, other than in a strongly paradoxical manner, is ever like that.

In reading a literary text, one hears multiple voices, some strident, some mute, their tonalities always fading and strengthening. The conventionality of a text is more adequately captured in the image of a voice than in that of a rule. Bakhtin's model of literary analysis suggests that the demands of reading literary texts are to hear multiplicity, to recognize diversity, to accept the inevitable fading in and out of literary language. The novelness of a text such as *Don Quijote* lies in its diversity of voice and signification. Its conventions, multiple and loose, come together from many directions and out of many traditions. In the midst of the world of antiromance, the world of romance remains, intact and perhaps enhanced (borne, in Ortega's image, like an embryo within the containing discourse of the novel's deflationary realism[43]), but the voices of other conventions, other networks of conventions, are to be heard as well. Pastoral enters into the novelness of *Don Quijote* in complex ways: only occasionally foregrounded, it nonetheless asserts itself, at least from the sixth chapter of the First Part, as a definite possibility, a mode of existence as well as one of textuality, present in its own right, as an aspect of romance conventionality (as it is also in *The Faerie Queene*) and as an aspect of the ongoing satire of romance. Properly to hear the voices of a literary text, as Bakhtin consistently reminds students of literature, it is necessary to allow the text its context: to respond actively to the resonances that echo along the corridors, both sinuous and interminable, of literary implicitness. It is a social phenomenon as well as a formal and purely textual one. Thus Susan Stewart writes of Bakhtin's translinguistics that the "rules" it seeks are "conventions of genre, conventions of voice, character, idea, temporality and closure which will be modified by the ongoing transformations of social life."[44] In *Don Quijote*, the novelness of the text manifests itself in a vast array of distinct literary conventions, in collaboration with, as well as in opposition to, each other. Furthermore, that novelness necessarily embodies the social background of Renaissance literature, with its privileging of certain conventions, its clear grasp of rhetorical tradition, its humanistic education stressing classical literature and its multiplex narrative conventions, its cultural and political institutions. Somewhere, at some level, the voices of *La Galatea* echo within the *Quijote*.

The distinction between convention and rule, between a set of flexible assumptions and a dissimilar set of inflexible assumptions, though primarily methodological in purpose, serves several important aims. It attempts to bring some precision into an ongoing discussion that often seems marked by brash conflations. The distinction does not prohibit the conclusion that literary texts may be games in several ways: that they may incorporate empirical games, that they may mark off the playground of the author's personal gamefulness, that they may engage the reader in textual games as well as in wordplay, that they may be constituted as games (whatever the author may wish or think) by the reader's own game playing, and even that they may be transformed into games by the rulelike procedures of interpretive criticism. The distinction argued in this chapter aims only to upend the instable equation between text and game, convention and rule, insofar as this formal equivalence claims to provide useful knowledge about either the structure or ontological status of literary texts. Game, and its many subordinate terms (an entire *spielraum*), will be with literary discourse for some time to come; hence it makes sense to clarify the strategic potential that it entails. Denied clarity, the concept of game will behave rather like a chesspiece transformed by the exigencies of a child's informal play into a simple plaything, or like a gameless shuttlecock.

CHAPTER 4

The Archetype of Bamboozlement

godgames and labyrinths

I take the tragic view of categories.
—John Barth, *The Friday Book*

It is much easier to bury a problem than to solve it.
—Ludwig Wittgenstein, *Philosophical Investigations*

LITERATURE DIVIDES READILY into categories. The history of literary studies appears to be a long, convoluted process of inventing categories: revising them, burying them, restoring old ones, striking and restriking new ones, and always studiously basing interpretations upon them. Genres, or kinds, are categories that subsume many diverse texts, but technical labels (rhetorical terminology, for example) are equally categories. As categories they are no less instable than are larger, more encompassing sets such as pastoral or Greek romance. If a reader, rhetorically educated and sufficiently sharp, can recognize an epanorthosis, then that is what he may perceive in "Januarie" of Spenser's *Shepheardes Calender*, but it is unlikely that any modern reader, even one educated in rhetoric, would be able to see that particular use of the trope as "pretty" in quite the same way that E.K. claimed to do in his gloss published in the original edition.[1] As John Barth writes, categories are "indispensable [but] more or less arbitrary."[2] They shift wildly, disappear from sight, and then, in either a revisionary or a reactionary age, reappear none the worse for having lain fallow. Yet they are how literature is constituted as a discipline (or as a field): according to different theoretical models, different interpretive frameworks, different approaches, different questions, different strategies of reading. It sometimes seems that the play of categories may be (the dice cast, the cards dealt, checkmate having been given) the only textual game.

The currently much-used term *postmodern* precisely illustrates the problem of categories. It claims to solve the difficulty of naming the present moment in Western culture, drawing evidence from more than one aspect of contemporary culture (this is a methodological weakness as well as a strength), both in contrast to a previous period, modern, and by indicating a range of communicative, stylistic, and structural devices employed by contemporary writers, artists, architects, and communicators generally. Postmodern thus constitutes a paradigm of contemporary Western cultural strategies: bearing, as Ihab Hassan writes, upon "problems of cultural modeling, literary periodization, cultural change."[3] For this reason it is an attractive term that promises taxonomic precision (*now* is different than *then*), a battery of subordinate analytic terms possessing immediate applicability, and a self-congratulatory charge of contemporary hype. In her preface to the second edition of *Narcissistic Narrative: The Metafictional Paradox*, Linda Hutcheon writes that, having formerly rejected the term, she would now accept postmodernism because "it would be foolish to deny that metafiction is today recognized as a manifestation of postmodernism."[4] Hutcheon's late acceptance of postmodernism, based largely on the evidence of architecture (where it is a normal term in professional and critical writings), reveals two of the difficulties inherent in the use of the postmodern category. It may indicate some broad, underlying or informing characteristic of the contemporary period that, having been discovered, both reveals the truth about this period and serves to knot together otherwise loose threads of critical analysis. Or postmodernism may be seen as the sum of its aspects, a totalization of numerous, separate devices that characterize the creation of works of art, including both buildings and literary texts.

Consider the following parabolic (double, biformed, irresolvable) distinction. First, literature is the body of stories that express a people's history and culture. It is what defines them, helps to bind them together, and is part of their educational development. Literature possesses vast, tentacular sociocultural functions. Second, literature is a large, though indeterminate, number of forms, techniques, and conventions that make possible the telling of any story. Literature is also an immeasurable, and equally indeterminate, elastic pool of motifs, of basic story materials. It is only the repertory of what Umberto Eco calls "intertextual frames," that is, the immense replication of itself that makes further replication possible. Literature is what makes the human capacity for narrative actual, and it is *always* transnational. Any convention, any motif, will find its place, useful and fruitful, in any national literature.

The first way of thinking about literature instructs one in the deep, interwound root system of a literature within its national culture. Every culture has its literature—oral, written, or both—and this literature is the traditional record of what has happened, what is important, what is obligatory, what is valuable, what is sad, and what is funny for one group of people. A culture is as much, perhaps more, its customary images, sayings, and stories as it is artifacts, laws, and sanctions. People learn what they may become, what they should not become, and what they ought to strive for (in short, who they *are*) through the stories they are told as children, the stories they hear, those they read, and eventually those they themselves learn to tell. Anthropologists study traditional narrative, both myth and anecdote, as well as ceremonial enactments to learn about a culture. Travelers read the literature of a place to learn more about it. Scholars make systematic efforts to read a people's literature in depth to place their claim upon them. (Any scholar may reach the point when she believes that she must understand a people better than any of them do themselves.) Learning a people's body of stories is one way to dominate them. In his *Renaissance Self-Fashioning*, Stephen Greenblatt tells a story that exemplifies the ways in which the Spanish conquerors of the New World used their superior grasp of narrative purpose to penetrate the storytelling traditions of aborigines in order to exploit them. The Spanish, Greenblatt argues, in common with other Europeans, possessed a narrative mastery that allowed them not merely to tell their own stories well but to grasp the stories of others, much as Iago captures and exploits Othello's story, to pervert them, to turn them to Spanish, not aboriginal, uses.[5] Narrative is culture-bound, the collective work of a people, national in a profound sense: a means of learning how to be a certain kind of person; a means of actualizing a culture's repertory of social roles and possible types; a means by which to dominate that culture, either from within or without.

The second way of thinking about literature instructs one in the openness, elasticity, and adaptiveness of narrative. Stories, in being told, must fall into some form. They are dilated, elaborated, brought toward that ideal of fullness that Renaissance writers knew as *copia*, made to take countless shapes, more or less fantastic. It is a principle of narrative analysis, for example, that any story may be told in any number of forms, in any conceivable medium. Opera, ballet, song, puppet shows, cartoons, films, even tarot cards, any medium, can bear a story's weight. Take any Renaissance text, *Othello*, say, or *Don Quijote*, and consider the immense complexity of generic forms, conventions, and strategies. Then ask, where did these come from? Does it make sense to claim that they are merely, or purely, English or Spanish? Which novels did the first novelist read to learn his craft? What had Cervantes read before writing *Don Quijote*? (He had read widely in European narrative, perhaps especially Italian, the traces of Ariosto's *Orlando Furioso* being everywhere apparent in the *Quijote*, but he had not read novels.) Literature rejects boundaries, escapes from them, overleaps them. It proclaims its Titanism. As Renaissance literature parabolizes, literary texts encode the openness of frontiers. Literature is transcultural, polymorphous, nomadic (perhaps vagrant), and always piratical.

The first way of thinking about literature instructs one in the deep specificities that bind texts to their times and places. As Greenblatt observes, social actions "are themselves always embedded in systems of public signification, always grasped, even by their makers, in acts of interpretation, while the words that constitute the works of literature that we discuss . . . are by their very nature the manifest assurance of a similar embeddedness."[6] The study of literature proceeds within the deliberate awareness of the interplay of symbolic structures in a particular place and time. As a disciplined investigation, it calls attention to the vibrant strands in a literary text—cultural, social, historical, biographical—that formal analyses tend, no doubt inevitably, to reduce, even to ignore.

The second way of thinking about literature instructs one in the innumerable connections that link each text to the larger context of the world, human civilization, and human history. It opens the narrowly blinkered vision of nationalism, of local place and custom. The study of literature proceeds within the deliberate awareness of transnational currents, of influences that have come from outside, of purely literary structures that have begun somewhere else, or perhaps no single place, and have become diffused, like light or wind. As a disciplined investigation, it calls attention to the massive weight of transnational influences, of model-borrowing and model-peddling, that constitute literary texts at any time and in any place.

There are always many such transnational currents. Indeed, some periods of literary history, such as the Renaissance, seem to be little else:

critical and theoretical controversies, particular forms (the sonnet, the epic), innovations (the novel), all swirl in a literary ocean in which the precise textual shapes privileged within national traditions often seem to be little more than momentary configurations of waves. And yet there are also, always and already, particular places, determinate local areas of human life and language: individual cultures that are defined by their distinct solutions to biological and ecological problems. Cultures that possess—that *must* possess—their distinct histories, their own records of what has taken place, and with what significance for them, for their future, for all time.

Postmodernism bears the biform nature of literary studies and categories in its inherent duality of use. It is usefully a period concept, naming either now or the postindustrial, multinational stage of international capitalism that has evolved since the end of World War II. It is also usefully a formal, analytic term, naming a number of artistic and specifically textual conventions. Thus it is not surprising that postmodern possesses two distinct archives of secondary commentary and explication. In the first archive one finds writers concerned with the interpretation of (their, our, contemporary) culture. These writers, accepting either the basic Marxist notion of an economic infrastructure or the Althusserian notion of underlying ideological structures, see literary texts as indexes of the cultures that produce them. More particularly, they read texts as evidence for the nature of the Western capitalist civilization (containing many specific cultures) as it currently exists. Terry Eagleton, for example, uses *postmodern* as a term to point out the obsessions of international capitalism and the illusory delights of commodity fetishism in general.[7] Fredric Jameson writes that the postmodern is a "cultural dominant" in "present history," an aspect of the general commodification of industrial products in this phase (late, multinational) of capitalism. "What has happened," he writes, "is that aesthetic production today has become integrated into commodity production generally: the frantic economic urgency of producing fresh waves of ever more novel-seeming goods (from clothing to airplanes), at ever greater rates of turnover, now assigns an increasingly essential structural function and position to aesthetic innovation and experimentation."[8] Thus artworks (the texts, say, that writers of the second archive consider to be innovative, fresh, experimental) are seen as commodities fetishized within a consumer-indoctrinated society. Paul Bové, asserting a somewhat different slant on contemporary culture, argues that the truly distinct (the ineluctably different) arises from the "counterlogic of postmodern society" in terms of which a number of "counterhegemonic" discourses such as feminism and ecology (but also including some aspects of literary theory) work to modify the dominant, hegemonic discourse of the capitalist power structure.[9]

The exclusionary concerns of the first archive are to establish postmodern texts and other artworks (Jameson writes often about the visual arts, both painting and film) as evidence of cultural commodification. The second archive contains commentary that focuses directly on texts and artworks. Writers in this archive may not altogether ignore the cultural context, even agreeing largely with Jameson's analysis of the consumer orientation of Western society, but they tend to see texts as, in themselves, primary objects of analysis. It makes sense to say that the first archive is essentially contextualist; the second, textualist. These two archives are not incompatible, though critics may often write as if they thought they were. Many critics in the second archive, such as Linda Hutcheon and Ihab Hassan, normally seem to want to have their postmodernism in both senses: a sweeping cultural designation, revealing something at once profound and distinctive, *and* a useful term by which to sum up the complex range of technical devices that are used in contemporary art. One can define postmodernism, Allen Thiher writes in the course of initiating what is perhaps the most brilliant discussion of the topic yet written, "as tightly or as loosely as one needs for one's particular purposes."[10] In the tight sense, largely corresponding to the second archive, postmodernism does the same conceptual work as other terms, less historically or culturally bound, such as *metafiction* or Hutcheon's own term, *narcissistic.*

All such terms, though they fail to constitute a cultural and period category, have an advantage over *postmodernism* in being inarguably transhistorical. They name particular acts of self-consciousness in which artists, reflexively, call attention to their work, their techniques, or themselves. David Lodge once proposed, with English bluntness, that fiction arising out of self-consciousness and distrust of traditional realism should be called "problematic."[11] Hutcheon's candidate, *narcissistic,* is offered as an imprecise synonym for a series of other terms, including *self-reflective, self-reflexive,* and *autorepresentational.* The most common term for this literature, certainly the most analytic and perhaps the most useful, has been, at least since William H. Gass coined it and Robert Scholes gave it currency, *metafiction.*[12] This clearly indicates a kind of fiction that comments on fiction, that foregrounds, lays bare, and then either explicates or mocks the literary conventions that make writing fiction possible. Metafiction occupies a place with regard to fiction that meta-anything (metalinguistics, say) fills: a commentary, theoretically informed, abstract, even notational, upon some cognitive operation in terms of which that operation's ordinary procedures are questioned, made explicit, and formulated. Such commentaries are, in Gass's words, "lingos to converse about lingos." (Self-)evidently, one may contrive for any discourse (or lingo), including fiction, another metadiscourse.

Self-conscious acts, whether they are globally distributed within a work (thematizing the difficulties of writing in a *kunstlerroman*, say) or limited to one or more reflexive devices (a play-within-the-play or a *mise-en-abyme* narrative), may be found in the literature and art of any historical period. Since one may always inquire after the material conditions of possibility, the cultural bases of human expression in symbolic systems, it is a reasonable question why such self-conscious devices are popular in certain periods (the Renaissance, say, or the mid-twentieth century). Still, even if they have been precisely noted and categorized, and even if they can be correlated to some definite aspects of cultural materiality, an inventory of self-conscious devices can serve only inadequately to establish a historical period. What is common to many historical periods, if not to all, can hardly constitute the differentia of a single period. Jameson argues that the postmodern is characterized by a number of aesthetic mannerisms, such as the "new kind of flatness or depthlessness, a new kind of superficiality," the "waning of affect," the weakening of genuine historicity and the enthusiastic acceptance of new industrial technologies as the constitutive bases for the creation of art, all of which serve to place the postmodern in the specific time frame of the current historical moment. Yet it seems that characters in the literature of many historical periods have led depthless, paracinematic existences and that affect has always been deliberately controlled. Spenser, to cite only one example, is remarkable for his craftiness in both mannerisms. Jameson also argues that the postmodern is characterized by intertextuality as a "built-in aesthetic effect" that generates a new "connotation of 'pastness' and pseudo-historical depth, in which the history of aesthetic styles displaces 'real' history."[13] It may or may not make sense to suppose a "real" history or a genuine historicity (it suits Jameson's ideology to suppose this), but it makes little sense to suppose that intertextuality is only a contemporary textual potentiality. (In Chapter 6 the discussion will return to intertextuality as a specific mode of textual play.) Renaissance writers "build in" intertextual effects with immense skill, and they do so both to play with the "history of aesthetic styles" and to supplement "real" history as they understood it. *The Faerie Queene* and *Don Quijote* are both highly sophisticated in, and permeated by, their vast intertextuality.

Writing about "postmodern American fiction" (thereby adding a spatial/cultural marker to an otherwise temporal/historical term), Charles Caramello argues that it often exploits "all available resources of the print medium, incorporates as narrative vehicles typographical variations, drawings, photographs, colored papers or inks, the shape of the page, even the binding of the book: one thinks of William Gass's *Willie Master's Lonesome Wife*."[14] One thinks of baroque, mannerist, and Renaissance experiments in writing. One also thinks of Spenser's *Shepheardes Calender*, with its woodcuts, archaic orthography, prose summaries, and mock wise glosses. One thinks of Bakhtin's theory of the novel. It is an explicit conclusion of Bakhtin's analysis of novelness that nothing must be, by definition or by genre prescriptions, excluded; it is, equally, a conclusion of contemporary textualist theory that discourse cannot be rigorously divided and that the properties of one kind of discourse penetrate, bear upon, and may be included by, any other kind of discourse.[15] What assumptions about the efficacy of categories does one make if, like Caramello, one employs an inventory of transhistorical devices to constitute a historical (and spatial/cultural) category? If an ambitious scholar were to make a complete inventory of all the self-conscious devices in Nabokov's *Ada* and then make one of Cervantes's *Don Quijote*, there would be, it seems likely, a high incidence of correlation between the two inventories, but few critics would call the *Quijote* postmodern.

Allen Thiher argues that it is something in the late modern psyche, the shared mentality of many Western people, that makes the range of self-conscious, reflexive devices attractive: the distrust of language, the deep, corrosive belief that "language articulates the world and that language cannot reach the world." Language, he writes with reference to a famous episode in Sartre's *La Nausée*, "fails in the presence of the tree root." In the absence of conviction with regard to the sufficiency of language to represent the world (and both authenticity and reference having been demystified), all that remains (though this is already much) is play: "Play's autonomy promises, if faintly, the possibility of creating a necessary order in the midst of absurd fallenness."[16] Barth seems to enact this proposition as well as to provide an analeptic commentary when he writes that postmodern "describes a very approximately shared inclination among numerous writers and other artists in the second half of our Western twentieth century: an inclination to work out in their individual ways, as I have put it elsewhere, not the next best thing after modernism, but the *best next* thing after modernism. However, that inclination cuts across national lines; what's more, smarter people than myself have let me know that what *I* mean by postmodern fiction isn't what the term really means at all. So forget it."[17]

In dealing with the range of self-conscious techniques in contemporary literature, critics have available two taxonomic strategies, one historical (postmodernism) and one transhistorical (metafiction). Hassan explicitly calls postmodernism a "boundary genre" in the sense that it marks the edges between historical periods (our "heteroclitic age" set against all that has gone before) and between ways of reading, of approaching textuality in general. As an artistic, philosophical, and social phenomenon, Hassan writes, "postmodernism veers toward open, playful, optative, provisional (open in time as well as in structure or space), disjunctive, or indeterminate forms, a discourse of ironies and fragments, a 'white ideology' of absences and fractures, a desire of diffractions, an invocation of complex, articulate silences."[18] But it is an indeterminate, boundary genre in a more fundamental sense: a term such as *postmodernism* calls attention to the problems of constructing, applying, and maintaining categories. *Postmodernism* self-inscribes the shifting play of categories.

I

> At the same time he admitted, with a self-deprecating smile, that a severe case of Porzellankrankheit prevented him from leaving her for good. The collection held him prisoner.
>
> —Bruce Chatwin, *Utz*

Collections, particularly in the form of lists, are common to all fiction. A catalog of ships, a roll call of heroes in epic narrative, a list of trees or of battle armaments are collections just as much as are a table of contents, an index, or a bibliography. Inventories add depth to fiction or enhance the "effect of the real."[19] They thicken the narrative text. Sometimes they may simply indicate the writer's command of certain narrative conventions as Spenser's catalogs of trees demonstrate that he is aware of epic conventions (*FQ*, 1.1.8–9, 2.7.52). Moreover, premodern literature provides many instances of writerly playfulness with the concept of a collection: Don Quijote's library, for example, in which the entire body of previous romance literature (which Cervantes's narrative displaces) has been collected, or My Uncle Toby's library of military architecture, which Sterne explicitly compares to Don Quijote's, or My Father's collection of books on noses, or even My Uncle Toby's model of the battle of Namur (since models are also collections). In postmodern literature, however, the concept of a collection takes on a different range and function. It is a convention that readily fits into the perspective (skeptical, intellectual, playful) that critics like to call postmodern, and it suggests how a specific textual device, transhistorical in essence, can undergo a significant metamorphosis when played from a distinct cast of mind.

Collections symbolize many aspects of human life and culture: like Don Quijote or My Uncle Toby, people collect what they love, and their idiosyncratic obsessions become evident in their collection-making activities; they also collect for the fun, for the spirit of, collecting. Hence a collection, any collection, may enter narrative at the level of characterization for many purposes, including the most sentimental. The absurdist theme, foolishness mingled with triumph, capturing the real-to-life ascendancy of all those proto-characters who, with obsessive monomania, collect *things*, possesses obviously powerful suggestiveness. George Brossard, a Québecois collector of bugs, describes his first experience of catching a butterfly: "So I was on the beach thinking, and a big black-and-red butterfly come flying by. And I thought *this is it*. So I chase him down the beach and kill him. With my hands! Then I start collecting like a mad dog."[20] There are more than eight hundred thousand species of bugs, and Brossard, now well on his way, intends to collect them all. Nearly everyone has met some person who collects, either out of an obsession or for the fun of it (or, most likely, both), pins, bits of string, matchboxes, the shells of nuts, bugs, hair, or severed hangnails. Walter Benjamin, acting from the great depths of an oceanic discourse, collected quotations, fragments of discourse, slivers of a mythic whole, way markers toward a reconstituted whole, and subsequently many critics, Marxists, postmodern, poststructuralist, and Bakhtinian, have collected him.

A collection also symbolizes all other human activities that attempt to fasten handles upon reality, to grasp and hold onto the dissolving certainties of human existence. If a collection is essentially conceptual (a schema, a framework, a model, a map of "reality"), then all concepts are also collections. They handle reality, so to speak, and draw its scattered fragments into illusory nets. Not merely butterflies but all reality (that word which Nabokov once observed is the *only* term that should always be placed within inverted commas) may be collected, its scattered bits or undifferentiated wholeness, drawn into conceptual nets. These latter may be (sadly, perhaps) our only hold on reality. Necessarily, they reflect the elaborate paradoxes of set theory, the slipping, breaking boundaries, the endless possibilities of multiple inscription, and the voracious cannibalism of categories (as when, as games do, and even texts, one category devours another). Susan Stewart observes lucidly that playing with a series is "to play with the fire of infinity. In the collection the threat of infinity is always met with the articulation of boundaries. Simultaneous sets are worked against each other in the same way their attention to the individual object and attention to the whole are worked against each other." The finite boundaries of collected objects, such as boxes and cruets that are themselves containers, she writes, are "played against the infinite possibility of their collection, and, analogously, their finite use value when filled is played against the measureless emptiness that marks their new aesthetic function."[21] The boundaries that bound, and do not bound, reality hold, and let fall, the fragments they collect. The paradoxes of sets, of categories, of all collections are identical to those that pervade, as Thiher argues, language itself. Hence the motif of a collection plays into the preoccupations of postmodern writing: it illustrates, reflexively, the inherent problems of language and of textuality. The abyssal distance between human concepts and the facts they collect seems to be one of the recurring obsessions of postmodern writers: the human grasp of reality will appear, ultimately, no firmer, stronger, more trustworthy, than the representational validity of a collection.

Two contemporary writers provide exemplary illustrations of the intricate textual potential of collection motifs and the discourse of museums. Both writers might be called (indeed, have been called) postmodern but, more interestingly, both represent the seldom invoked category of Commonwealth literature. That is, both writers, coming from odd corners of what used to be the British Empire, write in English but do so from outside the two main markets for modern English writing, London and New York. Commonwealth literature is an unstable, perhaps marginal, category (except, of course, for those who live, write, and attend conferences within its boundaries) that usefully offers a context for discussing writers, often magnificent ones, who do not normally fall into the normal workaday categories of American and English literary life, academic or journalistic.[22] The two writers are the Australian Murray Bail, who wrote *Homesickness* (1980), and the Canadian Robert Kroetsch, who wrote *Alibi* (1983).[23]

Both *Homesickness* and *Alibi* employ the concept of a collection for absurdist ends; as well, both novels use it as a vehicle for making serious (or seriously playful) comments on the nature, scope, and limitations of the human mind. The human inclination to construct collections can be quite funny, since anything may be collected in any conceivable manner, and it seems to demonstrate both the tenuous frailty of the human project and the triumphant spirit of domination and cognitive mastery. That is, for both Bail and Kroetsch, collections represent the absurdist paradox (the human person is both foolish and great, descendant even while ascendant). Yet in each novel the collection motif functions differently to display, even to emblematize, the limitations of human thought and language. If the handles on reality are slippery, elusive, arbitrary, and groundless as a collection (any and all), then what shall one say about that reality? What remains of it? How else can it be reached? What shall one say about fiction, the tradition of European realism, for example, that presumptuously claims to represent that reality?

Murray Bail's *Homesickness* narrates the adventures of a group of Australians (who are themselves, of course, a collection) making a world tour during which they visit museums in each stop. The museums are of all kinds, from the fanciful (an African museum of European handicrafts, the leftover detritus of colonialism) to the surrealistic, a museum of legs in Ecuador or one of gravity in the Soviet Union. The world can be and has been collected in countless ways. The image of the museum (a public, institutional collection, some of which must strike one as quite mad) is important, and not only because travelers commonly visit them. Museums are wonderfully absurdist: they claim not merely to collect but to have done so exactly, scientifically, and to document their collectivity in a neutral, objective, value-free nomenclature.

Bail's museums mock that claim to neutral, value-free objectivity. In an essay on Gustave Flaubert's *Bouvard et Pécuchet*, Eugenio Donato, having cited the passage in which Flaubert describes the two characters' early wanderings among the collections of Paris ("fossils fired their imagination, conchology bored them"), comments that the term "which is then representationally privileged, which allegorizes the series [of collections, from bric-à-brac shops to the Louvre], is the museum . . . an encyclopedic totality."[24] All collections may claim a kind of totality, if only implicitly, but the museum (founded on principles of objectivity and exactitude) makes a special claim to represent the world, the reality beyond the boundaries of its groups and subgroups. Museums are especially unmistakable collections. They are often located in large, attractive buildings, charging admission (a sign of confidence and public importance), yet they are only manifestations, if complex ones, of the concept of a collection.[25] Bail's narrative foregrounds the concreteness of the museum image, but the conceptual play revolves around the logically more primitive concept of collectivity. Either claim, whether the weak one to express the totality of a category by a metonymic projection or the strong one truly to represent reality, is undercut by the paradoxicality of collections: a claim to plenitude is mocked by the collection's evident emptiness.[26] Bail's novel plays upon the immense range of possibilities: "The world itself is a museum; and within its circumference the many small museums, the natural and the man-built, represent the whole. The rocks of Sicily, the Ufizzi, the corner of a garden, each are miniatures of the world at large. Look, the sky at night: the most brilliantly displayed and ever-changing museum of harmonic mathematics and insects, of gods and mythological figures, agricultural machinery. The catalogue is endless" (247).

There are two ways of interpreting the topos that the "world itself is a museum," both of which play roles in *Homesickness*. First, it is possible to see the world as a vast matrix of data, of fragmentary details and their endless recombinations. The rank, utter blankness of things waits to be known, to be collected, and resists these activities. It is always rather like the tree root in Sartre's *La Nausée*: thingness both inspires and frustrates the desire to know. Flaubert's two compilers of encyclopedias, visitors to and constructors of museums, Bouvard and Pécuchet, fail in every practical effort to apply their knowledge. The world, mere thingness, resists and frustrates them. In *Homesickness*, the Australians visit a museum of hair in London: "Collection of early shampoo bottles. Clippers. The stigma endured by albinoes and redheads. The extra length of male hair between world wars. They glanced at each other. 'That was all, wasn't it?' 'Who would have thought?' Shiela said, brimming with the extra knowledge. The high incidence of hairy wrists in English and Australian literature. 'Everywhere's a museum,' Sasha now complained. 'The whole world is a museum,' Gerald agreed" (246–47). The data are staggering, the sheer quantity of the matrix utterly inconceivable except abstractly and fragmentarily. Collections and models (which are purely cognitive, *structural* collections) knit the random fragments together in loose nets of signification. Hence museums, as Donato argues, the paradigmatic mode of human collection, symbolize both futility and courage. Human ambition (to get those handles on reality) is both foolish and wonderful. The fictional potential of this absurdist theme is obviously very large. Second, the notion that the world itself is a museum underscores the postmodern obsession with the arbitrariness of language, the abstractness of all concepts, the immeasurable distance that opens up between those handles, our conceptual/linguistic tools, and reality. Both interpretations are available in reading *Homesickness*. It is either (or both) a tremendously funny narrative in which the absurdist paradox is brilliantly captured or it is a densely intellectual account, in the manner of *Bouvard et Pécuchet*, of the hopeless futility of constructing cognitive tools for apprehending the world, whether these tools are maps, models, or museums.

Robert Kroetsch's *Alibi*, unlike Bail's cool and distanced third-person narrative, is told in the first person and is hotly confessional. The voice reminds one of most of Kroetsch's previous first-person narrators: male, involved, passionate, at once confessional and exuberant, always looking backward yet creating itself into existence by the act of narrating.[27] In *Alibi* the narrator, Dorf, recounts his experiences as the agent for an eccentric Canadian millionaire for whom he collects. Indeed, he seems to have collected not only a wide variety of collectible "things" but innumerable complete collections; that is, collections already made and enumerated but, as always, ready to be recollected for an even larger, more encompassing collection. (Late in the narrative, the reader learns that Dorf's qualifications to act as an agent for a collector of collections include his experience as "the curator of a county museum" in upstate New York and having written a Ph.D. thesis at the University of Iowa on cash registers as works of art.) The millionaire's pastime is "to collect anything that was loose" (7).

The narrative begins with Dorf flying back to Alberta from Sicily "with a collection of twenty-eight sets of dominoes" (7). At other times he has collected shrunken heads, Japanese armor, aphrodisiacs, stuffed tigers, ceremonial masks, walking sticks, locks, Central American birds' eggs, even once in Singapore "a dusty boxful of miniature Buddhas" (20). The full list of collections mentioned in *Alibi* would be extensive. The collections in Kroetsch's novel, however, are not intended for display in any museum. They go into warehouses where no one sees them: in the course of claiming that artists are collectors, Dorf insists that "Jack Deemer himself, my notorious employer, was an artist in his own right, a kind of looney sculptor intent on tacking together, or assembling in warehouses at least, all the loose pieces, all the high-class garbage of the riddling earth" (20). At another point, Dorf reflects, "Maybe, instead of just trying to buy the world, he was hoping to buy it and reassemble it too. According to his own design, of course" (37). Assembling and reassembling are key terms: constructs, products of design, exhibitions of pattern and the blessed rage to order, categories are never natural.

In the first chapter, as the collector's agent arrives back in Calgary, he is given a message: "Find me a spa, Dorf" (7). A spa is an item rather different to collect from the others that Dorf has already collected, even the most bizarre of them, since it would seem that spas cannot be moved or, if they can be, only at great expense and difficulty.[28] One may interpret this as an aspect of Deemer's characterization: the desire to handle the world, to bring it within the scope of a personal collection, transcends ordinary, merely physical, limitations. One may also interpret it as a comment on the essentially conceptual nature of all collections, even the most physically placed. Concepts, those loose nets of human thinking, collect, and members of the collection certainly do not have to be in any one place or even in any place. (It should be evident that one function of the collection motif is to thematize every problem, aporia, and paradox associated with set theory: not only may any item be a member of more than one set but every set may be subsumed by still other sets.) Dorf comments, "Deemer's collecting, and his collections, making no sense. So now against all the randomness, he wants to collect, possess, some special and immovable part of the earth itself" (58). Bail's novel coincides with Kroetsch's on this point. Collections, whether in museums or in warehouses, are often bizarre and certainly extraordinary, but this is a function of the collective scheme, the desire or madness of the collector, not of anything inherent in facts or in that elusive reality itself. Nothing is ordinary or extraordinary, but thinking makes it so.

There are several thematic parallels between the two novels. (This thematic analysis does scant justice to the narrative interest and excitement of the novels. Clearly, a great deal more happens in each than the manifestations of the collection motif. In particular, *Alibi* is a mystery novel with an international chase and a hidden conspiracy. Both novels are extremely funny, comic narratives. Yet, like any collection, a short analysis selects and reassembles its materials at the expense not only of other materials but also of all other possibilities for assemblage.) Both novels place the concept of a collection in the foreground. They not only employ collections as a theme, for whatever purposes of structure, characterization, or tone, but they make the very concept itself centrally significant. A museum or a warehouse is no more than a collection of collections.

Vladimir Nabokov once wrote a story about a visit to a museum in which the initial displays of such fragments of reality as insect dung give way to hidden interior labyrinths that seem to contain all possible collections in both time and space.[29] Nabokov's narrative suggests an important point about both Bail's and Kroetsch's use of the collection motif: collections carry an invisible baggage. The problem of boundaries, of the transposability of individual items, of the arbitrariness of the criteria for collecting, all play their inescapable roles.[30] On one hand, to unpack a museum would entail putting all of its collections onto the street, or into an adjacent lot, reducing it to the shapeless bric-à-brac into which the collections of Bouvard and Pécuchet inevitably dissolve; on the other, to unpack a museum would be to reveal the implicit, and ordinarily unself-conscious, criteria that secretly give it shape. Museums focus this set of problems (of unpacking collectivity) precisely. One can always ask about the curator, the curatorial principles and criteria, the nomenclature, the undisplayed collections. (Great museums, such as the Smithsonian, normally display only a tiny percentage of their holdings. The larger, undisplayed portion is usually located in a warehouse.) But even a warehouse exhibits, if less explicitly, the same set of problems. A collection obscures, but also betrays, its arbitrary foundations since its criteria are always, and already, in doubt: it is subject to modifications and substitutions (who, other than a professional curator, would dare to claim that the nomenclature of museums is, or could ever be, value-free, neutral, or objective?), and its boundaries can be collapsed or extended at will or whim.[31] Any object may belong to more than one collection, and any collection, like any set, may be included within another. All of Bail's museums, for example, might be collected within Kroetsch's warehouses. In fact, something like that happens in *Homesickness* when the Australian travelers discover, within the collection constituted by a railway station's Lost Luggage Depository, an abandoned railway station reflexively collected (and in which, no doubt, there must be another Lost Luggage Depository).

The concept of a collection, then, stands for (represents, may be collected as, leads to the fictionalization of) the wider one of language. What can be shown to be the case for the human desire to collect, to build museums or to fill warehouses, may also be shown to be the case for human thought generally. Donato comments bitingly on the normal claim made by museums to represent either a totality or a reality:

> The set of objects the Museum displays is sustained only by the fiction that they somehow constitute a coherent representational universe. The fiction is that a repeated metonymic displacement of fragment for totality, object to label, series of objects to series of labels, can still produce a presentation which is somehow adequate to a nonlinguistic universe. Such a fiction is the result of an uncritical belief in the notion that ordering and classifying, that is to say, the spatial juxtaposition of fragments, can produce a representational understanding of the world. Should the fiction disappear, there is nothing left of the *Museum* but bric-à-brac, a heap of meaningless and valueless fragments of objects that are incapable of substituting themselves either metonymically for the original objects or metaphorically for their representations.[32]

Language collects, as postmodern writers persistently observe, and (the gap between signifier and signified being the only absolute in which one may possess absolute confidence) it does so arbitrarily: discourse is a verbal collection, a lexical museum, much as a collection is an ocular discourse.

There is a parallel between the two novels in the way they treat the act of collecting, the pure subjectivity of the collector. Both Bail and Kroetsch suggest repeatedly that to collect is to play a game. As game, collecting would seem to have rules (though also conventions that determine modes of arrangement and expression) that are indemonstrable, even axiomatic. (From still another direction, the axiomatic nature of the rules that govern collections opens to the kind of analysis that Foucault has given: the organization of knowledge, whether in encyclopedias or in museums, differs in time according to hidden rules of formation. This is a problem in the history, or perhaps in the archaeology, of museums.) Both novels call the human propensity for imposing schematic forms, whether the principles, the labels, or the discourse itself, into doubt. Collections necessarily embody what might be called the curatorial fallacy: axiomatic necessity expresses subjective predilection. Deemer's mad desire to collect and reassemble the world in Kroetsch's novel is matched by the curatorial passion of Bail's collectors (the curator of the museum of legs in Ecuador, for instance, has had one leg amputated to call attention to his collection and to his role as its curator). The desire to reassemble the world, either in reshaping its contours and emphases or in transforming it into a mosaic of emblems, must lie implicit, always already, within the desire to collect.

One of Bail's most engaging characters, Zoellner, who had first appeared in a collection of short stories in the form of a series of definitions, reappears in *Homesickness* as a vendor of definitions.[33] Zoellner owns a little shop in London, near the British Museum, that he shares with Biv, a seller of maps. In the vast resources of their shop the congruencies between definitions and maps, as cognitive instruments for handling the world, become clear: "Zoellner & Biv had one of the finest collections of Collective Nouns to be seen anywhere. A regular Scriptorum; polyglot's trove" (259). The shop itself, set off from the disorganized clutter, the flow of uncollected facts, of London's streets, constitutes a refuge for the Australian travelers. Rather like the allegorical "houses" of Spenser's *Faerie Queene* in which the questing heroes encounter spatialized, or paradigmatic, representations of the moral virtues they seek, the shop is a self-contained world, a model of how collections work: "The storage of words, like the lines on a map, records and fixes the existence of things. Inside the shop, the repository, a feeling of serenity pervaded, as if the four walls contained the entire world and even what lay beyond, each part isolated, identified and filed. It was based upon facts, upon known quantities. Exactitude reigned. It contrasted casually with the chaos of forest impressions suffered by the travellers. It was a haven" (260). To contain the world within the four walls of a building, a room, or a display case suggests both the curatorial ambition and the triumph of human cognitive powers. Both Kroetsch and Bail link the collection to the desire to collect. The schemata that collect the world inevitably display the minds that construct them.

Kroetsch and Bail are local, regional writers. Kroetsch's evocative regionalism has been established by many Canadian critics. Bail's localism is less evident, at least to a North American audience, but it is there. No one could mistake him for other than what he is, an Australian writer. Consider the following exchange, which occurs in the middle of a number of ethnic comparisons and stale jokes (yet another collection):

> "What about the Canadians? Have you ever met an interesting Canadian?"
>
> The comparisons, their anecdotes. Gerald pursed his lips.
>
> "Yes, I'm not crazy about the Canadians."
>
> "I don't remember any," Violet mysteriously cracked. (225)

The concept of a collection, employed diversely by both novelists, illustrates the point that one way of looking at literature is as a transnational phenomenon, careless of frontiers. Regionalists, they are also transnationalists. The multiplicity, even the inevitability, of collections does not lead necessarily to their ready-to-handness as fictional themes. Not even the genuine looniness of collectors, or even the wonderfully smug official discourse of public museums, leads necessarily to fiction.[34] To make the concept of a collection the major theme of, even the basis for, a fictional narrative seems another matter: a deliberate, perhaps playful, move to transform a basic mode of human thinking into the materials for fiction. The eagerness that writers such as Kroetsch and Bail exhibit in playing upon the slippery groundlessness of discourse, exemplifying while enjoying the paradoxes that undercut even while constituting discourse, probably marks them as postmodernist writers as much as anything else. Playful self-consciousness, to which innumerable particular conventions and strategies may be subordinated, is, one suspects, the fundamental postmodernist mode. As a fictional theme, the concept of a collection must be taken as highly self-conscious: it unpacks the invisible baggage of a common, and probably basic, human activity and, in so doing, makes that activity less certain, its normally smug discourse undercut, even carnivalized. In the absence of certainty, as Thiher argues, play may be the most reasonable activity to practice.

II

> She looked around, spooked at the sunlight pouring in all the windows, as if she had been trapped at the center of some intricate crystal, and said, "My God."
>
> —Thomas Pynchon, *The Crying of Lot 49*

Modern literature is an immensely variegated fabric: its themes have been woven, and rewoven, in threads of illusion. As a body (that is, as a professional category, an area of knowledge, something that one can study, write about, offer courses in), modern literature seems overwhelmingly complex and elusive, but there is, at its core, a pervasive concern for illusion. All forms of illusion have been employed in the modern period: deception, metamorphosis, sexual masquerade, psychosis, obsession with (and of) the persona, tricks, tricksters, and all sorts of scheming schemata. Above all, modern literature seems to have been obsessed by the perceptual ambiguities of art itself. Much of the literature written since 1920 seems to incorporate the shifting fabric of appearance. Experience, whatever its context or apparent shape, has been seen to break down into multiple perspectives. Evident solids dissolve into their manifold hidden planes while observably stable ego relationships metamorphose into systematic configurations of role and play. The multiple perspectives themselves, which alone remain of a former faith in substantiality and intelligibility, prove to be no more certain than their subjective roots. Illusion has become stock in trade.

Few illusions in postmodern literature are as central, and few as overdetermined, as the godgame. In a godgame, one character (or several) is made a victim by another character's superior knowledge and power. Caught in a cunningly constructed web of appearances, the victim, who finds the illusion to be impenetrable, is observed and his behavior is judged. The name of this form of illusion, the godgame, must be attributed to the English novelist John Fowles. In his novel *The Magus*, the hero, a young Englishman teaching in an English-speaking school on a Greek island, becomes ensnared in an intricate net spun by a wildly experimental millionaire with a remarkable sense of play.[35] Conchis (whose very name suggests an inward labyrinth, the mandalic whorls of a seashell) creates a succession of illusions that make it impossible for the young teacher to grasp what is taking place around him. His true situation, as he is caught up in one clever and impenetrable illusion after another, is indeterminable. Fowles calls this situation a godgame by which he names, retrospectively, a narrative category that has existed since the tales of ancient mythology.

A godgame signifies a gamelike situation in which a *magister ludi* knows the rules (because he has invented them) and the character-player does not. A godgame occurs in literature when one or more characters creates an illusion, a mazelike sequence of false accounts, that entraps other characters. The entrapped character becomes entangled in the threads of (from his point of view) an incomprehensible strategy plotted by another character who displays the roles of both a gamewright and a god. The master of the game is godlike in that he exercises power, holds an advantageous position, will probably be beyond detection (even understanding), and may even be, like Oberon or Ariel in Shakespeare's plays, invisible. In this respect, the god of the godgame recalls the callous behavior of the gods toward human victims in certain ancient myths. Consider Semele, daughter of Cadmus, who is led innocently to her death by Hera's malign strategies.

Semele is chosen by Zeus to be one of his mortal lovers. As so often happens, this arouses the jealous anger of Hera. Seeking revenge, Hera takes the shape of an old woman and approaches the girl in the duplicitous form of another mortal, aged and wise, perhaps (as some versions of the tale have it) even as Semele's own nurse, but giving no indications of danger. In this trust-inspiring form, Hera causes Semele to divulge that the god Zeus is her lover. Then, filled with apparent sympathy for the girl and interest in her well-being, she asks if Zeus makes love to her in the same manner that he makes love to Hera herself. When Semele cannot answer this question, Hera suggests that she test the claims of her lover (for not every man is who he pretends to be) by exacting from him a promise and then requesting that he take her in his arms exactly as he does Hera. Zeus grants the abstract request for a promise; however, when he hears what it is to be, he tries to stop Semele's mouth, but she speaks too fast for him, and he finds himself, quite against his will, bound by his promise. He ascends onto Olympus and dresses himself in the panoply of thunder and lightning in which it is Hera's conjugal privilege to know him and returns to Thebes. And, although he wishes otherwise, and attempts to control the overwhelming power of naked godhead, he totally consumes hapless Semele.

The fate of Semele embodies the usual condition of humankind in the face of greater powers. She is uncomprehending, incapable of testing the illusion that Hera creates, falls into a trap without knowing that she has done so, fails to see the correct implications, makes the wrong decisions, embraces death unwittingly, even ironically, since it is contrary to her expectations of the moment. Her mind deals with the experience of superior power and cunning wholly inadequately: ignorance and bewilderment sum up her mind's capacity. Furthermore, she objectifies the natural human dread of puniness, of inadequacy, of becoming entrapped, of being played. For (this is the tale's exemplary lesson) Semele is actually played: she is encompassed in Hera's strategy and moved, as mindlessly as if she were a piece or a token, some (in Nabokov's phrase) "wooden materiality" or other.

The victim of a godgame finds himself in the bewildering necessity of having to think himself out of a context that he cannot understand. In comic godgames, the entrapped character may not even understand that he is in an illusion. He will simply react to the delusive shapes about him, as Christopher Sly does in the induction to *The Taming of the Shrew*, or as Prospero's sea-lost victims do in *The Tempest*, or as the Knight and his Squire in the Second Part of *Don Quijote* when they stumble among the Duke's clever snares. Whether comic or deadly serious, the godgame is a trap that subjects the character-player to a web of unintelligible incidents which are also, from the god's side of the play, cunningly opaque strategies, like the ruse that Hera plays on Semele. (Thus the godgame suggests the experience of chess from the pawn's vantage. And the victim may be said to feel in his marrow the pawn's conceptual vertigo.) The secret intransitivity of the godgame, in which intelligent rules are experienced as unintelligible, gives shape to the interiority of all game experience. In a godgame, narrative might almost seem to approach the play of a game from within. George Steiner remarks upon the "queer, still violence that chess engenders,"[36] and this expression captures the pure insideness of a godgame. It is often, as is Fowles's version in *The Magus*, an embodiment of exquisite violence and anguish. Human intelligence, once made conscious of its entrapment, struggles to understand the rules of the game in which it has been made a piece. It will fight stubbornly to avoid Semele's unhappy fate.

The godgame illustrates the paradox of defining the term *postmodern*. It is a term invented by a writer who is normally cited as postmodern, at least in much of his work, and the situation it names recurs frequently in postmodern writing generally. It falls easily into the discussion of games and, as either a narrative or a dramatic situation, embodies the ludic spirit of much postmodernism. In particular, the godgame constitutes an emblem of the postmodern obsession with uncertainty, ambiguous perception, and cognitive entrapment: the character-player in a godgame, granted its universal applicability as an image of human perplexity, encodes the reader's own cognitive difficulties in making sense of (or of playing through) the literary text. If any single convention marks postmodern literature, both by the obsessions it indicates and the fictional situation it creates, it must be the godgame. Yet the godgame, as the tale of Semele demonstrates, is unmistakably transhistorical. The godgame occurs in fiction from all periods, and it is always fascinating. It does not necessarily, though it may always be seen to do so, encode the perplexing difficulties of readership. The transhistorical nature of the godgame may be seen clearly in an examination of baroque fiction. Godgames recur persistently throughout baroque literature (Shakespeare, Spenser, and Milton are masters of the godgame's potential) and, except that one knows unmistakably that it also characterizes the postmodern period with equivalent accuracy, might be thought to be uniquely characteristic of the period. Pedro Calderón de la Barca's *Life Is a Dream*, an outstanding instance of a godgame in baroque literature, illustrates this point.

Segismundo, the hero of Calderón's play, has been imprisoned within a desert tower, not knowing that he is the son of the king of Poland, or that there is a world beyond his tower, or men other than his jailer. He has never been told that he has been imprisoned to avert the moral and political disaster that his father, an accomplished astrologer as well as king, has foreseen. In other words, the artificial reality of his tower, and his existence within it, seems to him (indeed, *must* seem to him) complete. In his first appearance, as he stands in the lighted doorway of his tower dressed in animal skins and weighed down with chains, Segismundo begins by posing questions. What crime has he committed against heaven to be treated in such a way? Or rather, as he rephrases the question, what crime, other than having been born, has he committed? He thus poses his existence as a problem. In the torchlit doorway, his sudden presence before the travelers indicates the operation of some hidden godgame and at once calls it, or its rules, into question. He goes on to tell the travelers that he has never seen a man other than his jailer and has learned nothing other than that which he has been able to teach himself: government from the animals, astronomy from the birds and the stars. His delusion is virtually complete for not only does he know almost nothing about reality, he knows nothing of his own identity or of the reasons for his imprisonment.

Later, the astrologer-king, Basilio, explains, but not to his son, that Segismundo was born under an eclipse and, in being born, had caused the death of his mother. Basilio had interpreted these signs to mean that Segismundo would prove to be a monster. He now intends to test his prediction by recalling his son. When Segismundo is brought back to the court, he is drugged. He is given no explanations. He simply awakes in bed attended by courtiers and is told that he is crown prince of Poland. His reaction parallels that of Christopher Sly in *The Taming of the Shrew*: he accepts the new illusion and begins immediately to live as crown prince. Why should he not, one might ask, since he possesses no way of judging the truth of the illusion or even of testing its illusoriness? Subsequently, the trial of Segismundo's character seems to prove that his father's auguries have been correct. Segismundo turns out to be violent, brutal, and vengeful, even to the point of throwing a disobedient soldier out of a window. Not surprisingly, Basilio does not inquire whether this behavior is that foretold by the auguries or merely a consequence of the barbaric treatment Segismundo has received since birth. Later, drugged once more, Segismundo is returned to the tower and told, upon awakening, that he has been dreaming. Indeed, even while he was living the role of crown prince he had been told that he might well be only dreaming. Thus it is easy for him to accept his keeper's word that he has been asleep. He opens his eyes, looks about him at the familiar cell, and exclaims, "God save me, what things I have dreamt."

The force of Segismundo's delusion is overwhelming: Calderón has left no point of reference outside the closed system of illusion, and he has provided that system with a built-in explanation for any apparent inconsistencies. Segismundo is *forced* to conclude that even in dreams one ought not fail to do good since it is impossible to distinguish a dreaming from a waking state. No doubt his conclusion indicates, as scholarly commentary has often argued, the inherent nobility of his nature. It also illustrates the logic of the illusion to which he has been submitted. Everyone dreams, he meditates: the king that he is a king, the rich man that he is rich, the poor man that he suffers poverty. "I dreamt," he concludes "that I saw myself in a carefree state and now I am dreaming that I am in this prison weighed down with chains. . . . All of life is a dream and dreams are always dreams."[37]

Later, when the rebellious soldiers come to free him and to make him king, Segismundo accepts their invitation. Bearing in mind that he may be dreaming once again, he sets out to confirm the truth of the heavens' auguries. If he is skeptical about reality, he nonetheless goes out to battle with an acquired control that he had not shown previously, convinced that even in dreaming one must act responsibly. He does not lose this conviction, controls himself, acts wisely and prudently, even to the extent of convincing his father that his nature will now pass tests of strictest scrutiny. At the end, he is established in his rightful place, the tower behind him forever, but he continues to believe that it may all be a dream and that he may awake at any moment in chains once more.

Life Is a Dream suggests that godgames build upon situations in which one dominant character—a magus such as Prospero (one must acknowledge how aptly Fowles named his novel, charged as it is with *Tempest*ian motifs), a powerful duke as in *Don Quijote,* or an even more powerful king as in *Life Is a Dream*—creates a web of illusions so powerful, and so thoroughly self-consistent, that the characters who are ensnared will not be able to extricate themselves. They will be led to accept illusion for reality, to act in terms of illusion, to reveal their beings in its terms and, if they attempt to think through the illusion, they, like Segismundo, will be frustrated. In certain respects the godgame recalls other common illusions of Renaissance literature. It has affinities with both the topoi of the enchanted garden and castle and with the trickster motif. The godgame, however, is significantly different from either of these. Unlike the enchanted garden (the Bower of Bliss, say, or Alcina's magical paradise in the *Orlando Furioso*), the godgame seems to be created neither for its own sake nor for giving pleasure. Furthermore, it need not take any specific form. The godgame is created solely for the victim and then only for the purpose of observing his behavior. On the other hand, the *magister ludi*, despite occasional resemblances, is unlike such trickster figures as Archimago, Don Juan Tenorio, or Milton's Satan. He does not create his illusion, as Don Juan does with Doña Isabel, to achieve a seduction, or for any precise or momentary purpose, nor does he break it or allow it to collapse, but rather he keeps it going through a series of linked incidents while he *observes* his victim. He seems far more like a "god" than a mere trickster.

There are several formal properties of the godgame that are indicated by, and may be derived from, *Life Is a Dream*. Brief reflection should suggest the applicability of these characteristics to other works of baroque literature such as *The Tempest* or the Second Part of *Don Quijote* and even to godgames that may be found outside of that historical period. These formal properties are extrapolations from the single text *Life Is a Dream*, but their applicability, as will be seen, is very general. They may be stated in a logical sequence, beginning with merely necessary conditions, of ascending sufficiency. First, there will be a series of incidents that, through their linkage, create an illusion. Second, these linked incidents will constitute reality for the victim. Third, the constructed illusion will be impenetrable. Fourth, the illusion will form a self-correcting and self-explaining system. Fifth, the illusion will be plotted and planned (looking at it from the standpoint of the god or gamewright), but to the character-player this plan will be unknown. The illusion, for the victim, will be more like choreography seen from inside the dance, or chess from the pawn's perspective. Sixth, the victim will act in terms of the illusion. He may be thought of as reacting, of course, but from his perspective he will be acting. Seventh, the character-player's actions will be observed and will be subject to judgment, although an actual judgment will not be strictly necessary. These observations are also open to the audience, the readers, ourselves.

The final property of the baroque godgame seems to be the most important; it is that in the absence of which the illusion might well be something less than a godgame, a trick or a mere joke.[38] The purpose of the godgame is to create a situation in which the character-player may be observed and his nature tested. This is precisely what Basilio reiterates throughout *Life Is a Dream*: the illusion is a test of human nature, its effects must be observed, and the revealed nature must be judged and either rewarded or punished. In a similar manner, Prospero's godgame variously reveals the natures of his shipwrecked countrymen and, as well, he imposes a judgment upon them. In a dissimilar manner, human nature is also tested, and implicitly judged, by the Duke's godgame in *Don Quijote*, but in that case the natures of the two victims are seen to rise above the petty nastiness of the gamewrights. In all three cases, the end of the godgame is to bring to light some truth about the character-players.

The presence of godgames in baroque literature coheres with the widespread incidence of illusion and perspectivism in that historical period. Nonetheless, godgames figure in all literary periods, including, strikingly, the modern and postmodern. Even a brief survey of the history of literature between the late seventeenth century and the second half of the twentieth century will make this point. The inescapable evidence of Goethe's *Wilhelm Meisters Lehrjahre*, in which the "insular" pedagogical community of the Tower (with its Masonic, and hence conspiratorial, undertones, rather like those of the second half of *The Magic Flute*) constitutes an educational godgame for the benefit of Wilhelm Meister's development, places the godgame squarely in the period of the Enlightenment.[39] Godgames, though often only mechanically conceived strategies of plot, occur frequently in Gothic fiction, as they do, a couple of generations later, in Victorian detective fiction, such as Arthur Conan Doyle's "The Redheaded League" and *The Hound of the Baskervilles*.

Low-level godgames are frequent in science fiction and generally in fantasy (though the distinctions between godgame, trick, and joke often fade). One thinks immediately of Arthur C. Clarke's *Childhood's End* or Ursula K. Le Guin's *City of Illusions*. Godgames were a recurring device in the television series "Star Trek"; and one British television series, "The Prisoner" (starring the incomparably apt Patrick MacGoohan as the character-player), was founded entirely on the premise that a secret "village" existed, in an elaborate, technologically enhanced godgame, for the single purpose of keeping, in an impenetrable state of ignorance and delusion, a number of prisoners who have made themselves difficult for their respective governments. (The opening two-minute montage of each episode of "The Prisoner," a model of narrative clarity that might still be viewed with enthusiasm by narratologists, establishes the background and the essential condition of the godgame and includes this paradigmatic exchange between an interrogator in the "village" and the character-player: MacGoohan's character demands, "Who are you?" and the interrogator responds, "I am number two," to which the character-player demands, "Who is number one?" and receives the enigmatic, power-saturated reply, "You are number six." The dynamics of power, entrapment, inquiry, and bafflement have scarcely ever been caught more crisply.) In the popular versions of the godgame ("The Prisoner" being a partial exception), however, there is little attention to the exploration of man's moral nature. The godgames of *The Tempest, Don Quijote,* and *Life Is a Dream* are, in pointing the reader toward a significant moral insight, sharply heuristic.

A number of modern (and/or postmodern) writers have employed godgames, or elements of godgames, in their fiction. Kafka's *The Castle* suggests, as do several of his short narratives such as "In The Penal Colony," a prototypical godgame in which the element of character revelation is subordinated, though not suppressed, to an account of the uncertainty and bafflement that characterize the illusion when it is seen from within. Modern American literature has produced several works, such as Charles G. Finney's *Circus of Dr. Lao* and Joseph Heller's *Catch-22*, in which the emphasis on games and gamewrights brings the narrative within the sphere of the godgame (indeed, any narrative that refers to, and ascribes responsibility to, an inexplicit "they" is likely to invoke some of the haunting qualities of a baroque godgame). Three modern writers, however, stand out as particularly important creators of godgames: Hermann Hesse, Jorge Luis Borges, and Thomas Pynchon.

Pynchon is the most systematic of these, for reasons that will become clear, but all three share an inclination to create situations in which one or more characters is subjected to a linked series of illusions that leads ultimately either to a revelation of the character-player's hidden nature or, as in Pynchon's fiction, to a modification of the character's essential nature. There is a fundamental pessimism and pervasive complexity to Pynchon's godgames: they reflect a post–World War II American understanding of the routine power of intellectual and administrative systems of all kinds, governmental and industrial. Pynchon's deluded victims are bewildered survivors (and in this sense close to the practice of Kafka) in an ongoing horror show. Even the "god" of the game becomes unanalyzable other than in terms of function, the amorphous, unthinkable *they* of bureaucracy and behavioral conditioning. Pynchon's fictional world seems appalling. It is markedly distant from the optimistic worlds of Hesse (in which characters are seen to possess "better" natures than have been achieved as the fiction begins) or the studiously withdrawn, sublimated, and cognitive worlds of Borges's fictions.

Godgames figure in several of Hesse's novels, particularly *Demian* and *Steppenwolf*. They are beneficent, psychologically oriented illusions in which the character-player is led to understand himself better and to realize a greater degree of his potentiality. Even in his last novel, *The Glassbead Game*, there are godgame elements insofar as the members of the pedagogical community are helped to self-realization, observed, judged, and either rewarded or punished. The secret communicants of *Demian*, the obscure benefactors of *Steppenwolf*, and the withdrawn educators of *The Glassbead Game* have much in common: they stimulate action, observe it, and in so doing help their victims (or clients) to higher levels of selfhood. The "gods" in Hesse's fiction are remote, mysterious, and in some respects unintelligible. One striking difference between baroque and modern godgames lies in the withdrawn, hidden (or disappearing) nature of the god in the latter.

Hesse's characters evolve under the guidance of obscure powers, through linked incidents that constitute chains of illusions, toward a realization of potential. In *Steppenwolf*, the central character is brought methodically away from a state of chronic depression that has arisen from his sense of dissociation. "Steppenwolf" is Harry Haller's term for the repressed "shadow" side of his personality; that is, the collection of violent, brutal drives that, in an active state, assume the traits of a single, coherent personality. In Haller's view of himself this personality is like a wolf from the steppes, voracious, hostile, an outlaw. Through a series of encounters that are never made entirely clear but must be taken as engineered, Haller is introduced, first, to the joys of uncritical sensuality which he had previously attempted to deny and, second, to the multiplicity of aspects embryonically latent within his being, all of which he had mistakenly grouped together as one under the inaccurate, pejorative shadow label "steppenwolf." In *Steppenwolf*, both the god and the nature of the illusions are unclear. Pablo may be thought of as a god or as a demiurge (at least), but he is in either case largely inexplicable. The narrative of the godgame, the step-by-step unfolding of its hidden intention, is clear enough: the benefactors lead the virtually deranged Haller to understand himself, to cancel out his restrictive self-censorship, and thus to recognize in the unexplored depths of his own shadow his manifold potential. Above all, the benefactors bring him to see, through the agency of the Magic Theater, that the "steppenwolf" label has been mistaken: his shadow has been neither single nor evil.

There are overt elements of Jungian allegory in Hesse's fiction, as critics have variously noted, that cause one to recall other writers, such as

Miguel Angel Asturias, Patrick White, Doris Lessing (in certain of her novels, such as *The Golden Notebook* or *The Summer before the Dark*), or Robertson Davies, who have adapted aspects of Jung's psychological model to the process of characterization.[40] The end toward which Hesse's novels move is that so frequently found in novels by White, Davies, or Lessing (among others, but excluding Asturias, whose cognitive scheme, though Jungian, does not focus in this manner): the Jungian desideratum of individuation. Furthermore, Hesse's characters discover depths within themselves (as do the characters of other writers mentioned) that, rendered paradigmatically, accord to the normal Jungian model of hierarchical and interdependent levels of conscious and unconscious activities. In other respects Hesse's emphasis on beneficent godgames that work, with more or less secrecy and mystery, toward the development of human potential recalls Goethe's similar stress in *Wilhelm Meisters Lehrjahre*. For example, the pedagogical community of *The Glassbead Game* suggests an obvious affinity. Yet, having allowed for the intellectual traditions to which Hesse's fiction belongs, and which serve to define its conceptual content, it is nonetheless possible to point to those formal, abstractable features that are godgamelike in their configurations.

The analysis of the structure of the godgame in *Life Is a Dream* indicates the presence of seven formal properties. The last of these—the god's observation of the victim—seems most essential. In modern godgames, however, such as those of Hesse, the observing god shrinks, withdraws, and becomes absorbed into the texture of the game itself. In the extreme case (that represented by Pynchon's fiction, say), the only evidence for the god's existence is that hinted at in the game's rules. Still, the function of observation remains entirely basic. It is shifted from the god to the audience of the game's playing and, most important, to the victim himself. An introspective character-player keeps a record of his experiences, like Harry Haller providing the journal of his enlightenment, reflects on it, and thus achieves what the most famous of baroque godgame victims, Don Quijote, believed he must leave to a benevolent sage. This is the case in *Steppenwolf*, in Fowles's *The Magus*, and commonly in Borges's fictions. Pynchon's character-players are developed from the third person, within the traditions of the psychological novel, in such a way that it is not merely the sequence of their reactions that the audience observes but also the interior record of successive, and parallel, states of consciousness.

Godgame situations are frequent in Borges's writing and usually follow a first-person narrative in which the narrator concludes in a revelation of his peculiar moral and intellectual temper. Even in "Death and the Compass," a godgame in which the narration is third person, the direction of the narrative is toward a comment on the protagonist's moral nature. "Tlön, Uqbar, Orbis Tertius" and "The Lottery in Babylon" are extremely clear instances of first-person narratives in which the narrator recalls confusing and complex experiences in which he has been involved; both fictions focus on the narrator's thinking, his inquisitiveness, and his recognition of hypotheses; both conclude with a revelation of the narrator's moral temper, established confessionally but indirectly through his attitude toward the outcome of his thinking. In "Tlön, Uqbar, Orbis Tertius," the narrator recounts how he learned that a late Renaissance conspiracy to create a secret, imaginary world has persisted into this century. The evidence for the conspiracy has come to him piece by piece, through successive coincidences, but he has been able both to penetrate the conspiracy and to understand the imaginary construct that is known as Tlön.

Over many years, the conspiracy has constructed Tlön out of a vast number of imaginative details, giving them internal coherence, and encoding the construct in the form of an encyclopedia. Tlön is an entire world inhabited by Berkleyan idealists in which mind necessarily precedes object and, most strikingly, objects come into existence in response to thought. The narrator then observes that various Tlönian objects, known as *hrönir*, have begun to appear on Earth and that a process through which Tlön will eventually replace Earth seems to be under way. "Tlön, Uqbar, Orbis Tertius" is an obvious godgame (a conspiracy, a construction of linked illusions, actions in terms of the illusions, and observation, the narrator's and the reader's), but what counts is the character of the narrator, who is also the character-player. He is at once surprised and inquisitive: he investigates, pursues his interest, fits together hypotheses, and finally withdraws from the threat of the encroaching Tlön. He does not care that Tlön will supplant Earth, he remarks, but will continue revising, in the quiet days of a suburban hotel, an ambiguous Quevedian translation of Browne's *Urn Burial* that he does not intend to publish.

The importance of the godgame has resided in its effects on the narrator. It has caused him to develop and to assert a specific moral and intellectual attitude. Similarly, the first-person narrator of "The Lottery in Babylon" recounts his experience as a victim:

> Like all Babylonian men I have been a proconsul; like all, I have been a slave; as well, I have known omnipotence, scorn, prisons. Look: my right hand lacks its index finger. Look: through this tear in my cape a bright red tattoo on my stomach can be seen:

> it is the second symbol, Beth. This mark, during the nights of the full moon, gives me power over men whose mark is Ghimel, but subordinates me to Aleph, who in moonless nights owe obedience to those of Ghimel. In the twilight of dawns, in dungeons, before a black stone I have slit the throats of sacred bulls.[41]

Existence under The Company (the unknown, unknowable system that, through its indefinitely complex lottery, introduces chance into a deterministic world) is open to the extremes of an arbitrary process of rewards and punishments. Every sixty days, each citizen of Babylon must accept a "prize" from the Lottery, and this prize may be anything from apotheosis to the most degrading form of death by torture. Even these prizes are subject to an unpredictable further series of qualifications through subsequent drawings. The narrator, who is looking back on his life in Babylon (evidently he is exiled already beyond Babylon in a ship waiting to sail from an unnamed port), examines a number of hypotheses concerning the origins of The Company and its operations. He can conclude nothing certain, but he does, in revealing his moral temper, indicate a posterior development of character: he accepts fully the consequences of the Lottery, likens the acts of The Company to those of God (he refers, for instance, to its "divine modesty" and explicitly compares its "silent functioning" to God's ways), and he rejects as *vile* every hypothesis that tends to demythologize The Company or leads to a denial of its existence. Borges's narrator is, thus, despite his investigative intelligence, the very type of an ideological devotee, a servant in the full sense, a man bound to the service of an idea who thereby accepts all of the consequences of that idea. Yet this, clearly, is no less a moral revelation than the conclusion of "Tlön, Uqbar, Orbis Tertius." The end to which the narrative points is the discovery (in the narrator) of a character-player's moral and intellectual nature.

In the fiction of Thomas Pynchon, the god is even more withdrawn than in Borges's tales. There are occasional hints of a named *magister ludi*, or of a precise conspiracy, such as that constructed by the behavioral psychologists in *Gravity's Rainbow*, who experiment with, and ultimately condition, the hero, Tyrone Slothrop, into rigorously predictable responses. In Pynchon's fiction, however, the god is typically absorbed into the operations of the game itself: its rules are his manifestation; the game and his existence are fused. In many respects, Pynchon recalls the work of Kafka. This resemblance is nowhere more apparent than in the way the ground of the illusion (its origins in whatever manipulative thinking, cruel or experimental) remains opaque to the bewildered, anguished, and impenetrating minds of the victims. *Gravity's*

Rainbow inevitably must suggest many provocative lines of comparison with the fiction of Kafka in which the closed psychic state of the character, entrapped within the anguish of incomprehension, stands bleakly in the narrative's central focus.[42]

Yet even in *Gravity's Rainbow*, the named psychologist, Dr. Edward W. A. Pointsman, is subordinated to, even enclosed within, much larger systems of godgamelike activity (of which he himself is merely a piece or token). From the standpoint of Pynchon's characters, the god is given the qualities of bureaucratic administration; the godgame itself, the routinized irreversibility of contemporary political or industrial bureaucracy. For Pynchon, as for other American writers, such as Heller, there seems to be little difference between political and industrial systems; apparent differences are actually functional transformations of a single, oppressive system that lies behind, though located nowhere specifically, and permeates Western society. (That point seems clearly made in *Catch-22* in the interchangeable activities of business and war, appears repeatedly in Kurt Vonnegut's novels, and is given nearly total lucidity in Pynchon's treatment of the Yoyodyne conglomerate in *V* and in *The Crying of Lot 49*, or, more graphically, in the fused metaphor of the Rocket, at once an industrial, scientific, political, and military system, in *Gravity's Rainbow*.) The purpose of the godgame in Pynchon's fiction remains analogous to that of the baroque exemplars, or to the practice of such modern writers as Fowles, Hesse, and Borges: to observe, or at least to display, the character's responses. Pynchon's special twist to the playing of the godgame occurs in the way the play seems to end with the modification of the character's psychology, not with a revelation as such of a potential, whether intellectual or moral, already in some sense present. In the extreme case, such as Slothrop in *Gravity's Rainbow*, the character is "conditioned" almost to the point of nonexistence. More typically perhaps, the character, like Oedipa Maas in *The Crying of Lot 49*, reacts to the play of a godgame by developing psychosis. Significantly, *paranoia* is a key term in Pynchon's writing.

Borges observes that "one of the great ambitions, or perhaps will-o'-the-wisps, of literature [is] the idea of writing a book, a book that shall be somehow all other books, a book of books, a book like that seashell of which Wordsworth speaks in his *Prelude*. . . . Many men have toyed with the idea, with the dangerous and divine idea, that a book might be written, a book that should be something of a Platonic archetype, a book of books."[43] He then cites the *Divine Comedy* as the book that contains all that can be said concerning guilt, repentance, and justice; *Ulysses* as the book that contains all the things that happen or may happen to a single man in a single day; *Leaves of Grass* as the book of democracy.

One can imagine additions to Borges's list (or his collection of textual collections): *Don Quijote* as the book of adventures (or of perspectives); *The Faerie Queene* as the book of allegorical conventions and of allegoremes; either *Tristram Shandy* or *The Faerie Queene* as the book of narrativity; Borges's own collected works as the book of paradoxes (or of labyrinths). And to this list one might readily add Pynchon's *Gravity's Rainbow* as the book of systems, and in particular the book of godgames.

Gravity's Rainbow contains an immense number of godgames: mazelike systems of predetermined behavior that run parallel to each other, overlap, integrate, and shape the narrative from beginning to (distant) end. Each of the several plots builds on its distinctive godgame, each subsumes other, smaller godgames, and each interconnects with the godgames of the other plots. All these godgames have in common an insistence upon the reiterated *they* (it is one of the most common words in the novel); that is, the unknowable, absorbed gamewright who is manifested only in the operations of the game itself. Each godgame, further, is centered on the behavior of its victims. The general formula for the narrative might be expressed thus: each character is either placed within a predetermined system of behavior or it is conditioned in terms of a stimulus which is then presented, or withdrawn, while its behavior is observed (by other characters, by the inferred *they*, by the reader). The consequence is a radical modification of the character's psychology.

The godgame also captures the reader in the expanding perplexities of the narrative and imposes the character-player's state of mind as a condition of readership. (This seems like a relatively constant factor in godgames, perhaps rather more so in narrative than in dramatic contexts, though it may be doubtful that many in Shakespeare's audience, whether readers or theatergoers, feel strongly the perplexities that Antonio, Stephano, and Trinculo experience in *The Tempest*. It is part of the accessible subjectivity of texts that incorporate godgames, and even a condition for experiencing them fully, to share the character-player's bafflement. This is as much the case with *Life Is a Dream* as with *The Magus*.) In *Gravity's Rainbow*, however, the reader, and the reader's perplexity, is encoded within the text in the form of a shifting, ultimately elusive second-person "you." *Gravity's Rainbow*, Brian McHale writes, "holds the mirror up not so much to Nature as to Reading. Whenever we open the novel we find images of our own behavior as readers and critics." McHale continues to argue for the irreducible "strangeness" of the text and of Pynchon's use of the second person. All the various interpretive hypotheses fail adequately to account for this strangeness. McHale concludes that Pynchon "solicits our participation at a higher, more abstract level of reading: 'the text constantly invites and then exposes the reader's imposition of meaning.' By confronting us with irreducibly ambiguous, or, better, multiguous features, such as the second-person pronoun, Pynchon compels us to ref.ect upon our own critical practices. . . . We are invited to become metareaders, readers of our own (and others') readings—and, more to the point, of our *mis*readings."[44] This irreducible strangeness belongs also to the godgame (as readers we are like Slothrop and must share his perplexed state of mind, but we are also like Segismundo, perpetually awakening and reawakening within his tower, confronting a dream that may be real or a reality that may be a dream) which is encoded within the text of *Gravity's Rainbow* as the shifting, defocused second person.

Something of the complexity with which Pynchon invests his godgame structures can be seen in the episode in *Gravity's Rainbow* in which Slothrop is placed in touch with the double agent (at least), Katje Borgesius. Sent to a French resort-casino on the Mediterranean by superiors in London who are fascinated by his ability to precognate the point of impact of German V rockets and who suspect that the explanation must lie in an assumed connection between Slothrop's childhood role of experimental guinea pig in the laboratory of the behavioral psychologist, who, in a later scientific incarnation, invents the plastic used in the nosecones of the German rockets, Slothrop is designedly brought into contact with Katje, the mistress (among other things) of the German officer in charge of the V rocket program. The agent of the introduction is an octopus trained in a London laboratory and positioned in the sea at the moment when both Katje and the unsuspecting Slothrop are near to each other on the resort's beach. The octopus predictably entwines Katje while Slothrop (with his ingrained chivalric values), equally predictably, attempts to rescue her. In the act of trying to kill the octopus, Slothrop is handed a crab with which to feed the octopus by another soldier with the injunction not to kill it. Released by the octopus, Katje predictably falls into Slothrop's arms, becoming for a short time afterward his lover. The crab, too markedly apposite, disturbs Slothrop, though he cannot see a solution to its apparent riddle:

> So it is here, grouped on the beach with strangers, that voices begin to take on a touch of metal, each word a hard-edged clap, and the light, though as bright as before, is less able to illuminate. . . . It's a Puritan reflex of seeking other orders behind the visible, also known as paranoia, filtering in. Pale lines of force whir in the sea air. . . . Pacts sworn to in rooms since shelled back to their plan views, not quite by accident of war, suggest themselves. Oh, that was no "found" crab, Ace—no random oc-

> topus or girl, uh-uh. Structure and detail come later, but the conniving around him now he feels instantly, in his heart.[45]

This catches the baffled consciousness of a character-player trapped in the impenetrable godgame of another character whose intentions have been skillfully cloaked. Slothrop senses that something is not right (the incidents have been too improbably linked), but he cannot think through surface manifestations, those "pale lines of force," to the now opaque "reality" that they hide.

Shortly afterward, having discovered no answer to the riddle posed by Katje, the octopus, and the crab, he is chased from the casino (the main room of which is called, significantly, the "Himmler *Spielsall*") by mysterious agents. He disappears in the obscure flux of the Zone (Pynchon's name for the uncertain, anarchic regions of a defeated, collapsing Germany), swallowed in the larger, encompassing godgames of war and its aftermath. His directed, or conditioned, pursuit of the plastic used in the V rocket nosecones is seen as, ultimately, only a single aspect of a vastly greater web of conditioned responses in which every character is, however unreflectively, a player. It is a web in which the reader also plays, though neither as spider nor as fly (but rather, to appropriate one of McHale's images, rather like a metafly), holding multiguous threads that, entangled and knotted, lead in diverse directions and may be followed to no single exit but seem always to loop back upon themselves.

Pynchon's fictions offer a profoundly pessimistic reading of what is worst in contemporary American society. Often funny, they are never joyful. In this full look at the worst, the godgame acts as the universal metaphor for the human condition. His second novel, *The Crying of Lot 49*, written in 1965, illustrates this proposition with a relentless precision. In its much shorter compass, it is nearly as remarkable an example of the godgame in narrative as the vast, cetacean *Gravity's Rainbow*.

Oedipa Maas, the heroine of *The Crying of Lot 49*, learns abruptly that she has been made a coexecutor of the will of a former lover, Pierce Inverarity, the immensely wealthy owner of an industrial conglomerate. An early image in the narrative projects the central idea of the novel and links it to the theory of godgames. As Oedipa drives down a hill toward San Narciso, the southern California community where Inverarity's multiple enterprises have their headquarters, she sees the community laid out before her like a "printed circuit." In one sense, this use of a printed circuit to describe a human community seems like a typical Pynchonian metaphor (like a rocket). It is a technological function, a servomechanism or an electronic conduit, superimposed upon a mental or cultural one, but in another sense the printed circuit focuses clearly the narrative's specific preoccupations. San Narciso, as Oedipa perceives it, is "less an identifiable city than a grouping of concepts." Society, then, is like a printed circuit in that it is essentially a network of suprapersonal abstractions each of which possesses a determinate function.

The social network, like Inverarity's interlocking conglomerate, is only so many interconnected functions operating independently of the individual's existence. Moreover, this conceptual network, human society, also resembles a printed circuit in that it is an informational system in two respects. First, it conveys information; that is, information is transferred from one part of the system to another. Second, the nodes, wires, and interchanges of society not only carry information but, in their own right, signify meanings. All that happens in the novel can be interpreted as an expansion of this primary image: society is an informational system, it can be interpreted, and it may generate, in the information it either conveys or signifies, a profound effect on the interpreter. Pynchon's victims are, to some degree, all interpreters, that is, they are receivers of information from the surrounding systems.

As the novel develops, Oedipa learns that there are really two systems in American society, each with its peculiar informational content. On one hand, there is the society of the successful, represented by the multimillionaire whose will she is to help execute. On the other, there is the society of the failed, the unsuccessful in business, love, science, and even revolution. (In the pseudo-Calvinistic terms that play an important role in *Gravity's Rainbow*, these two groups correspond to the elect and the preterite.) Further, Oedipa seems to learn that each society, each with its content of information, possesses a distinctive communication system. For the successful, orthodox society of achievers and winners, there is the regular United States Postal System. For the unsuccessful, the passed over, and the losers, there is a private system, known as W.A.S.T.E., which is an aspect (or "function") of a larger organization, the Trystero, that, dating back to the sixteenth century, exists in secret opposition to all regular postal systems. (W.A.S.T.E. actually makes an acronym out of the slogan, "We await Silent Trystero's Empire.") Oedipa begins to acquire a large amount of evidence for the existence of the W.A.S.T.E.: she observes its advertisements scrawled on the walls of lavatories, its use of a giant corporation's interoffice delivery system, wastepaper receptacles under freeway overpasses that function as mail drops, and drunken postmen who appear to walk aimlessly from pick-up to drop-off points. She also overhears anecdotes that seem to corroborate the existence of the W.A.S.T.E. Furthermore, the evidence for the parent organization, the Trystero, becomes equally impressive. Like "pale lines of force," the signs appear everywhere, forming a printed circuit as plain as that which she had noted originally from her car driving into San Narciso. In fact, it is an almost overwhelming pattern of evidence involving references to the Trystero in Jacobean drama, history books, memoirs, anecdotes, wall slogans, children's games, stamps, and philatelic catalogs. The symbol of the Trystero, a muted posthorn, begins to appear, with the solid predictability of the *hrönir* in Borges's fiction, in watermarks, tiepins, drawings, doodles, and labels.

The godgame aspect of the narrative emerges when Oedipa perceives that, for all the stunning array of evidence she has uncovered (or stumbled upon), the Trystero may be only a hoax cleverly engineered by her former lover to delude her. (Of course, this suggests the merely superficial analogy between a godgame and a practical joke with which some readers, no doubt, are content.[46]) Indeed, the counterevidence begins to appear, and it indicates that the books, the Jacobean play, the sources of evidence, the stamps themselves, may all have been fraudulent, deliberately constructed by the man whose will she has been named to execute. She is able to observe that in the counterpattern a suspiciously large number of places associated with the Trystero are owned by Inverarity's conglomerate. Earlier, Oedipa had recognized that Inverarity's will had been an "attempt to leave an organized something behind after his own annihilation."[47] Now she perceives that he might have "tried to survive his own death, as a paranoia; as a pure conspiracy against someone he loved" (134). The consequence of her double action and reaction (the inconclusive search for the Trystero and the recognition that it may be a hoax) is an increasing state of mental disturbance. Pynchon describes her situation graphically, in words that might well provide an epigraph for all godgames: "She looked around, spooked at the sunlight pouring in all the windows, as if she had been trapped at the center of some intricate crystal, and said, 'My God.'" (67). Oedipa's psychosis is induced by the baffling aspects of her experience. It is also important that she is aware of her mental state. One of the novel's motifs has been the recurring references to paranoia (a rock group, for example, names itself the Paranoids), and gradually Oedipa begins to embody this motif. Her incipient paranoia (totally absent from, even alien to, her psyche in the first chapter) is forced upon her. Her readings, or misreadings, of the printed circuit of society bring her irreversibly to the boundary of sanity. Even the fillings in her teeth begin to hurt. And in the close of the narrative, she is waiting, to one side, in a shaft of sunlight informed by rising and falling bits of uninterpretable dust, at the auction of Inverarity's Trystero stamps (the "lot 49" of the title), preparing a hysterical action/reaction.

The concept of an induced madness is central to Pynchon's preoccupation with behaviorally determined human personality. His characters are depthless, leading paracinematic existences, and their actions are invariably reactions to suprapersonal, or transpersonal, conditions. In the case of Oedipa Maas, one notes the element of experimentation (an element that suffuses *Gravity's Rainbow*). She is tested by her experiences, her nature is modified through a series of linked incidents which she knows may be either an illusion or her own delusion. So complete is her uncertainty, indeed, that she may be fairly compared with Segismundo in *Life Is a Dream*. Although *The Crying of Lot 49* does not provide an absolute criterion to determine whether the linked incidents are a hoax, a delusion, or a reality (the Trystero *might* exist), there is an overwhelming presumption that they are a hoax, a series of linked illusions carefully constructed by a powerful, intelligent industrialist with all the resources of American industry (including computerization of the "game") available to him. The test, the revelation (or modification) of personality, the openly available judgment (in sum, the necessary requirements of the godgame) are all present.

The formal similarities between diverse godgames, from distinct national literatures written at different times, indicate that the godgame is a genuine literary category available to writers and open to scholarly investigation. It is no more accidental within the history of literature than, say, the interior monologue or the epistolary novel. It can be isolated, abstracted, and defined in the same way that an episode, a soliloquy, or a literary dream can be; conversely, its function within a total work can be identified, its integrative importance explained. Furthermore, the godgame is related to other uses of illusion and perspectivism in literature though it is not identical with them.

The godgame recurs throughout Western literature from the Renaissance through the modern period to the present. It is possible to speak of godgames and narrative with distinct godgamelike elements even before the Renaissance: ancient mythology, and the literature based on it, might be said to contain the godgame as its kernel structure (exemplified by the story of Semele) and medieval literature suggests a number of romances in which godgames are important, even, as in the instance of *Sir Gawain and the Green Knight*, dominant.[48] Two historical periods stand out for the frequent use of complex and innovative godgames: the baroque and the modern era since World War I. There are significant differences in the modern versions of the godgame (such as the withdrawal of the god, or gamewright, into the game and the intense concentration on the character-player's introspection), but there are sufficient formal similarities to allow one to speak of the godgame as a common literary phenomenon. It is remarkably, even stunningly, transhistorical.

Behind every godgame, there lies a situation that recalls, with full power to evoke the appropriate feelings, the common human intuition of being made a victim, a scapegoat, or a sacrifice and of being made puny or deluded by someone superior, a *they* set over and against oneself. The unsettling potency of Pynchon's fiction stems in part from his successful linking of the character-player's predicament (being a victim caught in the intricate crystal of a godgame) to induced psychosis. Inevitably, one must suspect that this happens commonly enough: almost anyone can partially sense the "cold and sweatless meathooks of a psychosis" (98) that Oedipa Maas feels. Looked at in this way, the godgame seems to stretch back toward those ancient, archetypal notions concerning the race's origins and purpose. The gods' power over their subjects must seem, as Heraclitus remarks, to be play in which hidden rules organize the range of possible moves between opening and end, between creation and destruction. Cool, distant, its tone normally matter-of-fact, the narrative voice in *Gravity's Rainbow* observes, "But every true god must be both organizer and destroyer" (99).

Yet the godgame is also a literary structure that possesses a marked role in postmodern literature. It is both a transhistorical concept and a specifically postmodern concept. It underscores the instability of the category of postmodern (which must claim its uniqueness even while constituting itself according to the familiar conventions of aesthetic construction) and suggests an image for the tenuous, if inevitable, role of all classifications within human thinking. Purely within the discourse of postmodernism, the godgame displays an immense forcefulness. As a game situation manifesting the normal ludic, self-contained, and arbitrary properties of games, it serves to foreground the game/text analogy. Embedded within the text, the godgame poses the puzzles and paradoxes about the nature of reality and about the status of the text itself that preoccupy postmodern writers. It also embodies the strange relationship that McHale analyzes between a text and its readership. The reader, always already, is entrapped by the text he approaches, but the godgame highlights this entrapment, creates an embedded model of its processes, and makes strangeness itself the mode of the reading experience.[49]

The fascination with games characterizes postmodern literature and it may also, as Allen Thiher argues, correspond to an underlying distrust of language itself since, as he writes, "the very notion of system derives much of its plausibility from the way it is characterized as a game construct with ludic autonomy and rule-bound enclosure." A game structure constitutes an emblem (an embedded model, a recursive *mise-en-abyme* of the idea of a text) both of the literary text and of its hold upon, entrapping within its strangeness, its readers. In postmodern narrative, the godgame calls attention to the overall gamefulness of the text. To read, to write, Thiher argues, "is to play a kind of hopscotch, to leap from writing to writing in the never-ending play of codes that refer to codes."[50] In a stronger game metaphor than Thiher chooses in comparing reading to hopscotch (though thereby capturing resonances from Cortázar's novel), the text is a labyrinth in which the reader becomes entrapped. The way out entails the attempt to understand, drawing inferences, building hypotheses, testing possible accounts like pathways, often with no better thread to follow than one already used elsewhere (having mapped some *other* labyrinth), some bare interpretive model. Every godgame is a kind of labyrinth, for the reader as well as for the character-player, though not every labyrinth is, as shall be seen, a godgame.

III

> The solution to any problem is always relative to its formulation and . . . no problem can be completely formulated.
>
> —Elder Olson, "On Value Judgments in the Arts"

One summer in the late 1970s, a Canadian scholar set off to do research in a California library. For her reading on the flight, she chose John Fowles's novel *The Magus*. She had seen the wretched film that had been made from the novel and thinking (like a good narratologist) that behind the film narrative there might be an interesting story, she had determined to read the novel sometime when nothing else imposed itself. She had had no purpose in choosing *The Magus* for her in-flight reading other than her sense, based on having seen the film, that it might well be entertaining and suspensful. Yet in a curious way it belonged to a train of thought she had been following for several months before leaving for California. She had been pondering the difficulties of evoking mental activity in literature. More specifically, she had been analyzing the representation of thought in narrative and *The Magus* (to her surprise) belonged to this analysis and, at length, modified it significantly. Somewhere over the state of Washington, it struck her that Fowles's concept of the godgame was both intrinsically interesting and pertinent to her concerns.

The godgame (which the film version had not captured well and the complexity of which it had nearly submerged) suggested a narrative experience in which a victim thinks her way out of, or through, an ensnarement. Later, she realized that the godgame was every bit as much a dramatic as a narrative situation, but initially she took it to be quintessentially narrative. In *The Magus*, Nicholas Urfe, entrapped within a succession of illusions that have been created for the purpose of his ensnarement, finds it impossible to understand what is taking place around him. It is impossible for him to grasp his true situation; nonetheless, at all points he thinks, builds hypotheses, and never gives up his efforts to achieve cognitive mastery over his situation. When Fowles calls this predicament a "godgame" he seems to mean a gamelike situation in which one character knows the rules, because she has made them, while another character, the player, does not. It is much as if one were to put dice on a table and then leave the room making it "seem possible to the players that you were never in the room."[51] Thus, seen from inside the victim's consciousness, the experience of playing a godgame is a process of playing a blind game, of discovering hidden rules. For that reason, the godgame is massively cognitive, always an experiment in thinking, always a representation of thought.

By the time the scholar left the plane in San Francisco, she had begun to see the concept of a godgame in an extended context. From that moment the problem that she had been reflecting upon previously underwent a distinct change. She was no longer interested solely in how thought is evoked or represented in narrative. That problem had served to prod her toward the recognition of other problems of very different shapes: what kind of experience is a godgame? what kind of literary experience is it? What was interesting was not thought in general but specific situations in which thought occurs; not thinking generally, but determinate acts of thinking. What kind of thinking will be involved in a godgame and how will *it* be represented? The godgame, at least as Fowles employs it, seemed to provide a lucid instance of thinking at a very high level since the victim must think constantly and continually modify her thinking. This was the scholar's first reformulation of her thinking, moving from the general to the (comparatively) specific. She would encounter the necessity for subsequent reformulations as her research developed.

If, as it seemed to her, the godgame depended on a godlike character's creation of impenetrable illusions, then the analysis of the situation hinged on a logically prior understanding of the term *illusion*. That problem, however, in Wittgenstein's phrase, would be easier to bury than to solve. What constitutes an illusion within literature must be an important, even preludial, issue to almost any literary analysis, but the demands of a method intended to explore and make clear *illusion* present a labyrinth of choices, perplexities, and methodological paradoxes. The term itself derives from *illudere*, to play with or at, to make sport of, or to jest (the *Grande Larousse,* she noted, elegantly defines it as *se jouer de*), an ancestry that inescapably links illusion to concepts of play and game. Its oldest uses in English are associated with ideas of mockery and derision (the *OED* cites Wyclif in 1382 in this sense) and deception (1340 and Chaucer, in 1386, in "The Canon Yeoman's Tale"). It is, she concluded, a curiously elusive term. It might be said that it exemplifies itself.[52]

She read J. L. Austin's *Sense and Sensibilia* in which Austin examines the question of illusion at some length in an effort to exorcise the (demonic) concept of "sense data" from philosophic discourse.[53] Austin's analysis indicates a great number of traps that open upon the use of the term *illusion.* He is particularly pointed in distinguishing between *illusion* and *delusion.* No doubt, she thought, some such distinction must be kept, but its relevance to the analysis of literary texts seemed questionable and perhaps impossible to make stick. It struck her as unfruitful to insist, as Austin does, that "delusion" is primarily "a matter of grossly disordered beliefs" (29) and then to leave it at that. Thus she decided to use *delusion* to describe a state of mind (or awareness) and *illusion* to describe a state of things, the web of incidents itself. That, she reflected, is how one ordinarily uses the terms. It seemed closer to the experience of the terms' uses in literature than Austin's exiguous, if rigorous, distinction. She decided that throughout her analysis of the godgame she would use *illusion* to signify the constructed network of incidents through which, and by which, the victim is deluded. Of course, it is possible, she reasoned, to imagine victims who are deluded without a corresponding pattern of illusion: in Pynchon's *The Crying of Lot 49,* for example, one may suppose that the heroine is deluded without there being any illusion at all, but it is also possible to imagine either that she is deluded in a carefully fashioned fabric of illusions or that she is not deluded at all. She tried, at this early stage of her investigation, to make the distinction clear by a reference to *Don Quijote*: the Knight is often deluded (but whether this is an instance of "grossly disordered beliefs" is another matter) but not often subjected to illusions (the windmills, for instance, are not illusory giants); however, in Part II the Knight and Squire come within the power of the Duke and Duchess who *do* create illusions which *do* delude both characters. By beginning her investigations on the basis of a stipulative definition of *illusion,* however congenial to common sense, the scholar's initial methodological choice had been to bury, not to solve, the problem of illusion.

She had begun her analysis of the godgame by focusing on the "god" not the victim, the character-player. The godlike character who makes the hidden rules seemed to be a typical baroque figure (rather like Iago, Satan, or Don Juan), who, if tracked far enough, might reveal himself to be one of the important modes of heroic characterization within the period. She had begun her investigation by turning toward a speciously attractive, but extraneous, consideration. The allure of greater significance (ultimately, to provide a solution to a problem of maximum importance: to define a literary period and to make a contribution to literary history) had obscured the immediate problem of "seeing clearly" the actual configuration of the evidence. In several conversations during the first two weeks after she had arrived in California (one of which took place among Renaissance scholars in a café near the Ashland, Oregon, Shakespeare Festival), she held forth as an expert on her newly discovered topos. She was acting like a literary scholar with the scent up. She had no doubt that she had a fruitful problem under analysis, yet on her return to San Francisco from Ashland, something happened that forced her to reformulate the problem entirely.

She had been staying in a student residence on the Mills College campus in Oakland. It was summer and the residence was nearly deserted so she had become accustomed to silence, emptiness, and scholarly seclusion. Her habit was to wake up early, work until noon, go back to the residence for her swim suit, and then swim through the lunch hour until it was time to return to work. About a week after she had returned from the Shakespeare Festival, she observed an unusual number of cars parked in the half-moon driveway of the residence. As she walked closer, she was struck by the varieties of cars parked there: Lincolns, Cadillacs, and (she recalled specifically) a mauve Mercedes. There were also several Oakland police cars. In front of the main door, there was a swirling knot of excited people, including a number of policemen, all jabbering, shouting, and gesticulating, and all evidently tense with the awareness of hidden drama.

Only slightly intimidated, she walked through the entrance, edging her way past a crowd of superfly types in garish clothing and bizarre accoutrements. When she finally reached the inside hall, she could see that the attention of the crowd was directed toward the room directly opposite the doorway. There a gorgeously beautiful black woman, dressed in a scarlet pantsuit with a black flower pinned to the lapel of the jacket, was defending the door to the room against a young black man and two white policemen. She had never seen the black woman, nor any of them, but the woman was making it obvious that it was her room, that she lived there, and that the young man had no right to enter. She was afraid that he might kill her, she yelled repeatedly at the policemen. The young man, who was also screaming, kept insisting that he had a right to enter because he lived there too. There were innumerable threats of violence, imprecations, Jacobean curses, and loud appeals to justice, all uttered dementedly at the top of the voice. Through all this, the young black woman stood firm—the man could not come in. The bloodcurdling, demented tone of the curses astounded the scholar. She was also distressed that the policemen appeared to be taking the side of the man. The crowd of gawking, also yelling bystanders, and all the other policemen who were standing in the main doorway, added their own comments to the overwhelming cacophony. Worried, dumbfounded, and thoroughly rattled, the scholar grabbed her swim suit and departed through a back door. Later on she told a friend who taught at Mills College about the scene she had witnessed and she, too, was nonplussed. It was apparent, she said, that the hard drug scene in Oakland had crashed suddenly down upon Mills. That evening when she returned to the residence, all the frenetic figures of the forenoon had vanished, like spirits melted into thin air. The normal quiet reigned and the beautiful black woman was nowhere to be seen.

The next day, however, a similar scene took place just before noon. The cars were different (although the mauve Mercedes was there) and there seemed to be fewer policemen this time. The beautiful black woman was once again defending her door against the young man. Once more, curses and Jacobean threats filled the air. This time, however, the young man did not, it seemed, wish to enter the room (he no longer asserted that he lived there) but only to retrieve some expensive clothing he had left in the closet. He claimed that the woman had changed the lock on the door so that he could not get in (a fact the scholar, knowing that she lived in a student residence, found utterly baffling) and he was afraid that she would, or already had, sold his suits. This time the police seemed to be on the woman's side in keeping him out. Once more, the scholar was wholly astounded and just as afraid of the obvious potential for violence as she had been the day before, but this time she went into the building's lounge, which occupied one leg of a horseshoe structure overlooking the curved entrance driveway, so that she could study the scene from a side window. Inside the lounge, to her further consternation, she encountered a policeman sitting at a radio transmitter listening to incoming messages. From a chair across the room, she watched both him at the radio and the crowd outside. She had an overpowering feeling of having been cut off from reality, of not being able to understand anything in the complex situation surrounding her. After a few minutes, she overheard a message on the radio: a distant, static-masked voice was asking for confirmation of a report that a 1946 Plymouth had been stolen. She knew then, in an abrupt rush of intuition, that *something* had to be wrong with the supposed reality of what she had been witnessing. No one in California, in the mid–1970s, would steal a 1946 Plymouth, but if someone did, the police would not bother to look for it. She walked over to the policeman at the radio and asked him (an act which, until that moment, had not occurred to her) what was *really* taking place. It was, he informed her, a "domestic-intervention exercise" of the Oakland Police Academy, and he was a professor of police tactics (the stolen Plymouth had also been an exercise, of course). The superflies, the yelling gawkers, and the two young people had all been volunteer actors from the Oakland community.[54]

There were several lessons to be drawn from this firsthand immersion within a godgame, but she did not draw them all immediately. She did see, with great clarity, how impenetrable a godgame must be from the standpoint of the deluded victim. One needs an outside point of reference in order to crack a systematic illusion, and this vantage may be excluded by the rules of the godgame. Thc problem of the godgame, it then seemed, was evidently not the role of the god but the operation of the game itself. The gods in baroque godgames, such as Prospero, the Duke and Duchess in *Don Quijote*, or Basilio in *Life is a Dream*, have nothing in common, no single trait gathers them together, and they have no shared purpose beyond watching their victims' reactions. Once she had been confronted with an authentic godgame situation, it seemed clear that nothing could be gained by focusing on the role of the god, the maker of the hidden rules. Furthermore, it now seemed that the thinking of the victims must be peripheral to the analysis: for whether or not they thought about their entrapment, the illusion of the godgame would nonetheless surround them. The central problem now appeared to be to analyze the structure of a specific type of illusion. Her necessary reformulation of the problem, forced upon her by personal experience and not by the exigencies of analysis, committed two errors, one formal and one material. In the first place, she had now decided to attempt to analyze the structure of a phenomenon that she had already decided that she need not, or perhaps could not, define. It did not occur to her that her prior decision to assume a simple operational definition of *illusion* would make analysis of the specific phenomena constellated by the concept both arbitrary and unconvincing. In the second place, she had again leaped to a problem of large significance (structure) and, in so doing, she had precipitously overlooked certain rather obvious qualities of the evidence.

No *significant* problem can be completely formulated: trivial problems accept their forms with alacrity. (Although a solution must be relevant to the formulation of a problem in some sense, the relation need not be balanced, proportional, or exact. Indeed, it may come about less through deliberate strategy than through chance, luck, or inadvertence.) The spoor of the godgame was diffuse. It had seemed to raise a problem of historical periodization and then one of archetypal figuration. If it was a characteristic problem of the baroque period, then it was also a problem of the kind of central character that (for whatever reasons of cultural determination or confluence) the baroque period held dear, esteemed, and developed commonly in its literature. If it became a problem of structure in which the common features of all godgames could be analyzed, and perhaps placed in relation to each other within an interpretive model, then it was a question both of method and of corpus. How should the godgame be analyzed and what would constitute the appropriate body for such an analysis? Eventually, the Canadian scholar lost her historical blindness, her unexamined obsession with period, and came to understand that the godgame appeared in the literature of every literary period, though it might well seem more central to the concerns of one period than to another. The playing itself could not be successfully analyzed (except, it might be, as a recurring myth or a transhistorical archetype) since the evidence was too diffuse, the diversity of play too enormous.

She began to see, reflecting on godgames in modern literature, that the most adequate formulation of the problem would pose the godgame as a problem in narrative purpose: What are godgames good for? What do they accomplish? or What function do they fulfill? No model of the godgame could be complete unless it included the function of the character-player's mental state, the effect of the illusions on its narrative capacity for inference, hypothesis, and conclusion, and its potential to develop under these illusory exigencies. The godgame, she concluded ultimately, had more to do with the questions of characterization than with myth, archetypal resonances, or narrative structure (though these could not be altogether excluded from consideration), and no useful account could be given that did not proceed from a grasp of the theory of character. Perhaps she had been more completely bamboozled by the godgame into which she had stepped in Oakland than she had initially been aware. She had missed the genuine lesson embodied in that experience: not that the illusion is impenetrable but that the victim is limited and epistemologically befuddled. After all, she had been caught up in the web of illusion only through her own gullibility. Anyone familiar with police training techniques would have seen through it—as would anyone sufficiently quick on her toes to remark that the reality it seemed to present was flatly self-contradictory, with two versions, or scenarios, on successive days. She had simply been too innocent to penetrate the illusion. Like Don Quijote, she had been prompted by her reading to think in certain ways, but she had not been made more discerning.

Her final reformulation of the problem, however, seemed sharply in focus. Neither the godlike maker of hidden rules nor the game itself is strictly necessary to the godgame. What counts in the godgame, she concluded, is the victim, the character-player. For it, though not for it alone (since there are readers who play through the godgame on a secondary level), the narrator perplexes the narrative line into labyrinths. Linda Hutcheon captures the essence of the godgame in a single proposition when, referring to Fowles's *French Lieutenant's Woman*, she writes that the meaning of both power and the godgame is freedom: "The novelist is a creating god-figure, but freedom, not authority, dominates his image."[55] It had been a question of characterization all along, though not one that could be put in such absurdly simplistic terms as the baroque hero, that elusive ideal who, somewhat in the manner of the trickster, creates illusions for spite, gain, or the fun of it. It had been a problem concerning the author's choice of narrative strategies in dealing with her characters. Illusion can be heuristic. One need only recall how much Cervantes gains with regard to the characterization of his Knight by the entrapping illusions of chapter 3 of the First Part (long before the Second Part and the extended godgame of the Knight's sojourn in the Duke's palace) to grasp just how revelatory, how heuristic, an illusion can be.

IV

> All sorts of problems attach to the words "to know" and "to be clear."
>
> —Ludwig Wittgenstein, *Philosophical Investigations*

> Any truly comprehensive game theory would therefore have to include a thorough understanding of the human psyche.
>
> —Manfred Eigen and Ruthild Winkler, *The Laws of the Game: How the Principles of Nature Govern Chance*

All godgames are cognitive labyrinths, but not every labyrinth is a godgame. The godgame is a more intensive category than the literary labyrinth because it must include the notion of the character-player's awareness and is included within it as a species within a genus. Though conceptually less distinctive than the godgame, the labyrinth has been more visible, more eye-catching, in the history of literature. If the godgame has been a neglected, unformulated topos, the labyrinth stands out, a dominant rhetorical figure, as both a descriptive and a metaphoric commonplace. The labyrinth can constitute the underforming structure of a godgame: the successive decisions of the entrapped character may seem to follow a labyrinthine pattern of illusion, choice, and impasse. Thus the labyrinth, whether or not a particular instance is a godgame, suggests an evocative symbol, always a pattern of twisting (maze or meander), for the cognitive bafflement, the bewilderment, of the character-player wandering within a godgame and for its frustratingly hidden rules. The movement out of a godgame is a movement toward the hidden rules: it entails rational steps, testing, evaluating, constructing hypotheses, rebuilding them after they have crumbled, and always choice, decision, and the exclusion of one alternative in favor of another. The character-player struggles to reconstruct the world in which he is trapped from the exiguous (and normally contradictory) evidence available. The movement toward the hidden rules transcribes a movement toward hidden worldhood. Since the labyrinth, the genus that includes the godgame, can provide both the underforming structure and an evocative symbol, it seems evident that the range of interaction between labyrinths and godgames is complex.

Experience can be abstracted into increasingly broader and more empty forms. The fictional world within which a character is immersed can be transcribed into an abstract pattern or (if one is optimistic about these activities), by its restructuring, into homologous, but more rarefied, orders. The abstract pattern of an experience functions as an interpretive model (a commentary, a gloss, a conceptual map), and any interpretive model, even if it is discovered outside the text entirely, in the realm of ideology (or tradition), say, is a necessarily abstract pattern. Within a narrative, certain images can have the interpretive function of an abstract model; that is, they may point directly toward a precise pattern into which the narrative matrix itself might be transcoded. Embedded in the text, such images are coded directions toward a determinate range of interpretation. Early in *The Crying of Lot 49*, Oedipa sees San Narciso, where Inverarity's multiple industrial enterprises are located, laid out before her like a printed circuit. The intricacies of a printed circuit (the nodes, wires, and interchanges swelling up from a flat surface) can stand for the analogous intricacies of an interlocking conglomerate such as the dead industrialist's, but also for society which may seem to be essentially an intricate network of concepts. The initial image of the printed circuit predicts a great deal that is important to the narrative content of the novel. The solidly spatial image emblematizes the labyrinthine pattern that underforms Pynchon's narrative. Oedipa's experience within the fictional world constituted by *The Crying of Lot*

49 is, precisely, that of having been "trapped at the center of some intricate crystal" (67): a conscious bit of information within its circuit, or a pawn caught uncomprehendingly in the crystalline infoldings of a middle game, might feel much the same. The pressure of cognitive bafflement and of being trapped is so intense that even the fillings in Oedipa's teeth begin to hurt.

In *Don Quijote,* one of the great baroque exemplars of the godgame, there is a labyrinthine image embedded within the narrative that interprets (by recoding into spatial terms) the pattern underforming the godgame in the Second Part (chapters 30 through 57). In the ducal godgame the Knight and the Squire are subjected to a series of illusions that have been designed for them alone, cast into the terms of their private fantasies (since these, now public, have been read in the published First Part of the novel), and which are played upon them to make them play. The ensnaring illusions are difficult to penetrate, provoke bewilderment, and contain contradictory evidence. The character-players, Don Quijote and Sancho, do not examine the counterevidence because they are comic noninterpreters, players who are played without playing back, but it is clearly there for the reader to perceive. Carefully examined, the illusory incidents would indicate the presence of the gamewright himself, the cunning Duke, just as the incidents in Pynchon's novel lead back, though not perhaps inescapably, to Inverarity's conspiratorial designs. Though *Don Quijote* is a comic godgame, while *The Crying of Lot 49* is, despite comic enhancements, horrific, both narratives build upon analogous situations, mazelike in their fusion of perplexity and reason, in which cleverly constructed illusions hide the rules by which they could be interpreted.

Cervantes closes the godgame in the Second Part with an image that functions similarly to the printed circuit in *The Crying of Lot 49*. As Sancho returns, weary and defeated, from his eight days as governor of the Duke's "island," he falls into a deep pit that lies amid the ruins of a number of buildings. Both the Squire and his donkey tumble to the bottom. They survive the fall and eventually Sancho finds a small hole in the otherwise smooth wall of the pit which he enlarges and through which the man and his beast pass into a long cavern. "Sometimes he went in the dark and sometimes without much light," Cervantes writes, "but never without fear." Sancho himself thinks of the cavern, through which he travels for nearly a mile and a half, as "depths and dungeons."[56] When the Knight hears his Squire call for help, he immediately assumes that Sancho is calling from Purgatory. The episode is typically Cervantine: it embraces two kinds of misapprehension, the Squire's failure to see the entrance to the pit and the Knight's incorrect interpretation of the voice coming from the ground. In a narrative devoted to illusion and error, and to all manner of epistemological incertitude, a confusing pit and cavern system are evocative images.[57] Like the printed circuit in Pynchon's novel, the cavern is a maze, a spatial labyrinth embedded in the narrative, that embodies cognitive perplexities.

What account can be given of textual labyrinths? Do they possess distinctive structures? How would a labyrinth function if it were not a godgame? Could there be a general game of labyrinths that is different from (having, say, a distinct rule structure) the godgame? Could a textual labyrinth be a game (in any sense) without the entrapped character-player playing within it? The initial step toward an answer to these questions is to make a distinction: textual labyrinths fall into two separate, and remarkably distinct, categories. First, there are those labyrinths that create the illusion of physical appearance and suggest, at least in broad lines, the commonly recognized attributes of historical labyrinths, particularly the Daedalian labyrinth of the Theseus myth. These labyrinths mimic the commonplace and exterior properties of their historical models. There is an excellent instance of this kind of labyrinth in Borges's fiction "Abenjacán el Bojarí, Dead in His Labyrinth."[58] In that tale, there is a huge labyrinth constructed out of crimson brick (but now faded pinkly in time) that stands imposingly above the sea on a Cornish headland. It is circular in design and contains long corridors and a secret inner chamber. It looks like a labyrinth, and it is intended to look like one. It is, like other textual labyrinths in this category, a simulacrum: it is a mimic construction in words of walls, corridors, passageways, and rooms. Yet this kind of labyrinth follows no particular rule of structure (whatever architectural designs may have given structure to their historical models): jerry-built and slapped together out of physical images and historical clichés, they merely represent details of exterior appearances, specific configurations. They may be called mimic, or weak, labyrinths. Second, there are conceptual, or strong, labyrinths. This category comprises a bizarre range: strong labyrinths have no shape at all, or at least no necessary shape. They are purely conceptual mind-mazes, corridors of doubt, passageways of perplexity, forking paths of decision, "depths and dungeons" of bafflement, that underform godgames, giving structure but not receiving it. The printed circuit in *The Crying of Lot 49* and the dungeonlike pit in *Don Quijote* are strong labyrinths and, thus, powerful images for the godgames they abstract: they stand for turns, twists, meanders, and ambiguities that are wholly conceptual. Strong labyrinths are constructed out of alternatives, choices, a series of decisions, symmetrically opposed sets of criteria. They mimic nothing outside of the text unless it is the human mind itself.

The underforming principle of a strong, or conceptual, labyrinth may be expressed simply. (Indeed, it is the very spirit of simplicity: an unimposing proposition that formulates the sum of perplexity.) The order of a strong labyrinth is a sequence of alternatives; from the standpoint of the character within, it is a forking path, in which forward movement leads through sequential intersections and branches, of necessary decisions. The labyrinthine order is a series of exclusive disjunctions of the form "Either A or B but not both" or "A or B or N but only one." The movement through such a labyrinth proceeds by decisions progressively taken. Thus a strong labyrinth has no determinate shape; its actual shape, in any given fiction, merely manifests the sequence. The physical labyrinths of history, which weak textual labyrinths mimic, may have been built upon some analogous variant of this underforming principle, of course, though it is impossible to know if physical configurations, shaped in brick or stone, manifest a structure of potential cognitive movement, a sequence of decisions to be taken, or something else.

The Minoan labyrinth that suggested the mythic Daedalean construction (and which may have existed) was symbolized by the *labrys*, a double-headed ax. In any case, the name *labyrinth* appears to stem from the word for this kind of ax. Furthermore, the Daedalean labyrinth was built to contain the biform, double-natured monster, the Minotaur, who was not only a fusion of man and beast, as the son of Pasiphaë and a bull, but also the symbolic fusion of bestial appetite and reason. The term itself inescapably contains the suggestions of doubleness and alternatives. The disjunctive alternatives of the underforming structure of strong labyrinths reflect the metonymic associations of the classical (or archetypal) labyrinth.

Michael Ayrton, who might be supposed to know something about the subject (having both built a famous modern labyrinth and written a novel about Daedalus, *The Maze-Maker*), confidently argues that the labyrinth is merely a "model of the human condition," an attempt to represent spatially the human awareness of complexity. It attempts to reconstruct outside the body the known complexity of the body's inside: "the convolutions of the brain, the forest of the lungs, the long intricacies of the gut, the rivers of the arteries and their tributary veins, the caves and hills, valleys, ridges and furrows that individually we carry about with us."[59] Ayrton's argument involves a genetic fallacy (to suppose that what is chronologically more primitive must be less sophisticated, that man's first awareness of complexity must have been of something physical, not mental), but his definition of the labyrinth as a "model of the human condition" rings boldly, with the resonance of truth. The complexity that a labyrinth manifests is not, as Ayrton thinks, that of the physiological plumbing but rather that of the mind. Extending the minotauric concept of the labyrinth, Gabriel Josipovici remarks that it is "the dwelling place of demonic analogy."[60] The Minotaur, Guy Davenport observes, may be the "heart of the labyrinth": "where understanding fails the result is that we perceive a monster instead of an intelligible reality."[61] The labyrinth is the space of perplexed thought.

Any sequence of exclusive disjunctions, however it is manifested, is genuinely labyrinthine. It may be "demonic," in Josipovici's sense, since, like Pynchon's printed circuit or Cervantes's inexplicable pit and cavern, it deforms ordinary experience, reverses expectation, or even inverts normal thinking. Yet it does not seem necessary that a labyrinth should be demonic in this way (however often it may be): alternatives, decisions, even perplexity are normal enough. A labyrinth, reflects the narrator of Borges's fiction, "The Immortal," while experiencing the "intellectual horror" of trying to solve one, is "a house built to confound men; its architecture, prodigious in symmetries, is subordinated to that end."[62] It is made to confound men: thus Borges (*labyrinthorum magister artifexque*) has been able to conceive labyrinths in the form of books, libraries, lotteries, gardens, deserts, cities, polygons, the Tetragammaton, and even straight lines. Time is a labyrinth, infinitely ramiform, that space mirrors. All Borges's writing, it has been said, "is a multiplication of labyrinths."[63] What they share is the pattern of a character moving through a series of alternatives, presented as disjunctions, to a destination (which may be, of course, unforeseen, even undesired). That destination, corresponding to the central chamber in the Daedalian labyrinth, need not be reached. Mind-mazes and labyrinths, the underforming structures of godgames, are necessarily vehicles of cognitive bafflement, frustration, and anxiety. The victim in a strong labyrinth is more likely to end as Oedipa Maass, driven to the edge of psychosis, or as Semele, utterly destroyed, than as Theseus. Ariadne (standing exterior to the labyrinth), with her instructive thread, illustrates the infrequent exception.

The essential difference, then, between a strong and a weak labyrinth is simply that the underforming principle of the former can be identified while that of the latter cannot be. There may not even be one since the weak, or mimic, labyrinth requires only a certain slapdash and tinkertoying of images to succeed. The weak labyrinth is, like similar motifs in pictorial art, decorative and external; the strong labyrinth possesses a determinate order, is massively functional, even overdetermined in its textual significance, and is necessarily perceived from the inside. Having no necessary physical appearance, the strong labyrinth may be surprisingly simple even, as the narrator of "The Immortal" observes (describing a dream-labyrinth), "exiguous and nitid."[64] The reciprocity between godgames and strong labyrinths should be evident. The strong labyrinth must be experienced as a godgame.

The distinction between a strong and a weak labyrinth can be illustrated by an examination of two contemporary makers of textual labyrinths. The first, Alain Robbe-Grillet, has created a highly sophisticated instance of a weak labyrinth in his novel *In the Labyrinth*.[65] The second, Borges, is a builder of strong labyrinths and also gives them their clearest theoretical statement (scattered like bits of cut thread) throughout his writings. Borges has made both kinds of labyrinths and given them multiplex shapes. One of his fictions, "Abenjacán el Bojarí," has already been cited as an example of a weak labyrinth.

In his brief preface to *In the Labyrinth*, Robbe-Grillet insists that the reality of the novel is "strictly material" and that the reader should see only "the things, gestures, words, events" which are given to him without seeking further significance. This injunction upon the reader obliquely predicts the formal qualities of the narrative that unfolds. The labyrinth of the narrative is an unnamed European city, seen both as a network of exterior streets and squares and, in rigorous parallelism, of interior corridors and rooms. The victim is an unnamed soldier (bearing a number that is not his) who is attempting to deliver a box containing, the reader eventually learns, some personal belongings of another soldier who has died in battle. The narrative is presented in the voice of a doctor, who, evidently, watches the soldier's movements from an upstairs window and who also tries to imagine aspects of the soldier's experience that he has not, and could not have, seen. The doctor's voice is almost wholly submerged in the dispassionate, essentially bleak, focalization upon the unnamed soldier. Thus Bruce Morrissette seems perceptively correct when he writes that *In the Labyrinth* should be read "only as the mental content of an omnipresent narrator within the fictional field, and who is, in a sense, the real protagonist of the novel."[66]

The argument is a difficult one since it claims that the narrator, not the soldier, is the actual victim within the labyrinth. Yet this is consistent with the properties of labyrinths: to be caught between alternatives in giving an account of something (to confront the horns of whatever disjunctive possibilities) is also to act labyrinthinely, perhaps more so than to wander, baffled and lost, along the streets of an unnamed city. Morrissette extends his argument to the position that the narrator alone exists, isolated in his room writing a novel in which the task is to find "relationships capable of linking" the diverse materials of the narrative and for which "movement through the maze becomes the very design and form of the work itself."[67] If one follows the lines of Morrissette's *ludisme* (which is provocative if not forceful), then *In the Labyrinth* may seem ambiguously labyrinthine, strong insofar as the narrator confronts alternatives and must make decisions, but, since these are ramifications of his own thinking which he imposes upon himself and not the constructions of an *artifex* (or gamewright), only partially, or incompletely, so. If one rejects Morrissette, accepting the immediate indications of the narrative, then the conclusion seems clear that *In the Labyrinth,* in being "strictly material," is paradigmatically weak.

The narrator's account of the soldier's wanderings and death is entirely objective and incorporates, as commonly occurs in Robbe-Grillet's fiction, alternative or hypothetical versions. (The convention of "objective hypotheses," in which several versions of the same incidents are given without internal clues as to which should be accepted as correct, is perhaps best studied in Robbe-Grillet's and Alain Resnais's collaborative effort in the film *Last Year at Marienbad.*) The characterization of the soldier (the primary, or first-order victim, in any reading of the novel other than Morrissette's) is also entirely objective, existing fragmentarily in the narrator's focalizing. He is presented, to borrow another of Morrissette's observations, only "in situation . . . according to what he *is* and *does* at a given moment without framing his actions and psychological states with commentary on his thoughts or emotions, or with psychological analysis or explanation."[68] The situation that defines the soldier is, as Robbe-Grillet insists, both material and without "any allegorical value." It is obviously, though superficially, labyrinthine. The soldier wanders along streets that resemble each other, hunting for a street corner the name of which he cannot remember. It is snowing, at least some of the time, and the soldier feels weary, hungry, and cold. Even the snow is described in the physical terms of a labyrinth:

> The white dots, close and rapid, suddenly change direction; tracing vertical marks for a few moments, they soon pursue a direction close to the horizontal. Then they suddenly become immobile and begin, in an abrupt gust of wind, to hurry in an inverse direction, following the angle of a slight slope but headed toward the opposite side, so that at the end of two or three seconds, without more transition, they abandon their course in order to resume their initial orientation, tracing once again from left to right a zone of light against the windows without light.[69]

This grid pattern repeats itself throughout the narrative, as playfully recapitulative as a mirror image in a funhouse. A fly wanders fruitlessly in an attempt to escape from a lamp in which it is trapped, its shadow cast upward on the ceiling, paralleling the movements of the soldier on the streets. Images of biform duality persistently punctuate the novel, like regularly recurrent cards, or throws. One of the most important of these images is that dagger or bayonet (an image that necessarily recalls the *labrys* of Minoan legend) that begins the narrative and eventually is discovered in the box the soldier carries. Every narrative detail in the novel is obscure, unexplained (given no "commentary . . . psychological analysis or explanation"), parallel, recapitulative, and "strictly material." Surely, one must admit that, as the title promises, this does add up to be a labyrinth.

It does add up to a mimic, or weak, labyrinth. Robbe-Grillet's novel is unmistakably a simulacrum of a physical labyrinth. Yet it does not evidently manifest an underforming sequence of alternatives: no necessary chain of decisions, no constitutive rule (in Suits's sense), distinguishes Robbe-Grillet's labyrinth. The very "materiality" and objectivity that Robbe-Grillet emphasizes make a strong labyrinth impossible. The victim, defined wholly by his objective situation, cannot be said to make decisions or to feel cognitive anguish. He merely acts and reacts, wandering labyrinthinely, perhaps, but not decisively. The narrator does make certain decisions (one knows this because he occasionally comments "no" after describing one of the soldier's possible moves), but these are neither pervasive in the narrative nor disjunctive. When Morrissette calls the narrator the "real protagonist" of the novel, he points to an exciting, though elusive, renarration of the literal surface. The narrator, containing and attempting to shape the soldier's experience, becomes the labyrinth's second-order victim. Nonetheless, since the narrative does not depend on the narrator's negative decisions (those dead ends, impasses, twigless branches in the ramiform construction that make a strong labyrinth) but rather seems to incorporate the rejected accounts as further aspects of the whole, it is not possible to find the constitutive rule, the series of necessary decisions, of a strong labyrinth in the narrator's labyrinthine narrativity. Even at the level of the second-order victim, *In the Labyrinth* remains a weak labyrinth. To see how a strong textual labyrinth is made, one needs to turn to Borges.

Borges's fiction "Abenjacán el Bojarí, Dead in His Labyrinth," is exemplary. The primary labyrinth in the narrative (the one that is foregrounded) is obviously weak, built out of brick, circular in design, located spectacularly on a headland, containing a single circular chamber that can be reached only through miles of corridors; its resemblance to legendary labyrinths cannot be overlooked. In Borgesian fashion, the narrative contains labyrinths on other levels, and all of these are irreducibly strong. Each of them manifests the constitutive rule of strong labyrinths: there must be an underforming string of exclusive disjunctions which a character confronts sequentially. In "Abenjacán el Bojarí," Borges presents two conversations between two young Englishmen, Dunraven and Unwin, the former an unpublished poet, the latter a scarcely published mathematician. Dunraven explains that a large pink labyrinth (that had once been crimson) on the coast of Cornwall had been built more than twenty-five years previously, when he was a small boy, by the deposed leader of some unknown Nilotic tribe who had hoped to escape assassination. Abenjacán el Bojarí built the labyrinth, Dunraven explains, to escape the ghost of his former vizier and cousin, Zaid, a notorious coward whom he had killed but who now seeks revenge as well as the large treasure the sheik has carried away with him. Abenjacán el Bojarí hides in the labyrinth's central chamber until the day, a few years after its construction was completed, when Zaid's ghost arrives in a ship that appears to have been built by a cabinetmaker, so minutely fine are its parts. Zaid kills Abenjacán el Bojarí, his slave, and his pet lion, and all three are found dead in the labyrinth, their faces smashed. Up to this point, Borges's narrative presents a classic instance of a weak labyrinth employed for those purposes that such simulacra do well: hiding, wandering, a touch of mystery.

The foregrounded labyrinth (pinkly crimson on its Cornish headland) abruptly decomposes. In telling the tale, Dunraven notes that the good Cornish folk were scandalized by the idea of a foreigner building such a bizarre structure as a labyrinth on their soil and that the local rector had preached a sermon against labyrinths in which he told the tale of an Eastern king who was punished for having constructed one. Dunraven does not indicate the content of this old tale, but Borges recounts it himself in another place. It is very short but highly instructive. The king of the Arabs, having been baffled and humiliated in a labyrinth constructed by the king of Babylon, returns home, gathers an army, wages war against Babylon, conquers the king, and brings him back to Arabia. He then takes the king far out into the desert, where he frees him, saying only, "In Babylon you wished me to lose myself in a labyrinth of bronze with many stairs, doors and walls; now the Almighty has seen fit that I should show you mine, where there are no stairways to climb, nor doors to force open, nor tiring galleries to pass through nor walls to block the way."[70] The conquered king is then left in the labyrinth of the desert to die of thirst and hunger.

The strong labyrinth, infolded within the heart of Dunraven's narrative about the weak one, makes plain the distinction between the two categories and precisely indicates the constitutive rule of all strong labyrinths: each step that the king of Babylon must take embodies a decision between alternative steps (the way home being possible, but infinitely difficult, to find), between directions that are exclusive and disjunctive. Moreover, "Abenjacán el Bojarí" contains further instances of labyrinthine construction. Dunraven's narrative seems unconvincing (not merely because it hinges upon a ghost), and Unwin emphatically calls it a lie. The second conversation between the two young men occurs some time later in a London pub, when Unwin, having reinterpreted the details, renarrates Dunraven's original narrative. No one, he observes, builds a labyrinth in which to hide: labyrinths are traps. And, assuredly, no one would build a crimson labyrinth high on an ocean headland to hide in. Thus the builder, he argues, must have been, not Abenjacán el Bojarí but Zaid, the wretched vizier. He built the labyrinth of crimson brick to attract attention, expecting word to reach the sheik, and thus lured Abenjacán el Bojarí into the labyrinth, where he killed him. The crushed faces of the slave and lion were included, the young mathematician notes, only to provide the first two terms of a series that would be completed by the crushed face of the sheik. His objective, Unwin argues, was not to keep safely the wealth he had stolen from the sheik, since most of that would have been spent in constructing the labyrinth, nor merely to free himself of an ever-present threat of death, but to assume the identity of the dead sheik.

Labyrinthinely, the cowardly vizier discovered a way, in robbing another man of his identity, to become brave. This second narrative should appeal to everyone more than Dunraven's original narrative (indeed, it appeals to Dunraven more), but the important point is that Unwin's renarration transforms the weak labyrinth into a strong one. The labyrinth becomes a trap; its builder is also a gamewright; Abenjacán el Bojarí, a player within the labyrinth playing out a series of decisions. Further, the process of renarration (details, aspects of characterization, a plot) is, or can be, a kind of labyrinth, a series of steps taken between alternatives. Hence the weak labyrinth that Borges's narration foregrounds undergoes a metamorphosis, through being contained within Unwin's renarration, into a strong, conceptual labyrinth.

Labyrinthorum magister artifexque always, Borges gives an epigraph to his fiction, ascribed to the Koran, that states, "They [indeterminate] are comparable to the spider, which builds a house." This suggests the possibility of further labyrinths, weak and strong, implicit within, or enveloping, the narrative. The web, after all, must seem an obviously weak labyrinth from the outside, feeble and decorative at best, yet from the inside, perceived with fly's-eye bewilderment, it would have to be strong. Graphically, within Abenjacán el Bojarí's weak labyrinth (that is, the version of events attributed to him within Dunraven's primary, but weak, narrative labyrinth), there is a double image that recapitulates the epigraph: the sheik, having fled an uprising with Zaid, takes refuge in the tomb of a saint, sleeps, dreams that he is imprisoned in "a nest of serpents," and awakens to discover that the snakes' nest had been prompted by an actual spiderweb brushing his face. The weak labyrinth, in other words, has generated the strong dream labyrinth. Like the printed circuit in *The Crying of Lot 49* or the pit and cavern in the Second Part of *Don Quijote*, the web is an image, abstractable from the narrative, that transcodes the structure of the textual labyrinth in spatial terms. In Dr. Johnson's superbly spatial image, it serves to "perplex the labyrinth of uncertainty."[71] (To *perplex*, deriving from *plectere*, with its associations of interweaving, or weaving through, seems the most forceful term with which to name the characteristic twisting, infolding, and refolding of lines in space that creates a labyrinth.) J. Hillis Miller writes that the "paradox of Ariadne's thread" is that it "maps the whole labyrinth" rather than simply providing a unidirectional attack."[72] Miller further argues that the concept of the labyrinth assimilates (or folds into) the interwound concept of the web. In the perplexing terms of Borges's fiction, the spatial image of the web points twofoldly toward both categories of labyrinth. Either kind can contain, generate, or be transcoded into the other.

This doubleness seems essential to an understanding of labyrinths: twisting, bending, infolding, perplexing are the fundamental labyrinthine transformations of space. A strong labyrinth compels those within it to experience a bending of apparently straight lines, a perplexing of space, even while he attempts to straighten them. It is significant that in the initial description of the crimson labyrinth, Dunraven remarks that although it is circular its area is so vast that its curvature cannot be perceived. Unwin immediately remembers Nicholas of Cusa, who held that every straight line is an arc of an infinite circle. A labyrinth perplexes straightness; it bends directions, in the inescapable fusion of illusion and impasse, and involutes the empty potential of space. A desert, under the necessity of decision, becomes a labyrinth, but its primordial model is, as for all labyrinths, the web, the perplexed straight line that has been infolded upon itself.

Put most simply, a labyrinth expresses the solution to the problem of placing a disjunctive structure in space. The purely narrative dimension of the problem is to conceive a spatial arrangement in which such a disjunctive structure could be embedded (and so made manifest) while, at the same time, it can function as the pattern of characters' (and readers') experience. Seen from this angle, the labyrinth begins to evoke other problems dealing with spatial configurations and underforming structures in space. From above, for instance, seen as a flat surface, or as a net of exposed lines within a bounded space, the labyrinth becomes a mandala. As a mandala, a network of perplexed lines embedded in space stands for something outside itself (either cosmic or psychic wholeness, say) and points perception away from the immediate configuration in space. From any angle that displays the labyrinth's full three-space dimensionality, a spatial volume bewebbed by its own infoldings, it becomes a knot. As a knot, the network of lines is a problem to be solved from outside, and its significance lies in what that solution will make possible, in effect, what it will open. A strong labyrinth is like the Hercules knot (*nodum solvere*), or the Gordian knot, in presenting a problem in untangling, or deweaving, that is difficult to solve. Miller ties the labyrinth to the concept of knots ("a complex knot of many crossings").[73] In *Cymbeline*, Iachimo, slipping the bracelet from Imogen's wrist, reflects that it is "As slippery as the Gordian Knot was hard" (2.2.34): either the Hercules or the Gordian knot might symbolize conceptual difficulty, or cognitive bafflement, insofar as they may be considered as external problems, posed to (but outside) the solver. In being knotlike (or a knot), the labyrinth is also a problem in topology (though, like chess, it need not be considered as one). Knottedness presents a particular instance of the general "placement problem," the different ways in which a curved line may be embedded in three-dimensional space.[74] Though (as a network of perplexed lines) seen from outside it may be either a mandala or a knot, the labyrinth is fundamentally a doubleness to be experienced from the inside. In the absence of a character, an image of the human mind, that thinks its way along the labyrinth's infolded paths, then the network of lines, however intricate, cannot be a strong labyrinth. Similarly, a chessboard, viewed from above during a certain configuration in play, cannot be called a real game.

In many of his fictions, Borges specifies some of the possible shapes (out of an indefinite series) that a strong labyrinth might take. A labyrinth could be, as Erik Lönnrot explains to his personal minotaur, the criminal Red Scharlach, in the penultimate paragraph of "Death and the Compass," a straight line because the problem of finding another person on a single of the infinite number of points that make up a line would be an exercise in traveling, by way of making decisions, through a labyrinth.[75] In "The Garden of Forking Paths," Borges demonstrates that a narrative would be a labyrinth (the two concepts having become indiscernible and, hence, identical) if it incorporated, as does the Chinese novel alluded to in the narrative, all the possible alternative consequences of each action in a progressive bifurcation and branching. The total ramification of alternative possibilities would constitute a nonspatial, temporal (or narrative) labyrinth. Ts'ui Pên's novel is a labyrinth in words and time, not in stone and space, but it is essentially a labyrinth because its reader would be in the position of the entrapped character within a labyrinthine godgame. The novel's few readers had rejected it angrily, baffled by its apparent transgressions of narrative conventions, refusing to read under the demand that all possible alternatives be borne in mind. Other people had sought the labyrinth that he had proposed to build, puzzled that it could not be found, without realizing that, in the enwebbed narrative, they had held it in their hands. Set against Ts'ui Pên's novel, the mazelike garden of Borges's narrative seems little more than a weak, prolusory simulacrum.

The unhappy fate of Semele in the old myth casts a shadow forward upon subsequent literature. Like humankind generally, characters are often victims, though (suspended in narrative clarities) they are victims in a more schematic, far less visceral, manner than nontextual victims. One determinate form that this victimization takes in literature thrusts characters into some other character's conceptual ensnarement. To be invited onward unwittingly (or to be compelled) into a series of alternatives, into the necessity of having to decide between exclusive disjunctions when the rules of choice have been hidden, or made unknowable, is to play a godgame. The godgame, making the player both passive and active, played and playing, caught within a game structure even while creating it, is constituted by the structure of a strong labyrinth. Abstracted from its textual detail, the pattern of the godgame is labyrinthine; considered separately, as an abstracted image, the labyrinth symbolizes the godgame. All godgames subsume labyrinths; every strong labyrinth constitutes a minimal godgame. (That is, it abstractly traces a godgame's shape and suggests its potential scope.) The distinction between them lies in the amount of detail, whether of setting (southern California, say, in *The Crying of Lot 49*) or of character, the relative fullness of interiority, that a godgame incorporates and textualizes.

Given a definite structure (the sequence of disjunctive decisions) a labyrinth may be called a godgame, at least in the sense that it underforms the godgame, emblematizes it, and provides, ultimately, its constitutive rule. It can be an actual godgame only when, and if, there is a player who attempts, in a series of movelike decisions, to play his way through it. Normally, the player is a character in the narrative, but, as Borges's Chinese novel suggests, the reader may also play within the narrative. Indeed, the labyrinthine sequence of disjunctive decisions must inevitably recall the efforts by various narratologists, in particular Claude Bremond, to establish plot grammars and thus to provide schemata of narrative possibilities.[76] In his recent analysis of plot in English Renaissance drama, Thomas Pavel continues the narratological search for plot grammar to conclude with a definition of *plot* that, in echoing Bremond, clearly suggests the idea of an underlying sequence of disjunctive decisions (or, as he calls them, "moves"): "A *plot* is a structure of moves characterized by a stable number of actors and the exhaustion of a problem load by means of successful or unsuccessful solutions . . . a plot is a set of actions intended to overcome a certain number of problems, some of which can derive from actions initiated inside the plot itself. As long as the problems are not even tentatively solved, the plot is unfinished."[77] The reader may be drawn into the character's sequence of moves and compelled to think through the narrative structure in advance of the entrapped character (which is what happens emphatically in Fowles's *The Magus*) or he may, in reinterpreting an apparent experience (the literal surface of the labyrinthine narrative, say), become the only player in a labyrinth that he creates.

In this latter sense, Unwin plays through a labyrinth in his renarration of Dunraven's narrative. He displays (it might be said, as McHale claims that *Gravity's Rainbow* does for Pynchon) Borges's paradigm for the act of reading. And in this way, the reader is invited to become the third-order victim of Robbe-Grillet's *In the Labyrinth*, transforming into a strong labyrinth what had been, for both the unnamed soldier and the doctor/narrator, evidently weak. A narrative can be a labyrinth if it captures its readers in the perplexities of explication and interpretation. The intricacy of a plot, whether in narrative or drama, evidently varies. Given a simple plot (but a sophisticated reader), there can be little effect of entrapment. Pavel distinguishes between a plot and a pseudo-plot (the latter involves a coherent line of action but a constant set of actors who either make only a few moves or make only secondary moves), and his analysis indicates that English Renaissance drama, unlike earlier drama, such as *Everyman*, is centripetally dependent upon structures of successive decisions, or moves.[78] A reader, drawn into the plot, into the characters' sequence of disjunctive decisions, follows a parallel labyrinthine sequence. As if he were confronting Ts'ui Pên's imperceptible labyrinth, the reader will be required to bring together the available conventions of reading (from whatever directions) in order to constitute the narrative while playing it. The unfolding of a plot builds a specific labyrinthine structure in which the reader participates (however asymmetrically) on a coordinate plane of cognitive recapitulation. Furthermore, as every complex game swallows up its more rudimentary prototypes (North

American football swallowing rugby, for instance), the constitutive act of reading absorbs the godgame. Structure (by a paradox of hermeneutic compensation) must spring, then, from the reader's own playfulness and skill in matching the text's gamefulness: an achieved goal, it becomes the prize for having read.

The godgame seems inescapably central to the preoccupations of postmodern literature, but it is also markedly overdetermined. It shows the obsession for games, for entrapment, for duplicity (double-dealing and double-sidedness), for playing within an arbitrarily constituted field, for cognitive perplexity, and for epistemological aporia of all kinds. Above all, it brings into play the conflict of "worlds," or of cognitive domains, that both postmodernism and the contemporary criticism find fascinating.[79] The world of the gamewright, the god, powerful and capable of immensely skillful manifestations, always inherently monologic (since it seeks to impose itself, even when, as in *The Magus*, it is complex enough to include plurality), entraps, and thus confronts or plays against, the character-players' worlds. In attempting to play free, the character-players seek their own statement, rationalization, and freedom. If a fictional world is axiologically defined as a set of values, or psychologically as the interiority of a subject, then a godgame constitutes, among other things, a clash of hostile worldhoods. One might say, in Bakhtin's terms, that the godgame incorporates a byplay of voices (each of which entails, of course, a distinct world) that actually models the interaction of the monologic voice, striving for control, and the heteroglossic voices of others who strive to break free, evade the monologic center, and speak themselves.

The godgame embeds, in the actualities of particular texts, a spectrum of postmodern interests. Yet it is an essentially transhistorical notion, even if the term, now widely used to label narrative and dramatic situations of entrapment, is both modern and English.[80] This transhistoricality reflects the even more basic problem of the collection with which this chapter began. *Godgame* collects literary, or textual, experience, even if it does so retrospectively. It works as well, and as inadequately, for Calderón de la Barca or Cervantes as it does for Pynchon or Borges. One might easily imagine a textual museum composed of intelligently selected godgames: a collection that would follow closely the history of literature and represent (in some sense) most of its canonical texts. Rather like those museums that Murray Bail imagines, the godgame displays the critic's curatorial ambition and the triumph of his cognitive powers. Yet it poses a paradox that cannot be wholly solved by the analysis either of its transhistorical scope or its formal classificatory power. Nothing in the analysis of the godgame itself will quite explain how it can be transhistorical and still preeminently rooted in the textual experience of a particular, relatively short, literary period, the postmodern. It transcribes, then, the earlier paradox of postmodernism: how can a label (a mere curatorial strategy) name something as particular as a period and yet depend for definition on formal devices, techniques, or conventions that are found everywhere outside that period? The problem of postmodernism, a paradox that collects further paradoxes, indicates the intractable difficulties of dealing with the textual museum that literature makes possible. The godgame is certainly a textual game, but it is one that, however many times it is played, never entirely lays bare the range of its overdetermination.

CHAPTER 5

Gamefulness

notional areas, domains, and worldhood

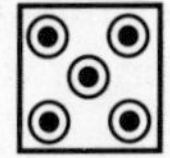

Concerning [parables] a man once said: Why such reluctance? If you only followed the parables, you yourself would become parables and with that rid of all your daily cares. Another said: I bet that is also a parable. The first said: You have won. The second said: But unfortunately only in parable. The first said: No, in reality: in parable you have lost.
—Franz Kafka, "On Parables"

PERHAPS ONE SHOULD simply admit that in the analysis of literature what one gains or wins in one place will be lost in another. Terry Eagleton, an incisive cartographer of modern literature's boundaries, maps succinctly the folds that mark the edges of inherently self-divisive activities: "Literature, that aporetic spot in which truth and error indissolubly entwine, is at once practice and the deconstruction of practice, spontaneous act and theoretical act, a gesture which in pursuing an unmediated encounter with reality in the same instant interprets that very impulse as metaphysical fiction."[1] Imagine literature as a large field divided into separate play areas: the rules that seem to make one activity possible preclude the playing of others. Or, drawing on a more commodious metaphor, think of it as a vast museum, with innumerable separate collections (activities that seem distinct and may be labeled), then it will be possible to see that understanding one collection provides no necessary help in understanding another. (It may help one in understanding how collections, as collections, are made and how the discourse of museums is constituted. It may help one become a theorist or, in the goal that Brian McHale holds out, a metareader, but it does not seem to provide an intercollective understanding that transfers readily from spot to aporetic spot.) Indeed, to understand one such collection may make the others tenuous: their boundaries, to use one of Derrida's images, may begin to tremble. The tenuousness and uncertainty of boundaries are, always and already, implicit in the notion of a collection.

One may understand some conventions of fiction (one or another collection in the museum), but actually lose the effort so far as fiction is concerned. Think of all those "readings" of novels and all those critical accounts of literary characters and characterization that simply, violently, and without regard invoke notions of "real" people and neglect, or underlook, the fictionality of characters. (Characters are always created out of, and made up from, conventions. But which ones? how does one discover them? where does one find them? how does one order them either in logical priority or historical precedence?) Similarly, to talk about space in fiction should not be confused with the dissimilar effort of talking about space in reality. Fictional space yet again shapes the puzzle of the collection. It is a certain fictional aspect, a problem in conventions (perhaps no more than a series of eruptions from within the system of fictional conventions, the total volume of which is unknown), a boundary within fiction but not its circumference, a mere fold but not the whole bulk.

Consider the following parable. Once upon a time, not so long ago, and not so far away, in a village on the pampas, on the prairies, along interminable Pacific beaches, there lived two brothers. They were like ordinary real-life brothers who got up each day and did what they were used to doing: eating normally, walking in more or less straight lines, feeling the winds of air and heat that blew, seeing within the variable translucencies of light, and living in the linear unfolding of time. Then one day they grew tired of this commonplace existence and began to invent fresh existences. The first brother began by asking whether it was truly necessary to walk in straight lines from one point to another. Perhaps, he reasoned, it might make more sense to walk in curved lines, since they might prove to be more interesting, or even (in the long run) quicker. After all, he reflected, the universe sometimes seems to be composed of chunks of curved space, so curved lines might make more sense than straight ones. He went on to think about other things that he had been taught to accept, all very ordinary things, but which might be only assumptions that could be changed: the notion that one line and only one line might pass through a given point, that planes have surfaces, that distances between points are constant, that time passes linearly. All these ordinary assumptions about human experience could be inverted, and strange, but profoundly exciting, innovations would follow. New worlds would emerge, open to exploration yet blankly closed to the commonplace vision of the rejected assumptions.

Meanwhile, the second brother began to weary of the undeviating predictability of ordinary life. He grew tired of the heaviness of gravity, of the solidity of substance, of the tedious ongoingness of cause and effect, and of the sensation of heated air that seemed to be the blowing of the wind. He began to imagine a world in which things floated or ascended at will, in which substance dissolved and then flowed together again like quicksilver, in which events called out meaningfully to each other but did not cause one another. He began to suppose that all human experience could be counterfactual. Suppose (he mused) that the wind were made of light. Suppose that the sky could be made of flowers and the clouds were bundles of soft petals, then rain might be the perfume of rose or of poppies. Let us suppose that the winds blow (or illumine) the embryos of our desires.

In this way the two brothers began to reinvent the world. But it is important to remark that they did so in very different ways without paying much attention to others, their precursors, who had tried to perform similar reinventions in the past. The first brother began by assuming a single proposition that was contrary to reason and to the likelihoods of human experience. The propositions that he invented were often antirational and counterintuitive, but he was able to draw from them fascinating consequences. Once he had made them, it seemed, extraordinary worlds became possible, and narratives about those worlds, before unimaginable, now flowed in his voice. All the it-goes-without-sayings of realistic fiction that he had grown up believing began to fade (either into insignificance or into the vast volume of literary conventions). Thus he was able to assume that a library could be infinite, that a man might lose his ability to forget detail (and hence to make abstractions), that God could suspend time for one man but not for others, that a coin could have only one side, that a book might have an infinite number of pages, not one of which could ever be rediscovered, or that there might be a world (call it Tlön) in which existence could depend on perception. Once he had invented these counterintuitive propositions, they began to function in his fresh accounts like axioms in fantastic geometries. Once one accepted them, one could not avoid where they led.

Now the second brother shared the desire to begin freshly and to discard what had become dustily commonplace. But he followed a dissimilar method of reinvention. He began by imagining spaces in which common and uncommon things existed side by side: men died, grew old, had children, were born, remembered, or forgotten; yet flowers rained from the skies, human persons metamorphosed into animals or exotic plants, ghosts and chimeras abounded, and human psychology lent the structure of its obsessions to things so that the world became, in its reinvention, a labyrinth of emblems. In the second brother's narratives there were no single axioms from which everything descended, or from which the world hung, but there were instead two codes that were interwound, twisted in a grip closer than blood and mind, in a tight choreography of antitheses. The one code put things into place quite normally (naturally and explicably) so that men were shot and died, had ambitions, were deserted, became lonely, and sought sublimations like, say, making silver fish. The second code organized events so that any number of strange things might occur: a man might be everywhere followed by butterflies, another might swim to the bottom of the sea and find lost villages where life continued or where ancient turtles lay by the thousands waiting to be eaten, still another might build a lighthouse out of ice. In the imagined space of the second brother's narratives, the possibilities of two worlds were always copresent (their codes mutually interwound) and clung fiercely to each other.[2]

Both brothers learned to tell narratives about their reinvented worlds with a straight face, without shrugs, secret winks, or other hints that it was, after all, just a tale (the world had not been reinvented, only temporarily disguised). Some people thought that their talent as storytellers was simply this knack of telling about their newly imagined worlds without drawing attention to them as out of the ordinary, of giving their worlds narrators who could never raise the question of how it could all be the way it is, who never raised problems or suggested that readers and hearers should look for explanations. There never were any explanations because none were ever required. Their worlds easily generated their own illusive belief.

No doubt there are always people (more than pedagogues, politicians, preachers, and policemen might care to admit) who would like to reinvent the world. If they cannot do it for themselves, except in sleep or when the fog is thickest, then they beg others to do it for them. So the two brothers quickly gathered disciples, followers like scattered knights, who swore to reinvent their own worlds according to the rules the brothers had formulated. As their following grew, the number of disciples increased, uncertainties stuck to the brothers' fame, they became associated with strangers, their origins lost, and (worst of all) they became confused with one another. There were some adventurers among the new worlds who said that the brothers were actually just one person who possessed a single magic formula; others, that they lived in this place or that and made gazetteers of all the real world's invisible cities; still others, that they were impostors, panvestites, masters of bunco and Buncombe. As often happens, a myth (a collective network of little myths) sprang up about the brothers and they became at once more and less than their true disciples knew them to be. They were everywhere and everyone spoke much of them and of their power and influence, but who were they? really, everyone asked, who really are they? really, who? (Perhaps that seemed too long for a parable: though a parable, unlike a limerick, is not known by its length.)

I

> Each narrative, fictional or historical, provides an alternative story set in a created "world" that is itself a fresh alternative to the "world" or "worlds" previously serving as boundaries of the reader's imagination.
>
> —Wayne Booth,
> *The Company We Keep: An Ethics of Fiction*

The two brothers in the parable reinvent the extratextual world and, in so doing, create new textual worlds. Their texts are fantastic variations upon the extratextual world or they are superadditions, supplements perhaps, to that world. To say that a literary text creates, or produces, a "world" is a commonplace, yet profoundly strange, notion. It accords with the experience of common readers and undergraduates who often claim that they become lost in the world of the story or reject certain forms of fiction (the short story, say) because its world, in being less fully developed, is either uninteresting or frustrating. The metaphors of penetration, exploration, dwelling within, inhabiting, and becoming lost (absorbed, swallowed, overwhelmed by) in the text describe the ordinary strategies of readerly articulation. *World* is also the term by which scholars and critics express their perception of the text's self-containedness and coherence. The "world of" *Don Quijote* or *Gravity's Rainbow* expresses both the sense of its enclosedness and the sense of its difference from the text and everything else. When scholars refer to the world of an author, however, Cervantes, say, or Pynchon, they normally mean either the extratextual world insofar as it has led to, borne upon, or become encoded within the author's texts, or they mean the author's production, viewed synchronically, as a totalized display of specific conventions, mannerisms, and characteristic choices in motifs, topoi, and themes.

World is evidently a term as rich in semantic applications, serving to identify and set apart any area of signification that can be thought independently of all others, and forceful in its connotations. It is, as C. S. Lewis observes, a word that conveys great concreteness. Certain uses of *world* in poetry, such as Keats's "Daffodils / And the Green world they live in" (or Shakespeare's "fleet the time carelessly, as they did in the golden world"), seem to possess an almost visceral emphasis while resisting exact translation into prose equivalents. When one calls any notional area a "world," Lewis argues, "we always suggest that it has some internal unity and a character that sets it apart from other areas." Thus any region "whatever can be called a *world* if it is being regarded, within a given context, as constituting a (relatively) closed system."[3] Other terms, such as *domain, realm*, or *field*, each bearing spatial connotations, might serve as synonyms, but *world* has become the normal term by which to describe the self-enclosedness of (in Lewis's phrase) a "notional area."

Literary texts are not the only notional areas that possess potential worldhood. Philosophers distinguish "possible worlds" from the actual one as conceptual entities that can be thought and access to which may be gained from the actual world. One might conceive a world, different only in a single salient aspect (that Notre Dame de Paris is painted blue, for example), from the actual world. Such a notional world would be accessible, asymmetrically, from the actual world. (It would be possible to think one's way there, but not to live there and think one's way here.) It would be a *possible* world. In a larger sense, the problems of discussing notional worldhood are inherent in the concept of signification. The interplay of concepts in discourse, whether the referents are taken to be actual or fictive, must tend to establish conceptual boundaries, as well as diplomatic corridors, that constitute notional areas. (The spatial metaphors are extremely deep and quite reasonable: a conceptual field in which different concepts are brought into play together, even though those concepts must be introduced diachronically, responds well to spatial imagery.[4]) From within, as a dimension of human experience (whether as reader, viewer, or thinker), the phenomenological aspect of space makes notional areas not only conceivable but also experiential. They take on distinct casts, shapes, and limitations all of their own (like a chess game or a Superbowl experienced from within to the exclusion of all impinging extraludic actuality), and they can be, in some real sense, felt, even seen in the mind's eye, as spatially independent. Hence Lewis's "notional area" may be taken as equivalent to a "spatial structure that acts as a secondary illusion" against the primary illusion of temporal sequence.[5] The distinct self-enclosedness and spatiality of notional areas (or secondary illusions) leads inevitably to analogies with games and to axiomatic systems. The problem of the third chapter, whether literary texts can be said to have rules or merely conventions, returns on the most general of all scales. Can a self-enclosed area of significance be said to have axioms? Does the presence of axioms (and consequent self-enclosedness) constitute worldhood? What are the minimal conditions for worldhood? Given the tremendous diversity of its uses, *world* is not necessarily always a closely examined term that has been made to survive the rigors of conceptual scrutiny.

One may mark in the following example from a Shakespearean commentator both ease and fluidity in the use of *world.* In analyzing the many acts of drawing, from observed words, gestures, and acts, inferences concerning absent truths (that is, the many acts of interpretation) in *The Winter's Tale,* Howard Felperin writes that we are "from the outset in a world of interpretation—the producer's and our own—where nothing can be either wholly dismissed or wholly believed, and nothing can be known for certain." Later in his argument, Felperin writes that "the world of the text and the text of the world, once securely because dogmatically defined, now become indeterminate because overdetermined."[6] Evidently, *world* is a word that Felperin uses with some fluency. One supposes that he does not expect its use to cause his readers difficulties. Yet it is clear that he uses the term in three distinct senses. The second passage cited posits a normal, if perplexing, distinction between the actual world (that concerning which there may be observations, experiments, and some agreement), which may be transcribed into a text, and a textual world that bears some relationship to the actualities of the first. Both can be "securely," if dogmatically, defined, and both can become, through interpretation, overdetermined. The "world of the text," despite the ease with which it is used, must give pause: what does it mean to say that a text has a world? how is it determined? can it be mapped? This use of *world* accords with common usage, though, because of the antithesis within which Felperin places it, its inherent uncertainties are neatly on the surface.

Felperin's initial use of *world,* however, is less common but still well within the boundaries of critical usage. A "world of interpretation" seems vastly different from, and must surely be constituted differently than, a simple "world of the text." It suggests a world (and here the problems of the term become aggressive: what synonyms are available? would *domain* work as well or better? what about *game*? doesn't Felperin mean only that certain kinds of actions, perhaps made possible by rules, dominate the "world of the text"?) in which the precise action of interpreting is the most important or, perhaps, the only action that takes place. *World*, in this sense, implies a semiotic domain, a conceptual area specifically constituted by a particular category of signifiying actions. A text, insofar as it is made up of heterogeneous kinds of discourse, each governed by specific axioms (or, as Thomas Pavel prefers, maxims), may manifest a number of domains.[7] Hence a literary text may normally contain a plurality of worlds, one of which might easily be a world of interpretation.

Yet this definition of *world* as a loose synonym for *domain* further entails that many texts will traverse each world. The "world of interpretation," for example, subsumes many texts, such as *Hamlet*, *Othello*, *Don Quijote*, *The Crying of Lot 49*, *Gravity's Rainbow*, or any number of Borges's fictions. Imagine all possible signification as an infinitely vast Rubik's cube in which the colored squares, constantly undergoing kaleidoscopic permutations, symbolize precise notional areas, or self-enclosed domains, and then call each square a world but also call every possible relationship between squares a world as well. What will be gained through this promiscuous emphasis? What lost? The problem of textual worldhood remains. (One might think that the idea of a semiotic world was clear enough yet still inquire after the conditions of fictional worldhood as a special case.) Felperin's fluid use of *world* involves a relatively complex, though perhaps accidental, byplay of concepts that diversely signify worldhood.

II

> The Buddhists sometimes picture the universe as a cobweb strung with beads of dew, each drop reflecting all the others. In the novelist's world, not only does every thing imply every other thing and each event every other event, as Leda's egg hatched the history of Troy; but the egg itself, the dew-strung web, is an artistic whole—distinct, harmonious, and radiant—as the actual real world is not.
>
> —John Barth, "How to Make a Universe"

The worldhood of literary texts is a fundamental, if seldom analyzed, dimension of the reading experience. It marks one kind of question: How are texts like worlds? How is *this* text like a world? What is it in the particular discourse of a text that leads one to confer worldhood upon it? The third question masks several others. One may always ask how the world of a text resembles the actual (or "real") world, for example, and to do that is partly to inquire after the semiotic indices in the text that evoke, more or less recognizably, that extratextual world. The ideology of literary realism may contaminate questions about worldhood (if it isn't *the* world, how can it be called *a* world?), though there is no necessity that this should be so. Readers often seem to respond to a literary text as if they had experienced it in world, or world-like, terms. Questions about worldhood often move back and forth from the textual indices that evoke the actual world and those that evoke a self-contained, experiential (in some sense) but splendidly nonactual world. Many literary texts, if not most, both point to the actual extratextual world and also create, at least minimally, another world specific to the text. One philosopher, Doreen Maitre, identifies a class of texts characterized by the "oscillation between could-be-actual worlds and could-never-be-actual worlds."[8]

Although one can certainly think of textual modes that constitute "could-be-actual" worlds and even some, such as fantasy, fairy tales, and fables, that evoke "could-never-be-actual" worlds, most texts seem to be mixtures, containing some indices of the actual world but insufficient to make a meaningful correspondence. They may be described, accurately, as oscillating between. Thus Spenser's *Faerie Queene*, a text that seems overwhelmingly to constitute a world that could never be actual, contains frequent references to parts of the actual world, including physical aspects of the setting, historical events, and human individuals, and has consistently inspired a line of interpretation, historical allegory, that seeks to correlate fictional characters (but also places and events) with people in the actual world. The *Variorum* Spenser contains many possible readings of this kind, not all of which are particularly obvious, and an excellent overview can still be found in Ernest de Sélincourt's introduction to the Oxford edition of Spenser's works. There one can learn not merely the easy correlations, such as Gloriana and Belphoebe both representing Queen Elizabeth I, but such comparatively arcane equivalences as "Marinell = Lord Howard of Effingham" or "Paridell = Earl of Westmoreland."[9] Historical allegory illustrates a kind of interpretation that can be applied to any text that can be imagined to have a history, fairy tales and Mother Goose prominently included.

Nonetheless, it seems apparent that the principles of organization in texts such as *The Faerie Queene* are not intended to mimic the organization of an actual world, even if certain parts seem to correspond. The cohesiveness, integrity, and organization of such a textual world are not apparently borrowed from the actual world (though Renaissance scholars might argue that, in Spenser's case, they are taken from current models of that world in the sense that it is hierarchical and providential), but depend upon text-specific assumptions that have more to do with Spenser's understanding of allegory, and his intention to "fashion a gentleman," than with his empirical observations. Such principles of world organization may be called axioms in the sense that the world that the text creates depends upon, but does not normally examine, them. They make possible (in some sense) the often impossible worlds of fiction. The possible nonactual worlds (or "pnaws," as Doreen Maitre calls them) that philosophers enjoy talking about do seem very different from the hyperbolically impossible nonactual worlds that readers can conceive (of) in fiction. *The Faerie Queene*, for example, constitutes a world in which characters are depthless, appear and disappear meaningfully but irrealistically, and in which both time and space are extremely variable, capable of irrealistic deformation, and essentially plastic. The textual assumptions that legislate these impossibilitics may be called axioms. But *axiom* possesses a dual signification with respect to literary texts. If it is taken as describing the way the text has been written, or has accounted for the organization of semiotic features in general (the phenotext as, following Kristeva, it is sometimes called), then, like rule, it has a doubtful applicability. Any text-specific assumptions might be modified and the text would still be recognizably itself and belong to whatever categories (such as pastoral or romance) it has normally been assigned. If *axiom* is taken as describing the way the experience of the text is governed, its interiority in reading, then it seems more accurate. Once certain assumptions have been accepted, as an aspect of the reading transaction, then their authority is pervasive. Since a text is not like a geometry (neither absurdity nor nonexistence follows upon the rejection of textual assumptions), but only experienced like one, it would make sense to call the fundamental text-specific assumptions *pseudo-axioms*.

The problem of represented space in literature (as opposed to the uses of actual page space, which can be, in certain texts, an interesting question in its own right[10]) prepares the way for the larger issue of worldhood. Space is only an element in the constitution of textual worlds, and not perhaps the most important (if any distinct element were *the* most important, it probably would be character), but it is an elusive element, as difficult to formulate as it is unavoidable. Gabriel Zoran puts the issue succinctly when he writes that "research in general on the subject is quite diffuse, and there are few assumptions that have become generally accepted."[11] There is a loose vocabulary (hardly a lexicon) containing terms such as place, distance, volume, coexistence, order, shape, and form, but there are *no* generally accepted propositions, not even that textual space exists. This book will assume that the experience of reading a literary text invariably shapes some spatial dimension. The problem of textual worldhood, its axiomaticity, and its analogy to games (in being also self-enclosed experiences) can be approached from an analysis of textual space.

Space (taken in its most primitive sense: a distance to be crossed, an openness between two points, one of which is occupied by a perceiving subject, filled by something, sunlight, moonlight, hot dust, cold mud, or emptiness, that one can traverse, or at least think about traversing) seems, for all of its elusiveness, virtually omnipresent in literary experience. Anyone can try the following simple experiment: ask a reader to describe the space in some narrative. Probably the reader will not be able to do this well. Yet if one asks the same person to *recall* the narrative, he will probably do so in spatial terms. These terms may be inexact and crude, but they will be spatial nonetheless: the place, the distance, the land, the world. Few readers possess an adequate vocabulary for talking about space. Yet it seems normal enough to recall literature in rudimentary spatial terms. One can easily observe that very sophisticated readers, such as literary critics, also talk about space in literature and recall texts in terms of spatiality. One can even turn the problem upside down and inquire what a reading of literature would be like if one did not think in spatial terms and did not recall the experience of reading in spatial terms. What, in the absence of space, could take place?

It is possible to distinguish at least six distinct ways of talking about space in literature. They are not equivalent and only the first two may seem to be literal, commonsensical ways of accounting for space and spatiality. The argument here is only that they are six distinct ways of talking about space and that they correspond to ordinary reading experience. One may observe—and even actively seek evidence among one's fellow readers—that readers, on every level of sophistication, do read in terms of spatial images, do interpret literature, and narrative in particular, as having taken place within space, and do tend to recall the action in terms of directions, places, worlds, and other kinds of spatial imagery. The six ways, then, though not perhaps exhaustive, nor precluding other ways of accounting for the problem of textual space, do correspond to elementary aspects of the reading experience.

First, it is possible to identify a level of microsemiotics in which the normal deictics of speech are used. Deictics serve to establish that a character is located spatially and that it experiences spatially: here, there, up, behind, below, far, close, and so forth. Deictics function in literary texts to make a certain limited experience of space possible.

One must read narrative deictics as doing what they normally do in extratextual speech (or "real-world talk"): pointing. They point within the experience of characters, including that sometimes neglected character, the narrator, and make their experience more clearly imaginable. No doubt, one could say, as speech act theorists like to claim, that they function "as if" the author had been referring to actual space; that is, deictics, along with all other aspects of language, may be held to be parasitic upon ordinary, extratextual language. This claim may fulfill the demands of ideology and it may not even be incorrect (in the sense that it offers a model of the interrelation between textual and extratextual language), but it is nonetheless exiguous. Readers respond to deictics by imagining the space in which they point.

Second, it is possible to distinguish a larger, more inclusive semiotic level upon which place is established. There can be, as a consequence of a number of descriptive phrases, or structural oppositions between one direction and another, one particular image and another, or as a consequence of the metaphors that are used, an emergent sense of a larger place in which the character lives, moves, and experiences. This seems less a direction of realistic descriptiveness than of literarity itself. The process of constructing the text's world (reading itself) invokes space, and the constructed world has a kind of being in space. Joseph Conrad's Pacific littorals are places, just as are Shakespeare's Belmont and Illyria or Spenser's Faerieland. Place is not in any important way a problem of reference, of where places actually are (or how one might reach them), but of signification. Certain theorists invoke the category of "fictive referents" (perhaps to placate the supposed demands of ordinary-language philosophers, who link meaning to reference and reference to existence), but that attempt to dull the edge of Ockham's razor falls into superfluous tangles.[12] (The "tragic view of categories," in Barth's phrase, holds that they fail even though they are necessary. The absurdist view would hold that they both fail and are unnecessary. The category of fictive referents probably exemplifies the latter view.) One could easily compile a dictionary of imaginary places, as has indeed been done, and no one using it as a reference tool would suppose that it directed him to actual places but only that it might help to clarify his reading experience.[13] Pavel writes that fictional texts, like theories, "refer as systems, and just as in physics it is often impossible to set apart 'genuinely' referential elements from the mathematical apparatus, in fiction one does not always need to keep track of pretended and genuine statements, since global relevance is apparent in spite of such distinctions."[14] Descriptive phrases, along with deictics, signify within the global experience of reading but not as guides to exact location. The effective test of narrative, Ricardo Gullón observes, is whether it affects the reader and makes him feel and "understand the meaning of the space in which the character exists."[15]

Third, on a level of macrosemiotics readers experience literary texts globally as "worlds." Space constitutes a fundamental, perhaps even an invariant, element of worldhood. Certainly a text is most likely to be recalled spatially—that is, as a world possessing distance, scope, volume, and coexistence—even if, as a textual artifact open to semiotic analysis, it can be shown that metaphysical, axiological, or psychological elements play a greater role in specifically determining its worldhood. The worlds of *The Trial*, of *The Faerie Queene*, of *Don Quijote*, of *Ulysses*, or of *Gravity's Rainbow* are built up from the operations of particular signifying moves on the first two, microsemiotic, levels and are experienced not merely as different (from each other, from all other fictional worlds, and from the extratextual world) but as distinctive. Spatial axioms, thus, are basic to fictional worldhood.

The argument that "an imaginative and imaginary world" requires the faithful observance of "the rules of logic and inner consistency" nowhere strikes a stronger resonance than in the consideration of textual space. (Whether the claim that texts, insofar as they make up worlds, possess axioms contradicts the claim in Chapter 3 that texts do not have rules, but more flexible operational assumptions, conventions, will be discussed further later in this chapter. Axiom is used here to indicate the broadest kind of text-specific assumption relevant to the constitution of the text's global experience.) Doležel, for example, describes the world of Kafka—of the stories considered collectively and of the three novels—as being "hybrid" in the strict sense that they are experienced in terms of the fusion of disparate principles: ordinary and bizarre, say, or normal and abnormal.[16] Hybridness, then, might be said to provide one axiom for the construction of Kafka's world in that it legislates the possibility of fusion for "realities" which are normally, in the extratextual world, distinct.

Similarly, the world of *The Faerie Queene*, in common with much Renaissance allegorical narrative, builds upon axioms that make possible a space that is open to enigmatic transformations. The same route (at least, the ways to and from the same places) can be either empty or full, swift and easy to cross, or slow and difficult. The route to the Bower of Bliss in the Second Book, for example, can be empty, in the sense that certain characters experience no difficulties in arriving there. Yet Sir Guyon requires a great deal of time (Spenser precisely indicates that Guyon's voyage across the Gulf of Greediness takes several days) and encounters a long catalog of maritime hazards and sea horrors

(2.12.2–25) of which, Spenser's narrator comments, there are "thousand thousands many more, / And more deformed Monsters thousand fold" (25). *The Faerie Queene* abounds in instances of variable time schemes and corresponding transformations of space. In Book I, after Red Cross deserts her, Una is said to have wandered "from one to other Ynd" (6.2), which both indicates the time lapse and the rigors of her search but also functions to distend (and declarify) the boundaries of Faerieland itself. After Orgoglio defeats and imprisons Red Cross, Una's dwarf sets out in search of her "to tell his great distresse" (6.19). He encounters Una almost at once, but in their return journey to rescue Red Cross they take longer to reach Orgoglio's castle than the dwarf had taken alone. This dilation of narrative time parallels a corresponding deformation of space:

> Long tost with stormes, and bet with bitter wind,
> High over hils, and low adowne the dale,
> She wandred many a wood, and measurd many a vale. (7.28)

The space of the return journey, marked by topographical diversity, is full while that of the dwarf's trip from the place of Orgoglio's castle had been empty. The distances between places are, like the local spaces themselves, open to transformations.

In *The Faerie Queene*, plasticity and metamorphicity are spatial axioms. Thus the plasticity of routes, each projecting variable distances depending upon which character is traveling and for what purposes, corresponds to the plastic capacities of inner spaces. In *The Faerie Queene*'s world, dragons and other monstrous creatures possess bodies that open to extremely plastic cavities and that do not manifest a consistent anatomy: wings, tails, and mouths, for example, may be of any size and may undergo transformations. The Blatant Beast is said to have a hundred tongues (5.12.41) but later Sir Artegall observes that it seems to have a thousand (6.1.9). Insofar as the axioms that govern spatial capacity are concerned, it might have both these numbers of tongues. In Spenser's allegorical space, the inside of a place may be greater than its outside as if the interior had folded outward to incorporate the exterior. In fantasy literature, such axioms of spatial plasticity are not uncommon. In the BBC television series "Dr. Who," the doctor travels through time and space in a TARDIS which appears to be, from the outside, an ordinary English police call box but, from the inside, is actually a spacious time-space vehicle. Either the TARDIS or the Blatant Beast's oral cavity might provide an emblem for the notion of textual space: a limited semiotic exterior (so many signs arranged according to a definite system) opens out into the vastness of interior experience.

Fourth, it has become common, at least among American critics, to speak of "spatial form." When readers of literature claim that they have experienced their reading as spatial or that the text possesses a spatial form, they mean that the normal temporal unfolding of narrative provides an inadequate basis for giving an account of their experience. Certain texts, it is argued, are too discontinuous to be experienced diachronically (although, on the level of text sequence, they must be read in this way) and must be reconstructed into a simultaneous, or spatialized, whole. They must be grasped, if at all, in a single synchronic act of comprehension. In Ricardo Gullón's words, the reader "must spatially connect temporally unconnected references."[17] Joseph Frank first argued this view with respect to Djuna Barnes's *Nightwood*.[18] He generalized the argument to make all modernist narrative spatial in this sense: that is, because discontinuous, narratively intercut, anything but "unfolding," it had to be experienced as simultaneous, as capable of being held in a single grasp, perceived in "a moment of time." Frank's argument can be further generalized to apply to all literature. If all literature is discontinuous (as poststructuralism insists and all readers, not ruled by organicist metaphors, tend to believe), then to some degree the experience of it must be synchronic or, in Frank's weaker term, simultaneous. Spatial form, in Frank's sense, "far from being restricted to the features which [he] identifies in [modernist] works (simultaneity and discontinuity), spatial form is a crucial aspect of the experience and interpretation of literature in all ages and cultures."[19]

Spatial form thus seems inescapably linked to the problem of readerly recollection. (Once again, the experiment is openly available: all one has to do is to ask a reader, a student, or a child, for example, to recall a literary text that he or she has read and then observe the distortions, the formulas, and the metaphors that will underscore the spatiality of the reading experience.) Gaston Bachelard argues that memory in itself is spatial—that is, associated with images of place—and this certainly does seem to be the case with memories of textual experience.[20] Intricate diachronic complexities come to be collapsed into simpler spatial arrangements. Georges Poulet makes a similar point: memories and places, changes in time and changes in space, spatial image and temporal phase, all intersect in Proust such that the recapturing of lost time is also, or is possible only under the form of, the rediscovery of lost places.[21]

The recollected world of *Hamlet* may seem to be all dark and interior, associated with specific places such as battlements, courtrooms, stairways, graveyards, and not at all a linear time sequence of so many acts and scenes, so many inferred days and weeks: not the unfolding time of the play's action but the spatial images associated with the separate actions. Similarly, the world of *Lord Jim* seems easy to recall as oceanic and insular, a constant interplay between open and enclosed places, between oceanic exteriors and insular interiors, the vast topography of the Pacific from India to Australia and the cramped enclosures of courtrooms and ship cabins, but it is more difficult to recall it in terms of Conrad's dazzling time shifts, his narratively constructed embedding of voice within voice, time within time, diachronic unfolding within diachronic unfolding. As Bachelard argues, memory is ordinarily spatial such that to recall a complex narrative under the form of its temporal strategies alone demands a difficult reading discipline.

Fifth, it is possible to see spatial form*s* (which is not at all the same as perceiving spatial form) within particular texts. All kinds of patterns—shapes, configurations, paradigms, geometrical forms, figural presences—run through literary texts. They are discovered in time since they must unfold in the course of physical text sequence and become apparent within the reading time of the reader's experience. Such patterns are understood in, and recalled in, spatial terms. Diversely exemplified, but structurally unmodified, they persist unchanged through both text sequence and textual diachronicity and, to be understood, all their parts need to be grasped together. They can overlap and intersect (both spatial metaphors), take place anywhere or spread themselves through. W. J. T. Mitchell writes that some "patterns will be so simple as to seem self-evident, virtually identical with the genre of the work. One of our most common spatial equivalents for literary action is the image of a wheel whose revolutions mark not just the time-line but the fortunes of the hero."[22] Roland Barthes makes a similar distinction when he contrasts "character" with "figure." Character is only the distribution of semiotic bits within a text—many bits, obviously, for certain characters, minimally few for others—united by the specious identity of a proper noun. A figure, while discovered temporally and therefore, in some sense, distributed, is experienced as always the same, always known, always what it is, neither to be supplemented nor to be reduced.[23] Amputation of a trait does not shrink a figure.

One understands such figures in allegorical narrative without much problem (the figure of Error in the First Book of *The Faerie Queene*, say), but Barthes's point is that readers also experience them in realistic fiction, even in the closed, readerly (*lisible*) texts of canonical French novels. Borrowing a figure from Barthes's analysis of Balzac's "Sarrasine," one may discern the spatial pattern (a figure) of the narrator in both *Hamlet* and *Lord Jim*. Someone speaks, tells stories, and someone hears: pervasively, there is a scene of telling, of narration. Narrators and narratees are interlocked in a semiotic (as well as a narrative) dance of tongue and ears. *Lord Jim* is a novel in which multiple spatial patterns, distributed recursively throughout, emerge. J. Hillis Miller, taking an image from one of Conrad's letters, compares the narrative method to a knitting machine: "It is a chain of repetitions, each event referring back to others which it both explains and is explained by, while at the same time it prefigures those which will occur in the future. Each exists as part of an infinite regression and progression within which the narrative moves back and forth discontinuously across time seeking unsuccessfully some motionless point in its flow."[24] This adequately describes the way in which patterns become spatialized (that is, distributed, variously exemplified, demanding a total grasp of discontinuous particulars) in a highly complex narrative such as *Lord Jim*. The specific example of the narrator/narratee transaction evokes a spatialized figure in which all the many instances of narration, involving different narrators and narratees (who occasionally exchange places), flow together in a confluence of common characteristics and are capable of being recalled in terms of the single figure of one character telling another (something). It can be recalled as a scene of narration.

There are many possible spatial forms. The labyrinth constitutes one such spatial form pervading, structuring, and summarizing certain narratives. All of Borges's labyrinths, for example, are spatial forms—even when, as in "The Garden of Forking Paths," they serve to thematize problems of time—and all of them, lucidly and unmistakably perceived, create error and confusion in the experience of characters: a labyrinth is, after all, only "a structure compounded to confuse men" the architecture of which, though rich in symmetries, is "subordinated to that end." Labyrinths are, Gullón writes, "spaces that are confused and are identified with the metaphor that they create and which in turn defines them—metaphor spaces, self-sufficient in their reduction of everything to an image."[25] Hence the labyrinth, which is a topographical place in certain texts, is a spatial form in Borges's fiction: a paradoxical fusion of geometrical clarity and experiential obscurity that recurs.

Sixth, there is a way in which any literary text may be thought of spatially as invoking a larger space than it occupies. Although this may sound paradoxical, it, too, corresponds to the way literature is experienced. Barthes refers to "stereographic space" (*l'espace stéréographique*), the volume of the textual plural, of intertextual *enchaînement*, in which one text, or bit of text, leads to, associates itself with, pulls into its own textual space, some other text, or bit of text.[26] The space of one text, whether thought of as its topographical places or as its inscribed forms or as its world, invokes the space of another one. Stereographic space is the field, or complex place, of textual inscription. In Derrida's discussion of this problem, space appears as the relational *habitation* for all of our sign systems and it is this, the universe of textuality, of inscriptions and inscriptibility, that produces the "spatiality of space."[27] In reading one may see not only a world in words, a world in a text, but also worlds in the textual world. A text, considered as a world, can contain multiple textual worlds. In Barthesian phrase, the text, like an egg (*un text-oeuf*), is always full. Reading for worldhood is as intricate an experience as seeing a merely singular world in a grain of sand.

Not everyone will agree that these six modes of spatiality are equally copresent in the experience of literature, nor that they are equally concepts of space. The argument here is only that in these ways readers do seem to experience literary texts and do often claim to have read literature, and to remember it, in one or all of these spatial modes. The one kind of space that has not been discussed is the space of the cosmos or the ideas of this space that philosophers have formulated. This is not because the space of the extratextual world never enters into literature or because there are never any ideas of space in literary texts. Both propositions would run against common sense. Ideas of space are only themes, among others, that can enter into literature. Whether the space of the actual world is absolute or relative, vortexical or solid, infinite or finite, flat or spherical, contrasted to chaos or not, a form of perception or a form of things, a container of things or their essence, a perceptible receptacle or a receptacle of perceptions, a mode of God's being or of His absence, are all potential themes: ideas that might be inscribed, in a vast number of ways, within the text. Anything can become a theme. The themes that characters discuss, that narrators introduce, or that patterns of imagery establish are distinct from the question of how readers experience. How space is experienced in literature and how it is recalled in the memory of that experience are different problems from the ideas of space that may (or may not) be inscribed within particular texts. Even if an idea of space, transformed into a theme, coincides with the experience of space—as it might on the level of world—it should still be possible to distinguish between the idea of space and the spatiality of the text. For this reason the argument here does not require a seventh mode of spatiality.

An analysis of a short literary text will indicate the interaction of multiple spatiality. All six modes of spatiality need not all be copresent equally or equally significant. To make *that* case would require a particularly freewheeling interpretive argument. Consider the first two paragraphs of Conrad's "The Secret Sharer":

> On my right hand there were lines of fishing-stakes resembling a mysterious system of half-submerged bamboo fences, incomprehensible in its division of the domain of tropical fishes, and crazy of aspect as if abandoned for ever by some nomad tribe of fishermen now gone to the other end of the ocean; for there was no sign of human habitation as far as the eye could reach. To the left a group of barren islets, suggesting ruins of stone walls, towers, and blockhouses, had its foundations set in a blue sea that itself looked solid, so still and stable did it lie below my feet; even the track of light from the westering sun shone smoothly, without that animated glitter which tells of an imperceptible ripple. And when I turned my head to take a parting glance at the tug which had just left us anchored outside the bar, I saw the straight line of the flat shore joined to the stable sea, edge to edge, with a perfect and unmarked closeness, in one levelled floor half brown, half blue under the enormous dome of the sky. Corresponding in their insignificance to the islets of the sea, two small clumps of trees, one on each side of the only fault in the impeccable joint, marked the mouth of the river Meinam we had just left on the first preparatory stage of our homeward journey; and, far back on the inland level, a larger and loftier mass, the grove surrounding the great Paknam pagoda, was the only thing on which the eye could rest from the vain task of exploring the monotonous sweep of the horizon. Here and there gleams as of a few scattered pieces of silver marked the windings of the great river; and on the nearest of them, just within the bar, the tug steaming right into the land became lost to my sight, hull and funnel and masts, as though the impassive earth had swallowed her up without an effort, without a tremor. My eye followed the light cloud of her smoke, now here, now there, above the plain, according to the devious curves of the stream, but always fainter and farther away, till I lost it at last behind the mitre-shaped hill of the great pagoda. And then I was alone with my ship, anchored at the head of the Gulf of Siam.
>
> She floated at the starting-point of a long journey, very still in an immense stillness, the shadows of her spars flung far to the eastward by the setting sun. At that moment I was alone on her decks. There was not a sound in her—and around us nothing moved, nothing lived, not a canoe on the water, not a bird in the air, not a cloud in the sky. In this breathless pause at the thresh-

> old of a long passage we seemed to be measuring our fitness for a long and arduous enterprise, the appointed task of both our existences to be carried out, far from all human eyes, with only sky and sea for spectators and for judges.

In the first place, the deictics of this passage—the pointing indications of direction and spatial relationship—are prominent. There are a large number of them by any count. They create the impression of the perceiving character's distance from, and relationship to, a number of spatially distributed positions. The narrator remembers looking to his right, to his left, and to his front and having perceived a number of things in relation to himself. He (or "it") even points to relational positions in the distance (the tug sails "right into" the land, becomes lost to sight beneath the level of the horizon, and the smoke from its engines is "now here, now there, above the plain") so that it appears that the use of simple deictics in this passage is quite complex. Still, they do not in themselves entirely create the sense of topographical place.

A reader would not immediately know whether the narrator remembers facing north or south (though it may well seem that he is likely to be facing north since the "westering sun" occurs in a sentence introduced by the deictic "to my left" though it does so only after a semicolon has divided the sentence: so the direction in which he had been facing at the time the action is remembered to have taken place is not altogether explicit), but he would know that the narrator remembers seeing a number of things, at varying distances, on his left, right, and in front. The deictics come together only in the final phrase when the reader learns where the narrator had been—at "the head of the Gulf of Siam"—and then, but only then, the reader can know that he had been facing north. This is the opposite of what normally takes place in ordinary speech: one usually hears deictics within an already established context ("Look up!" "Go left!" or "Turn behind you!" would be, for example, used within a context which both speaker and hearer must already understand and agree upon). No such requirement governs the use of deictics in literature. As in the passage from Conrad, deictics may very well function to create a sense of place, not to reflect their dependence upon it. Conrad's narrator remembers perceiving, and is precise about how and to what extent he did perceive, before the reader can have a sense of the place. One often interprets deictics, as in this passage, in a radically decontextualized manner: they point toward but they do not place. Deictics in literary texts do not seem to be equivalent to the designation of place. They usually are (what they seldom are in ordinary speech) aspects of characterization.

In the second place, once one has read to the end of the first paragraph of "The Secret Sharer," the sense of local topography has become very strong. Not only is it the head of the Gulf of Siam (an actual place, unlike many textual places, which a reader could check in an atlas—though it would have to be an out-of-date atlas since that actual place is now known as the Gulf of Thailand), but it is a place with definite characteristics. It is divided between land, water, and sky. The sky is described as an "enormous dome" under which the sea and land meet. The place possesses positive characteristics only insofar as the narrator perceives it: it is entirely focused by his recollection of perceptions, and it serves, reciprocally, to characterize him. Furthermore, it is a place divided and subdivided in many ways. The narrator remembers it as having been divided and readers probably experience it in terms of dividing lines, boundaries, and thresholds. On the narrator's right hand there are "lines of fishing-stakes" that resemble fences and are both incomprehensible and "crazy" (in either the shipbuilding or the ceramic sense but surely not in its usual clinical sense). The flat shore joins the sea "edge to edge" in what also appears to be "an impeccable joint." A number of objects in the narrator's field of perception are said to be "marked" by other things (gleams of water, for example, mark the windings of the river). In the second paragraph there is a striking spatial image (one that is typically Conradian) in which the shadows of the ship's spars are flung upon the still sea by the "westering" sun. The image invokes the contrast of dark shapes upon a lighter blue, the contrast between sky and sea, between east (where the spars must point) and west (where the sun lies), between shadow and substance, the image of the ship and the actual ship.

The proliferation of edges and boundaries is greater than one might suppose at a first reading: many of the boundaries are hidden within the descriptive imagery; for example, there is the nomadic tribe of fishermen, who did not exist but who might have traveled to the "other end of the ocean." Furthermore, the ship itself and the narrator-character (who must be a captain since the reader learns that the ship is "his") stand on the "threshold" of a long passage, at the "starting-point" of a long journey, which will be a "task" that will be judged "far from all human eyes." Hence there seems to be a boundary between where the ship presently rides and where it will go next and, in between these two points, the area of the "task," which will be "far from all human eyes." Finally, the sense of topographical space, of local place, that the narrator creates is both specific (a ship at the head of the Gulf of Siam) and intricate: it is a place of many boundaries and divisions, some obvious, some hidden. A place characterized by divisions and boundaries is also a place with many possible coordinates. It is a navigational space.

In the third place, readers do normally recall their reading of Conrad's fiction in terms of a world. The worlds of *Lord Jim*, "The Secret Sharer," *The Nigger of the "Narcissus"* or any other of his seafaring narratives are constituted by descriptions of the sea, of weather, of ships, of problems in navigation and accounts of men in these situations who act against a background of moral discipline. There are many aspects to these worlds and they are not constricted to the sense of local place, though this is normally, as in "The Secret Sharer," exceptionally strong. Scholars respond to Conrad's evocation of worldhood by exploring the sociology of seafaring in the nineteenth century, by discovering the "real" ships behind Conrad's fictional ones (much as other scholars seek the "real" people behind Shakespeare's characters), by establishing the professional codes that ruled men at sea, and (all in all) by seeing in Conrad's writing a definite world and by seeing in that world the actual world of the past century. It is impossible to say whether this is a good or a bad undertaking—a proper concern of literary scholarship or a professional will-o'-the-wisp—but it is certainly possible to cite these preoccupations to suggest that Conrad's readers do normally respond to his fiction by postulating worlds.

The world adumbrated in the first two paragraphs of "The Secret Sharer" is larger than the topographical space that is explicitly indicated, though it is clearly suggested in this local account. It is a world in which directions can be established and in which these cognitive lines can be followed (that is, navigated) across boundaries to destinations. It is a world in which things are far from or close to each other and the distance between them can be crossed. It is also a world divided between comprehensible and incomprehensible systems, between rational and irrational, and one in which actions (usually the crossing of boundaries by rational navigation) can be, and normally will be, judged. They will be judged even when there are no human eyes to make the judgment. One must conclude that the larger world of navigational space is also one of professional ethics (a sense of duty, say) in which the relevant ethical codes may be internalized. Every character in this world will be his own judge and, if he will not be, then there will be, as Lord Jim so notably discovers, a profession to judge him for himself. This world of divided and subdivided navigational space is also a world that contains ethical (or professional) boundaries. It is a world constituted by the axiom of boundaries.

In the fourth place, it might seem that the concept of spatial form would be inapplicable to the analysis of the two initial paragraphs of

"The Secret Sharer." It is, after all, an account of a place that is not evidently discontinuous. Still, one must remember the arguments of critics such as Mitchell who believe that spatial form is, to some degree, always a consideration. One may note, for instance, that the careful unfolding of discrete perceptions—on my right, on my left, in front of me, there, over there, above, under, and so forth—undercuts the impression that it claims to create. The painstaking development of perceptions, finally to create a sense of place, is unlike the moment of experience that the captain must have had and which he methodically recalls. In that moment of experience (if the reader can imagine it), the captain must have perceived the place in a single, if complex, moment of perception. Hence the passage turns upon its head the order of experience and requires its readers to experience one thing (the wholeness of place) in terms of its opposite (a series of perceptual fragments). To have some sense of the experience that the captain recalls having had, one would have to reread the passage to hold all those discrete perceptions together in a single grasp. One would have to reestablish the normal order of experience that begins with a sense of knowing where one is, of knowing where "here" is, and of running distinct perceptions together holistically. There is, at least in terms of rereading, a strong sense of spatial form. The unfolding series of fragmentary perceptions can be reread synchronically as spatially distributed perceptions that must have been, and still can be, experienced within a moment's comprehension.

In the fifth place, there is a particular spatial form that emerges distinctly from the passage. Everywhere, the figure of the edge stands out: it pervades and divides the passage, cuts it into pieces and unites it. To be sure, one could also claim that there is a spatial figure of enclosure in the passage. There are smaller places enclosed within larger ones, insides opposed to outsides (the homeward voyage is projected as a series of enclosures, of stages, in which each stage is an inside that must be crossed to reach the outside that is the boundary of the next stage), but these enclosures are made possible by the logically prior edges. The navigational space of Conrad's narrative is filled with, even crowded by, the presence of lines and divisions that, like fences, separate one local place from another, all the insides from the outsides. Topographically spatial units lie edge to edge and are marked by lines, not always straight, that distinguish them. Furthermore, there are numerous symbolic edges. There is an edge between day and night and, significantly, between stillness and noise, the still quiet of the inside of the present moment and the unstill unquiet of the outside world and the outward voyage. Even the homeward journey is described by the image of a threshold which is a starting point to be crossed that divides an inside stage from an outside stage. (Only a few paragraphs after this introductory passage the captain recalls the journey as a series of phases, "my mind picturing to myself the coming passage through the Malay Archipelago, down the Indian Ocean, and up the Atlantic. All its phases were familiar enough to me, every characteristic, all the alternatives.") It does seem possible to read this short passage and to discover spatial forms, even one dominant spatial figure.

In the sixth place, if one can grant the third sense of space—a world that is built up from the microsemiotic plane—then there should be little difficulty in seeing the possibility of "stereographic space." The world is always present in the place. Beyond the edge of the threshold, the larger world, with its tasks, its professional codes, its impersonal judgments, looms to provide challenges, to offer rewards and punishments, the opportunities for success or failure. The world invades the place, crossing the edges of enclosure in the reverse direction from that of the captain's perceptions, traveling backward along the line of the journey. Thus the captain's awareness of stillness is broken (it is always already broken from the moment his account begins) by his professional concerns, his worries, his apprehensions both about his upcoming voyage and about his "appointed" tasks. His observation that "I was left alone with my ship" is far from neutral: he has been left with the loneliness of command.

The invasion of place by world (focused here, as so often in Conrad's fiction, upon the mental loneliness, the psychological edginess, of the professional seaman) makes "horizon" the most important manifestation of the figure of edge. The world is not only just beyond the horizon (the "monotonous sweep" of which is always deceptive), but it is already present in the local place. The world, as one knows from reading other of Conrad's narratives, is always a world of story. Even in this narrative, there are invasive stories that unsettle the captain's awareness of his place. Later Leggatt tells his version of a story about edges (physical, existential, professional) that took place elsewhere, beyond the immediate horizon, and that Conrad plays against a different version of the same story that the skipper of the *Sephora* tells. As much as anything, Conrad's narrative concerns the way the captain reads these two narrative versions of the same story and then chooses between them on the basis of which seems more consistent, more satisfactorily coheres, with the world as he understands it.

The world's invasion of place marks a characteristic of all of Conrad's narratives. His fictional worlds are rich worlds of stories. Every character brings from the larger world beyond the horizon stories to tell. Conrad's fiction, to borrow a phrase that Todorov uses to describe *The Thou-*

sand and One Nights, is a world of narrative men.[28] Place is always charged by the vast world of stories. For example, in *Heart of Darkness*, Conrad not only retells the story that Marlow told the group of friends gathered on the *Nellie* but he has Marlow introduce *his* narrative by alluding to the many other narratives that he might tell or that might have been told. *Lord Jim* is a narrative that not only includes many other narratives, told by several characters but incorporated into Marlow's own, but it is also an investigation, a search after truth, conducted by means of narrative. Its narrative premise is that the world contains narratives, stories to be told, and if one listens to a sufficient number of them, then one ought to be able to tell a correct version. This view of the possibilities of narrative (a view that the world is constituted by its stories) runs through all of Conrad's writing.[29] Even in his autobiographical writing, Conrad is insistent that the world is full of stories. There are more stories than have been told, or at least remembered in written narrative. It is the potential of telling the world's stories that makes the world valuable, even perhaps comprehensible. In *The Mirror of the Sea*, Conrad refers (in words not unlike Marlow's) to the Mediterranean as "that old sea of magicians, slave-dealers, exiles, and warriors, the sea of legends and terrors, where the mariners of remote antiquity used to hear the restless shade of an old wanderer weep aloud in the dark."[30] He writes in *Notes on Life and Letters* that his art was "this snatching of vanishing phases of turbulence, disguised in fair words, out of the native obscurity into a light where the struggling forms may be seen, seized upon."[31] Similarly, he remarks in the Preface to *The Nigger of the "Narcissus"* that his narrative was a "rescued fragment" that had been "snatched from the remorseless rush of time."[32] The enveloping world of stories fills place, awareness of place, and the minds of those who perceive place. Always, before the particular perception of a place begins, and already, before it can be expressed in narrative, the possibility of story exists and fills the world. Thus Barthes's concept of "stereographic space," which is essentially intertextuality, or the discursive space of texts (that is, a space of inscriptions, of multiple writing), accords with Conrad's own conception of narrative space.

Textual space proves to be overdetermined, and conclusions about it, as Gabriel Zoran observes, diffuse. There could be other ways (including Zoran's own tripartite classification) to mark the modes of textual spatiality. One reason for this, as Zoran argues, is that "the spatial dimension of the text has no autonomous existence." There is nothing in the text corresponding to extratextual space to which one can point with anything like the assurance with which one points to time. Indeed, as Zoran writes, following Kant's argument, space is "unique in that here the transformation from an object to a system of signs involves also a transformation from a spatial arrangement to a temporal one."[33] To be understood, spatial arrangements (which in the extratextual world might be perceived synchronically) must be given a temporal succession. Thus the first paragraph of "The Secret Sharer" presents the numerous spatial details, which perceived together function to build a precise topographical place (a definite, if intricate, spatial unit), both under the form of text sequence and of the elapsed time of the narrator's remembering. This difficulty in talking about textual space reflects an ineradicable epistemological problem, but it also makes plain the vast difference between the exterior semiotic features of a text and the interiority of its reading. The experience of space in reading, like the even more complex experience of worldhood, cannot be given an adequate account merely on the basis of quantifiable deictic and descriptive passages. The aspects of a text that possess spatial import can be identified, enumcrated, and correlated, but this process does not explain how space is experienced. The interior spatiality of a text may be made possible, even prestructured, by a range of diverse signifying practices, but it cannot be reduced to them. The difference between the objective aspects of a text and the experiences that they make possible corresponds to the difference between the constant features of a game (rules, board, pieces) and the interior absorption that these generate. Ajax and Achilles, absorbed in the play of backgammon, are entrapped by the experience, not by Palamedes' board and counters that have made it possible.

It is as reading experience that literary texts most resemble games. The capacity to become absorbed within the text and the capacity to reconstruct, on the basis of its semiotic system, not only space but time, events, agents, and actions, are the paracursive conditions of reading. A literary text may be called a game with respect to the ways in which it is read. The axioms (or pseudo-axioms) of literary texts are effective in making possible, and in directing, the experience of a world. One can suppose that Spenser might have written *The Faerie Queene* without the axioms of plasticity and deformation and that Conrad might have written "The Secret Sharer" without recourse either to the axiom of boundaries or to the incremental use of deictics. Like all conventions, such strategies are flexible and open to modification. Once in place, however, they function exigently to direct the reading experience. Such text-specific assumptions, once accepted in reading, exert a constructive force. Their axiomaticity, if any, constitutes the text's interiority.

The phenomenology of reading is gamelike in that the reader, like a player, is "run away" with, in Huizinga's phrase, or "caught up" in the narrative. Kendall Walton puts this idea precisely: literary texts are games of make-believe in which the reader becomes a participant, at least insofar as he is present as an observer.[34] The duration of reading corresponds to the duration of play and, for however long it lasts, the make-believe, made possible by the text, is experienced as real. Pavel provides this scholium to Walton's account: "Now when a group of children play with mud, they simultaneously touch globs of mud—in the really real world—*and* offer one another tasty pies in the world of make-believe, which is real within the game. Running away from tree stumps in the real world becomes, for the same children, a flight from dangerous bears in the world of make-believe."[35] Similarly, extending Walton's account, it is possible to argue that the semiotic features of the text, such as deictics and descriptive phrases, are taken, in reading, as props for a more or less complex game of make-believe and, for the duration of this game, they are accepted as real. Deictics are real enough, or sufficiently real, to provoke a response on the reader's part. The response is one in which semiotic features, such as deictics, are transformed into the experience of space—direction, distance, size, volume, and coexistence—and ultimately, in their complex totality, into the experience of a world bearing some (minimal) degree of completeness and self-enclosure.

III

> The blowfly on its bed of offal is but a variation of the rainbow. Common forms are continually breaking into brilliant shapes. If we will explore them.
>
> —Patrick White, *Voss*

Although semioticians normally approach the topic of possible worlds as a problem in the analysis of propositions and in the logic of propositional modes, phenomenologists discuss textual, or fictional, worlds as a dimension of human experience. Something happens to the propositions that make up a text when the text is read and experienced. This process of transformation cannot be adequately explained simply in terms of the meanings of words, the syntax that arranges them, or their normal use values (their pragmatics) in ordinary speech. Characters who from a merely semiotic perspective are fictional entities, like the so-called worlds they inhabit, become quite real, or real enough to be taken as actual, and their actions are perceived, felt, and judged in strong, if perhaps odd, ways. From the one perspective characters are traits, diffused semes, gathered together by the superaddition of a name; from the other, they are "open" constructs, capable of provoking significant responses, including the reader's fascination and continuing concern.[36] The boundary between these two perspectives is imagination.

On one hand, one may analyze the kinds of "pnaws" that are conceivable and their relation to the actual world. This is largely a question of thinking through the varieties of propositions about conceivable worlds and ordering them in maximally significant paradigms. Saul Kripke, for example, has mapped the set of possible worlds, K, in their relationships, R, to the actual world, G. On this basis it would be methodically straightforward to place any conceivable pnaw into the map such that its conceptual difference from G would be mapped as spatial distance.[37] In any such map there will be a basic distinction between accessible and inaccessible worlds; that is, when the conceptual difference is too great, that distance will be uncrossable. "We have," Pavel writes, "access to possible alternatives but are cut off from impossible worlds."[38] Further, scholars can devise typologies of possible worlds. Pnaws are of very different kinds (some differing from the actual world on the basis of one or more extrinsic traits, others on the basis of axiological variation and so forth) and one important way to deal with them is to classify them.[39] On the other hand, one may observe that fictional worlds are normally impossible, that their accessibility from the actual world is either nonexistent or extremely tenuous, and that in thinking about them peculiar problems arise.

A fictional world raises several problems that a merely possible variant of the actual world does not. Two problems that assert themselves in every literary text, insofar as it is experienced as a world, are, first, the minimal size of a world and, second, the amount of coherence it requires. One's usual intuition about literary texts is that the worlds they postulate are incomplete, fragmentary, and, in many important respects, empty. Space, which is "realistic" in Conrad's fiction but has a puzzling plasticity in Spenser's, may well be absent in a given fictional world or, if not entirely absent, barely perceptible, reduced to a minimal use of necessary deictics. Furthermore, texts postulate worlds that are, by actual-world criteria at least, noncoherent. A reader must somehow "be" within them and accept their constitutive conventions as axioms.

On the first problem, Pavel comments that one cannot make the "dimensions of the text depend on those of the world about which it speaks." Short texts, incorporating few textual details, may be experienced as vast, but other texts, packed with the giganticism of naturalistic detail, may be experienced as relatively truncated, narrow, and spatially cramped. The fictional world of a narrative by Borges, Pavel writes, "may exceed in size the worlds of *Remembrance of Things Past*." Quantity of detail does not bear a direct correlation to the experiential size of a fictional world. Indeed, sheer detail may work to limit the imagination and to cause an experiential blockage. The "opacity to inference," in Pavel's phrase, which readers may encounter in imagining fictional worlds, and which keeps these worlds from "expanding indefinitely along irrelevant lines," would not seem to constitute a property of merely possible variants upon the actual world.[40] In the latter case, one would assume that a world differing from the actual world in only a single detail (in possessing a blue Notre Dame de Paris, say, or talking donkeys) would contain all of the actual world's indefinitely great detail. Fictional worlds are largely empty (as are, of course, fictional characters, who often possess no physical traits at all[41]), but they can be experienced as vast, immeasurable, and open.

The comparative emptiness of fictional worlds makes inevitable the problem of coherence. If very little is given, then the interrelationship between details must seem equivalently empty. Things hang together in fictional worlds but not usually in terms of laws or explanatory models. And as the consideration of texts such as Spenser's *Faerie Queene* makes clear, they often hang together despite evident departures from any of the explanatory models available for determining the coherence of the actual world. Nonetheless, they are *experienced* as coherent. Maitre argues that a fictional world is "seen as a totality, a coherent whole: it satisfies certain *coherence* criteria, as does the actual world, and in our attempts to understand it we employ certain plausibility criteria."[42] This seems like a perfectly adequate account of what happens in reading literary texts, but it does not follow that either the plausibility criteria or the consequent coherence are actual-world dependent.

Worldhood results from surprisingly little. It is a property of imaginative experience and not of the texts that underlie this experience. Imagination posits "non-actual states of affairs, it enables us to consider what alternative states of affairs *could* be the case."[43] Texts can be thought of, in Walton's terms, as props, or even as necessary conditions; they are not, however, sufficient conditions for the experience of worldhood. For that, the reader must bring to bear the resources of the mind's eye: a fund of presuppositional knowledge, a capacity to suppose connections and causes, the skills required to draw inferences, and, above all, the imaginative power to project lines of development. Consider the following passage from Pynchon's *Gravity's Rainbow* in which Slothrop, the centrally focalized narrative agent (one hesitates to say hero) in the novel, is being brought to the White Visitation, a collection of parapsychologists and ideational eccentrics who conduct a kind of intelligence activity. The White Visitation is located in an old house, a "folly," somewhere along the edges of London: "Overhead, on the molded plaster ceiling, Methodist versions of Christ's kingdom swarm: lions cuddle with lambs, fruit spills lushly and without pause into the arms and about the feet of gentlemen and ladies, swains and milkmaids. No one's expression is quite right." The passage then goes on to describe the "Whig eccentricity" that had led to the construction of this folly. The rooms are oddly shaped, "triangular, spherical, walled up into mazes." Portraits, frescoes, floor mosaics everywhere present different versions of "Homo Monstrusus."

The interior of the folly is a maze of archways, grottoes, walls, those oddly shaped rooms, and balconies that "give out at unlikely places, overhung with gargoyles whose fangs have fetched not a few newcomers nasty cuts on the head." Then as Slothrop approaches the house, the description continues:

> Topiary trees line the drive for a distance before giving way to larch and elm: ducks, bottles, snails, angels, and steeplechase riders they dwindle down the metaled road into their fallow silence, into the shadows under the tunnel of sighing trees. The sentry, a dark figure in white webbing, stands port-arms in your masked headlamps, and you must halt for him. The dogs, engineered and lethal, are watching you from the woods. Presently, as evening comes on, a few bitter flakes of snow begin to fall.[44]

Pynchon's camera-eye movement from outside to inside, from detail to detail, contributes to the intricacy of the description, but it is not simply a question of descriptive conventions. The house, located within the general fictional world of the novel (flakes of snow, larch and elm trees, London, World War II), projects further worlds. It does this from the basis of fragmentary detail. The overhead plaster ceiling on which swarms a Methodist allegory, or the frescoes and mosaics on which appear humanoid monsters, or even the labyrinthine interior topography of the house, are all constituted by a minimal use of textual details. The overall structure of the house is not given, no blueprint is available, the materials out of which it has been constructed are not indicated: the house, taken as a number of signs, a definite process of signification, is mostly empty. Nevertheless, the few signs for which the reading mind might imagine signifieds are both intricate and diverse. In a sense they are prolific, or, at least, they interrelate prolifically. They point toward several imaginable worlds, or toward notional areas (Methodist allegory, neoclassical grotesquerie) that possess a graspable worldhood.

Texts are experienced as worlds only when narratees, as readers or as hearers, are brought within the text and experience its sign system from within and accept its conventions as having the force of axioms. Considering the immense density of physical detail alone in the actual world (leaving aside the psychological detail implicit in the human subjectivities who inhabit the world) and the complexity of models required to explain it, the sheer minimalness of details necessary to constitute fictional worldhood seems astounding. From what is demonstrably little, much (in many successive variations) can be constructed. The White Visitation occupies a house that immeasurably exceeds the minimal textual details that serve as its props.

In his *Actual Minds, Possible Worlds*, the psychologist Jerome Bruner investigates the psychological bases for the human capacity to imagine worlds or, in general, fictional entities. Bruner argues that this capacity is so fundamental as to be considered innate: experiments have shown that even extremely young children seem able to attribute both causation and intention to actions. There may be such things as random thoughts, but no one thinks the world randomly. What happens in fiction, according to Bruner, is that the mind is set into action along purely natural (for human beings) lines. In telling a story, he writes, "one has the selection restriction of representing a referent in the eye of the protagonist-beholder, with a perspective that fits the subjective landscape on which the story is being unfolded, and yet with due regard for the action that is going on."[45] The phrase *subjective landscape* names the minimal spatiality that the mind can imagine for any action. It also, as Bruner uses the term, suggests the peculiar kind of self-enclosure that such imagined landscapes possess. Events happen, objects appear, and characters act in ways that are distinctive and text-specific, but once that is recognized, any number of additional objects and events can be made to "fit," to cohere within the whole.

Bruner goes on to discuss what he calls *constitutiveness* or the "capacity of language to create and stipulate realities of its own." Constitutiveness, he writes, "gives an externality and an apparent ontological status to the concepts words embody: for example, the law, gross national product, antimatter, The Renaissance. It is what makes us construct proscenia in our theater and still be tempted to stone the villain."[46] From within, the worlds of fictional texts are experienced as having this constitutiveness: ontological status is accorded, freely and (perhaps) naturally, to the signifieds brought forward to the mind's eye by the textual sign system.

The minimalness necessary to constitute worldhood might be compared to a primitive theater (which is more or less Bruner's own metaphor) in which not only the inadequacy of the props, whether actors or setting, is evident, but the conventions are unmistakably bare. A puppet show is "realistically" primitive, but it possesses the power to captivate, to entrap, an audience. The audience need not be composed merely of gullible children (a statement that an adult reader can test merely by watching a puppet show). Sophistication in dealing with literary texts does not necessarily prevent readers or viewers from being caught up in the illusion of primitive textual forms.

Cervantes's Knight, whose sophistication pervasively counterbalances his gullibility, exemplifies this point. In Chapter 26 of the Second Part, Don Quijote and Sancho encounter the galley slave, Ginés de Pasamonte, whom they had freed in the First Part. Disguised as maese Pedro, a puppetmaster, Ginés presents a show in which the story of Don Gaiferos and Melisendra is enacted by puppets. Interrupted from his absorption in a game of backgammon (*tablas*) by the Emperor Charlemagne, Don Gaiferos is commanded to free Melisendra from her captivity in the court of the Moorish king, Marsilio. Don Quijote attends the show, but he is, as always, an extremely critical narratee of the stories that others tell. He breaks into the narration that accompanies the action on the stage to fault it for its failures in verisimilitude. Nonetheless, as Don Gaiferos makes his escape with Melisendra, the Knight leaps up and assists him in his escape by attacking the Moorish soldiers who have given chase:

> Matching his actions to his words, he unsheathed his sword, and at a single bound planted himself in front of the show. Then with swift and unparalleled fury he began to rain blows upon the puppet-heathenry, knocking down some, beheading others, maiming one, and destroying another; and, among other thrusts, he delivered one down-stroke that would have sliced off Master Peter's head as if it had been made of marzipan, had he not ducked and crouched and made himself small.[47]

Despite the primitive nature of the puppet show, which he has severely criticized for its shortcomings, Don Quijote is swept away by the illusion (he is swallowed by it, or run away with) and reacts characteristically as he might in confronting any opportunity for heroism. The frame of the puppet show is like a dividing line between two worlds. Within, the puppet show encloses, José Ortega y Gasset writes, a "fantastic world, articulated by the genius of the impossible." Outside the frame there is a very ordinary world, inhabited by unsophisticated men, including a "fool, a knight from the neighborhood."[48] For the reader of *Don Quijote*, the text makes possible both worlds at once. It is not even clear that the one world contains the other. They are copresent and equally accessible.

The capacity to become absorbed in an illusion, or secondary reality, even though both its illusoriness and its conventions are apparent, must seem inseparable from literary experience. The paradox of the puppet show underscores not merely an audience's relation to a text or a performance but, as well, the fundamental property of all fictional worlds. An excess of textual detail, or "opacity to inference," may obscure the capacity to experience a fictional world, but a contrasting deficiency of detail does not prevent the imaginative reconstruction of a fictional world. The mind's capacity to enter into a fiction, fragmentarily and discontinuously presented, and experience it as a whole, entire and continuous, constitutes one of the important themes of Renaissance literature.[49]

The paradigmatic mode for this theme in Renaissance literature is probably the ekphrasis: a verbal description of a work of fine art which, normally in Renaissance literature at least, tells a story. (There is a full discussion of ekphrasis as a narrative strategy in Chapter 8.) An ekphrasis that occurs in *Don Quijote* makes the point clearly. On their way back to their village, the Knight and Sancho lodge in a room (of an inn that is truly an inn and not a castle) the walls of which are decorated by poorly painted, old cloth hangings upon which are depicted the stories of the rape of Helen and of Dido's love for Aeneas. The paradox of the puppet show functions in this scene as well. Don Quijote both comments upon the inadequacies of the depictions and enters into the experience that they make possible. He remarks that he could have prevented the two women's sorrows simply by killing Paris.[50] More elaborate ekphrases, such as those in *The Faerie Queene* or in Shakespeare's *Rape of Lucrece*, all make the same theoretical point.[51] The necessary conditions (or props) for fictional worldhood can be extremely, even astoundingly, few, but the interior experience of that worldhood can be vast indeed.

Borges's "Tlön, Uqbar, Orbis Tertius" casts a brilliant light on this paradox. Tlön is an entire world in the literal sense of being a planet; it is also a fictional world, the source of all stories told in the country of Uqbar (which is also, of course, a fictional world); finally, it is the product of a conspiracy. The hidden conspirators undertook to write an encyclopedia in order to create Tlön. The forty volumes of the First Encyclopedia of Tlön (twice the length, Borges notes pointedly, of the relevant edition of the *Britannica*) are to provide no more than the basis for a more complete version which will be written in one of the languages of the fictional planet/world. The immense scope of the project is staggering, though clearly not impossible.

In *Exemplars*, Rodney Needham links Borges's invention of an invented world to an actual instance of fake enthnography in the eighteenth century, George Psalmanazar's *An Historical and Geographical Description of Formosa* (1704). In the face of its total falsity and some direct criticism by people who knew better, Psalmanazar's work enjoyed great popularity, successive editions, and devoted readers. Needham concludes that it is relatively easy to fake an ethnography (which is a convention of contemporary science fiction, the outstanding instance of which is probably Le Guin's *Lefthand of Darkness*) since neither the quantity of detail nor the internal coherence of the work can serve as an adequate criterion of its plausibility. "Mere internal consistency is not enough," he writes, "and this is demonstrated moreover by professional responses to the structural interpretation of ethnographic data: if the analysis proves to be consistent, it is suspiciously neat; if inconsistencies remain, these are contradictions which invalidate the analysis."[52]

In other words, coherence tells the reader little or nothing since even "real" ethnography may have inconsistencies and any inconsistency may be rationalized. Later, in a discussion of Carlos Castaneda, Needham writes that coherence "is in itself no evidence either for or against authenticity; a clever writer of bogus ethnography will easily make his inventions coherent, and a cleverer one perhaps will contrive to make them just as inconsistent as may be plausible."[53] As a monument to cognitive ambition, the conspiratorial First Encyclopedia of Tlön is conceivable. If one considers the history of literature, which records such gigantic world-making ventures as *The Faerie Queene, The Remembrance of Things Past*, or *The Lord of the Rings*, the First Encyclopedia of Tlön is, at a second glance, not even particularly astounding.

The paradox inherent in Borges's short fiction is, simply, that the First Encyclopedia of Tlön does not exist. Tlön, in the richness of its Berkeleyian idealism and its extravagant materialities, arises upon the slender, unfolding spine of Borges's narrative. To be imagined, Tlön does not actually require the First Encyclopedia, only the bare adumbrations that Borges provides. Tlön is a labyrinth, Borges writes, but one that has been raised by men and is destined to be deciphered by men.[54] Labyrinths, it was argued in Chapter 4, depend upon situations in which necessary decisions must be made, not upon physical complexity; fictional worlds depend upon significant detail, not upon the quantity of textual detail. The point here is not that "Tlön, Uqbar, Orbis Tertius" is like a puppet show, or the wretched ekphrasis that captivates Don Quijote, but that it exemplifies an analogous claim upon the imagination. The story's potential for interior experiential complexity exceeds, by an immeasurable factor, its textual detail.

What seems to be required to experience a text as a fictional world is that there should be a minimal "landscape." If there are text-specific assumptions that can be understood, some indications of spatiality, a time sequence that can be grasped (not, needless to say, a chronology), a narrative agent, events that have some bearing on each other, and the presuppositions of coherence, then the story can be transformed into a world. Indeed, "story" (the *fabula* of Russian formalism), when it is analyzed into necessary components, such as events and existents (Chatman's terms), or colligatory motifs, or incidents and potential time sequences, can be seen to constitute the actual basis for fictional worldhood.

The paradox that complex fictional worlds arise on the basis of minimal semiotic foundations indicates no more than that the mind grasps a story (or fails to grasp it) in the first place and narrative elaboration (the "dilation" that Renaissance writers admired[55]) only continues down the lines of projection. The paradox, after all, is not that elaborated narratives do not project worlds but that only minimally developed narratives *can* project such worlds. The reader, given a graspable story, may be said to play within the worlds made possible or, in Martínez-Bonati's acute phrase, to play "contemplatively" within his imaginative projection.[56] (Or, as Kendall Walton puts it, he may be said to play at make-believe.) In any case, the reader's entry into (his play within) a fictional world, though made possible by the text, does not seem to be narrowed by the text's limitations. The potential interiority of a literary text, like that of a game, is inevitably, if strangely, boundless.

IV

> I think that every novel is unique and that it isn't unique. And this again relates fiction to game and play. I suspect that I haven't thought enough about this business of special emotions that go with games. It is a very sobering thought, actually. It breaks down the concept of mimesis even further. If it is true that there are special emotions that go with games, which there well may be, then I think that it must be good for us as human beings to expand our range of emotions through reading.
>
> —Robert Kroetsch, *Labyrinths of Voice*

When Don Quijote first erupted upon the horizon of European literature, bearing the dust of Spain on his body and the golden worlds of chivalric romance in his mind, a cataclysm convulsed literature. An episteme had been shattered and a new one (of ambiguous interiors, doubtful validations, and declarified certainties) called for its exemplars. They were not long in appearing: Gil Blas, Parson Adams, Mr. Pickwick, Prince Myshkin, Emma Bovary, Quentin Compson, Voss. A host of offspring appeared and, even now, themselves part of a dying episteme, continue sporadically to appear.[57] Their precursor, Don Quijote, the Knight himself, is endlessly instructive. A brief consideration of Don Quijote, as a fictional entity that has been characterized in certain ways, will help one to grasp the reasons for the misidentification of the two brothers in the parable that began this chapter.

In Chapter 72 of the Second Part of his adventures (published about ten years after the First Part), Don Quijote encounters Don Alvaro Tarfe and converses with him. Don Alvaro Tarfe is a character invented by another writer, not Cervantes, and he has stepped out of the pages of another book: in fact, he has arrived in the same inn as Don Quijote and Sancho from the pages of the False Sequel, a piratical continuation of the successful First Part. In effect, Cervantes has hired him (to use Flann O'Brien's term for an author's deliberate transworld borrowings) to meet Don Quijote in the true continuation and swear, after their conversation is over, that the Don Quijote with whom he has just enjoyed such a wise discussion was not, and could not be, the Don Quijote whom he had previously met in the False Sequel. It is enough, Robert Alter comments, to give the reader "ontological vertigo."[58]

The bizarre encounter in the inn illustrates an important point about fiction: something new may come along, smash common prejudices, offer a new mode of narrative, but be extremely difficult to get straight, indefinable at its core. (And as the two brothers in the parable have been thought occasionally to be panvestites, bunco artists who have stolen rules from long-dead fantasists, so even Don Quijote, perhaps the freshest of all fictional characters, has seemed to some only a carryover from the self-parody of the romances or a fugitive from sixteenth-century comedy.) Don Alvaro Tarfe pays homage to the elusiveness of Don Quijote (not merely the freshest, but the most imitated character in European literature), to the difficulties of getting straight his novel fusion of exterior and interior, of dust and golden flecks.

Don Quijote is, Michel Foucault observes, "himself like a sign, a long thin graphism, a letter that has just escaped from the open pages of a book. His whole being is nothing but language, text, printed pages, stories that have already been written down. He is made up of interwoven words; he is writing itself wandering through the world among the resemblances of things."[59] He was new, became a model (acquired his knights), was borrowed, brought European literature into its modern phases. Don Quijote evokes literary desire. He gave, and continues to give, as scholars such as Alter delight in demonstrating, the modern novel its narrative tasks. Composed out of stories, a microcosm of language, a text, a graphism, a sign himself, Don Quijote ought to have been precisely imitable, a narrative character splendidly reiterative. Yet he was not wholly so.

The irreducible uncertainty of literary history must be that paradigms are essentially playful, freely metamorphic, never hinged upon a didactic center. (At its best, some would say, literature is always unhinged.) Literary paradigms possess immense plasticity. They disregard visas and other credentials when they cross frontiers (like the Petrarchan sonnet or the picaresque novel), but that does not show that they are easily naturalized. They often seem to remain, like resident aliens, within their host culture, but always unassimilated. Furthermore, old paradigms inspire weary variants of themselves, ghosts that flicker too wanly for fear while new ones evoke doubles, phantasmal figures that, with folded wings, lurk within other figures, like distorted mirror images. Unlike the process of paradigm shifts that Thomas Kuhn has mapped for science, in which new paradigms arise out of a genuine need to resolve anomalies and radically displace what had previously been accepted, the paradigm shifts in literary studies usually seem more like the shifts of dancers within an intricate choreography: neither lost nor forgotten, old positions may be resumed.[60] Don Quijote, the most imitated characterization in modern European literature, was already in his conception the most unimitable; trapped, netted, enmeshed, reenmeshed innumerable times, but never captured.

Now what of the two brothers who grew tired of ordinary experience and set out to reinvent the world? Are there actually two? Where do they come from? Are they (as some think) panvestites who have passed off a dead gamewright's rules as their own fresh game? First, the two modes of reinventing the world are two distinct modes of fantasy, both of which are relatively common in contemporary literature. Both oppose themselves to canonical realism: to "dun-colored" fiction (in a mocking phrase that Patrick White has made famous), to the literature of the scruffy earth. Both modes of fantasy are easily confused with each other. Still, it may be possible to separate them. Whenever two ways of writing appear too similar to distinguish, or their common oppositions seem to bring them together into one enterprise, then it makes sense to examine them on the level of common literary elements. How such fundamental and recurring concepts as voice, plot, character, time, or space function can tell scholars where the uncertain boundaries are to be drawn.

The two brothers metaphorize not only two distinct modes of fantasy but two ways to create narrative spatiality. The secret of the first brother's reinvention of the world seems to be no more than to extend the common method of making text-specific assumptions (pseudo-axioms) that, like Spenser's assumption of multiplex interior spaces, such as the

Blatant Beast's oral cavity, make possible determinate spatial effects. The extended version of this method allows for the assumption of a single axiom, both nonexperiential and counterintuitive, from which a number of coherently interrelated consequences flow. Instances can be seen in Borges's assumption of Berkeleyan idealism in "Tlön, Uqbar, Orbis Tertius" or his assumption, in "The Garden of Forking Paths," of the proposition that an infinitely bifurcating time determines the possibilities of space. In one of the most remarkable novels that Borges ever wrote (to lift a witticism from Gore Vidal), Italo Calvino's *Invisible Cities*, Marco Polo creates for a weary Kubla Khan an atlas of fictional cities, each one of which is constructed upon the axiom that the spatial arrangements of a human city can follow from, or build upon, a single human quality in a total projection.[61] In a thin city everything must be thin, including aspiration, hope, and desire. In a city of signs not only do all buildings signify, but they do nothing other than signify. The empire of Kubla Khan, Brian McHale writes (borrowing a term from Foucault), is a *heterotopia*: "Radically discontinuous and inconsistent, it juxtaposes worlds of incompatible structure."[62] *Invisible Cities* magnifies the plural worldhood of the puppet show in *Don Quijote*, but it does not modify the principle of imaginative copresence.

The second brother's secret is very different. In his reinventions of the world, space is necessarily dual. In his fantasies, there is always the normal space of realism (in all its equivocal representations of extratextual space), but there is also something abrupt and deformative. The second brother creates the spatial effects of magic realism, a third kind of space in which the spatial effects of canonical realism and those of axiomatic fantasy are interwoven. The second brother might seem to have thrust a difficult task upon the imagination. Surely, as Ortega observes, reality "has such a violent temper that it does not tolerate the ideal even when reality itself is idealized."[63] The third space of magic realism must seethe with contradiction and the intractable hostilities of mutual rejection. Yet this does not seem to be the case.

One way to describe this third space is to borrow the phrase Lubomír Doležel employs to characterize the world of Kafka's fiction: in magic realism, space is hybrid (opposite and conflicting properties are copresent). Typically, the fictional world does beg comparison with an extratextual world more or less as Conrad's "The Secret Sharer" does (but as neither *The Faerie Queene* nor *Invisible Cities* does). It may even, very much in the manner of canonical realism, seem to offer a kind of translucent windowness through which the reader perceives reality. The secondary illusion of an extratextual space may be noted in magic realist narratives as diverse as *One Hundred Years of Solitude* or Salman Rushdie's *Midnight's Children*. An excellent example (because unusual and too little read) of this dual spatiality can be seen in Robert Kroetsch's careful evocation of an Alberta springtime in the opening passage of *What the Crow Said* and his painstaking account of rural life on the Canadian prairies.[64] The hybrid nature of Kroetsch's space, as in magic realism generally, becomes apparent in the natural way in which abnormal, experientially impossible, and empirically unverifiable events take place. It is as if they had always been there, and the possibility of their abnormality had been promised from the moment that the fictional world could be imagined. One might say that in the hybridness of space eruptions occur normally, or that abrupt folds crease the seemingly predictable (the illusively extratextual) surface.

The opening passage of *What the Crow Said* illustrates the principle of spatial folding. Kroetsch immediately establishes the common features of spring in Alberta: "The crocuses bloomed in spring as they had always bloomed, the buffalo beans cracked yellow, the violets and the buttercups and the shooting stars took their turn." Kroetsch then causes a magiclike fold to break this even surface. Vera Lang, asleep in a "swarm of wild flowers," is raped by a swarm of bees. Where the bee swarm comes from; why it chooses Vera as its queen; how her anatomy can conceive a child from such an impregnation; nor even how her cry, terrified and ecstatic, can reach the town more clearly than a locomotive whistle: these are not questions that are asked. In the neutral voice of the narrator, they are not even questions that could be asked. The text simply excludes them. The world of *What the Crow Said* is hybrid in much the same way that, according to Doležel, the world of Kafka's fiction is hybrid. It is as if there are two worlds (wholly distinct, following dissimilar laws) which interact, interpenetrate, and interwind, unpredictably but in a fully natural manner.

One consequence of this world interpenetration in Kafka is the creation of a number of bizarre creatures who owe their natures to both worlds at once. (One might see the bee swarm in Kroetsch's novel as a single hybrid creature in this way, human *and* apiarian, belonging to two distinct worlds, the possibilities of interpenetration always present, never explained. And one can also clearly distinguish between this kind of fantastic hybrid and the monstrous chimeras of axiomatic fantasy, such as the Blatant Beast, who belongs to one world only.) The fold occurs when the one world, evidently following its own axioms, erupts into the other world. At such moments, it seems as if two systems of possibility, two modalities of cause and effect, have enfolded each other. The consequence is not only a hybrid organism but also a hybrid time and space. Even the textual mode in magic realism is hybrid: one kind of writing writes over, and into, another. Consider this tentative hypothesis: magic realism is the name that one gives to the fictional space created by the dual inscription of incompatible geometries; it is also the name to be given to texts that doubly inscribe incompatible kinds of writing.[65]

In magic realism, world interpenetration takes place in a variety of ways. It would be completely feasible to compile an atlas, a kind of fictional geology, of folds. It is at least possible to suggest the range of world interpenetration by one distinction and two examples. On one hand, the hybrid constructions of magic realism arise, in some texts, as they do in the first chapter of *What the Crow Said*, when something different, even inconsistent, arrives. It comes from outside an already established world (crocuses and buffalo beans, say) and informs it temporarily. On the other hand, one world may lie hidden within another. Then the hybrid construction emerges from a secret already inscribed within, forming an occulted and latent aspect of the surface world. This is what commonly happens in the fiction of Gabriel García Márquez. The pattern may be seen (to take only one example) in his tale *Innocent Eréndira*. In that narrative the principle of hybrid construction manifests itself most clearly in the green blood that lies occulted, but always waiting to be revealed, within the veins of Eréndira's minotauric grandmother. In the depths of an always reconstructible labyrinth she lurks; within her, the always natural, yet neither seen nor foreseen, green blood (perhaps like the gems that wait occulted within the oranges that Ulysis and his father grow and smuggle). This pattern of the one world waiting secretly within the other seems too apparent to miss: the hybrid construction, then, is always already present.

The world interpenetration that distinguishes magic realism from both axiomatic fantasy and canonical realism suggests a model for textuality itself. The magicalness of magic realism lies in the way it makes explicit (that is, unfolds) what must always be present. The magic is simply the foregrounding of narrative's essential literariness. The world interpenetration, the dual worldness, the plural worldhood even, of magic realism is the total projection of a hybrid spatiality that is probably more difficult to suppress than to express. Canonical realism might be seen as a more difficult mode of literary production simply because it must run consistently against the grain. Realism's typical limpidity arises from the muscular suppression of narrative potential. The second brother in the parable has been successful, perhaps more so than the first brother, because he has discovered what literature does best.

Magic realism emblematizes the poststructuralist textual model. The plural worldhood that one encounters in certain texts, such as *One*

Hundred Years of Solitude, Midnight's Children, or *What the Crow Said*, makes visible, in a particularly striking manner, what Barthes calls "stereographic space." Stereographic space, which has been discussed as the ground of intertextuality, can be seen as the complex place of textual inscription. It is the mere presence of sign systems, the universe of textuality itself, that produces the "spatiality of space." The plural worldhood of magic realism reflects and exemplifies the textual theory of inscriptibility: the one world lies always already present, though hidden, within the other, just as one text lies latent within another text. (One way to reinvent a world is to inscribe its normal sign systems upon the inscriptions of another world or worlds.) It is the possibility of inscriptions being reinscribed upon others, or multiplexly upon each other, that, in Derrida's thinking, generates the human concept of space. In this view, there seems to be no single, freestanding, uncontaminated, pure text, only the weaves, the nets, the threads, and the labyrinths of textuality. Similarly, there seems to be no pure, single-formed space in literary texts. World interpenetration may be seen as the model, the metamorphic image, of writing. In texts that may be placed within the (instable) category of magic realism, the plural worlds, like distinct kinds of writing, like parabolic trajectories, always approach each other but never actually merge. (Their fusion occurs, if at all, only in the reading experience.) The fascination that surrounds magic realism springs from its emblematic congruence with the post-structuralist model of textuality. In important respects, it must seem the most fundamental mode of storytelling, neither recent nor ancient, but inevitably the present shape of fiction.

The analysis of spatiality in literary texts reveals that, leaving to one side the question of the extratextual spatial existence of the book as a physical object, space is a function of the reading experience. It is made possible by the textual sign system, as a number of necessary conditions or as an observable prestructuring of response, but it exists in reading's interiority only. The text's world takes shape, both complexly and variably, in the reading experience. The reader may be said to play, even to play a *game*, but it is evident that there are several notions of play involved. One may say, following Walton, that the reader plays a game of make-believe or that he plays, as Martínez-Bonati puts it, contemplatively (in the sense that he explores, and takes pleasure in the activity of cognitive exploration, associated with the imaginative reconstruction of a text's semiotic potential). In either case, the parallel between the interiority of reading and the interiority of playing a game (during which secondary, aesthetic, or ludic emotions are often said to be significant) is evident. The gamefulness of reading falls into two major categories:

on one hand, the text, very much like any board game, can be experienced, in its imaginative reconstruction, as pure self-enclosed interiority; on the other, it can be played like any field as a network of potentialities in which clues, echoes, and threads are picked up and followed. The latter sense of textual play corresponds, obviously enough, to the generalized concept of stereographic space and, in particular, to the Kristevean concept of intertextuality. In this intertextual space, the reader plays a game (still in the sense that Suits argues) because he makes the text respond to rules which he, in reading, imposes. The constitutive rules that shape the energies of play come from the direction of the reader, though they may be largely borrowed from an available interpretive model, giving (what is like) a secret structure to the reading experience. It is to intertextuality as play, or as a difficult form of interplay, that Chapter 6 turns.

CHAPTER 6

Interplay

narrative allusiveness

(il y en a tant et tant eu) —Roland Barthes, *S/Z*

THE OPPOSED VIEWS of human play that were, in Chapter 2, associated with Derrida and Bakhtin help to define the shifting problem of how texts relate to each other. Literary texts bear upon each other in many complex ways. How they do this, to what extent, under what conditions, the ways in which answers to these questions affect one's reading and understanding, have been among the most recurring of theoretical problems in recent years. If play is taken to describe an involuntary system of movement (whether of light or of signification), as it is in Derrida's textualism, then the playful relations between texts must be seen as possessing systematicality. A vast system, which one may call "literature" (or even "literarity"), pervaded by its own resonances, constituted by narcissistic echoes, precedes and determines specific textual expressions. A literary text, seen in these terms, is rather like a momentary configuration of waves, transient, intricate, and bearing the potentiality of oceanness in its fleeting shape: the ocean plays through its waves. If play is taken to describe a voluntary semiosis (of whatever kind of signifying system), as it is in Bakhtin's translinguistics, then the playful relations between texts must be seen as intentional. They will still presuppose a system, literary, linguistic, and cultural, but the systematicality between texts will be limited. A literary text, in these terms, is always a wholeness that incorporates difference. Its difference, between levels and kinds of signification, actually constitutes it. The relation between texts is playful, but it is a playfulness that emerges from human intention, purposeful and constructive. The waves still play, but they bear within them a conscious life.

The complex ways of bearing upon that correlate texts may be classified in different ways. It has become possible, with the help of a sharpened theoretical vocabulary, to distinguish between source, influence, quotation, citation, allusion, and intertextuality. The latter concept is the one that seems to cap the others: all aspects of literary "bearing upon" may be seen as instances of intertextuality if, as Jonathan Culler argues, "intertexuality is the general discursive space that makes a text intelligible."[1] This discursive space is filled by (or is the realm of) echoes, iterability, repetitions, reinscriptions, permutations, resonances: the locus of the reader's active mind. It is an involuntary, systematic free play of shapes, forms, and structures. Textual possibilities touch each other, recall each other, careen from each other into yet further forms, always in themselves recapitulations and echoes: they play like waves.

In the first chapter, it was claimed that games (paradigmatically, board games) exemplify a primitive intertextuality. Games recapitulate the structures of other games. Backgammon, for instance, might be seen as always resonating with the intensity of the game that Achilles and Ajax played once on the windy plains of Troy. Every chess game contains positions, partly resumed, imperfectly actualized, of the "Immortal Game." What games exemplify comparatively simply, literary texts manifest in extremely diverse ways. Within a mind that is reading, the intertextual space (a discursive space of citations, echoes, and allusions, not necessarily consciously articulated) is the condition of signification and intelligibility. One could no more read outside of such an involuntary system of free play and cross-signification than one could speak outside the vastness of a language. In Michael Riffaterre's words, intertextuality is a "modality of perception, the deciphering of the text by the reader in such a way that he identifies the structures to which the text owes its quality of work of art." Intertexual reading, Riffaterre continues, is either the "perception of similar comparabilities from text to text" or the assumptions that "such comparing must be done even if there is no intertext at hand."[2] Readers, one must admit, confront a number of hard cognitive tasks.

The concept of intertextuality, first formulated by Kristeva in 1969,[3] reflects the textual revolution in literary studies. This postulates (as Saussurian linguistics does in the logically prior question of language) a system for literature, a spacious conceptual field in which all literature is necessarily, if invisibly, related, and out of which (or back into which) particular textual manifestations slip. (One may say, of course, that they *play*, although that begs the question: intertexuality may be defined as, even grounded upon, a precise concept of play, but play, elusive and *labile*, cannot be grounded on intertextuality.) The concept of literature's systematicality marks a revolution in literary theory (though one that may be unaccepted, short-lived, or prove to be, like non-Euclidean geometries, of interest only to an intellectual elite) and, in being revolutionary, it has made possible perceptions that previously had been unavailable. One such perception is that of an intertext (a corpus with flexible boundaries that the reader brings to mind when he reads),[4] in terms of which invisible, though necessary, connections may be discerned. Their force must be felt. All the versions of intertextuality in narrative theory since Kristeva claim to define a dimension of cognitive self-consciousness with regard to reading and the discursive space in which it takes place. An accurate formulation (always a self-conscious act) makes explicit the diverse modes of "bearing upon" in which another text, a part of a text, a genre of texts, or a conceptual space filled by many texts can be discerned in the particular text being discussed. In this sense intertextuality is an analytic, isolating tool of considerable power. Furthermore, as such an analytic tool, intertextuality projects the possibility of discovering empirical relationships between actual texts, and it predicts, as Riffaterre's second formulation of reading claims, the discovery of intertexts even when these are obscured, hidden, inaccessible, or otherwise "not at hand." (Laurant Jenny considers the modes of representation according to which nonverbal texts, such as paintings or mosaics, can serve to inform written texts.[5] The concept of intertextuality subsumes the transpositionality of semiotic systems.) It is important to observe that this concept, for all of its useful analyticity, presupposes a textual system that constitutes itself as a condition of all literature, whether considered as individual texts or as reading. The system plays through texts, and though it may be discerned (in part, given sufficiently analytic formulations), it cannot be controlled. The constructive intentionality that Bakhtinian translinguistics ascribes to textual interplay must be an illusion.

The reader's task in discovering an absent intertext, always perplexing, can never be more difficult than in those cases when the orectic, sought-for text is inaccessible because it is nonexistent. The empty register of untold stories (that is, the never narrated, the textually nonexistent), whose actual absence can be perceived to exert a force within a text, provides a touchpoint for the investigation of textual bearing upon as play. If a text can be shown to hang upon, or to be constituted by (even in small part), an absence so utter that it is empty, filled not by resonances but by inferences, then its playfulness, either the way in which it *is* play or may be played in reading, may turn out to be extremely active. Clearly, this would not be the activity that Gadamer sees in the text or artwork. (For Gadamer, as the discussion in Chapter 2 indicated, the active to-and-fro playfulness of a text is self-contained, unconnected to the analogous to-and-fro activity of other texts, a fundamental aspect of the text's organic being.) It is, however, an activity that would cohere with Bakhtin's theory of dialogism that makes a place for the human mind inevitably struggling to draw inferences from the incomplete evidence of discourse in order to reconstruct the fuller contours of a hidden world. The question seems to be whether the concept of an intertextual system as the condition of reading and signification leaves room for the mind's active participation. Can a model of reading incorporate both Derridean notions of systematic, involuntary play *and* Bakhtinian notions of intentional, voluntary play?

I

> The original game state has a tendency to disappear, to be supplanted by qualitatively new, initially nonexistent forms of game interaction. For the agar, substitute the Protocosmos, and for the bacteria, the Protocivilizations, and you obtain a simplified view of the New Cosmogony.
>
> —Stanislaw Lem, *A Perfect Vacuum*

The problem of the untold in narrative may be described initially as a special case of allusiveness (it is, as well, an instance of the problem of implicitness in literary texts) rather than as intertextuality in the most general sense. There will be an allusion to something, or to the hint of something, but the prior text(s) either does not exist or is inaccessible. Nonetheless, its force will be experienced, its absence marked. Such are the paradoxical qualities of literary texts that a story does not have to be told or to be accessible for it to exercise a powerful force, both structural and signifying, within the narrative that alludes to it. (Consider the Ghost's narrative in *Hamlet*, 1.5.13–22, in which he first lists the probable effects of a story upon his narratee, then refuses to tell it, and finally tells another, quite different, story.) For the reader, an allusion to an untold story must work strangely. His difficulties in making sense of an unanchored allusion might be compared to those which Socrates demonstrates to be inherent in Ion's rhapsodic practice, even though Ion had never perceived them previously. In the *Ion*, Socrates, leading him through a swift series of gambits and snares, compels Ion to admit that his interpretations of Homer (for which he has won prizes and acclaim) must involve him in speaking about things he does not understand and in making judgments on aspects of the Homeric narrative that have been merely adumbrated. Similar pits open silently before any reader since a narrative must contain elements that are only suggested, implications of possible significance that have been left undeveloped, conceptual fields that lie beyond the horizon's edge. Most important, a narrative may allude to other possible (but untold) narratives. If Hermes, that tricky patron of literary exploration, occasionally grants hermeneutical blessings, he more often lays snares. Ion's dilemma (what to make of that which is unknown, perhaps unknowable, conceptually unpresent) is one such trap.

Allusiveness is a commonplace event in narrative. At any moment in reading, a distant space may glimmer uncertainly through a sudden fissure in the text's linearity: like undergraduates reading *Hamlet* and abruptly plunged by the Player King's narrative into the matter of Troy, the violent, archaic world of the *Aeneid* and *The Metamorphoses*, and then thrust back again into the distinct action of the play, enveloped in its chill irony, readers of narrative may experience the bewilderment of allusiveness. Such allusiveness may be classified in different ways. There are instances in which known works are cited. (A literary citation is often similar to the old metajoke about the monks who had heard each other's jokes so often that they had coded them numerically so that one monk had only to shout "fifteen" or "twenty-five" to stimulate laughter.) An allusion may be as elaborate as an embedded fragment, a piece of discourse that runs for some length and possesses a self-contained distinctiveness, or it may be as simple as a single word, a syllable, a splintered sound. Allusions may be made to archetypes, each of which is embodied in its cloak of known stories, or they may be to structure (the strictest sense of intertextuality) as well as to content. Allusions, however, granted their empirical variousness, are often to stories that have *not* been told elsewhere though they may be grasped intuitively as narratable. Something, perhaps a single motif, or two or three hanging together, a single character trait, the tiniest glimpse of a fictional world, will suggest the possibility of being told, a narratable (even if never narrated) story. At all these junctures one is, as a reader, caught up in the interplay of stories.

One version of the trap into which Ion steps so easily is the difficulty of making sense out of a narrative that contains allusions to stories that are not told, not retrievable as narratives, but are recognizably stories that could be, or might have been, narrated. *The Faerie Queene*, a narrative that is exceptionally rich in narrative allusiveness, offers a number of instances of unnarrated stories.[6] In Book IV, canto 4, Sirs Triamond and Cambell fall in with Sirs Blandamour and Paridell and the four, with their respective ladies, ride some way together, and as they ride, the narrator remarks that they spoke of "deeds of armes abrode, / And strange adventures, all the way they rode." Yet no such adventures are actually narrated. The passage is minimally allusive: the adventures remain hidden in the vastness of unactualized story. Nonetheless, there is a hint of something, a glimmer of narrative anachronism, a simple potentiality that, though unactualized, characterizes both the tellers and their uneasy journey together. One can recognize that they might have told stories and even, at least as readers of this kind of narrative, grasp what kinds of stories they might have told ("of courtesies and many a daring feat"). A less minimally allusive instance occurs at the end of the second canto of Book II when Sir Guyon tells the knights and ladies gathered in Medina's castle the story of the babe with bloody hands (that is, the story of Mordant, Amavia, and Acrasia) and the narrator describes Guyon's narrating act in this manner:

> Night was far spent, and now in Ocean deepe
> *Orion*, flying fast from hissing snake,
> His flaming head did hasten for to steepe,
> When of his pitteous tale he end did make. (46)

Guyon's story, too, is untold. But it is more significant, more narratively dense (as it were), since it does allude to a story the outline of which has been told and it does characterize the narrator (Sir Guyon) as a man of both art and feeling. As these examples from *The Faerie Queene* indicate, narrative (the told) can easily contain, both significantly and strikingly, the nonnarrated (the untold). The problem for the reader is how to recuperate this often minimal allusiveness. What sense of play does this transient relationship to the untold imply? Is the reader played by the system of textual citation or does he play, actively if uncertainly, from what he reads to what he cannot read?

The problem of intertextuality in general, repeatedly discussed and reformulated in current metacriticism and theory, divides into two radically opposed positions. A text's relation to that "sedimentation of prior texts"[7] which one calls intertextuality (or occasionally transtextuality) can be seen as either unconscious (the system plays) or as chosen (the reader and writer play). It is with this latter sense in mind that Linda Hutcheon collapses intertextuality into a "synonym" of parody, a "form of inter-art discourse."[8] The opposition might be imagined in terms of an untold story from the matter of Troy (perhaps the only important one remaining) that explores the mind of Aeneas as he carries his father, Anchises, from the firestorms of Troy. In one version (the repeatedly told one), he cheerfully follows the command of his mother, Venus, and begs Anchises to ride on his shoulders. In another (the untold), he feels harrowed by the thought of Creusa left to burn in the fallen city. In one version, Aeneas helps Anchises onto his back; in the other, Anchises, like a Kafkaesque father, all unrelenting power and ferocity, hurls himself upon his son's back and rides triumphantly to safety. Intertextuality appears in both these guises. First, the writer chooses the texts to which he makes allusion, skillfully adopts certain citations, and creates, as a matter of craft and cunning, an allusive field in which his own narrative plays. Second, the "sedimentation of prior texts" takes on a ferocious visage and emerges, inexorably and undesired, from the vast field of literature to play out its role on the back of the text. In the first version, the reader passively, even unconsciously, allows his mind to become the echo chamber of prior textualization, iterating and replicating the resonances of literature's total volume. In the second version, the reader acknowledges, or fails to acknowledge, the precise textual moves that the writer has made, adding to (no doubt) or substracting from the intertextual field that has been invoked. The latter postulates the conscious playfulness of those writers and readers who have something to create; the former, the free play of an involuntary system. The ineludable problem for the articulation of a theory of play in literature is whether one may have both Bakhtin and Derrida, free play and dialogism, in a single inclusive model.

If one begins narrative analysis at a comparatively simple level, inquiring about moves, techniques, conventions, and strategies, then allusiveness must seem, in the first place, to be a convention, like others, to be used with cunning and craft. An allusion to an untold story (such as the Ghost's in *Hamlet*) exploits, consciously, the distinction between story and discourse. It is, in narrative practice only, a knowing and calculated move. In the history of narrative there is one massively central instance of allusiveness to untold story. (It serves here as a fragment to invoke a comprehensive catalog.) In the eleventh book of the *Odyssey*, Odysseus meets the prophet Tiresias on the edge of the Underworld and Tiresias tells him that after reaching Ithaca he will undertake yet a further voyage in which he will encounter a people who do not know the sea, who eat their food without salt, and who are ignorant of ships and seafaring. Odysseus will recognize them, the prophet adds, because one of them will mistake the oar that Odysseus will carry over his shoulder for a scythe. This story, alluded to in the Homeric narrative, is not narrated. Yet even though it is untold, it is included within the told and powerfully affects it. Indeed, any commentary upon the whole of the

Odyssey that failed to discuss its function would be, to that extent, inadequate.

The force of the untold story of Odysseus's second voyage can be gathered from the subsequent attempts to tell it or to comment on it. In the twenty-sixth canto of the *Inferno*, Dante narrates this second voyage, sending Odysseus beyond Gibraltar on a hubristic exploration to damnation. Tasso alludes to the second voyage and Tennyson comments on its possibilities without telling it, though he clearly suggests that, if told, the narrative would incarnate heroic idealism. Of this continuing extrapolation from the possibilities of an untold story, George Steiner observes that Odysseus survives the stories that have been told about him to reappear in further narrative: "The mariner's ghost . . . would not stay put. It rose from damnation to assume countless shapes in Western art and literature. Most of these shapes—even those given it in our time by Joyce and Kazantzakis—are already implicit in the first Odysseus."[9] At this point one must note the complexities: Homer alludes to a story but does not narrate it (it has no existence within the Homeric narrative other than as an unanchored allusion), other writers do tell the story within *their* narratives, and these secondary narratives are comments on the original narrative in which the story remains, always, untold. These subsequent narratives, however many there are, fail to exhaust the story's potential. Its narrative possibilities continue unclosed. Thus the story of Odysseus's second voyage is a significant aspect of the *Odyssey*, but it is not present in the narrative. It is untold, though it demands commentary. And the commentary, which normally has been a telling of the story, can never be closed.

Considerations such as these are basic. A narrative actualizes certain aspects of a story (a story matrix, in effect). In so doing, it gives them an arrangement, a shape, a disposition. If one thinks of narrative as the actualization of possibilities (making definite specific potentialities within a given matrix), then one might say that every narrative is a crystallization. Narratives crystallize possibilities but continue to hint at story matrices which exist in logical antecedence and cannot be exhausted. (The technical, formal notion of story, once it is expressed as a matrix, begins to suggest an analogy with game: a limited system of rules, or necessary elements, the permutations of which are indefinite, virtually innumerable, practically endless.) It is one of the intriguing problems of literary theory that readers can recognize the matrix of a story, can even sense that parts of it are missing or have been transformed. A reader's sense of story involves a recognition of related possibilities: a number of colligatory motifs that could be, and perhaps have been, narratively crystallized. A simple comparison will indicate the balance of this relationship: narrative is to its story matrix as an itinerary is to a trip. An itinerary might be said to crystallize the possibilities of a trip (this way, not that way, via this place, not that, and so forth), but unactualized aspects of the trip may continue to haunt the traveler's imagination. Signs in an airport, distances to other spots indicated at different points along the itinerary, ads and other images of places one has missed, all combine to remind one of the other possibilities of the trip that have been left unactualized by the exigencies of an explicit itinerary. A traveler can recognize the trip, or the potential of the trip, as a number of colligatory motifs, through the particular disposition of his actual itinerary. Every experienced traveler has an intuition about what he might have done, where he might have gone, even though his itinerary has excluded those possibilities. The comparison between itinerary and narrative (or discourse) suggests that, even though narrative analysis has typically been concerned exclusively with modes of disposition (time, plot, characterization, voice, mood, texture, and structure), the presence of an untold story must inform even rigidly crystallized narratives. Untold story can function even more evidently in those playful, self-aware narratives that make the most of their relationship to their own story matrices.[10]

It should be apparent that all the tangled threads of the story/discourse distinction have led, almost exclusively, to the analysis of narrative: that is, to the side of device, convention, construction, disposition, and *agencement*. Seymour Chatman stands out among contemporary analysts of narrative in attempting to discover ways to approach story outside of, and independently of, narrative categories. Chatman points out that far more is involved in story than incidents underlying plot (events) since there are also existents, the possibilities for character and setting.[11] Jonathan Culler is probably closer to theoretical orthodoxy when he argues that "story" is merely a "heuristic fiction": something that is postulated from the evidence of a narrative to explain the particular arrangements, or disposition, of a text. Analysis of narrative requires one to "treat the discourse as a representation of events which are conceived of as independent of any particular narrative perspective or presentation and which are thought of as having the properties of real events."[12] One might say that, following Culler, "story" is only a back formation, a hypothetical postulate. It comes into existence much as one might postulate a plan to account for the cityscape of any modern urban grouping and to allow the analyst to refer to specific architectural usages as if they indicated strategic choices. David Lodge adopts a similar view when he limits the distinction to its bare formalist statement (*fabula* vs. *sjužet*) and, like Culler, he also insists on its status as a heuristic fiction. The *fabula*, he remarks, is something that we, as readers, *conceptualize*: "It is important to realise that the *fabula* is not the same as the source of a story . . . [it is] a hypothetical extrapolation from the *sjužet*."[13] Although the position that Culler and Lodge take seems orthodox, and even unexceptional, it may be possible to argue that *story* is meaningful in a positive way (as even those minimally allusive stories in Spenser indicate) and that a great deal can be said concerning its relationship to narrative.[14]

The reason that a great deal can be said about *story* is that the term means more than one thing: several things more, in fact. The ordinary sense of *story* (as in "Tell me a story" or "I like that kind of story") is unstable but linked, through divagations, by a continuous thread. There are three interconnected meanings to the ordinary usage. First, the word may signify only the events of a narrative in a presumptive natural order (the chronological order restored to *Tristram Shandy*, say) which is, more or less, the way the Russian formalists understood *fabula*. In ordinary usage, one might respond to a narrative (an oral presentation, for instance) by saying, "Tell it right!" or "Don't mess up the story!" or "That's right! *That's* the right story." Children, as anyone who has ever read out loud much may observe, often respond to narrative (rather like the editors of small literary magazines) in this manner. Second, story ordinarily may refer to all the possible arrangements, or dispositions, for the events and existents in a narrative. In this sense it signifies the ways things might have been composed but were not. Story, in this second sense, may signify either another narrative (one that has been told elsewhere and which the reader knows) or one that has not been told but recognizably might be told sometime, someplace, by someone. In either case, story consists of a body of motifs, events and existents, that one can recognize as belonging together. For example, a child might say, "Tell me the story of Odysseus's scar." It would be apparent that the request pertained to Odysseus's homecoming and not to the adventure of the wooden horse or to the feigned madness. Even if this ordinary usage were pushed to a very high level of abstraction (to define story as, say, a cluster of colligatory motifs), it would still be the case that story entails a number of things that one can recognize as belonging together. This ordinary sense of story accords well with such common English locutions as "an old story," "Tell me a story," "a familiar story," "that would make a good story," "Do you know that/the story," "to tell sad stories of the death of kings," and so forth. Story is not simply the linear order of incidents, but a larger, synchronic collection of motifs that belong together, any one of which might serve to call up the others, and that can be recognized as interdependent.

Third, a short conceptual skip onward, *story* signifies all the aspects of a narrative that are allusive. In this sense, it entails intertextuality. A narrative may allude, in any of countless ways, to archetypes, to mythic materials, and even to highly abstract (or nearly empty) concepts. In such cases the narrative texture, its total disposition including its time scheme(s), must appear contrived, even arbitrary. One can hear, in the told story of *Hamlet*, the differently told stories of Orestes, the told and the untold stories of the Bitter Fool, and even stories that must remain untold, irretrievably obscured. Gilbert Murray heard in *Hamlet* all this and much more:

> The things that thrill and amaze us in *Hamlet* or the *Agamemnon* are not any historical particulars about medieval Elsinore or prehistoric Mycenae, but things belonging to the old stories and the old magic rites, which stirred and thrilled our forefathers five and six thousand years ago; set them dancing all night on the hills, tearing beasts and men in pieces, and giving up their own bodies to a ghastly death, in hope thereby to keep the green world from dying and to be the saviours of their own people.[15]

This is a good deal to have heard in *Hamlet*, but it is not unlike the ordinary experience of readers (and hearers) who perceive in narrative more than has been explicitly told, but do so only because, having heard more elsewhere, they can see more motifs belonging together than have actually been used. In this third sense, story can be thought of as flecks of carbon shadowing from within the crystallization of narrative: shadows of an incompletely actualized matrix of the narratable though never narrated.

The continuous thread that links all three ordinary uses of story is the possibility of recognition. Narrative is always already a "transactional phenomenon"[16] in which a narrator proposes to hold the attention, even to charm the ears, of a narratee while the latter offers to hear, even to hear through, what is being told. One aspect of the transaction must be to hear through the narrative to its range of possibilities, its variants as well as its intertext, and to what may be perceived as its story matrix. One knows that one is in the presence of a story matrix when one recognizes that a narrative has been told before, that it could have been told before (in some disposition), or that it might be told, either once again or for the first time. It seems to be a fact, a matter of empirical record, that readers can recognize more narrative possibilities than have been actualized in a particular instance. They can recognize the clustering of motifs, their quality of hanging together, their mutual implicitness.

Why this should be so makes one of the fascinating, if entirely marginal, problems in literary theory. (Even to pose it thrusts one immediately into the windy spaces between the Borgesian hexagons.) First, it may be argued that certain facts of experience are recognized without the mediation of rational demonstration. When children call for a story, no one needs to demonstrate to them that certain motifs, and only those motifs, belong together. One may call this intuition, but only in the sense that experience often brings a capacity to recognize in immediate, not mediate, ways. (An experienced driver, observing that another car has changed lanes without signaling, perhaps playing the "king of the freeway" game, and is hurtling toward him, makes certain "right" maneuvers, without thinking, but based on past experience and acquired skills, rather like encoded rules. Later, but only then, he can explain, step by step, what he had done to save his life.) What the reader (or hearer) recognizes is a cluster of colligatory motifs, whether events or existents, or perhaps only one or two plus their inevitable implicitness.[17] Furthermore, the concept of colligatory motifs entails the proposition that there can be a sufficient number of motifs for narrative disposition. Not everything that can be conceived need be told: indeed, everything that can be conceived is evidently much too much for narrative. Thus the narrator's own intuition concerning the possibilities of story should keep him to a mean of sufficiency and allow him to avoid both the defect of using too few motifs in a story (Odysseus's scar, say, but not the old nurse to perceive its significance) and the excess of using too many (not only the scar, but the name and pedigree of the boar that gave the original wound along with the nurse's family's history).[18] Intuition is nonrational but not irrational. Second, it may be argued that stories, defined as colligatory motifs, inhere in certain cultures. As one inherits a culture, through education and other modes of intracultural experience, one learns about the possibilities of story. The interconnection of motifs (that is, their mutual implicitness) comes with cultural experience and may be said to precede, even if never previously told, recognition.

It must also be true that certain conceivable stories cannot be told at all. They defy recognition because they possess no motifs that belong together. A title, one might say, is conceivable, but not the story itself. Thus one cannot tell the story of "How the Irresistible Force Met the Immovable Object," nor can one tell the story of "How the Circle Was Squared" (though one might tell the story of the obsessional fanatic who attempted it). The genus of story divides according to the differentia of narratability. On the side of the untellable, or nonnarratable, belong inconceivable stories (mere titles) for which no knowledge is available and, above all, those stories that would involve the narrator in irresolvable contradictions. A logical impossibility, clearly, is altogether distinct from a mere technological impossibility (the "magic" of certain hyper–science fiction): one can narrate a story of faster-than-light travel, or even of synchronic travel (as in Le Guin's *The Dispossessed*) but not the story of a voyage that is completed both synchronically *and* diachronically (or which also fails to end and never begins, or all these possibilities at once).[19] To attempt that would be to enter blindly into the kind of narrative labyrinth that Borges evokes in "The Garden of Forking Paths." Noting that "contradictory objects" do occur in fiction (as, for example, in "Borges' metaphysical stories or in contemporary science fiction"), Pavel writes: "The presence of contradictions effectively prevents us from considering fictional worlds as genuine possible worlds and from reducing the theory of fiction to a Kripkean theory of modality. Contradictory objects nevertheless provide insufficient evidence against the notion of *world*, since nothing prevents the theory of fiction from speaking, as some philosophers do, about impossible or erratic worlds. Contradictory worlds are not so remote as one might expect."[20] Still, a physically erratic world is different from a contradictory one (in which, say, all circles are square or every identity is also a nonidentity) and it may make more sense to say, simply, that such stories can be conceived as titles or as programs for storytelling but that their relevant motifs do not belong together and necessarily fail to cohere (that is, they are noncolligatory) such that no *thinkable* story matrix exists and no narratives are possible. One can easily imagine, of course, a metafictional narrative in which two independent, and contradictory, stories are intercut and the illusion of a single story emerges. That would be essentially the textual modality known as magic realism discussed in Chapter 5.

Furthermore, certain stories cannot be conceived simply because their motifs are not encoded within a particular culture. At some level of conceivability, motifs are encoded within a culture and, in their cultural absence, no stories can be conceived without them. But motifs, like conventions, are transnational. They can, like nomads or migrants, cross boundaries, though they are likely to undergo metamorphoses, of both scope and purpose, as they fit themselves into the literary structures of another culture. Renaissance Italian writers, for example, borrowed freely from the matter of France and contemporary North American writers have discovered that many of the customary motifs of Latin American fiction can be borrowed, transformed, and profitably reemployed.

Culler's formulation of story as a "heuristic fiction" (a back-formed postulate to ground a certain kind of narrative analysis) seems correct but restricted. Certainly, the distinction between story and discourse *is* a methodological requirement: it allows narrative analysis to begin *as if* there had been a story (encoded and constructively disposed) within, as well as prior to, a particular narrative. To make the distinction in the terms of that bare-bones methodological formulation leaves much hanging. The concept of story, the postulated side of the distinction, allows for a story matrix (intuitively recognizable), on one hand, and an actualizing system of conventions and possible textual moves, on the other. The interaction of the two (in a narrator) produces a narrative. One slender problem of literary theory, then, replicates that at the center of Plato's *Ion*. How, when one talks about narratives, shall one talk about those things that seem to be there but about which nothing much is said: knowledge, belief systems, important information, or further possible narratives? How actively does a reader react to these absences? Can he be said to play, constructively and consciously, with these absences or does the prior textual system, constituted in part by its own incompleteness, play? Shall we say, perhaps, that both of these questions deserve affirmative answers?

Granted the concepts of story matrix and an actualizing system, a number of modes of relationship between story and discourse, and between narrative and the stories to which they allusively point, are possible.[21] A narrative may call attention to the possibilities of story embedded within its discourse. Hints of other stories (outside the main, homodiegetic line of the narrative), glancing references that function as coded phrases, scenic descriptions, metaphors, characters' names, and even character types, all call attention to the possibilities of story outside the narrative. All these narrative sparks exclaim to the reader that there are other stories that could be told (there have been "ever so many" stories in the world, Barthes observes), stories that can be heard elsewhere, stories that have been told, might have been told, might still be told, should be told: stories in the subjunctive mood.

Subjunctivity is the mode of relationship that, typically, obtains in *The Faerie Queene*. Against this mode of entailment (so to speak), one may distinguish a relationship in which story and narrative are, by the narrative's strategic moves, pitted against each other in ironic contrast. Bakhtin writes that "differences in plot follow from differences in values."[22] The most minimal shape given to a disparate (or heterodiegetic) story within a narrative will hint at contrasting values, at worlds quite, even utterly, different from that shaped within the main line of narrative. A narrative may call attention to an untold story, or to a body of stories, but it may do so only to establish the distance between the told and the untold. The untold possibilities of story that have been invoked have the purpose (in an ironic narrative) of indicating how far this narrative has advanced from them, how far it has left them behind, or to one side, how great a conceptual abyss divides them. It may also indicate how ironic an act narrating may be: that is, how uncertain and caught between polarities is the very act of telling through which shaped narratives come into existence. Stories, untold as well as told, can be made into vehicles of values: to choose one over another, or one narrative expression over another, may imply, as Bakhtin argues, an explicit value judgment. To narrate a story that invokes contrasting stories is to make a value judgment, but it may also be an act in which the nature of value judgments is called into question. This is what happens (preeminently, one might say) in *Don Quijote*.

II

> Here, too, we see that the myths of the nineteenth century retain all their power; the great novelist, the "genius," is a kind of unconscious monster, irresponsible and fate-ridden, even slightly stupid, who emits "messages" which only the reader may decipher.
>
> —Alain Robbe-Grillet, *For a New Novel: Essays on Fiction*

The Faerie Queene contains many allusions to stories other than the one being narrated: stories that have been told elsewhere, stories not yet told, stories that might have been told, but always stories that are recognizably narratable. The allusiveness of *The Faerie Queene* is crowded by hints, suggestions, glancingness, and the full scope and play of self-conscious intertextuality. It is also, to use Frank Kermode's expression, the realm in which secrets appear.[23] Though hidden in the allusiveness of narrative, stories can be followed, or even chased, but the reader must recognize them first. In *The Faerie Queene*, Spenser's allusiveness displays a great knowledge of previous narrative (of the "sedimentation of prior texts"), craftiness in the possibilities of intertextual play, and skill, like the Ghost's in *Hamlet*, in the use of untold stories to prompt narrative effects in the reader's mind.

One of the specific narrative strategies that Spenser learned from Ovid, or from the common pool of Ovidian convention that all Renaissance storytellers inherited through the romance-epic tradition (as well as from classical narrative), is ekphrasis, the description of a tapestry or other work of art, which, often in truncated ways, alludes to a well-known, previously narrated story.[24] An example of this convention can be noted in Book VI of the *Metamorphoses* in which the arrogant but hapless Arachne duels with Minerva. She weaves a tapestry upon which she depicts, doubly to shame the goddess, a series of pictures alluding to the wanton lechery of the gods. Arachne's tapestry shows a series of rapes performed (in this order) by Jove, Neptune, Phoebus, and Bacchus. One needs to observe that in Ovid's account of Arachne's tapestry little detail is given. There is only allusion to the story. Thus, describing the rapes by Neptune, Ovid writes (in Arthur Golding's translation) that Arachne showed him

> in lusty Stalions shape . . . covering there
> Dame Ceres with the yellow lockes, and hir whose goldne heare
> Was turnde to crawling Snakes: on whome he gate the winged horse.
> She made him in a Dolphins shape Melantho to enforce.
> Of all these things she missed not their proper shapes, nor yit
> The full and just resemblance of their places for to hit.
> (lines 146–51)

It is evident that, his claims of performance notwithstanding, Ovid does not attempt to give the "full and just resemblance" of the things he evokes: *that* is work for the mind's eye, which cannot see if it has not already heard. Readers of Renaissance literature will recall many other instances of the ekphrastic convention. The shield, "War's targe," that Thomas Sackville's narrator in the "Induction" to *A Mirror for Magistrates* observes in his stroll through Hell bears as its intricate device, with full classical resonance, depictions ("depainted there") of ancient battles with the final seven stanzas of the ekphrasis being given to the Trojan War. The narrator observes,

> But how can I descrive the doleful sight
> That in the shield so livelike fair did shine?
> Sith in this world I think was never wight
> Could have set furth the half, not half so fine. (lines 470–71)

The wide green sleeves of Hero's garment, in Marlowe's *Hero and Leander*, are

> bordered with a grove
> Where Venus in her naked glory strove
> To please the careless and disdainful eyes
> Of proud Adonis, that before her lies. (lines 11–14)

Shakespeare's use of ekphrasis in *The Rape of Lucrece*, the "piece of skilful painting" depicting "Priam's Troy," stands out both for its complexity and detail and for its psychological depth in paralleling the state of Lucrece's mind after she has been raped.[25] *Lucrece* is a magnificent instance of Renaissance rhetorical playfulness and elaboration: the ekphrasis, one of several precisely employed techniques to achieve maximal dilation (among the others are Tarquin's psychomachia, or "split awareness," and Lucrece's three Ovidian interior monologues), develops at length not merely the treacherous situation when the wooden horse is carried within Troy's gates but also a focalization on Hecuba that allows Lucrece to parallel her griefs to those of Trojan queen.[26] The most masterly practitioner of this Ovidian convention must be Spenser. So much is this the case that while one may rightly call this erotic-mythological narrative convention "Ovidian" in consideration of the Renaissance backward perspective, one would do better to call it "Spenserian" in looking forward to later writers, such as Keats, who learned their Ovidianism from Spenser.

A striking instance of Spenserian ekphrasis occurs in Book II of *The Faerie Queene* when Sir Guyon and the Palmer arrive at the gate to the Bower of Bliss. This gate, through which they must pass to complete Sir Guyon's quest, is made of ivory upon which, in a work of "admirable wit," appears *all* "the famous history / Of Jason and Medea" (12.44.3–4). Spenser's narrator explains that the story is written ("ywrit") but one may certainly suppose it to have been carved or otherwise incised (ekphrasis does not depend on a particular medium for the work of art to be described). The "famous history" moves from a description of Jason to a picture of Medea in her "furious longing fit," and then proceeds, incident by incident, from the conquest of the Golden Fleece to the "enchanted flame" that killed Creusa. "All this and more might in that goodly gate / Be red," the narrator comments (46.1–3). Yet there is no indication of what the "more" might comprise: perhaps Medea's rejuvenation of Aeson, her murder of Pelias, the flight to Corinth, or her murder of her children, all colligatory motifs that belong to the story matrix (and which a reader, certainly a Renaissance reader, should recognize), but which are not narrated in *The Faerie Queene*. "All this and more" appeals to the mind's eye, to the reader's larger experience of narrative. Spenser's readers are asked to know more than the narrative explicitly tells. Referring to the ekphrasis of Arachne's and Minerva's weaving contest that occurs in *Muipotmos*, John Bender writes that the "passage is a forceful narrative, but it is not visually precise."[27] That, one would suppose, is necessarily the case with ekphrases. The important question should be how it, or any ekphrasis, becomes a "forceful narrative" when it must seem that the "narrative" is itself little more than a spare, fleshless collection of incidents or, in effect, narremes. In part the answer appears to be that Spenser's readers must bring to the reading of an ekphrasis a prior knowledge. The abstract quality of the story incised upon the gate does not weaken its effectiveness in the narrative. It evokes echoes of a story, untold here but elsewhere told and retold, of a mad passion, cruel lust (one must think, if the mind's eye can hear, of all the deaths associated with Medea's savage love for Jason), and the tragic conclusion. Itself a gate of sorts, this narrative allusiveness opens out upon the Bower of Bliss in all its moral implicitness.

The Third Book of *The Faerie Queene*, following the triumph of temperance over lust in Book II, concerns chastity. In so doing, it also concerns sexual appetite, lust in a variety of shapes and resolutions. Book III constitutes an exploration of the diverse effects of sexual appetite embodied in behavior that ranges from the morally excellent to the appallingly debased. This seems appropriate for a long narrative dealing with chastity since, as Socrates makes plain to Ion, the person who claims to know the good, in whatever category of action, must also know the bad. Book III begins with the Knight of Chastity, Britomart, accompanied by the hero of the First Book, Red Cross Knight, seeking a night's lodging in the Castle Joyeous, ruled by Malacasta, the Lady of Delight, where sexual promiscuity is the normative mode of behavior. Britomart does not know what kind of place she has entered, but there are certainly striking indications. For one thing, as the two knights cross the great chamber of the castle, they observe the "image of superfluous riotize" (1.33), for the walls are covered with costly tapestries from Arras and Tours upon which are depicted scenes from the story of Venus and Adonis. The description of these tapestries occupies five stanzas (34–39) and reduces the familiar story to an ordered series of essential narremes, ending with the "dainty flower" into which Venus transmutes Adonis and which "in that cloth was wrought as if it lively grew" (38). One must be clear about what happens at this point: a series of woven illustrations are described (but not, obviously, made accessible to the reading eye); they depict a small number of incidents corresponding to a known story but not narrated as incidents in a narrative normally would be since there are no embellishments, no dilation, the plot is no more than sequentiality, and characterization is minimal. The whole is a stark account, left at the level of discontinuous narremes and narrative agents, that the narrator *claims* to be rich and skillful. The ekphrasis calls a story into existence (to be heard, if at all, in the mind's eye), but it does this only to the extent that the story is already familiar. The effectiveness of the ekphrasis does not depend on the reader having read any particular version of the story, in Ovid or anywhere else, but only on the reader's familiarity with the story matrix.

Although the ekphrasis is a poor narrative (and not a picture at all), a mere narrative skeleton at best, the function of its allusiveness is resonantly significant. Both its thematic weight and its structural force are great. It generates a narrative linkage for the whole of the Third Book, since recursive echoes of this story will be heard frequently. The most abstract account of the Venus and Adonis story, that a sexually appetent female attempts, unsuccessfully, to seduce a reluctant male, reflects the very relationship that Britomart finds developing between herself and Malacasta. The ekphrasis also informs the reader about something the characters themselves do not understand. Indeed, in this latter sense, the function of the ekphrastic narrative seems largely ironic since neither of the two heroes grasps the import of what the tapestries reveal: the light it casts upon the essential mode of the Castle Joyeous. For readers who know the story matrix (though not necessarily only readers of Ovid), Spenser manages to call forth another narrative to thicken the fabric of his own. If the mind's eye had not already heard, however, the strategy would be ineffectual.

Spenser's most labyrinthine use of embedded allusiveness (of unnarrated, though narratable, story) occurs in the final two cantos of the Third Book. Britomart has crossed an enchanted fire surrounding the castle of an enchanter, Busirane, in an effort to rescue the enthralled Amoretta and return her to her lover, Sir Scudamour, who waits outside the castle, beyond the fire that he himself cannot cross. (There are several allegorical motivations, not directly to the purpose of this discussion, that explain why Britomart, the Knight of Chastity, can cross the fire but Sir Scudamour cannot.) Busirane represents a massive development from the simply lecherous Lady of Delight in the first canto. He perverts knowledge and intellectual skills, symbolized by his vast powers of magic (the emblem of which is Amoretta's heart, excised from her body, split by a dart, yet still living), to the satisfaction of sexual appetite. On the level of appetite Busirane is an appallingly evil figure, recalling Iago, Iachimo, or Edmund in unswerving selfishness of intention, while Malacasta is little more than a Doll Tearsheet with a castle. The intricate adventures of Book III, all variants on the theme of sexual appetency, have pointed toward Busirane and Britomart's meeting with him. The castle of Busirane encloses a space that fills with a culminating conflict.

As Britomart crosses the hall of Busirane's castle, she encounters three distinct story matrices, ranging from recognizably narratable story (because it has been narrated elsewhere) to empty, though abstractly colligatory, motifs. Each story matrix is functionally appropriate to the context and to the mode of Busirane's castle. First, she observes tapestries, "woven with gold and silke," upon which are depicted, in powerfully realistic images, *all* of "Cupid's warres." In what should be taken as a symbol of secret significance, of the way in which allusiveness works, the gold thread of the tapestry shows "unwillingly" through the silk of the weave like "a discolourd Snake, whose hidden snares / Through the greene gras his long bright burnisht backe declares" (28.8–9). Jove is shown roving the world "in straunge disguize" in order to "slake his scalding smart" (11.30): in a ram's form for Helle, a bull for Europa, a golden shower for Danaë, and so forth. The tapestry in the hall of Busirane, it seems, might have been woven by Ovid's Arachne for it covers nearly the same incidents. (It adds Saturn to the series and reverses the order between Neptune and Phoebus, but it is clearly a tapestry analogous to, and strongly evocative of, the one that Ovid attributes to Arachne.) A recursive ekphrastic rendering of another ekphrasis, Busirane's tapestry is a deliberate transcription within the possibilities of allusive interplay. Spenser's narrative represents narrative visual art telling stories that imitate verbal narrative (Ovid's) that represents narrative visual art telling stories. The obsessive reflexivity of Renaissance literature could hardly discover a more telling emblem.

Second, after Britomart has crossed the hall, she enters a room in which there is a further series of unnarrated stories (11.51–52). These are worked in gold, not in "painfull" weavings, and evoke, not known stories, but raw story-stuff: episodes of grotesque passion, "wild Antickes," and a "thousand monstrous formes" such as love often wears. All of these depicted scenes appear to share a common feature in dealing with the cruel effects of sexual appetite and its "mercilesse intent." At this point Spenser's narrative alludes to unnarrated stories that, though recognizable as story, or as the colligatory motifs of stories, call to mind no particular narrative. For the mind's eye to hear them at all, it must have had a wide narrative experience, though not necessarily to have heard a given story told. Nonetheless, the thematic, as well as the structural, significance that these representations in gold possess, allusion adding the weight of suspense to plot, seems unmistakable. Britomart is struck by the series of visual figures for she stares at them intently though she fails to "satisfie / Her greedy eyes with gazing at long space" (53).

Third, she passes through another iron door into another room, where she witnesses the Masque of Cupid. The Masque issues once a day from yet a further room where Busirane keeps the captive Amoretta in the bonds of magic spells. The Masque consists of a series of personifications, followed at last by Amoretta herself, "her brest all naked, as net ivory," with her heart, still trembling, cut from her breast and laid in a silver basin transfixed by a dart. The Masque is puzzling from the point of view of narrative theory since, though it is "enranged orderly" (12.5), it tells no particular story. It is merely a sequence of personified passions that bear forcefully upon the concept of love in all of its metamorphoses. The personifications are relevant both to the main idea of Book III and to the special behavior of Busirane: for example, there are figures of Fancy, Desire, Doubt, Danger, Fear, Hope, Grief, Fury, and many more. They all embody emotions associated with human desire, appetency and love. All, though belonging to no particular story matrix, could easily assume sufficient texture to play a large number of narrative roles. Any experienced reader would recognize them for what they are: motifs that belong to all the "ever so many" stories of human sexual appetite.[28]

What happens at this point in Spenser's narrative is certainly strange, but it is indicative of his complex skills in storytelling. The story materials, embodied in the Masque, are pushed to an extremely high level of abstraction even while being given the local habitation of actors. The Masque of Cupid comprises a typology of possible emotions, typical actions, and typical passions, but no explicit stories are suggested. Although the allusive story materials are not crystallized in narrative (far from it), they do evoke a matrix for the actual narrative of Book III of *The Faerie Queene*. It is a remarkably reflexive, and hence playfully self-conscious, act: Spenser's narrative calls forth its own story matrix, stripped of, and beyond, any actual narrative, including its own. In this instance, story means a number of colligatory motifs, not incidents, that a reader may recognize as belonging together, though in countless permutations, and offering the bases for any number of possible tales. (The Masque of Cupid, then, constitutes the purest, though not the most helpful, illustration of the formulation of story given in this chapter.) The embedded allusiveness of Spenser's narrative becomes more abstract through each of the three sets of representations, more logically primitive, even as the narrative of Britomart becomes increasingly particularized, always more sharply crystallized. At this point, the mind's eye, to hear the allusive story materials, must not only have heard prior stories but must have understood them, on several levels of their deepest entailments, as well. If the mind's eye fulfils the requirements for recognition, then it may fill with striking sounds.

Spenser's skills in using never-narrated story materials to evoke either a narrated or a narratable story, and so to enrich and thicken his own narrative, exemplify the intricate uses to which the interplay of stories may be put. A story does not have to be narrated to function forcefully in a narrative. And this proposition indicates that to limit the formulation of story to a "conceptualization" or a "heuristic fiction," though a fruitful methodological move, does not do justice to its paradoxical solidity. Spenser's narrative practice makes plain that stories do not have to exist in any narrated form to be effective and to be recognized as intuitively coherent. Their motifs need not be narrated for them to be recognized. All that is necessary is that they be encoded in a common culture or, more narrowly, in a literary tradition. Furthermore, an analysis of the temporal function of embedded narratives within a containing narrative would seem to support this argument.

An embedded narrative (that is, any narrative that is contained within another narrative either through the voice of a character, abruptly transformed into a narrator, or through the use of some other convention such as the inclusion of extraneous discourse in the form of letters, messages, journals, or any other heterodiegetic inscription) breaks the time scheme of the narrative that incorporates it. It opens a fissure in the narrative order of the text that, whether one thinks of this sequence as chronological or as radically perturbed (where, say, the chronology could be restored only on the level of story), introduces a different time scheme into the narrative. Intertextuality, as Jenny remarks, is a "mechanism of perturbation."[29] Thus embedded narratives construct a textual anachrony that is different from the anachrony (if any) that the containing, homodiegetic narrative may possess. Yet even the most minimally narrated story can create this effect. It will have its *own* time: the fissure in the text takes one there, elsewhere, and elsewhen. Furthermore, narrative proclaims its plural worldhood. Each narrative possesses, however minimal the indications are, not merely its own time but its own space as well. It is, in a rich sense of the term, a world. To narrate a story is to express a fictional world. Even the merest story materials, existing only in shadowy allusiveness, will create this effect: they will lay the foundation for a distinctive time, space, and worldhood. When, as in Spenser's case, the allusive story matrix is presented as visual (and is *viewed* by a perceiving character), then it might be argued that the allusive materials are essentially descriptive and, hence, timeless. Chatman writes (rather casually given the intricacies of the problem) that "what happens in description is that the time line of the story is interrupted and frozen. Events are stopped, though our reading- or discourse-time continues, and we look at the characters and the setting elements as at a *tableau vivant*."[30] If, however, one examines the time functions of embedded narratives or (even) the simplest story-stuff, it should appear evident that this is *not* what happens. The story materials, no matter how minimal the narrative crystallization, do not freeze discursive time but rather shunt it to another sequence. Even the Masque of Cupid achieves this effect. Since the personifications are intuitively recognizable as belonging together, their potential for varied permutations is also evident.

Minimal as they are, mere story-stuff at best, they project an indefinite series of metonymic combinations. And they create the possibilities of different time schemes. Thus the embedded allusions to stories, as clearly is the case with embedded narratives, should probably be considered as having a temporal order and duration in themselves. In the realm of narrative allusiveness, there are many odd nooks, mirages, impasses, and broken labyrinths: all project distinct time schemes and the potential for worldhood.

III

> I trust the reader appreciates the strangeness of this,
> because if he does not, there is no sense in writing poems,
> or notes to poems, or anything at all.
>
> —Vladimir Nabokov, *Pale Fire*

The allusive interplay in *The Faerie Queene* supports, and thickens, the containing narrative. The allusive stories are always congruent thematically to the main, homodiegetic narrative line, however distinct and anachronic they seem.[31] It is also possible for allusive stories to have a sharp edge, an abrading incongruence. Rather than evoking a large expense of parallel or congruent story matrices, the interplay can set off the containing narrative in dialogic contrast. The untold, or the barely told, will seem so different from what is actually being narrated that the possibilities of contrast (of contradiction and irony) become aspects of the narrative. David Lodge has noted the way the "realm of Fancy" plays within the unlovely materials that the narrative of *Hard Times* actualizes.[32] Charles Dickens uses this interplay to create a system of echoes of traditional motifs from fairy tales. Not only do specific characters in *Hard Times* seem to be derived from "the staple ingredients of the fairy-tale," but there are many other allusions to these folkloric story matrices. All the circus folk are "persistently associated with legend and myth" (Pegasus and Jack the Giant Killer, for instance). Furthermore, Cissy Jupe tells Mr. Gradgrind that she used to read to her father about "the fairies . . . and the dwarf, and the hunchback and genies." (It is a confession that, needless to observe, astounds Mr. Gradgrind.) All of these allusions to the "realm of Fancy," to the world of the fairy tale, to nursery rhyme, to the stories of the pantomimes, to ogres, witches, giants, dragons, fairies, and the cow with the crumpled horn, allusions with which, as Lodge writes, the text of *Hard Times* is "saturated," function consistently to place the utilitarian, industrial world of the containing narrative into a deep and ironic contrast. The told is so unlovely; the untold (but evocatively hinted), so lovely. Dickens achieves,

Lodge argues, a powerful effect by making the "inhabitants of this drab, gritty, Victorian mill town re-enact the motifs of folk-tale and legend." Further, Dickens is able to draw attention in this way to the repression of imagination (or Fancy), which he "believed was the culturally disastrous effect of governing society according to purely materialistic, empirical criteria of 'utility.'" This double contrast, Lodge writes, is epitomized in Dickens's "recurrent description of the factories of Coketown as 'fairy palaces.'"[33] Clearly, unlike the congruent interplay that Spenser creates, contrastive interplay between stories and narrative proposes a discursive space more difficult to map: a space that is crowded with sharp obliquities. How much this is the case can be seen by considering the way in which allusiveness functions in that most ironic (and most dialogic, it may be) of all narratives, *Don Quijote.*

Don Quijote can scarcely be seen innocently. Too much has been written, too much is known, too much assumed for most readers to approach the narrative without the conviction that they have already understood it. Like one of Shakespeare's tragic heroes, Cervantes's Knight advances across the reader's horizon preceded by his reputation. Thus readers commonly assume that *Don Quijote* is a satire of the Renaissance predilection for discontinuous chivalric romances (to which tradition Spenser's *Faerie Queene* is the appendant). Occasionally, critics have argued that there is nothing more to the narrative than that or, even more strongly, that there *cannot* be anything more since Cervantes seems to have made it plain that satire is his objective in writing. After all, it is said, Cervantes does claim in the Prologue to the First Part that he should "keep [his] aim steadily fixed on overthrowing the ill-based fabric of these books of chivalry, abhorred by so many yet praised by so many more; for if [he] achieve[s] that, [he] will have achieved no small thing."[34] First, one must observe that Cervantes does not say that irony cuts in only one direction. The lines from the Prologue are actually the words of a Friend who offers the Author advice. The possibility remains open that the advice is not followed, or that it is inadequate. (Irony, as well as its militant mode, satire, can cut more ways than one and in the *Quijote* it typically cuts more ways than a sword in battle.) Second, the evidence of the narrative seems repeatedly to stress the viable presence of the values represented by chivalric romance within the present moment of narrative action. The chivalric values function effectively as criteria for moral action, and, to the extent that they do so, it is impossible to see the chivalric romances as merely the butt of a narrow satiric thrust. It may be argued that the romance values coexist in permanent opposition to the Knight's other set of effective values, those of Home and Household, more or less as an irresolvable split in his consciousness.[35] If this is a correct account, then the possibilities for ironic interplay between contrasting categories of story are evidently quite large.

In the *Quijote* the web of allusions to chivalric romance is dense and tentacular. It manifests itself on every level of discourse: proper names, titles of books that are cited, situations that parallel romance topoi, parodic treatments of typical romance characterizations and situations, snatches of ballads, incorporated narrative of romance materials (such as maese Pedro's puppet show in the Second Part), and many romance motifs such as the Helmet of Mambrino or the figure of Merlin. The values of the romances are everywhere apparent. Still, the most forceful use of the traditional romance materials occurs in the way in which the Knight can discursively shape narratives that are complex, indebted to the conventions of chivalric romance, well formed, and yet do not derive from any particular prior narrative text. They display "sedimentation" but only of the story materials and the normal conventions of the genre. Of course, one might argue that the purpose of these embedded narratives is satiric only, but it is difficult to ignore the way they give expression to a set of values that are credible (the Knight and other characters believe in them), admirable, and evidently imitable. Martínez-Bonati observes, "Far from closing itself off, the imaginary world of the *Quijote* blends its boundaries with historical reality and other imaginary worlds."[36]

In three key passages the Knight creates romance narratives out of the story matrices that his reading has made available. (He is, paradoxically perhaps, precisely the kind of reader that Renaissance critics theorized as an ideal.)[37] These passages are, first, chapter 18 of the First Part, in which the Knight describes to Sancho the composition of two vast armies which are about to engage in battle; second, the systematic account of chivalric adventure that the Knight tells the Canon in defense of his profession in chapter 50 of the First Part; third, chapter 28 of the Second Part, in which the Knight narrates his adventures in the Cave of Montesinos. In each of these embedded narratives, something entirely new is shaped from antecedent story matrices. The manner of telling (that is, its style) indicates that Don Quijote has grasped the conventions for this kind of narrative. (One should recall that, as early as the first chapter of the First Part, Cervantes's narrator observes that the Knight might have successfully completed the unfinished narrative of Sir Belianis if other preoccupations had not prevented him: clearly, style, as distinct from the inventory of motifs, is also something that may be learned.) Indeed, everything about these narratives is consistent with the way stories are normally told in chivalric romance, but the narratives do not point to any text or prior narrative. There is a great deal of allusive interplay between stories, but this interplay, as it stretches outward into the conceptual field of romance narrative, touches nothing precise and remains as unanchored as the "wilde Antickes" or the pageant of personifications that Britomart observes in the house of Busirane.

Chapter 50 of the First Part is exemplary. The Knight's devotion to chivalric romance has been attacked by the Canon, who favors narratives that have a historical basis; that is, narratives which derive their verisimilitude from an extrinsic knowledge of certain (presumptive) facts. The Knight responds to this attack by creating a typical romance narrative: "Be silent, sir, do not speak such blasphemies; and, believe me, if you take my advice you will be acting like a man of sense. Only read these books, and you will see what pleasure you get from them. For, tell me, could there be anything more delightful than to see displayed here and now before our eyes, as we might say, a great lake of pitch."[38] He then continues to narrate a tale that both springs from, and is a commentary on, the chivalric tales that have been told but is not actually one of them. In this narrative a knight, undistinguished except by his courage and decisiveness, hears a voice challenging him from a lake of boiling pitch, dives into the lake, and descends to the bottom, where he discovers "flowry meadows" more beautiful than the Elysian fields and all manner of riches. At the flowery bottom of the lake, the knight meets a number of extremely beautiful young women who escort him to a castle where he is attended and entertained (much as Sir Lancelot is said to have been entertained in the popular ballad that the Knight loves to quote), and invited to a great feast. Then a maiden, lovelier than any of the others, unexpectedly enters the hall, sits down beside him, and begins to tell him "what manner of castle it is, and how she lives there under a spell, and other things which surprise the knight and astonish the readers of the story."[39] The courageous knight is trapped; the readers of his tale are trapped (as are the intratextual narratees). The Knight has been trapped by other narratives of that kind and all of his auditors find themselves trapped by the sylleptic tale that he tells but does not conclude.[40]

A reader of *Don Quijote* might read this typical romance narrative and infer that it provides further evidence that the Knight is mad (it does that) or that it is a satire on the romances (it is that, too). The text of the *Quijote* certainly permits such simple reading strategies. If he reads as the Canon listens, then those must be his only conclusions. On the other hand, the reader might listen a bit more closely to what the Knight himself says about the consequences of reading narratives such as this one that he has begun to tell: "Believe me, sir, I repeat, and read these books. You will see how they drive away the melancholy, and improve your temper if it happens to be bad. I can say of myself that since I became a knight errant I have been valiant, courteous, liberal, well-bred, generous, polite, bold, gentle and patient, and an endurer of toils, imprisonments and enchantments."[41] One readerly conclusion should be that if the romances have this effect (and Cervantes's narrative indicates, overwhelmingly, that they do), then they cannot be quite so bad (not so morally bad, certainly) as many characters in the narrative, not only the Canon, have claimed. The Priest and the Barber who burn the better part of the Knight's library, this conclusion would suggest, make a mistake: they misunderstand the effects of narrative entrapment.

What happens in this passage is fundamental to Cervantes's narrative. The allusiveness emerges from a perspective that is treated ironically (there *is* an ongoing satire of chivalric romance in the *Quijote*), but at the same time the ordinary experience of routine life, of job, commercial and professional purposes, is put into a perspective which, viewed from the direction of romance, treats *it* ironically. The embedded allusiveness in the *Quijote* engages its containing narrative (much as the voice of the Knight engages the Cervantine narrator) in a counterpoint of ironies. The narrative consequence of this interplay between distinct voices is a kind of heteroglossia. The language of the *Quijote* comprises different levels, and varying formulations of these levels as well, in an active (that is, ironic) interplay. One could almost claim that in the *Quijote* Cervantes achieves such mastery in the novel, even in inventing it, that his characters coexist polyphonically. (In Bakhtin's terms, polyphony designates an open narrative mode in which distinct voices, reflecting the correspondingly distinct values of unique worlds, are set against each other.) Nonetheless, within the active interplay of voices (stating, undercutting, denying, reaffirming, building two opposed worlds of value out of continuous reformulation and reembeddings), something does emerge rather like Bakhtin's account of polyphony in the novels of Dostoevsky. The "all-devouring consciousness of the hero," set against an objective world, constitutes a field of actions in which a character becomes aware of himself and of the values he embodies. All comments on the hero are, in a polyphonic novel, transferred "into the field of vision of the hero himself, thus transforming the finalized and integral reality of the hero into the material of the hero's own self-consciousness."[42] If it is not quite polyphonic in this sense, the *Quijote*, in its complex interplay of distinct voices, comes as close as, if not closer than, any novel between Cervantes and Dostoevsky.

Ortega writes that the realistic, ironic narrative of the *Quijote* contains within it the materials (the "stuff" or the story matrices) for another kind of narrative, the chivalric romance it displaces. Thus the Knight, Ortega adds, in a phrase that finds a later echo in Martínez-Bonati, "stands at the intersection" where the worlds of literary romance and literary realism "meet forming a beveled edge."[43] The Knight possesses a "frontier nature" and encloses within himself a double worldhood, much as the narrative in which he appears encloses an analogous doubleness. It is a doubleness that persists in permanent contrast: an ironized irony of irresolvably conflicting values for which, if they are not equally reasonable, a reasonable case might equally be made. Ortega further argues that although the realistic novel, that literary stepchild of *Don Quijote*, was "born in opposition to the so-called novel of fantasy, it carries adventure enclosed within its body."[44] One reason that it does this lies in Cervantes's self-conscious play with the narrative potential of romance story matrices and their normal actualizing conventions. All of romance narrative, one might say, springs forward into the *Quijote*'s foreground in those allusive tales that the Knight tells. And romance narrative, its voice perhaps never so lucidly nor so distinctively heard than in the *Quijote* (undercut, carnivalized, continuously reformulated), undergoes a permanent metamorphosis.

In their different ways, both *The Faerie Queene* and *Don Quijote* exemplify the complex relationship that obtains between story and discourse. On one hand, the allusive, embedded story materials may function to extend the scope and play of the narrative (the untold thickening the told) either along a homodiegetic plane of incident, characterization, and signification or along a heterodiegetic plane of different incidents and characterizations that, in both cases, underscore thematically congruent parallels. On the other hand, the allusiveness sets itself against the narrative along a discontinuous plane, as a means of focusing the detail (of whatever category), either in a single direction of contrast, as in *Hard Times*, or in a double swing and counterswing of mutual ironization, as in the *Quijote*. In both cases, the ekphrases in *The Faerie Queene* or the syllepses in the *Quijote*, the allusions to recognizable story matrices fall short of the actual embedding of an integral heterodiegetic narrative. Still, the matrices that narrative allusiveness evokes are intuitively graspable, do execute a positive function within the narratives that contain them, and, in possessing their own (potential) time schemes, do contribute to an overall anachronic effect.

Conrad's narratives, it was argued in Chapter 5, are traversed by the echoes of other stories. The sense is always strong that the world, the fictional world of each narrative, is to some extent formed by the body of untold story that it represents. *Heart of Darkness* begins with Marlow yarning on the deck of the *Nellie* in the context of the stories that

Roman seafarers might have told about their experiences on the river Thames. *The Nigger of the "Narcissus"* contains not merely the story of the *Narcissus* sailing home from Bombay, with all its problems of personalities, storms, the authority of officers, and the power of decision making, but also the larger story, indefinite in its possiblities, of the sailors' lives and untold stories. It is, Conrad says in his Preface to the narrative, the story of "all the disregarded multitude of the bewildered, the simple and the voiceless."[45] Similar comments appear throughout Conrad's prefaces and autobiographical writings. They are very precise formulations of what seems always to be the case, always one of the conditions of narrative. Other texts, such as *The Faerie Queene* and *Don Quijote*, specifically call attention to the vastness of narrative, the "ever so many" human stories, self-consciously alluding to the intertexual field that they cannot actually incorporate. In general, it may be said that an analysis of never-narrated stories in these two Renaissance texts suggests the extent to which story, defined as a number of colligatory incidents (or motifs) that can be recognized as such, can be a constructive force in narrative, a positive concept, however slippery, and not merely a methodological requirement. The concept of story, though clearly an important tool for literary analysis, points toward some of the hidden, recessed but narratively compelling, depths of fictional writing. (The solution to Ion's dilemma, then, must be to slip between its horns.)

Thus *story*, understood in its functional opposition to *discourse*, indicates ways in which the intertextual space of literature, the vast corpus of the always-shifting intertext (paradoxically filled not only by texts but by nontexts, or by the never textualized), can be precisely manifested: perplexed into the labyrinthine movements of narrative. The complex interplay between text and the never textualized is both an unclosable free play through, and among, the vastness of narrative discourse (even when described narrowly as the possible matrices that a particular culture makes available) and a more limited play (a truncated metonymy, say) between matrices, as between worlds, or between motifs having the potentiality for worldhood, for the stakes of meaning.

CHAPTER 7

(Para)lude

Swiftly, above the scrub the bright birds sweep and dive. Shadows swirl over the ground. Stunted trees stretch raggedly. The birds fly low, close to the ground, only infrequently rising to the tops of the squat, ugly trees. Their feathers are luminous. Their wings are muscular and steady. Their eyes, like hidden suns, are sunken. As they fly, they sing melodiously. Their sharp bell-tones fill the opaque air. The bright birds, their short wings beating furiously, wheel in narrowing circles. They are almost lost in the dark scrub.

—Metafictionist Parable

THE FINAL PAGES of a book about play/game theory might be called a postlude or even a postludium.[1] A reader who has persevered until this point, following the argument's irregular ways, might well have expected to encounter a postlude. Instead, there is (best qualified by parentheses) only a paralude. To have a (para)lude is to admit that the large issues that have driven the discussion have not been wholly resolved. Indeed, conclusiveness might appear embarrassingly inappropriate. Literary texts do seem to be like games in many important respects, and games are powerfully textlike. Yet, as argued in Chapter 3, they are not the same, however many cognitive affects, on the side of the author or the reader, the gamewright or the player, they seem to share, and they should not be confused. As networks of signs, semiotic constructs built upon specific organizing assumptions, they are distinct. Perhaps they are not as distanced from each other as, say, recipes and geometries (two other semiotic systems) are, but the fundamental difference between rule and convention marks them as apart, related but leading separate existences. Nothing has run through this discussion quite so pervasively, so paracursively one might say, as the dual perception that literary texts are, and are not, like games. Games, though they manifest unmistakable textual features (a kind of primitive textuality), are not literary texts. Yet they often seem to be precisely that.

Other problems with important roles in the discussion have also run along together, occasionally touching but, one hopes, never quite tripping each other. Each of the eight positions available to play/game theory that were introduced in the first chapter has had a place in the discussion, some far more than others, but no single one has been predominant, and none can be said to have wholly dominated the argument. Play seems to be both education and self-expression, controlled and limitlessly open; game, both trickery and pedagogy, rationally designed activities and the helter-skelter moilings of tactical opportunitics, taken and missed. Play and game seem interrelated, almost as inside and outside, energy and structure, but clearly distinct. Above all, the four positions in play/game theory that this discussion has examined, Derrida, Bakhtin, Gadamer, and Suits remain open to further extrapolation. Derrida and Suits represent extreme, perhaps incompatible, positions (for Derrida, play loses itself seeking its salvation in game; for Suits, play scarcely seems to exist outside of the structures that constitutive rules make possible), but the force of the discussion has been to show that they are both important to the clarification of play/game theory. Yet in some of its manifestations play also seems very much like a social, public exchange, as Bakhtin argues that carnival must always be, and yet a private, work-specific reiteration of fundamental being, as Gadamer claims. The four positions do not displace each other, nor does one achieve mastery. Each casts a significant light on the complex phenomena of play and game. At times, both play and game seem to bear directly upon the extratextual reality of the world (as Bakhtin and Gadamer claim) even while bearing away from it (as Suits and Derrida argue).

Gregory Bateson, in an argument that resonates with Huizinga's seminal discourse, defines play as a separate, self-contained reality, parallel to the (as it were) reality of the world. "What is characteristic of 'play,'" he observes, "is that this is a name for contexts in which the constituent acts have a different sort of relevance and organization from that which they would have had in non-play." It may even be, Bateson continues, "that the essence of play lies in a partial denial of the meanings that the actions would have had in other situations."[2] Given certain cues, signs that mark cognitive and physical boundaries, one may step off into another dimension while employing, *sub specie ludi,* some (or all) of what one has learned in the parallel dimension of nonplay. The similarity to the theory of fictional worlds, discussed in Chapter 5, is suggestive: in both cases, a set of semiotic markers, functioning as cues, indicate a boundary between an actual, empirical world (both extratextual and extraludic) and a parallel (in some sense, alternative) textual or ludic world; the boundary may be crossed mentally and affectively to allow a reader or a player to experience, as self-enclosed and coherent, an imaginative or stipulated alternative. The access to fictional worlds, Lubomír Doležel observes, "requires crossing of world boundaries, transit from the realm of actual existents into the realm of fictional possibles."[3] Bateson's theory of play, if only because of its resemblance to normal textual models, has proved to be instructive, since literature, too, may be defined as a separate and parallel domain into which the reader, having received a set of cues to point the way, steps off bearing along all that has been learned in the extratextual world. Ultimately, the central problem of *In Palamedes' Shadow* (whether literary texts are, or resemble, games) has been given a number of varied answers, functions of disparate perspectives, all of which mutually cohere into a plural account. None would be altogether incompatible with Bateson's simple two-domain model.

The discussion has shown that there are several ways in which literary texts may be considered to contain games, to be modeled upon games, and even to be games in themselves. They may be thought of as the result of play—an author's, a reader's, or an entire culture's—and, insofar as they are perceived as being playful, as either conscious or unconscious. In the form of textual games, play may seem deliberate, as in the crafty self-consciousness of metafiction, or as welling up, quite unmediated by any act of conscious intelligence, from an author's unconscious in paronomasia, word games, and wit. Wit itself provides a small paradigm for the difficulties of defining (getting straight, or even just pinning down) play. It indicates an intellectual capacity to twist words from their normal meanings and to comment upon, as in capping or parodying, someone else's words. A professional fool's wit, remarks Viola in *Twelfth Night,* is as "full of labor as a wise man's art" (3.1.66). While in a psychoanalytic perspective wit is often seen as unconscious, the upwelling contribution of the unconscious to comic byplay, it can also be seen as the imaging in words of conscious, even cruel, intelligence. Peter Farb remarks that "playing with words does not refer solely to entertainments like anagrams or crossword puzzles. Nor is 'word play'—which usually refers to riddles, puns, jokes, wise sayings, verbal dueling, and so forth—a trivial pastime."[4] Wordplay can be conscious, deliberate, and very serious (as when one remarks that another person's wit is "pointed" or carries an "edge"), a cause of pain and triumph as well as fun. Like play, wit is a cognitive mode with diverse origins and purposes and thus, like play, it prompts diverse explanations.

Play may take the shape of a challenge flung in a reader's face, or of a challenge that an author makes to himself (Farb, thinking narrowly, believes this to be impossible) either to test his knowledge of conventions, as one supposes that Spenser must have done, or, as Roussel is believed to have done, to free an otherwise inchoate notion. Following Suits's analysis, play can be seen to become game when the presence of a constitutive rule, the otherwise impractical consequences of which are accepted by players so they can enjoy the playing, transforms the energies of play into order and pattern, random indeterminacies into prescription and prediction. Furthermore, it is possible both to bring sophisticated play/game theory(ies) to bear upon literary texts to describe, analyze, and interpret them and also to incorporate such theories into the literary texts themselves. Anything may become a theme, but when play and game concepts are threaded into narrative discourse it seems to cut close to the heart of the literary experience. There is *something* in the game/text analogy (reduced to irresolvable paradox in Chapter 3) that seems hard to deny even if it is also hard to get straight. When play and game concepts metamorphose into themes, or lend their shapes to plot moves and episodic patterns (as in the godgame) or serve to characterize narrative agents, or merely provide symbolic interludes, they generate a fundamental reflexivity. To write about games or about play is (the textual bloom replicating the contours of the indehiscent depths) to write about writing. Even the unexploited game of chess in Shakespeare's *The Tempest* seems to have this effect, and other literary texts, such as Pope's *The Rape of the Lock,* Carroll's *Through the Looking-Glass,* and Cortàzar's *Hopscotch,* might almost be said to turn upon the image of the narratively embedded game.

In Chapter 2, the allegorical narrative in section IV puts theories of play and game into the foreground. It creates a playfield where concepts of play and game are argued and itself becomes a highly gamelike trap for the dourly rational editor. A community of intellectuals, all of whom articulate complex theories of textuality (some parts of which have to do directly with play and game), may itself not be playful, but it is certainly possible to perceive it as such, more or less as Ainslie does. Philosophical discussion, if its intensities are sufficiently isolated from interruption, may easily become a field of play. In the narrative, the philosophers have a great deal to say about both play and game, but it is Ainslie, caught up in ("run away with") the intellectual ambience, who experiences their discourse, increasingly from within, as game. He collects, savoring but always reinscribing, anecdotes about Barthes discovering *moulinologie,* Kristeva seeing Martine Gruss perform (leaping garters) at the circus, or Todorov falling from his bicycle, ascribing to them a coherence and interdependence, a cerebral hanging-togetherness. On the other hand, the stolid editor, whose level sentences fall into place like pieces of Lego, eventually becomes absorbed into the ludic spirit himself, though without recognizing his metamorphosis, constructing a hypothesis that would be startlingly absurd outside the playfield onto which he has stumbled.

The allegorical narrative transforms intellectual disputation into the field of play and then allows the account itself, in the hands of its distant editor, to become a textual field. Ainslie's discontinuous notes, his splintered or raveling anecdotes, are self-enclosed, traversed and filled by intertextual resonances, and wholly open (vulnerable, indeed) to critical penetration. Above all, they constitute a text that can be read and interpreted. The editor's act of reading Ainslie's fragmentary reportage creates a coherent world in which events happen that would be improbable normally but which, from within the field, seem to meet plausibility criteria of some kind. Certainly, the editor takes pains to argue that his interpretation of the text is plausible, having met (his) rational criteria. Concepts, and the characters who hold them, function like tokens to be shifted from one area to another. The editor's fascination with the construct before him (which he, a *bricoleur* of notions, rather like the protagonist of Coover's *Universal Baseball Association Inc., J. Henry Waugh, Prop.,* has fashioned out of bits and pieces that he has received, already fashioned differently, from Ainslie) manifests the absorption verging upon madness that games can inspire. Locked within the interiority of a game, as within the experience of a literary text, whatever is outside slips away. A world with its own space and time, its own actions and agents, its lucidly defined, if fantastic, hypotheses, comes into being and is felt as distinct, self-enclosed, and actual. It is a private world, but since it is textual it is also potentially public. Any reader can enter a textual world, following its pathways, edging through its labyrinths, however it came into being in the first place, whatever alien playfulness first gave it life. The stolid/mad editor, displaying his close affinities with J. Henry Waugh and Nabokov's Charles Kinbote in *Pale Fire,* allegorizes reading.

Consider the two parabolic brothers in Chapter 5 who, weary of their actual lifeworlds, set out to reinvent those worlds. They follow different methods (the methods of two kinds of fantasy), but the results are analogous. Both make assumptions that run counter to common experience and knowledge and then draw the inevitable conclusions. In the case of the first brother, there is always only a single counterfactual proposition; in the case of the second, there are extended interweavings of opposed codes so that many different but similarly encoded events correspond to each other. In both cases, the results are fictional worlds that can be experienced as distinctive, whole, and coherent. In their interiority, the two brothers' reinvented worlds hang together within themselves, make sense (though this will never be the sense of the extratextual world), and may even displace the actual world. From the inside, the assumptions that the brothers make, however variable, arbitrary, or fantastic, have the force of axioms. The parable of the two brothers leads to the conclusion that the flexible, conventional structures of the imagination, expressed as literary texts, function, in reading, with the force of pseudo-axioms. The parable also underscores the playful inventiveness of the imagination. The brothers, slipping a number of extratextual fetters, exercise the exploratory, heuristic scope of imagination. In this sense, they exemplify what writers as diverse as Kurt Riezler, Harry Berger, and Patricia Yaeger (cited in Chapter 1) mean when they speak of the seriousness of play, its importance as a mode of exploration and reinvention. One may suppose that the brothers begin in play, weariness with their lifeworlds brightened suddenly by a playful flare (whether glimmer or bolt) in the imagination. What they produce, following still another mode of play, the experimental shaping of conventional structures, are occasions for further play. In the text's interiority, their readers play games of make-believe, cultivating old fantasies, building new ones, exploring the possibilities of the fictional world and, perhaps, of themselves as well.

A fictional world's inevitable self-enclosure, exemplified by the fantastic axiomaticity of the brothers' reinventions, marks the closest correspondence between literary texts and games. From the outside, considered as semiotic systems, the one governed by inflexible rules, the other by flexible conventions, they seem essentially unlike. The differences between games and texts seem both massive and unmistakable. Yet once either games or texts are engaged, in play or in reading, they create separate domains of experience that have distinct worldlike properties: their own space and time, their specific actions, even their distinctive emotions. Like games, fictional worlds are made, not "discovered in some remote, invisible or transcendent depositories," but necessarily "*constructed* by human minds and hands."[5] Conventions and rules are the directional criteria for their construction, the set of instructions that the reader, or player, must grasp prior to crossing the boundary between the extra and the intra (textual/ludic).

In contrast to the self-enclosure of texts and games, one must always distrust the supposed playfulness of external situations. There is little genuine play in having a text, even *Don Quijote,* read out loud against one's will. A game that one has been compelled to "play" has about as much playfulness as a forced march through rain and sleet. Many external situations in contemporary American society, theme parks and technobowers, say, lure people inside (often exacting an entrance fee) with promises of fun. Such external situations enclose, physically and legally, but they cannot offer self-enclosure. Spontaneity is rigidly controlled. Neither dance nor song could spring from the heart without a security guard clamping it down, thrusting it back out of sight. There would be nothing personal in the guard's hostility, only the manifestation, in the mode of regulation and protection, of the vast commercial system that causes these physical enclosures to exist in the first place. A commercial system of exchange and profit, largely hidden from those within, underforms the surface, merely apparent, system of excitement and fun. Its illusory play can be scarcely more than a controlled instrument of exploitation. Typically, a technobower offers the chance to be manipulated, to be directed and channeled, not to play. Schiller, one suspects, would have seen little in either theme parks or technobowers to delight him, little to suggest that human beings might reach their fullest potential there. Jameson's gloom over the "waning of affect" in postmodern society could draw its most powerful instances from such external, depthless enclosures. In carnival, Bakhtin observes repeatedly, genuine spontaneity occurs; the individual values of people, their "worlds" in some sense, are expressed in a free social exchange. The masks that customers assume in theme parks, technobowers, or (most radically awful) casinos are normally empty forms, as blank and characterless as noodles. In contrast, the interiority of both games and texts makes possible, in the richness of make-believe, playfully exploratory roles. Their masks have blood and bone behind them: the flesh of players and readers.

Fictional worldhood, whether in the attenuated experience of games or the denser overlayerings of texts, can be highly compelling, even overwhelming. The entrapping power of worldhood can be seen most clearly in the godgame. In a godgame, the character-player not only discovers a monstrous, inescapably personal entrapment within the fabric of a constructed illusion, but also reacts delusionally. In the constricting grasp of an illusion, the option of simply stepping aside never occurs. Pynchon's Oedipa Maas does not abandon her search for the Trystero to return home, Don Quijote does not leave the Duke's castle, the simplest of all moves for a wandering Knight, and Fowles's Nicholas Urfe does not board a plane for London when his experience on the Greek island becomes baffling. Borges's character-players pursue their labyrinthine entrapments to ultimate cognitive barriers, even, as does Lönnrot in "Death and the Compass," to death. The scholar (the narrative of whose actual-life godgame exemplifies the theoretical analysis in Chapter 4), caught in the police exercise which, from her limited, interior perspective, seems totally, though inexplicably, real, simply cannot think her way out of the illusion that surrounds her. The discussion of entrapment, strikingly illustrated by the godgame, points the way into the analysis of space, spatiality, and fictional/game worldhood in Chapter 5. In turn, that analysis points towards the discussion in Chapter 6 of intertextuality as the interplay flowing between texts.

Throughout *In Palamedes' Shadow,* the intercut narratives paracursively make the point that the experience of fiction requires remarkably little to ground its possibility. It is a proposition that Renaissance literary texts repeatedly exemplify: a world (in some sense) rises upon relatively little information, but it is experienced in temporal, spatial, and axiological complexity. Don Quijote looking at the wretched cloth hangings on the walls of an inn, and Britomart viewing with fascination and bemusement the ekphrases in the house of Busirane, both underscore the proposition that the power of signs to evoke worldhood exceeds their measurable semiotic features. Thus, the allegorical narrative in Chapter 2 plays with the possibilities of a dual evocation. In the first place, it attempts to allegorize the deceptive interiority of the reading experience. The editor is caught up in a number of fragmentary texts, constructs a textual whole (for which he claims, as do all editors, an authority), and on this basis provides an interpretation (a "reading") that goes far beyond the inferences that the fragments actually validate. Like Don Quijote, the editor is a reader for whom the inside of the text is unpredictably rich. It is very much like the inside of a game: a discursive space, possessing a distinctive time scheme, in which it is possible to become absorbed to the degree that everything that is outside, or "extra," is excluded. The stolid/mad editor resembles Achilles and Ajax, lost within a game of backgammon, in his textual absorption.

In the second place, the allegorical narrative also attempts to evoke a certain place (Paris) and a certain kind of discourse. Neither place nor discourse needs to be fully represented (if that were possible) to be experienced as such. Text-space, like game-space, is experienced as self-enclosed and full, even though it may be more exiguous than the starkest landscape, the emptiest ellipsis. "The space of a game bends inwards," a character in a fiction (outside this book) remarks, "and the time is closed. . . . The inside of a game, when you play it, is closed off, tight, always ending, but tighter as it develops, always bending in upon itself. Then new interiors show up in the folds like hollow worlds."[6] In the House of Busirane, Britomart momentarily finds herself enthralled by a complex succession of worlds in rudimentary forms. Ainslie finds himself enthralled within a kind of discourse, and within the magic of thinking, but he does not need to see ideas whole (all their entailments made evident) to become absorbed in his experience. When he writes home, not only does his experience appear in fragments, or at least it is discovered in that wholly normal form, but he is, in essence, fragmentary. He knows little but makes much of what he knows. His editor knows less but makes even more of it. (What *did* happen to Ainslie, murdered or seined, dispatched by or to be a terrorist, is largely beside the point, though not beyond the possibilities of an open narrative.) The worlds of scholarship, which are only precisely interplayed notional areas, arise fragmentarily upon the much larger, denser fictional worlds. The latter are, at best (even if we possessed *all* of Ainslie's anecdotes, say), founded on a semiotic sparsity. The extratextual world seems always to sweat its ungraspable thingness.

The allegory in Chapter 2 moves along parallel courses. The interiority of reading, in which fragments may be experienced as worlds, grounds itself upon an overwhelmingly intense sparsity. A world seems such a vast entity, the properties of its worldhood so massively felt, and yet it needs, in order to exist, only the inescapable exiguousness of signs. Fragments, mere slivers and microsemes of a supposed totality, are all that Ainslie possesses (all, for that matter, that Don Quijote and Britomart possess), and what he leaves behind must be less, but those fragments are sufficient for his editor to construct a world (different from Ainslie's) that is, though mad, coherent. The congruence between text and game, considered as experience (as interiority only), can be seen explicitly.

Play is something worth thinking about reflectively; and keen players, of whatever games, do normally meditate upon their play and the happiness that it brings. Many players of such structured games as chess or bridge would probably agree with the nineteenth-century chess master Wilhelm Steinitz, who is reported to have said that chess, like love and music, has the power to make one happy. In one sense, all of *In Palamedes' Shadow* has been an attempt to reflect deeply, if discontinuously, upon an obvious problem of human existence: play does take place; there is something that one may call a play element (in Huizinga's term) in human culture; this does take on the shapes of games and does, indeed, seem to slide imperceptibly into fiction and textuality. Nonetheless, the twin phenomena of play and game, whether considered only as sociocultural or prototextual problems, have never been explored adequately across the entire range of their exuberant diversity. This book has not, of course, succeeded in accomplishing that much. The history of play/game remains to be written and the theory has been, even now, adumbrated only obscurely. Still, *In Palamedes' Shadow* has tried to reach into the dark corners of play/game discourse, in particular the analogy with fictional texts, that have seldom seen much light. The book's method has been both discontinuous and narrative: otherwise solid blocks of discursive analysis have been allowed to split open to incorporate narratives. The method may be called, in a phrase both descriptive and provocative, *ficto-theory.* A narrative, as most writers seem to have known up until the end of the Renaissance at least, may tell an apparently simple story, display its own narrativity, provide a commentary on another text, whether fictional or not, and exemplify a complex spectrum of ideas. All these motivations are likely to be taking place within the same text, as they do in the works of most Renaissance writers, such as Spenser, Cervantes, Shakespeare, and Milton. In ficto-theory, the boundaries between narrative and theory become unstable and may even collapse. No natural barriers divide and delimit these separable domains, the one flowing always into the other, except for the traditions of literary studies and the unexamined insistences of the academic discipline of literature. Ficto-theory acknowledges Kant's famous dictum that concepts without percepts are empty while percepts without concepts are blind (perhaps even more famously put by Lenin as a distinction between theory and practice): the most fruitful way to "do" literary theory is through fiction, to write fiction with theory sharply in mind.

In the parable that heads this (para)lude, the bright birds, wings luminous, eyes like suns, are almost lost in the dark scrub they seem to be exploring. One can be swallowed in all cognitive activities. Perhaps the metafictionist parable speaks directly to the dangers, the threats or potential entrapments, of dirty realism, of minimalism and the too slavish attention to sparseness, but it also speaks obliquely to the absorbing delights of notional areas, of semiotic domains (always, so to speak, waving their signs to command attention), of every *hortus conclusus.* For this reason, the (para)lude may be read back through the entire discussion. The intercut narratives break up the sequence of the argument (and this may have seemed like a frustratingly wrongheaded strategy), but they do this as paradigms and exempla to shift the discourse from plane to fruitful plain. One may suppose (even hope) that a discussion partially about the potential worldhood of limited semiotic systems (of slivers, fragments, tokens, and pieces) can bear a certain amount of interruption and discontinuity. The discussion has been meant to have its own (in abundant, if deceptive, measure) intellectual coherence beneath the edgy moves of its narrative intercutting. The force of parables, as of all fictions, even when these play an indeterminate role in a conceptual hybrid called ficto-theory, is to gather together the echoes of widely scattered, (dis)jointed similitudes.

Notes

CHAPTER 1

1. J. D. Beazley, *Development of Attic Black-Figure* (Berkeley: University of California Press, 1951), p. 65.

2. R. R. Wilson, "Godgames and Labyrinths: The Logic of Entrapment," *Mosaic* 14 (December 1982): 6. See Bernard Suits, *The Grasshopper: Games, Life and Utopia* (Toronto: University of Toronto Press, 1978). The account of a "lusory attitude" in "Godgames and Labyrinths" purposefully exceeds that which Suits provides: a formal account of the mental condition required to make the voluntary acceptance of inefficient rules explicable.

3. Johan Huizinga, *Homo Ludens: A Study of the Play-Element in Culture* (Boston: Beacon Press, 1955), p. 10. The power of Huizinga's analysis of play and the play element in Western culture can be traced through innumerable subsequent writings on play and games. Sura P. Rath, for example, writes, in true Huizingaean spirit, "Le jeu commence quand on s'évade de la réalité quotidienne et cesse quand on retombe dans la routine." See "Le Jeu et les jeux dans la fiction romanesque: Un nouveau paradigme de la critique," *Diogène* 136 (October–December 1986): 128–42.

4. Plato, *The Republic*, VII, 522, trans. B. Jowett (New York: Random House, 1937), p. 781.

5. *The Myths of Hyginus*, trans. Mary Grant (Lawrence: University of Kansas Press, 1960), pp. 84, 92.

6. *Godgame* is John Fowles's term for the literary situation in which one character of superior intelligence and cunning creates a context of contrived bamboozlement that forces another character to struggle, as within a complex cognitive trap, to discover the godlike gamewright's hidden rules (that is, to think his way out or to "play through"). See "Foreword," *The Magus*, rev. ed. (Boston: Little, Brown, 1977), pp. 5–10; Fowles discusses the concept of the godgame in *The Aristos: A Self-Portrait in Ideas* (Boston: Little, Brown, 1970), p. 19.

7. George Steiner, "Introduction," in Huizinga, *Homo Ludens: A Study of the Play Element in Culture* (London: Paladin-Granada, 1970), p. 12.

8. Caillois's influential and widely applied taxonomy of games divides games into four distinct categories: conflict or agon, chance or alea, simulation or mimicry, and vertigo or ilinx. Caillois also introduces a definition of "game," founded on presumptatively invariant features, that expands upon Huizinga: games, Caillois argues, are always free, separate, uncertain, unproductive, rule-governed, and make-believe. See *Les Jeux et les hommes: Le masque et le vertige* (Paris: Editions Gallimard, 1958), English ed., *Man, Play and Games*, trans. Meyer Burash (New York: Free Press, 1961).

9. Erik Erikson, *Toys and Reason: Stages in the Ritualization of Experience* (New York: Norton, 1977), p. 63. Cf. Erikson, *Childhood and Society* (Harmondsworth: Penguin Books, 1965), p. 204: "Play, then, is a function of the ego, an attempt to synchronize the bodily and the social processes with the self. . . . The emphasis, I think, should be on the ego's need to master the various areas of life, and especially those which the individual finds his self, his body, and his social roles wanting and trailing."

10. Anselm Strauss, ed., *The Social Psychology of George Herbert Mead* (Chicago: University of Chicago Press, 1956), p. 228.

11. Christopher Lasch, *The Culture of Narcissism: American Life in an Age of Diminishing Expectations* (New York: Norton, 1979), p. 100.

12. Oswald Spengler, *The Decline of the West*, trans. Charles Francis Atkinson (New York: Knopf, 1932), 2:103.

13. In *The Culture of Narcissism*, Lasch's chapter "The Degradation of Sport" follows Spengler in employing games, sports, and other play activities as a basis for the examination of culture. See also Lasch's "The Degradation of Work and the Apotheosis of Art," *Harper's* 268 (February 1984): 43–45.

14. Friedrich Schiller, *On the Aesthetic Education of Man in a Series of Letters*, trans. Elizabeth M. Wilkinson and L. A. Willoughby (Oxford: Clarendon Press, 1967).

15. Kurt Riezler, "Play and Seriousness," *Journal of Philosophy* 38 (September 1941): 513. Writers on literature, both scholars and critics, have often stressed the seriousness of play. In his *Revisionary Play: Studies in the Spenserian Dynamics* (Berkeley: University of California Press, 1988), Harry Berger, Jr., speaking of the ethical function of play, writes that Spenser's "fabulous narrative is to be taken seriously, not evaporated into ideological correlatives; *but it is to be taken seriously as play* (p. 60). Patricia Yaeger urges the development of a serious, exploratory "feminist aesthetic of 'play' [in order to] understand how women have been able to transform and restructure a literary tradition that forbade them the right to speak" (*Honey-Mad Women: Emancipatory Strategies in Women's Writing* [New York: Columbia University Press, 1988], p. 18; chapter 7 is entitled "Toward a Theory of Play" [207–38]).

16. Sigmund Freud, "Lecture 5," in *Introductory Lectures on Psycho-*

analysis, trans. James Strachey (Harmondsworth: Penguin Books, 1973), p. 128.

17. For an example of this mode of analysis, see Edmond Radar, "A Genealogy: Play, Folklore, and Art," *Diogenes* 103 (Fall 1978): 78–99. Radar argues that "the manifestations of play" unfold in the imagination, give form to time and space, and are governed by the pleasure principle (p. 79). Although the bibliography of works devoted to the analysis of the relationships between psychoanalysis (in all its formulations) and literature is vast, Meredith Anne Skura's *The Literary Use of the Psychoanalytic Process* (New Haven: Yale University Press, 1981) is an especially helpful introduction to a complex set of problems.

18. Eugen Fink, "The Oasis of Happiness: Toward an Ontology of Play," trans. Ute Saine and Thomas Saine, *Yale French Studies* 41 (1968): 24–25.

19. Jean Piaget, *Six Psychological Studies*, trans. Anita Tenzer (New York: Vintage Books, 1968), p. 23. For a critical extrapolation of the Piaget model, see Dennis J. Huston, *Shakespeare's Comedies of Play* (New York: Columbia University Press, 1981).

20. For a discussion of the influence of Jungian analytic psychology on characterization in modern fiction, see F. L. Radford and R. R. Wilson, "Some Phases of the Jungian Moon: Jung's Influence on Modern Literature," *English Studies in Canada* 8 (September 1982): 311–32. The archetypes of the unconscious may be said to "play" through the conscious levels of the psyche and to find their expression in roles that are played on the conscious, or surface, level. Role-playing is a distinctive aspect of characterization in all fiction influenced by the Jungian psychological model. (This is, for example, overwhelmingly the case in the fiction of Patrick White.) For a recent example of criticism that examines literary role-playing, see Eileen Jorge Allman, *Player-King and Adversary: Two Faces of Play in Shakespeare* (Baton Rouge: Louisiana State University Press, 1981).

21. The "game analogy" appears in two ways in Wittgenstein's *Philosophical Investigations*, trans. G. E. M. Anscombe (Oxford: Basil Blackwell, 1953). First, discrete activities are called games; for example, the "reporting of slabs" game (p. 10e, para. 21). Second, Wittgenstein singles out games as instances of separate activities that possess a "family resemblance" but not a definition (pp. 31e–32e, para. 66). The availability of "family" resemblances is opposed to the futility of definitions; however, the term has taken on constructive functions in contemporary discourse in order to express close relationships between specific concepts. See Renford Bambrough's "Universals and Family Resemblances," in *Proceedings of the Aristotelean Society* 63 (1960–61): 207–22; reprinted in George Pitcher, ed., *Wittgenstein: The "Philosophical Investigations"* (Garden City, N.Y.: Anchor Books, 1966), pp. 186–204. Highly formalized analysis of Wittgenstein's notion of language games can be found in Jaakko Hintikka and Jack Kulas, *The Game of Language: Studies in Game-Theoretical Semantics and Its Applications* (Dordrecht: D. Reidel, 1983). The second usage is, perhaps, the most famous instance of the "game analogy" in Wittgenstein, but it is the

first that has promoted a line of subsidiary analysis. See Gabriel Josipovici, *The World and the Book* (London: Macmillan, 1971). More recently, the notion of "language games" has been used with great effect by Jean-François Lyotard in *The Postmodern Condition: A Report on Knowledge* (1979), trans. Geoff Bennington and Brian Massumi (Minneapolis: University of Minnesota Press, 1984). The usage is carried on in Lyotard and Jean-Loup Thébaud, *Just Gaming* (1979), trans. Wlad Godzich (Minneapolis: University of Minnesota Press, 1985).

22. Although the relationship between speech act theory and Wittgenstein could be contested, the importance of the "game analogy" does not seem to be in doubt. See J. L. Austin, *How to Do Things with Words*, ed. J. O. Urmson (New York: Oxford University Press, 1965); John Searle, *Speech Acts: An Essay in the Philosophy of Language* (Cambridge: Cambridge University Press, 1969), and *Expression and Meaning: Studies in the Theory of Speech Acts* (Cambridge: Cambridge University Press, 1979). The game analogy (especially with regard to how "rules" work) runs through *Speech Acts* (see pp. 33–42, 63–64). A number of attempts have been made to apply speech act theory to the study of literature (it has been called everything from "the most sophisticated theory of literature available" to a "banal system of taxonomy"); see, for example, Wolfgang Iser, "The Reality of Fiction: A Functionalist Approach to Literature," *New Literary History* 7 (Autumn 1975): 7–35. The most fully developed examination of speech act theory in relation to literature is Mary Louise Pratt, *Toward a Speech Act Theory of Literary Discourse* (Bloomington: Indiana University Press, 1977). The emphasis on isolatable, discrete activities, each possessing its constitutive rule (hence making a separate "game") seems to appeal to those who prefer atomistic (empirical and particularizing) modes of analysis.

23. Thomas Pavel, *The Poetics of Plot: The Case of English Renaissance Drama* (Minneapolis: University of Minnesota Press, 1985), p. 14.

24. For example, see George de Forest Lord, *Heroic Mockery: Variations on Epic Themes from Homer to Joyce* (Newark: University of Delaware Press, 1977), pp. 17–18, 40. For a discussion of Lord's use of game theory terms, see R. R. Wilson, "Three Prolusions: Toward a Game Model in Literary Theory," *Canadian Review of Comparative Literature* 8 (Winter 1981): 79–92.

25. See Elizabeth Bruss, "The Game of Literature and Some Literary Games," *New Literary History* 9 (1977): 153–72. See also Bernard Suits, "The Detective Story: A Case Study of Games in Literature," *Canadian Review of Comparative Literature* 12 (June 1985): 200–219.

26. Robert Alter, *Motives for Fiction* (Cambridge, Mass.: Harvard University Press, 1984), p. 92.

27. See Oskar Morgenstern and John von Neumann, *Theory of Games and Economic Behavior* (Princeton: Princeton University Press, 1944). There exists an extensive bibliography of expositions of game theory and its applications to specific situations. See Anatol Rapoport, *Fights, Games and Debates* (Ann Arbor: University of Michigan Press, 1960), and Rapo-

port, ed., *Game Theory as a Theory of Conflict Resolution* (Dordrecht: D. Reidel, 1974). Paul Diesing's *Patterns of Discovery in the Social Sciences* (Chicago: Aldine, 1971) contains an excellent account of mathematical game theory (see esp. pp. 42–46). For a discussion of game theory from a philosopher's point of view, see Richard B. Braithwaite, *Theory of Games as a Tool for the Moral Philosopher* (Cambridge: Cambridge University Press, 1955).

28. See Warren F. Motte, Jr., *Oulipo: A Primer of Potential Literature* (Lincoln: University of Nebraska Press, 1986).

29. Ann Swinfen, *In Defence of Fantasy: A Study of the Genre in English and American Literature since 1945* (London: Routledge & Kegan Paul, 1984), p. 3. This proposition is, of course, common to analyses of fantasy. See W. R. Irwin, *The Game of the Impossible: A Rhetoric of Fantasy* (Urbana: University of Illinois Press, 1976).

30. Félix Martínez-Bonati, *Fictive Discourse and the Structures of Literature: A Phenomenological Approach* (Ithaca: Cornell University Press, 1981), p. 92.

31. Derrida's "version of play . . . wants to do without ontological anchors" (Frank Lentricchia, *After the New Criticism* [Chicago: University of Chicago Press, 1980], p. 168).

32. James S. Hans, "Derrida and Freeplay," *Modern Language Notes* 94 (1979): 809, 823.

33. Jacques Derrida, *L'Ecriture et la différence* (Paris: Editions du Seuil, 1967), p. 423; *Writing and Difference*, trans. Alan Bass (Chicago: University of Chicago Press, 1978), p. 289.

34. Jacques Derrida, *De la grammatologie* (Paris: Editions de Minuit, 1967), p. 73; *Of Grammatology*, trans. Gayatri Chakravorty Spivak (Baltimore: Johns Hopkins University Press, 1974), p. 50.

35. Jacques Derrida, *Positions* (Paris: Editions de Minuit, 1972), p. 38. See also "Living On: Border Lines," in *Deconstruction and Criticism*, ed. Harold Bloom et al. (New York: Continuum, 1979), in which Derrida observes that there is no "shore" or "edge" to discourse but only continuous deferral (p. 82) and that hence a text must be taken as a "differential network, a fabric of traces referring endlessly to something other than itself, to other differential traces" (p. 84). Clearly, within Derridean deconstruction, this constitutes an inescapable (though not, of course, "central") proposition.

36. Vicki Mistacco, with unmistakable echoes of Roland Barthes, provides the following definition of *ludisme*, which seems to capture the textual possibilities of free play: "The open play of signification, as the free and productive interaction of forms, of signifiers and signifieds, without regard for an original or an ultimate meaning." See "The Theory and Practice of Reading Nouveaux Romans: Robbe-Grillet's *Topologie d'une cité fantôme*," in *The Reader in the Text: Essays on Audience and Interpretation*, ed. Susan R. Suleiman and Inge Crosman (Princeton: Princeton University Press, 1980), p. 375, n. 2.

37. See Brian Edwards, "Deconstructing the Artist and the Art: Barth and

Calvino at Play in the Funhouse of Language," *Canadian Review of Comparative Literature* 12 (June 1985): 264–86.

38. Howard Felperin, *Beyond Deconstruction: The Uses and Abuses of Literary Theory* (Oxford: Clarendon Press, 1985), p. 131.

39. Suits, "Detective Story," p. 218.

40. Frank Kermode, *The Genesis of Secrecy* (Cambridge, Mass.: Harvard University Press, 1979), p. 17.

41. For a valuable bibliographical discussion of empirical games in literature, see Elisabeth Frenzel, "Spieler," in *Motive der Weltliteratur* (Stuttgart: Kroner, 1980), pp. 633–43.

42. Peter Hutchinson, *Games Authors Play* (London: Methuen, 1983), p. 14.

43. For a narrative written in questions that is not itself a question, see David Arnason's brilliantly Oulipoesque "Do Astronauts Have Sex Fantasies?" in *The Circus Performers' Bar* (Vancouver: Talonbooks, 1984), pp. 95–98.

44. "Game, Play, Literature," *Yale French Studies*, ed. Jacques Ehrmann, 41 (1968). An examination of the 208 items in James A. G. Marino's "Annotated Bibliography of Play and Literature," *Canadian Review of Comparative Literature* 12 (June 1985): 306–58, reveals that the great majority of entries were written after the 1968 issue of *Yale French Studies*.

45. M. M. Bakhtin, *Rabelais and His World*, trans. Hélène Iswolsky (Cambridge, Mass.: MIT Press, 1968); Hans-Georg Gadamer, *Wahrheit und Methode: Grundzüge einer philosophischen Hermeneutik* (Tübingen: J. C. B. Mohr, 1960), *Truth and Method*, trans. Garrett Barden and John Cumming (1975; rpt. New York: Crossroad, 1988). For discussion of *The Grasshopper* see Wilson, "Three Prolusions."

46. Felperin asserts that deconstruction is "the only poststructuralist definition and defence of literature on offer" (*Beyond Deconstruction*, p. 220), but most theorists would disagree. The textual revolution is, *tout court*, the radical transformation of all notions of text and textuality (a revolution that is, much as Kant called his philosophy, "Copernican") by a number of thinkers from the late 1960s on. Derrida is, no doubt, the most widely known, but he is certainly not alone. Roland Barthes, after a certain point in his career, and Julia Kristeva were especially momentous in fomenting the textual revolution, but many contributors to *Tel Quel* played a hand or two. The account of *Tel Quel*'s influence given by Jonathan Culler in 1975 remains immensely helpful: "'Beyond' Structuralism: *Tel Quel*," in *Structuralist Poetics: Structuralism, Linguistics, and the Study of Literature* (Ithaca: Cornell University Press, 1975), pp. 241–54. Roland Barthes's overview of the textual revolution, written as an article for the *Encyclopaedia Universalis*, is invaluable: "Theory of the Text," trans. Ian McLeod, in *Untying the Text: A Post-Structuralist Reader*, ed. Robert Young (Boston: Routledge & Kegan Paul, 1981), pp. 31–47. Young's introduction to his collection provides a readable summary of poststructuralist textual positions.

47. Julia Kristeva, *Séméiotikē: Recherches pour une sémanalyse* (Paris: Editions du Seuil, 1969). For a bibliography on the problem of intertextual-

ity, see Don Bruce, "Bibliographie annotée: Ecrits sur l'intertextualité," *Texte: Revue de critique et de théorie littéraire* 2 (1983): 217–58.

48. The unwritten history of play and game would probably reveal not only that games appear, are played enthusiastically, and then disappear (following determinate sociocultural shifts), but that the continuing process of rule transformations makes new games out of old ones. North American football developed from rugby through a series of historically verifiable transformations of the rules. On the campus of the University of California at Berkeley there is a statue, tucked away in a grove of eucalyptus trees, by Douglas Tilden that honors the "prize of superiority in football won by the University of California in 1898 and 1899." The statue depicts two young men in a heroic stance, more like a statue for ancient warriors than football players, in which one kneels to bind the calf of the other. No doubt, Tilden made use of the wrong conventions or, more likely, did not know any conventions appropriate to football. Even more interesting are the uniforms of the two players and the ball the standing figure holds. They are clearly dressed as rugby players, and the ball, large and thickly ovoid, is a rugby ball. Tilden may have achieved this bronze manifestation of the shadow-turf between two games, the one evolved from the other through a gradual transformation of the rules, only because of his ignorance of North American football (he cast the statue in Paris), but the effect is striking. The statue seems to capture one game at a moment when it was still, in an important sense, its own precursor. It is as if a memorial replaying of a famous early modern chess game, the "Immortal," say, between Adolf Anderssen and Lionel Kieseritzky, was reconstituted on an Ashtapada board according to the rules of Shatranj. Other games, such as the Royal Game of Ur, clearly significant to the unwritten history of games, are known only through their wooden materialities, their rule structures unknown. Whether, for instance, the Royal Game was a precursor (or analogue) of chess or of backgammon may never be known with certainty.

CHAPTER 2

1. Jorge Luis Borges, *Ficciones* (Madrid: Alianza, 1974), p. 89; *Labyrinths: Selected Stories and Other Writings*, ed. Donald A. Yates and James E. Irby (New York: New Directions, 1962), p. 51.

2. Borges, *Ficciones*, p. 90; *Labyrinths*, p. 52.

3. Felperin, *Beyond Deconstruction*, p. 123.

4. Joel Weinsheimer, "Theory of Character: *Emma*," *Poetics Today* 1 (1979): 195.

5. Mihai Spariosu, *Literature, Mimesis and Play: Essays in Literary Theory* (Tübingen: Gunter Narr Verlag, 1982), p. 13. Although the history of play concepts has not been written, Spariosu's book, particularly the first chapter, "Literature and Play: History, Principles, Method" (pp. 13–52), adumbrates such a history. No single bibliography has captured the complex range of discussions about play and game concepts in the social sciences. In

the social sciences the differences between diverse formulations of the concepts are as important, and perhaps more rigidly argued, as they are in literary studies. An interest in play or in simulation games in sociology, or in play as an aspect of learning processes in psychology does not reflect the same conceptual framework as does an interest in mathematical game theory in economics or political science. For the latter (which is utterly remote from any discussion of play), see Rapoport, *Fights, Games and Debates*, and Rapoport, ed., *Game Theory as a Theory of Conflict Resolution*. For an interesting discussion of play in anthropology, see "The Anthropological Study of Human Play," ed. Edward Norbeck, *Rice University Studies* 60 (Summer 1974). Though primarily devoted to literary studies, James A. G. Marino's "Annotated Bibliography of Play and Literature" includes a number of significant items from the social sciences and from philosophy.

6. Gadamer, *Truth and Method*, pp. 93, 110. As the argument of this chapter makes clear, there are affinities between Gadamer's and Derrida's accounts of play's conceptual kernel: that play is, fundamentally, a process of reciprocal motion. Thc *OED* partially agrees with both Gadamer and Derrida; it observes that "all uses of 'play' are seen to arise naturally from a primary notion 'to exercise, bestir, or busily occupy oneself', the line of development having been determined by the recreative or directive purpose of the exercise."

7. Jacques Derrida, *La Dissémination* (Paris: Editions du Seuil, 1972), p. 177; *Dissemination*, trans. Barbara Johnson (Chicago: University of Chicago Press, 1981), p. 153.

8. Lubomír Doležel, "Truth and Authenticity in Narrative," *Poetics Today* 1 (Spring 1980): 21; Alain Robbe-Grillet, *Pour un nouveau roman* (Paris: Editions de Minuit, 1963), p. 9; *For a New Novel: Essays on Fiction*, trans. Richard Howard (New York: Grove Press, 1965), p. 9; David Lodge, *Working with Structuralism: Essays and Reviews on Nineteenth- and Twentieth-Century Literature* (Boston: Routledge & Kegan Paul, 1981), p. 15.

9. Vladimir Propp, *Morphology of the Folktale*, trans. Laurence Scott (Austin: University of Texas Press, 1975).

10. Lubomír Doležel, "Kafka's Fictional World," *Canadian Review of Comparative Literature* 11 (March 1984): 61–83.

11. Christine Brooke-Rose, *A Rhetoric of the Unreal: Studies in Narrative and Structure, Especially of the Fantastic* (Cambridge: Cambridge University Press, 1981), pp. 311–38; Gérard Genette, *Figures III* (Paris: Editions du Seuil, 1972), pp. 188, 265; *Narrative Discourse: An Essay in Method*, trans. Jane E. Lewin (Ithaca: Cornell University Press, 1980), pp. 168, 259.

12. The distinction between story and discourse seems basic to the formal analysis of literature and perhaps to common sense as well. It does not need to be defended, but, like any analytic concept, it can be clarified. Although it is implicit in Aristotle's *Poetics*, contemporary formulations derive from the work of the Russian formalists. Their distinction between *fabula* (story-stuff) and *sjužet* (plot), it has been said, moved the study of

prose fiction "off dead center" and set the stage "for work on the history and theory of the novel" (*Readings in Russian Poetics: Formalist and Structuralist Views*, ed. Ladislaw Matejka and Krystyna Pomorska [Cambridge, Mass.: MIT Press, 1971], p. 21). The distinction has made possible, among other things, the analysis of narrative according to models of textual codes and grammars. Every use of the distinction as a methodological tool has assumed that *story* is an empty concept or merely an analytic device to make certain kinds of critical investigation possible. Thus Jonathan Culler argues (*The Pursuit of Signs: Semiotics, Literature, Deconstruction* [Ithaca: Cornell University Press, 1981], p. 170) that *story* is only a "heuristic fiction." The extent to which *story* may be more than a heuristic fiction (a discoverable prototype, an archetype, a set of colligatory motifs, or even a potential for narrative) is one of the implicit problems of literary theory and it will constitute one of the lines of discussion in this book. See especially Chapter 6.

13. See Linda Hutcheon, *Narcissistic Narrative: The Metafictional Paradox* (London: Methuen, 1984), pp. 118–37, quote on p. 121.

14. Gadamer, *Truth and Method*, p. 93.

15. For a discussion of the difficulties in translating Bakhtin's idiosyncratic Russian, see Caryl Emerson, "Translating Bakhtin: Does His Theory of Discourse Contain a Theory of Translation?" *University of Ottawa Quarterly* 53 (January–March 1983): 23–33. See also Emerson's valuable glossary of Bakhtinian terms in Michael Holquist, ed., *The Dialogic Imagination: Four Essays by M. M. Bakhtin* (Austin: University of Texas Press, 1981), pp. 423–34.

16. Tzetvan Todorov, *Mikail Bakhtine: Le principe dialogique* (Paris: Editions du Seuil, 1981), p. 7.

17. *Translinguistics* is the normal term in English by which to signify Bakhtin's linguistic theories. The term, however, belongs to Bakhtin's English translations. In their biography of Bakhtin, Katerina Clark and Michael Holquist note that Bakhtin calls his theories "metalinguistics," but they translate Bakhtin's term as "'translinguistics' because the term *meta* has become so banal in the West" (*Mikhail Bakhtin* [Cambridge, Mass.: Harvard University Press, 1984], p. 10). See also Gary Saul Morson, "The Heresiarch of *Meta*," *PTL* 3 (October 1978): 407–27.

18. Michael Holquist, "The Politics of Representation," in *Allegory and Representation: Selected Papers from the English Institute, 1979–80*, ed. Stephen J. Greenblatt (Baltimore: Johns Hopkins Press, 1981), p. 164.

19. Clark and Holquist, *Mikhail Bakhtin*, p. 217.

20. Mikhail Bakhtin, *Problems of Dostoevsky's Poetics*, trans. Caryl Emerson (Minneapolis: University of Minnesota Press, 1984), p. 6; Holquist, ed., *Dialogic Imagination*, p. 52.

21. Michael Holquist, "Bakhtin and Rabelais: Theory as Praxis," *boundary 2* 11 (Fall–Winter, 1983): 13.

22. Like the history of play, the history of carnival is largely unwritten. Specific aspects of carnival have been investigated as have carnivals in par-

ticular countries. Comments on carnival as a sociocultural phenomenon in France are made in Natalie Zemon Davis, *Society and Culture in Early Modern France* (Palo Alto: Stanford University Press, 1975). An examination of one historical carnival can be found in Emmanuel Le Roy Ladurie, *Le Carnaval de Romans: De la Chandeleur au mercredi des cendres, 1579–1580* (Paris: Editions Gallimard, 1979). The carnival in Paris is examined in Alain Faure, *Paris Carême-prenant: Du carnaval au XIX siècle, 1800–1914* (Paris: Hachette, 1978). An account of carnivals in Spain is given in Julio Carlo Baroja, *El Carnaval: Analysis historico-cultural*, 2d ed. (Madrid: Taurus, 1979). A general view of contemporary carnivals in Europe and South America may be found in Shaïtane, *Carnaval* (Paris: Editions Fernand Nathan, 1979). Marie Chicoine et al., eds., investigate a number of traditional North American carnivals in *Lâches Lousses: Les fêtes populaires au Québec, en Acadie et en Louisiane* (Montreal: VLB Editeur, 1982). To write the history of carnival would be a vast undertaking. A start toward that end was achieved during an exhibition devoted to European carnivals held in Paris at the Centre Pompidou during the spring of 1984. It ranged historically back to Roman *saturnalia* and synchronically across modern Europe. Slide shows were presented for each aspect of the subject, including each European country with a significant carnival experience. A portion of this sociocultural depth is captured in the catalog for the exhibition.

23. Bakhtin, *Problems of Dostoevsky's Poetics*, pp. 122, 130; Bakhtin, *Rabelais and His World*, p. 4; Andrew McKenna, "After Bakhtin: On the Future of Laughter and Its History in France," *University of Ottawa Quarterly* 53 (January–March 1983): 68.

24. Holquist, ed., *Dialogic Imagination*, p. 58; Bakhtin, *Rabelais and His World*, pp. 11–12.

25. Michael Holquist, "The Carnival of Discourse: Bakhtin and Simultaneity," *Canadian Review of Comparative Literature* 12 (June 1985): 220.

26. See Davis, *Society and Culture*, and Dominic La Capra, *Rethinking Intellectual History: Texts, Contexts, Language* (Ithaca: Cornell University Press, 1983).

27. The appropriation of Bakhtin's theory to the uses of practical criticism and interpretation has been widespread. For a few instructive examples, see the following: Linda Hutcheon, "The Carnivalesque and Contemporary Narrative: Popular Culture and the Erotic," *University of Ottawa Review* 53 (January–March 1983): 85–92; Edith Kern, *The Absolute Comic* (New York: Columbia University Press, 1980); Peter Petro, *Modern Satire: Four Studies* (Berlin: Mouton, 1982). Marie-Anne Macé's discussion of Alejo Carpentier, the Cuban novelist, is particularly interesting in its use of Bakhtinian notions, "Le Siècle des lumières ou les turbulences baroques," in Daniel-Henri Pageaux, ed., *Quinze études autour de "El Siglo de las Luces" de Alejo Carpentier* (Paris: Editions L'Harmattan, 1983), pp. 187–204. Brooke-Rose's *Rhetoric of the Unreal* tends to thematize the Bakhtinian concept of carnival, but in this, as in so many other respects,

deserves perusal. Instances of comparatively unsophisticated appropriations of Bakhtin in criticism are abundant.

28. Kristeva, *Séméiotikē*, pp. 144, 161, 160 (my translation).

29. Brooke-Rose, *Rhetoric of the Unreal*, p. 105; cf. p. 338.

30. Gadamer, *Truth and Method*, p. 100.

31. Joel C. Weinsheimer, *Gadamer's Hermeneutics: A Reading of "Truth and Method"* (New Haven: Yale University Press, 1985), p. 103.

32. See Chapter 1, note 36.

33. Derrida, *De la grammatologie*, p. 73; *Of Grammatology*, p. 50. In the passage cited, Spivak translates Derrida's *jeu* as *game.* I have revised her translation to read *play* because *game* does not seem to fit the conceptual context of the argument at this point. Spivak's footnote to Nietzsche, Heidegger, Fink, and Kostas Axelos provides evidence for strongly preferring *play* to *game*.

34. Derrida, *L'Ecriture et la différence*, p. 423. Two English translations of this important text exist: *Writing and Difference*, trans. Alan Bass, p. 289, and (with the original questions and answers of the 1966 Johns Hopkins conference) in Richard Macksey and Eugenio Donato, eds., *The Structuralist Controversy*: *The Languages of Criticism and the Sciences of Man* (Baltimore: Johns Hopkins University Press, 1972), p. 260.

35. Derrida, "Living On: Border Lines," in Bloom, *Deconstruction and Criticism*, pp. 82, 84; Derrida, *L'Ecriture et la différence*, p. 413; *Writing and Difference*, p. 211; Derrida, *Positions*, p. 38; *Positions*, trans. Alan Bass (Chicago: University of Chicago Press, 1981), p. 26; Jonathan Culler, *On Deconstruction: Theory and Criticism after Structuralism* (Ithaca: Cornell University Press, 1981), p. 99; Roland Barthes, *S/Z: Essai* (Paris: Editions du Seuil, 1970), pp. 171, 12; *S/Z: An Essay*, trans. Richard Miller (New York: Hill and Wang, 1974), pp. 165, 5.

36. Derrida, *Dissémination*, pp. 181, 182; *Dissemination*, pp. 157, 158.

37. Geoffrey Hartman, "Monsieur Texte: On Jacques Derrida, His *Glas*," *Georgia Review* 29 (Winter 1975), 760–61; Hartman, "Monsieur Texte II: Epiphony in Echoland," *Georgia Review* 30 (Spring 1976): 174.

38. Spariosu, *Literature, Mimesis and Play*, p. 22.

39. Schiller, *On the Aesthetic Education of Man*, p. 107.

40. Fink's *Das Spiel als Weltsymbol* (Stuttgart: G. Umbreit, 1960) has not been translated into English. A French translation is available: *Le Jeu comme symbole du monde* (Paris: Editions de Minuit, 1966). An introduction to Fink's thinking on the subject of play can be found in Fink, "The Oasis of Happiness," pp. 19–30. Spariosu discusses Fink's ideas in *Literature, Mimesis and Play*, pp. 26–29.

41. See the discussion of this point in Chapter 1.

42. Roman Jacobson, "Two Aspects of Language and Two Types of Aphasic Disturbances," in *Fundamentals of Language*, ed. Jacobson and Morris Halle (The Hague: Mouton, 1956), pp. 55–82; see also Jacobson, "Closing Statement: Linguistics and Poetics," in *Style in Language*, ed.

Thomas A. Sebeok (Cambridge, Mass.: MIT Press, 1960), pp. 350–77. Ladislav Matejka observes that Jacobson early recognized that the "opposition between paradigmatic and syntagmatic procedures" was connected with the two "fundamental poles dominating the verbal operation: the metaphoric pole, making use of similarity, and the metonymic pole, making use of contiguity." Jacobson pursued this "connection" between lingusitic and literary categories, beginning with his study of Pasternak's prose (1927), through many discussions ("The Formal Method and Linguistics," in *Readings in Russian Poetics*, ed. Matejka and Pomorska, pp. 293–94). An excellent discussion of Jacobson's use of linguistic methodology in semiotics may be found in Terence Hawkes, *Structuralism and Semiotics* (Berkeley: University of California Press, 1977), pp. 76–87. See also Culler, *Structuralist Poetics*, pp. 55–74.

43. See James S. Hans, *The Play of the World* (Amherst: University of Massachusetts Press, 1981); see also Hans, "Derrida and Freeplay," p. 809.

44. Michael Holquist, "Answering as Authoring," *Critical Inquiry* 10 (December 1983): 311; rpt. in *Bakhtin: Essays and Dialogues on His Work*, ed. Gary Saul Morson (Chicago: University of Chicago Press, 1986), pp. 59–71. The metaphor of language as an ecosystem clearly appeals to Holquist because he uses it elsewhere. See "The Carnival of Discourse," p. 233, and his coauthored *Mikhail Bakhtin*, p. 227.

45. La Capra, *Rethinking Intellectual History*, p. 294. Bakhtin's comment can be found in Holquist, ed., *Dialogic Imagination*, p. 194.

46. La Capra, *Rethinking Intellectual History*, p. 301; Milan Kundera, "Afterword: A Talk with the Author," in *The Book of Laughter and Forgetting*, ed. Philip Roth, trans. Michael Henry Heim (New York: Penguin Books, 1981), p. 232. Kundera elaborates this point in an essay, "The Novel and Europe," trans. David Bellos, in the *New York Review of Books* 31 (July 19, 1984): 15–19. As Clark and Holquist point out, the musical analogue had already occurred to Bakhtin's friend Ivan Ivanovich Sollertinsky; see *Mikhail Bakhtin*, p. 266.

47. Clark and Holquist repeatedly argue that Bakhtin shared a specific *zeitgeist*, a complex moment in world history, with many other thinkers, including Einstein and Heidegger, so that it is not surprising to them that he should manifest so many concerns, preoccupations, and ideas developed by other thinkers of the early twentieth century. See *Mikhail Bakhtin*, p. 94.

48. Holquist, ed., *Dialogic Imagination*, p. 324.

49. In *Reflections on the Hero as Quixote* (Princeton: Princeton University Press, 1981), Alexander Welsh analyzes certain situations in which the Knight is "played with" or manipulated by another character who is in a cognitively superior position. He sees these narrative situations as practical jokes, but the more accurate designation, more specific and more consistent with contemporary narrative analysis, would be "godgame." See R. R. Wilson, "Review of Alexander Welsh's *Reflections on the Hero as Quixote*," *Modern Philology* 82 (August 1984): 120–24. For a full discussion of the concept of a godgame, see Chapter 4 below.

50. Jorge Luis Borges, "Sobre *The Purple Land,*" in *Otras inquisiciones* (Madrid: Alianza Editorial, 1976), p. 138; "About *The Purple Land,*" trans. Ruth L. C. Simms, in *Borges, A Reader*: *A Selection from the Writings of Jorge Luis Borges*, ed. Emir Rodriguez Monegal and Alastair Reid (New York: Dutton, 1981), p. 136.

51. L. S. Vygotsky, *Mind in Society*: *The Development of Higher Psychological Processes*, ed. and trans. Michael Cole et al. (Cambridge, Mass.: Harvard University Press, 1978), p. 103. See also Caryl Emerson, "The Outer Word and Inner Speech: Bakhtin, Vygotsky, and the Internalization of Language," in *Bakhtin*, ed. Morson, pp. 21–40.

CHAPTER 3

1. Kermode, *The Genesis of Secrecy*, p. 17.

2. Textual movements, motions, and moves may suggest different phenomena. Moves presuppose an intention. In a board game, moves reflect the player's prior thinking. Hayden White and both neorhetoricians and poststructuralists point out the "running to and fro" that the etymology of *discourse* implies (from Latin *discurrere*, to run back and forth). See White, *Tropics of Discourse* (Baltimore: Johns Hopkins University Press, 1978), 3–4. Patricia Parker, writing in the same spirit, analyzes Shakespeare's use of rhetorical tropes as textual motions and moves that seem to be functions of the text. In her discussion of the figure of *hysteron proteron* in the Clown's language in the fifth act of *The Winter's Tale*, she writes that the Clown may "take us . . . to other Shakespeare plays which play with the idea of following and succession, of 'naturall' or ordered sequence." See Parker, *Literary Fat Ladies*: *Rhetoric, Gender, Property* (London: Methuen, 1987), p. 68.

3. "Now, with the increasing systematization and regimentation of sport, something of the pure play-quality is inevitably lost. . . . The spirit of the professional is no longer the true play-spirit; it is lacking in spontaneity and carelessness" (Huizinga, *Homo Ludens*, p. 197). See also Christopher Lasch, "The Degradation of Work," pp. 43–45.

4. Huizinga writes, "No other modern language known to me has the exact equivalent of the English 'fun'" (*Homo Ludens*, p. 3). No doubt, *fun* is an ideal word with which to describe the complex motivations for play (pleasure, spontaneity, freedom, purposeless purposiveness, and so forth), but it tends to play down the rich range of human playfulness. Would one play a demanding game of chess merely for "fun" (as opposed to some more intricate concept of pleasure) or set oneself the gamelike task of writing a Petrarchan sonnet "just for fun"?

5. Istvan Szabó, *Square* (Budapest Film Studios, 1963; distributed by Hungarofilm, 35mm, color, 5 minutes).

6. Wittgenstein, *Philosophical Investigations*, p. 31e, para. 66.

7. Suits, *The Grasshopper*, p. 34.

8. John Rawls, "Two Concepts of Rules," *Philosophical Review* 64 (1955): 3–32.

9. Kathleen Blake defines *game* as occurring at "the point where it takes two to play and one will win" in *Play, Games and Sport: The Literary Works of Lewis Carroll* (Ithaca: Cornell University Press, 1974), p. 19. (It is a commonplace, though not one that Blake had heard, that in chess the best games are normally draws.) Elizabeth W. Bruss asserts that "the basic fact [is] that games require parity; a game, by definition, is the encounter between equally matched and equally creative participants" ("The Game of Literature," p. 154). Anyone who has seriously played a game, other than a child's game of pure luck, would perceive that these definitions are ludicrous. Neither definition expresses a necessary condition of game playing; neither will provide an account of what *goes on* in games as diverse as chess or ring-a-ring-a-roses. Whereas Blake seems to think that games can never be draws, Bruss thinks that they are or should always be draws. The momentous difficulties of basing an analysis of the possible gamefulness of literary texts on a game model without any definition of game, or even an understanding of the activity, are exemplified in Carolyn L. Dinshaw's "Dice Games and Other Games in *Le Jeu de saint Nicolas*," *PMLA* 95 (October 1980): 802–11. Dinshaw argues that the medieval world was characterized by a pervasive interest in games. Yet, other than a loose formula borrowed from Huizinga (that rules delimit a game and create a "sphere" of activity), Dinshaw provides no definition of, and no conceptual focus on, her key term, *game*. Dinshaw's failure to consider the problem of definition leads her into the unrewarding position of holding that a game can be predetermined (all of its options fixed in advance) and still be a game. The "cosmic game" of God's history is said to be a game precisely because its unfolding (its "rules, boundaries, the action itself") has been predetermined. It is difficult to say whether, in these and similar cases, the poor theory or the poor observation is most at fault.

10. Suits, *The Grasshopper*, p. 152. A glance at James A. G. Marino's "Annotated Bibliography of Play and Literature" will indicate how may articles claiming to analyze game elements in literature, of the game side of the game/text analogy, are little more than extrapolations of a few simple notions, drawn primarily from Huizinga and Caillois, and ultimately add up to little beyond the unreflective use of an incantatory critical vocabulary. In his article "The Detective Story," Suits addresses the problem of defining exhaustively the possible ways in which a literary text might be a game. He refers to this task, quoting his own Grasshopper on "loose talk," as "dealing with one of my own chickens that has come home to roost" (200).

11. Susan Sontag, *Against Interpretation and Other Essays* (New York: Dell, 1961), p. 33; Gabriel Josipovici, *The Lessons of Modernism and Other Essays* (London: Macmillan, 1977), p. 122; Steiner, "Introduction" to Huizinga, *Homo Ludens*, p. 12; Steiner, *On Difficulty and Other Essays* (New York: Oxford University Press, 1978), p. 39; Arthur Koestler, *The Act of Creation* (London: Pan Books, 1970), p. 39.

12. Vladimir Nabokov, *The Defense*, trans. Michael Scammell (New York: Capricorn Books, 1970), pp. 91–92; *The Annotated Alice*, ed. Martin Gardner (New York: Bramhall House, 1960), pp. 11–12.

13. Paul Valéry, "Au sujet d'Adonis," in *Oeuvres*, vol. 1, ed. Jean Hytier (Paris: Bibliothèque de la Pléiade–Editions Gallimard, 1957), p. 481 (my translation).

14. Kermode, *Genesis of Secrecy*, p. 53. Kermode employs *game* and *rule* with an analogous nonchalance in his "Secrets and Narrative Sequence," *Critical Inquiry* 7 (Autumn 1980): 89. Game concepts are a marginal concern in Kermode's writing, yet the casualness with which they are used suggests a symptomatic attitude. William H. Gass, *Fiction and the Figures of Life* (New York: Knopf, 1970), p. 124.

15. Suits argues that there are 1,023 possible ways in which literary texts might be actual games. See "The Detective Story," p. 216.

16. David Hume, *A Treatise of Human Nature*, ed. L. A. Selby-Bigge (Oxford: Clarendon Press, 1978), pp. 490–91.

17. The scholarly discussion of the concept of convention has been extensive in recent years. The following are important for anyone interested in tracing its configurations: Harry Levin, "Notes on Convention," in *Refractions: Essays in Comparative Literature* (New York: Oxford University Press, 1966), pp. 32–61; David Lewis, *Convention: A Philosophical Study* (Cambridge, Mass.: Harvard University Press, 1969). (In an analysis along the lines established by Hume, Lewis states the concept of convention as an instance of the general set of coordination problems. A valuable discussion of Lewis's position may be found in Margaret Gilbert, "Notes on the Concept of Social Convention," *New Literary History* 14 [Winter 1983]: 225–51.) Claudio Guillén, *Literature as System: Essays toward the Theory of Literary History* (Princeton: Princeton University Press, 1971); Bernard E. Rollin, "Nature, Convention, and Genre Theory," *Poetics* 10 (June 1981): 127–43. Two special issues of *New Literary History* have been devoted to the concept of convention: 13 (Autumn 1981) and 14 (Winter 1983). An important analysis of the concept occurs in the chapter entitled "Conventions" in Thomas Pavel's *Fictional Worlds* (Cambridge, Mass.: Harvard University Press, 1986), pp. 114–35. It would be impossible to acknowledge fully the many arguments, often expressing dissimilar positions, on the concept of convention that have been both helpful and provocative in the writing of this chapter.

18. Pavel, *Fictional Worlds*, p. 127. Pavel grounds his discussion of coordination games, as instances of convention-governed behavior, on the analysis in Barbara Herrnstein Smith's *On the Margins of Discourse* (Chicago: University of Chicago Press, 1978).

19. Huizinga employs the notions of the spoilsport and the false player (the cheat) in *Homo Ludens*, pp. 11–12. In *The Grasshopper*, Bernard Suits introduces the notion of the trifler.

20. The hypothesis that all human laws, theories, and models are conventions is known as conventionalism. See Peter Alexander's article "Conven-

tionalism" in *The Encyclopedia of Philosophy*, ed. Paul Edwards (New York: Macmillan, 1967; rpt. 1972), 1: 216–19. For another overview, see Hilary Putnam, "Convention: A Theme in Philosophy," *New Literary History* 13 (Autumn 1981): 1–14. Reflecting on the two special *New Literary History* issues on convention, E. D. Hirsch, Jr., distinguishes between strong and weak conventionalism ("Beyond Convention?" *New Literary History* 14 [Winter 1983]: 389–97).

21. Guillén, *Literature as System*, p. 63; Culler, *Structuralist Poetics*, pp. 5, 28–31. In his essay on the concept of convention in speech act theory, Culler refers to "conventional rules"; see Culler, "Convention and Meaning: Derrida and Austin," *New Literary History* 13 (Autumn 1981): 16. The conflation is commonplace and may be located on either side of ideological boundaries; see Gerald Graff, *Literature against Itself: Literary Ideas in Modern Society* (Chicago: University of Chicago Press, 1979), pp. 155, 157, 168. When Graff accuses Culler of acting "as if there is no question of the nature of the convention to be applied" (p. 168), it seems that he has missed Culler's point: there are many questions about the nature of convention, but Culler, equating convention and rule, does not raise them; his definition, if any, would be implicit in his discussion of Saussurian linguistics. It should be evident that, as the argument of this chapter maintains, the issue of definition is not fundamental (though the absence of any attempt to provide even operational definitions, as in the discussions of many literary scholars concerned with gamefulness in literary texts indicates, certainly does suggest something about the writer's ways of thinking). Even the precise definitions that emerge from several of the essays in the two special issues of *New Literary History* cannot close the gaps between definition and text. Perhaps the most fruitful approach would be to say, following Umberto Eco, that concepts such as convention (*a fortiori*, game or text) require encyclopedias, not definitions. See Eco, "Metaphor, Dictionary and Encyclopedia," *New Literary History* 15 (Winter 1984): 255–71.

22. Jay Schleusener, "Convention and the Context of Reading," *Critical Inquiry* 6 (Summer 1980): 669–80, esp. 674.

23. Baldassare Castiglione, *The Book of the Courtier*, trans. Charles S. Singleton (Garden City, N.Y.: Anchor/Doubleday, 1959), p. 62.

24. Paul Alpers, "Convening and Convention in Pastoral Poetry," *New Literary History* 14 (Winter 1983): 277.

25. Miguel de Cervantes, *El Ingenioso Hidalgo Don Quijote de La Mancha* (Madrid: Ediciones Castilla, 1963), p. 935. All translations of the *Quijote* given in the text are from *The Adventures of Don Quixote*, trans. J. M. Cohen (1950; rpt. Harmondsworth: Penguin Books, 1984), p. 902.

26. Cervantes, *Don Quijote*, p. 55; Cohen trans., p. 61.

27. Cervantes, *Don Quijote*, p. 84; Cohen trans., p. 85.

28. Walter W. Greg, *Pastoral Poetry and Pastoral Drama* (London: A. H. Bullern, 1906), p. 5. See also Maurice Evans, *English Poetry in the Sixteenth Century* (London: Hutchinson University Library, 1967), p. 89; Harold Toliver, *Pastoral Forms and Attitudes* (Berkeley: University of California Press,

Press, 1971), p. 3; Renato Pogglioli, *The Oaten Flute*: *Essays on Pastoral Poetry and the Pastoral Ideal* (Cambridge, Mass.: Harvard University Press, 1975), p. 2.

29. *Pastoral Poetry*, Greg, pp. 5, 7; Toliver, *Pastoral Forms*, p. 3; Alpers, "Convening and Convention," pp. 284–87.

30. Cervantes, Don Quijote, p. 935–36; Cohen trans., p. 902.

31. Robert Coover, *Pricksongs and Descants*: *Fictions* (New York: New American Library, 1969), pp. 46–60. It is significant that Coover names his dystopic shepherd "Morris" since the Morris dance was associated with traditional pastoral games. Titania's account of the decay in human customs, which some Shakespearean scholars suppose to be topical, that has followed upon the rift between herself and Oberon specifically mentions that "The nine men's morris is filled up with mud" (*Midsummer Night's Dream*, 2.1. 98).

32. Hallett Smith, "Pastoral Poetry: The Vitality and Versatility of a Convention," in *Elizabethan Poetry*: *A Study in Conventions, Meanings and Expressions* (Cambridge, Mass.: Harvard University Press, 1964), pp. 10, 8.

33. Borges, *Ficciones* pp. 47–59. "Mi solitario juego esta gobernado por dos leyes polares" (p. 55) (my translation). For English translation, see James E. Irby, trans., in *Labyrinths*: *Selected Stories and Other Writings*, ed. Donald A. Yates and James E. Irby (New York: New Directions, 1962), pp. 36–44.

34. Howard Felperin, *Beyond Deconstruction*, p. 123.

35. John Searle, in *Speech Acts*, makes this distinction. See also Alpers, "Convening and Convention," p. 304 n. 41.

36. W. K. Wimsatt, "How to Compose Chess Problems and Why," *Yale French Studies* 41 (1968): 74.

37. See the entry on the "Fairy Problem" in *The Oxford Companion to Chess*, ed. David Hooper and Kenneth Whyld (Oxford: Oxford University Press, 1984), p. 110.

38. *The Annotated Alice*, ed. Gardner, pp. 170, 172. Gardner points out that, since Carroll, many writers, particularly writers of science fiction, have used the idea of a chess problem as an underforming narrative structure.

39. Huizinga, *Homo Ludens*, p. 8.

40. Nabokov, *The Defense*, p. 8. For the moves of the Immortal Game, see *The Oxford Companion to Chess*, p. 150.

41. Tzetvan Todorov, *The Fantastic*: *A Structural Approach to a Literary Genre*, trans. Richard Howard (Ithaca: Cornell University Press, 1975), pp. 24–40.

42. Motte, *Oulipo*.

43. José Ortega y Gasset, *Meditations on the Quijote*, trans. Evelyn Rugg and Diego Marín (New York: Norton, 1963), pp. 136–37.

44. Susan Stewart, "Shouts on the Street: Bakhtin's Anti-Linguistics," in *Bakhtin*, ed. Gary Saul Morson, p. 46.

CHAPTER 4

1. *The Shepheardes Calender*, "Januarie," 1.61 gloss, in *The Poetical Works of Edmund Spenser*, ed. J. C. Smith and E. de Sélincourt (Oxford: Oxford University Press, 1912; rpt. 1966), p. 423.

2. John Barth, *The Friday Book: Essays and Other Nonfiction* (New York: Putnam's, 1984), p. 257.

3. Ihab Hassan, "Pluralism in Postmodern Perspective," *Critical Inquiry* 12 (Spring 1986): 504; rpt. in *The Postmodern Turn: Essays in Postmodern Theory and Culture* ([Columbus]: Ohio State University Press, 1987), pp. 167–87.

4. Hutcheon, *Narcissistic Narrative*, p. xii.

5. Stephen Greenblatt, *Renaissance Self-Fashioning: From More to Shakespeare* (Chicago: University of Chicago Press, 1980), pp. 225–29.

6. Greenblatt, *Renaissance Fashioning*, p. 5.

7. Terry Eagleton, "Capitalism, Modernism and Postmodernism," in *Against the Grain: Essays, 1975–1985* (London: Verso–New Left Books, 1986), pp. 131–47. This essay first appeared in *New Left Review* 152 (July–August 1985). See also Eagleton's *The End of English: The Pratt Lecture, 1986* (St. John's: Memorial University of Newfoundland, 1986).

8. Fredric Jameson, "Postmodernism, or the Cultural Logic of Late Capitalism," *New Left Review* 146 (July–August 1984): 56.

9. Paul Bové, "The Ineluctability of Difference: Scientific Pluralism and the Critical Intelligence," in *Postmodernism and Politics*, ed. Jonathan Arac (Minneapolis: University of Minnesota Press, 1986), p. 17.

10. Allen Thiher, *Words in Reflection: Modern Language Theory and Postmodern Fiction* (Chicago: University of Chicago Press, 1984), p. 7.

11. David Lodge, "The Novelist at the Crossroads," in *The Novel Today: Contemporary Writers on Modern Fiction*, ed. Malcolm Bradbury (Manchester: Manchester University Press, 1977), p. 105.

12. William H. Gass, "Philosophy and the Form of Fiction," in *Fiction and the Figures of Life* (New York: Knopf, 1970), p. 25; Robert Scholes, *Fabulation and Metafiction* (Urbana: University of Illinois Press, 1979). In recent years many books and articles have been written on the subject of postmodernism and/or metafiction. Some of these in English are Margaret Rose, *Parody/Metafiction: An Analysis of Parody as a Critical Mirror to the Writing and Reception of Fiction* (London: Croom Helm, 1979); Steven Kellman, *The Self-Begetting Novel* (London: Macmillan, 1980); Christine Brooke-Rose, *Rhetoric of the Unreal;* Inger Christensen, *The Meaning of Metafiction* (Bergen, Nor.: Universitetsforlaget, 1981); Charles Caramello, *Silverless Mirrors: Books, Self and Postmodern Fiction* (Tallahassee: Florida State University Press, 1983); Jerome Klinkowitz, *The Self-Apparent Word: Fiction as Language/Language as Fiction* (Carbondale: Southern Illinois University Press, 1984); Alan Singer, *A Metaphorics of Fiction: Discontinuity and Discourse in the Modern Novel* (Tallahassee: Florida State Univer-

sity Press, 1984); Patricia Waugh, *Metafiction: The Theory and Practice of Self-Conscious Fiction* (London: Methuen, 1984). Several of Ihab Hassan's many writings on postmodernism over twenty years have been collected in *The Postmodern Turn*. The topic, by one name or another, has become pervasive in French criticism. For a starting point, see Lucien Dällenbach, *Le Récit spéculaire* (Paris: Editions du Seuil, 1973). Brooke-Rose's *Rhetoric of the Unreal* analyzes in depth the metafictional elements in contemporary French fiction, particularly that of Robbe-Grillet.

13. Jameson, "Postmodernism," pp. 60–61, 67.

14. Caramello, *Silverless Mirrors*, p. 4.

15. Hassan observes that traditionally "genre assumed recognizable features within a context of both persistence and change; it was a useful assumption of identity upon which critics (somewhat like Stanley and Livingstone) often presumed. But that assumption, in our heteroclitic age, seems ever harder to maintain. . . . In boundary genres particularly—and certain kinds of criticism may have become precisely that—the ambiguities attain new heights of febrile intensity" ("Pluralism in Postmodern Perspective," p. 509). The notion of permeable, or semipermeable, boundaries, open to transgression, always already broken and crossed, both everted and invaginated, is a poststructuralist topos. It is particularly commonplace in deconstruction, which considers rupture and invagination the conditions of boundaryhood. See Jacques Derrida, "The Law of Genre," in *On Narrative*, ed. W. J. T. Mitchell (Chicago: University of Chicago Press, 1981), pp. 51–77.

16. Thiher, *Words in Reflection*, pp. 93, 95, 156.

17. Barth, *The Friday Book*, p. 256.

18. Ihab Hassan, "Toward a Concept of Postmodernism," in *The Postmodern Turn*, pp. 93–94; first published in *The Dismemberment of Orpheus: Toward a Postmodern Literature* (New York: Oxford University Press, 1971; rev. ed., 1982).

19. Roland Barthes, "The Reality Effect," in *French Literary Theory Today: A Reader*, ed. Tzetvan Todorov (Cambridge: Cambridge University Press, 1982), pp. 11–17.

20. Mark Abley, "Bugged," *Saturday Night* 102 (February 1987): 36–37. Umberto Eco refers to "incontinent collectionism." See *Travels in Hyperreality: Essays*, trans. William Weaver (London: Picador, 1987; 1st ed., *Faith in Fakes*, London: Secker & Warburg, 1986), p. 22.

21. Susan Stewart, *On Longing: Narratives of the Miniature, the Gigantic, the Souvenir, the Collection* (Baltimore: Johns Hopkins University Press, 1984), p. 159. In her *Nonsense: Aspects of Intertextuality in Folklore and Literature* (Baltimore: Johns Hopkins Press, 1978), Stewart discusses the paradoxes inherent in the concept of a boundary.

22. Kendrick Smithyman calls the category of Commonwealth literature a "handy fiction." See "The Commonwealth Experience, the Common Response," *Journal of Commonwealth Literature* 6 (June 1971): 6. Indeed, the initial editorial of the *Journal of Commonwealth Literature* noted, with considerable insouciance, that it was only a "convenient shorthand" that

doubtless should not be taken too seriously. See "Editorial," 1 (September 1965): v. Yet despite the uncertainties of its boundaries, and although, as Smithyman remarks, one seldom finds a person "who is a Commonwealth writer or finds a piece of professedly Commonwealth writing" (p. 6), Commonwealth literature does exist. It is a possible professional category (with its own journals and conferences and its appointed slots at conferences such as the MLA) and it does serve, valiantly and well, to collect writers who, in normal literary studies, seem to be consistently marginalized, even excluded.

23. Murray Bail, *Homesickness* (London: Macmillan, 1980; rpt., Melbourne: Penguin Books, 1981) (subsequent references are given in the text); Robert Kroetsch, *Alibi* (Toronto: General Publishing, 1983) (subsequent references are given in the text).

24. Eugenio Donato, "The Museum's Furnace: Notes toward a Contextual Reading of *Bouvard and Pécuchet*," in *Textual Strategies: Perspectives in Post-Structuralist Criticism*, ed. Josué V. Harari (Ithaca: Cornell University Press, 1979), p. 220.

25. The smug official discourse of museum curators would be worth a study in itself. Museum catalogs and brochures commonly illustrate the fundamental human pleasure in self-congratulation. For a striking example, see William Jacob Holland, "Museums of Science," in *The Encyclopaedia Britannica*, 11th ed., vol. 19 (Cambridge: Cambridge University Press, 1911), pp. 64–69. Holland, the curator of the Carnegie Institute, cites his own institution ("the most magnificent foundation for the advancement of science and art in America which has yet been created") as a model of what a museum should be. He includes the plan of the first floor of the Carnegie Institute, which reveals a high degree of heterogeneity (the Gallery of Sculpture, for example, runs parallel to Geology and Minerals and at right angles to the Gallery of Useful Arts, Ceramics, and so on) and thus suggests an adventitiousness that the curator's claims deny.

26. Museums of natural history typically build into their exhibits a paradoxicality that other museums can hardly obtain. In paleontological displays, the bones, which are fossils, may or may not be real. Most likely, they are fiberglass or lightweight plastic simulacra and the real bones are kept safely elsewhere. They may also be reconstructions, curatorial projections of what the skeletal frame of a whole animal *must have* looked like, or they may be combinations, probably not color-coded, of both fossil materials and plastic. A fossil is, of course, only a natural simulacrum—a permineralized displacement of what once may have been a real bone. Documentation in paleontological exhibits also contains an extraordinary amount of paradoxicality. Contradictory accounts (dinosaurs died out gradually; they died out suddenly; they did not entirely die out but became birds) are normally given, under the name of science, as if they were all true. In other words, conjecture plays the role of fact. See R. R. Wilson, "The *Struthiomimus*'s Tale: Discourse in the Tyrrell Museum," *Alberta: Studies in the Arts and Sciences* 1 (1988): 75–95. Umberto Eco recounts his explorations of various

American museums in which the distinction between a copy and an authentic item is not merely lost but deliberately obfuscated. He concludes that the "real fake" lies at the heart of museum practice in the United States: museums often seek an authenticity that is not historical but purely visual. See *Travels in Hyperreality*, pp. 3–58.

27. For a general biocritical discussion of Kroetsch's writing, see Robert R. Wilson, "Robert Kroetsch," in *Dictionary of Literary Biography*, vol. 53, ed. W. H. New (Detroit: Bruccoli Clark–Gale, 1986), pp. 240–55.

28. When a version of this part of the argument was presented at the Seventh Triennial Meeting of ALCLALS (Association of Commonwealth Literature and Language Studies), held at the National University of Singapore in June 1986, the Australians in the audience found this point in Kroetsch's novel both funny and (possibly) incomprehensible. In Australian lingo, a "spa" is a hot tub. The word collects reality rather differently in Australian and North American English. The actual place name, the spot in Belgium that, historically, gave its name to various sources of hot water, remains overlooked (that is, uncollected) in either version of modern English.

29. Vladimir Nabokov, "The Visit to the Museum," in *Nabokov's Quartet* (New York: Pyramid Books, 1966), pp. 109–25.

30. In her *Nonsense*, Susan Stewart discusses many aspects of the "boundary problem." In particular, see her chapter "Play with Boundaries" (pp. 85–115).

31. I once visited the Indian Museum in Calcutta, struggling through the crowds along Chowringhee one hot morning, and encountered in its vast, and essentially heteroclite, collections several instances of physical boundaries that had been transgressed. The street had poured into the museum as large numbers of beggars and street people had paid the half-rupee admission so they could sleep in relative comfort under the display cases. When I entered the room specifically marked as containing the invertebrate collection, the first thing that caught my eye was the immense skeleton of an Irish stag. Boundaries are never stable, never secure, and may be crossed in all manner of ways. Eco draws an analogy between the clutter of many museums and the Baroque *wunderkammer* in which "a unicorn's horn would be found next to the copy of a Greek statue, and, later, among mechanical crèches and wonderous automata, cocks of precious metal that sang, clocks with a procession of little figures that paraded at noon" (*Travels in Hyperreality*, p. 5).

32. Donato, "The Museum's Furnace," p. 223.

33. Murray Bail, "Zoellner's Definition," in *Contemporary Portraits and Other Stories* (St. Lucia: University of Queensland Press, 1975), pp. 65–74.

34. There are also fictions about museums that *do not* thematize the various paradoxes, whether curatorial or exhibitional, of collections. Brian Moore's *The Great Victorian Collection* (Toronto: McClelland and Stewart, 1975) is extremely playful about the idea of a collection of Victorian bric-à-brac, but does not evoke any paradoxes other than the principle that proclaims the identity of indiscernibles.

35. Fowles, *The Magus* (rev. ed.). Fowles uses the term *godgame* frequently in the novel, though perhaps with more emphasis on the *god* element than on the *game.* In the "Foreword" to the revised edition, Fowles notes that the alternative title for the novel, which he regrets not having used, was "The Godgame" (p. 10). He discusses the concept in the *The Aristos*, p. 19.

36. George Steiner, *Extraterritorial: Papers on Literature and the Language of Revolution* (New York: Atheneum, 1971), p. 53.

37. Pedro Calderón de la Barca, *La Vida es Sueño*, vol. 2 of *Comedias*, facsimile ed. (Madrid, 1636), ed. D. W. Cruikshank and J. E. Varey (London: Greggs International in association with Tamesis Books, 1973), p. 18 (my translation).

38. Welsh, *Reflections on the Hero as Quixote.*

39. For a discussion of godgames during this period of literary history, see Patricia Merivale, "Learning the Hard Way: Gothic Pedagogy in the Modern Romantic Quest," *Comparative Literature* 36 (Spring 1984): 146–61.

40. See Radford and Wilson, "Some Phases of the Jungian Moon."

41. Borges, *Ficciones*, p. 71 (my translation).

42. It is interesting that in Helen Weinberg's *The New Novel in America: The Kafkan Mode in Contemporary Fiction* (Ithaca: Cornell University Press, 1970), there is only a single reference to Pynchon. No American writer better deserves the epithet "Kafkan."

43. Jorge Luis Borges, "Walt Whitman: Man and Myth," *Critical Inquiry* 1 (1975): 708–10. Borges first gave this paper in English to a group at the University of Chicago.

44. Brian McHale, "'You Used to Know What These Words Mean': Misreading *Gravity's Rainbow*," *Language and Style* 18 (Winter 1985): 93, 113. The embedded citation in the passage quoted from McHale is from Maureen Quilligan, *The Language of Allegory: Defining the Genre* (Ithaca: Cornell University Press, 1979), p. 277. McHale asserts that "Quilligan's treatment of the reader in Pynchon (pp. 265–77) bears comparison with the kind of metareading I have undertaken here" (p. 118 n. 57).

45. Thomas Pynchon, *Gravity's Rainbow* (New York: Viking, 1973), p. 188.

46. Texts may be read, not only as McHale argues they should be, on many levels of simplicity.

47. Thomas Pynchon, *The Crying of Lot 49* (New York: Bantam, 1967), p. 58. Subsequent references are given in the text.

48. Many distinctions are possible. Chaucer's "The Miller's Tale" is a practical joke, much as Welsh uses the term, but *Sir Gawain and the Green Knight*, a complex fabric of many distinct games, is, in its essential episode, a godgame. For a discussion of the pervasiveness of gamefulness of *Sir Gawain and the Green Knight*, see John Leyerle, "The Game and Play of Hero," in *Concepts of the Hero in the Middle Ages and the Renaissance*, ed. Norman T. Burns and Christopher J. Reagan (Albany: State University of New York Press, 1975), pp. 49–82.

49. In *Narcissistic Narrative*, Linda Hutcheon argues that metafiction normally encodes (or "internalizes") certain "recurring structural models" (p. 31) that both metaphorize the narrative being written and direct the reader to be constantly aware of difficulties in reading. She identifies four such "diegetic models" that metafictional texts may be said to internalize, one of which is games, or "game structure" (the others are the detective story, fantasy, and the erotic). Her illustrative texts are Sollers's *Drame* and Coover's *The Universal Baseball Association Inc., J. Henry Waugh, Prop.*, but her analysis would have wide applicability: any text that incorporates game structures seems to provide an internal model of its own narrative procedures and may be allowing "the reader to enjoy the same creative processes as those in which the writer had originally indulged" (p. 33). The godgame, then, merely encodes to a further degree, and (often) in a more intricate manner, the general problem of the reader's entrapment and cognitive participation in the text.

50. Thiher, *Words in Reflection*, pp. 158, 183.

51. Fowles, *The Aristos*, p. 19.

52. For an instructive discussion of the philosophical difficulties implicit in the term *illusion*, see R. J. Hirst's article "Illusions," in *The Encyclopedia of Philosophy*, ed. Paul Edwards (New York: Macmillan and the Free Press, 1967), pp. 130–33. Hirst's article provides a useful bibliography.

53. J. L. Austin, *Sense and Sensibilia* (Oxford: Clarendon Press, 1962).

54. The painful difficulties of penetrating a skillfully constructed illusion, even when one has had some experience in godgames, were impressed upon her a few years later when a friend, who had read an essay she had written on godgames, totally deluded her with an illusion of his own design. She found herself accused of stealing a valuable Aztec coin, and even though she knew she had not done so, she could not see who else, in the circumstances, would have stolen it, or even how it could have been stolen at all unless she herself had committed the crime. She spent a great deal of time wondering where the coin had gone, who had stolen it, and how the theft could have been accomplished, without once thinking of the only possible solution: she was being cleverly deluded by someone who understood (because he had read her essay) the nature of the godgame.

55. Hutcheon, *Narcissistic Narrative*, p. 67.

56. Cervantes, *Don Quixote*, Cohen trans., pp. 824–25.

57. For a more detailed discussion of epistemological incertitude in the *Quijote*, see R. R. Wilson, "Drawing New Lessons from Old Masters: The Concept of Character in the *Quijote*," *Modern Philology* 78 (November 1980): 117–38.

58. Jorge Luis Borges, *Obras completas*, vol. 3 (Buenos Aires: Emecé Editores, 1968), pp. 123–34. An English version may be found in *The Aleph and Other Stories, 1933–1969*, ed. and trans. Norman Thomas di Giovanni (New York: Dutton, 1978), pp. 115–25.

59. Michael Ayrton, "On the Meaning of the Maze," *Labrys* 1 (February 1978): 16. The theory of labyrinths, or of literary labyrinthiness, that is

being argued in this chapter finds support in J. Hillis Miller's analysis of bifurcation, perplexed decisiveness, and spatial disposition in "Ariadne's Thread: Repetition and the Narrative Line," *Critical Inquiry* 3 (Autumn 1976): 57–77.

60. Josipovici, *The World and the Book*, p. 307.

61. Guy Davenport, "The House That Jack Built," *Salmagundi* 43 (Winter 1979): 145, 144.

62. Borges, *Obras completas*, 3:15 (my translation).

63. Ernest H. Redekop, "Labyrinths in Time and Space," *Mosaic* 13 (Spring–Summer 1980): 97. Redekop offers an empirical-descriptive account of some of Borges's labyrinths, but he does not venture to specify their underforming structures or to state their constitutive rules. For other studies of labyrinths in Borges's writing, see Ana María Barrenechea, *La Expression de la irrealidad en la obra de Borges* (Buenos Aires: Paidós, 1967), and Carter Wheelock, *The Mythmaker: A Study of Motif and Symbol in the Short Stories of Jorge Luis Borges* (Austin: University of Texas Press, 1969).

64. Borges, *Labyrinths*, p. 107.

65. Alain Robbe-Grillet, *Dans le labyrinth* (Paris: Editions de Minuit, 1959). An English translation by Richard Howard is available in *Two Novels by Robbe-Grillet: "Jealousy" and "In the Labyrinth"* (New York: Grove Press, 1965).

66. Bruce Morrissette, *The Novels of Robbe-Grillet* (Ithaca: Cornell University Press, 1975), p. 163.

67. Morrissette, *Novels of Robbe-Grillet*, p. 166.

68. Morrissette, *Novels of Robbe-Grillet*, p. 167.

69. Robbe-Grillet, *Dans le labyrinth*, p. 34 (my translation).

70. Jorge Luis Borges, "Los dos reyes y los laberintos," in *Obras completas*, 3:135–36 (my translation).

71. Samuel Johnson, "Pope," in *The Lives of the Most Eminent English Poets*, vol. 3 (Chicago: Stone and Kimball, 1896), p. 124.

72. Miller, "Ariadne's Thread," p. 70.

73. Miller, "Ariadne's Thread," p. 73.

74. Knottedness may be thought of as a "property that is intrinsic not to a curve but to the embedding of a curve, that is, the way the curve lies in three-dimensional space" (Lee Neuwith, "The Theory of Knots," *Scientific American* 240 [June 1979]: 110). The problem of space in literature has been analyzed by a few theorists with provocative, if perplexing, results. See the discussion of space and spatiality in Chapter 5.

75. Borges, *Ficciones*, p. 162: "I know of one Greek labyrinth which is a single straight line. Along that line so many philosophers have lost themselves that a mere detective might well do so, too. Sharlach, when in some other incarnation you hunt me, pretend to commit (or do commit) a crime at A, then a second crime at B, eight kilometers from A, then a third crime at C, four kilometers from A and B, half-way between the two. Wait for me afterwards at D, two kilometers from A and C, again halfway between both.

Kill me at D, as you are now going to kill me at Triste-le-Roy" (trans. Donald A. Yates, in *Labyrinths*, pp. 162–63).

76. Claude Bremond, *Logique du récit* (Paris: Editions du Seuil, 1973). See also his "La logique des possibles narratifs," *Communications* 8 (1966): 60–76.

77. Pavel, *Poetics of Plot*, p. 118.

78. Pavel, *Poetics of Plot*, p. 57.

79. One needs to remember Linda Hutcheon's aphorism that "literature creates its criticism" (*Narcissistic Narrative*, p. 45).

80. Clearly, John Fowles's neologism *godgame* works splendidly in English. The situations that one may name by that label, or the conventions that are relevant to the construction of textual godgames, would require other labels in other languages. It is not clear that one would invariably stress the "god" aspect of the notion, though the "game" aspects might be thought to be invariable. Following a suggestion by the Chilean scholar Christian Hunuus, I wrote an essay in Spanish on the subject in which I translated the Fowlesesque phrase as "El juego del Hacedor." "Hacedor" (Maker) captured the notion of a "god" (in the sense that Borges's Spanish uses the term to indicate the maker of second nature, of art and culture, a sense largely lost to English since the late Renaissance though it might always be available as an archaism, as it is in the poetry of Wallace Stevens), but it also paid due homage to Borges, for whom "hacedor" is (like "laberinto") a favorite term. The Puertorriqueña literary review *Sin Nombre* accepted the essay and for several years proclaimed it as forthcoming and then, in a fateful godgame, folded before the publication of my essay.

CHAPTER 5

1. Eagleton, "Capitalism, Modernism and Postmodernism," in *Against the Grain*, p. 137.

2. The model of two entwined codes evidently fits magic realism. See Amaryll Beatrice Chanady, *Magical Realism and the Fantastic: Resolved versus Unresolved Antinomies* (New York: Garland, 1985).

3. C. S. Lewis, *Studies in Words* (Cambridge: Cambridge University Press, 1960), p. 260. On Shakespeare's use of "golden world," see J. Leon Livsay, "Shakespeare's 'Golden World,'" *Shakespeare Association Bulletin* 13 (1938): 77–81, 260, 258. Lewis's chapter on worlds is an excellent summary of the term's etymological variety.

4. The point, recurrent in contemporary literary theory, that time sequences must be spatialized but spatial arrangements temporalized to be grasped derives from Kant's *Critique of Pure Reason*. See Alexander Gelley, "Metonymy, Schematism, and the Space of Literature," *New Literary History* 11 (Spring 1980): 468–87.

5. Jeffrey R. Smitten, "Approaches to the Spatiality of Narrative," *Papers on Language and Literature* 14 (Summer 1978): 303.

6. Howard Felperin, "'Tongue-tied our queen?': The Deconstruction of Presence in *The Winter's Tale*," in *Shakespeare and the Question of Theory*, ed. Patricia Parker and Geoffrey Hartman (New York: Methuen, 1985), pp. 8, 14.

7. Pavel, *Poetics of Plot*, pp. 44–45. "The specific point where the present proposal differs from other suggestions already present in the field is that according to this proposal, a plot is split into *more than one* narrative domain, and is accordingly divided into several distinct sets of propositions or maxims. The nature of these propositions is heterogeneous" (p. 45).

8. Doreen Maitre, *Literature and Possible Worlds* (London: Middlesex Polytechnic Press, 1983), p. 79.

9. *The Poetical Works of Edmund Spenser*, pp. lii–liii, n. 1.

10. For a discussion of the spatial properties of the empirical (i.e., existing in actual space-time) book, see Carl Darryl Malmgren, *Fictional Space in the Modernist and Postmodernist American Novel* (Lewisburg, Pa.: Bucknell University Press, 1985).

11. Gabriel Zoran, "Towards a Theory of Space in Narrative," *Poetics Today* 5 (1984): 310.

12. The notion of a purely "fictional referent," touching nothing in the extratextual world, might seem to be as lexically superfluous as existentially nugatory, a way of co-opting the terminology of post-Russellian philosophers without granting their primary demand for real world existence as a necessary condition for adequate textual reference. See, however, Linda Hutcheon's essay "Metafictional Implications for Novelistic Reference," in *On Referring in Literature*, ed. Anna Whiteside and Michael Issacharoff (Bloomington: Indiana University Press, 1987), pp. 1–13. See also Doležel, "Truth and Authenticity in Narrative."

13. *The Dictionary of Imaginary Places*, ed. Alberto Manguel and Gianni Guadalupi (Toronto: Lester & Orpen Dennys, 1980).

14. Pavel, *Fictional Worlds*, p. 25.

15. Ricardo Gullón, "On Space in the Novel," *Critical Inquiry* 2 (Autumn 1975): 19.

16. Ann Swinfen, *In Defence of Fantasy*, p. 3. Lubomír Doležel, "Kafka's Fictional World," *Canadian Review of Comparative Literature* 11 (March 1984): 61–83.

17. Gullón, "On Space in the Novel," p. 21.

18. Joseph Frank, "Spatial Form in Modern Literature," *Sewanee Review* 53 (Spring, Summer, and Autumn 1945): 221–40, 433–56, 643–53; rpt. in *The Widening Gyre: Crisis and Mastery in Modern Literature* (New Brunswick, N.J.: Rutgers University Press, 1963), pp. 3–62. See also Frank, "Spatial Form: An Answer to Critics," *Critical Inquiry* 4 (Winter 1977): 231–52.

19. W. J. T. Mitchell, "Spatial Form in Literature: Toward a General Theory," *Critical Inquiry* 6 (Spring 1980): 541.

20. Gaston Bachelard, *The Poetics of Space*, trans. Maria Jolas (Boston: Beacon Press, 1969), pp. 9–10.

21. Georges Poulet, *Proustian Space*, trans. Elliott Coleman (Baltimore: Johns Hopkins University Press, 1977).

22. Mitchell, "Spatial Form in Literature," p. 556.

23. Barthes, *S/Z: An Essay*, pp. 67–68, 94–9[illegible].

24. J. Hillis Miller, *Fiction and Repetition: Seven English Novels* (Cambridge, Mass.: Harvard University Press, 1982), p. 34.

25. Gullón, "On Space in the Novel," p. 18.

26. Barthes, *S/Z: An Essay*, pp. 15, 21.

27. Derrida, *Of Grammatology*, p. 290.

28. Tzetvan Todorov, *The Poetics of Prose*, trans. Richard Howard (Ithaca: Cornell University Press, 1977), p. 70.

29. On Conrad's general notions of history, see T[homas]. McAlindon, "Conrad's Organicist Philosophy of History," *Mosaic* 15 (September 1982): 27–41.

30. Joseph Conrad, *The Mirror of the Sea* (London: J. M. Dent, 1946), p. 176.

31. Joseph Conrad, *Notes on Life and Letters* (London: J. M. Dent, 1949), p. 13.

32. Joseph Conrad, Preface, *Nigger of the "Narcissus"* (London: J. M. Dent, 1957), p. x.

33. Zoran, "Towards a Theory of Space," pp. 312–13.

34. Kendall L. Walton, "Fearing Fictions," *Journal of Philosophy* 75 (January 1978): 5–27; Walton, "How Remote Are Fictional Worlds from the Real World?" *Journal of Aesthetics and Art Criticism* 37 (Fall 1978): 11–23. Walton develops the basis in general for his position in "Pictures and Make-Believe," *Philosophical Review* 82 (July 1973): 283–319. The importance of make-believe as a component in the play of games was already present in Caillois.

35. Pavel, *Fictional Worlds*, p. 56.

36. The proposition that fictional entities, such as characters, are "open constructs" is more or less explicit in all phenomenological approaches to fiction. It has been developed, with great incisiveness, from the side of semiotics and narratology by Seymour Chatman in *Story and Discourse: Narrative Structure in Fiction and Film* (Ithaca: Cornell University Press, 1978).

37. Pavel, *Fictional Worlds* (esp. pp. 44–47), discusses Kripke's model of possible world relations. See Pavel's bibliography for references to Kripke's writings.

38. Pavel, *Fictional Worlds*, p. 44.

39. Citing it as the "most complete and suggestive classification of fictional worlds," Pavel (*Fictional Worlds*, p. 155, n. 5) refers to Félix Martínez-Bonati's "Towards a Formal Ontology of Fictional Worlds," *Philosophy and Literature* 7 (October 1983): 182–95. An exhaustive taxonomy (not cited by Pavel) may be found in Lubomír Doležel's "Towards a Typology of Fictional Worlds," *Tamking Review* 14 (1984–85): 261–76.

40. Pavel, *Fictional Worlds*, pp. 94–95.

41. The definitive analysis of the emptiness of fictional characters remains Gass, *Fiction and the Figures of Life*, pp. 34–54.

42. Maitre, *Literature and Possible Worlds*, p. 29.

43. Maitre, *Literature and Possible Worlds*, pp., 117, 119. Maitre acknowledges her debt to Sartre's analysis of imagination. Another important philosophical study on imagination that she cites is Edward S. Casey, *Imagining: A Phenomenological Study* (Bloomington: Indiana University Press, 1984). In his subsequent book (the "sequel"), *Remembering: A Phenomenological Study* (Bloomington: Indiana University Press, 1987), Casey observes, relevant to the argument of this chapter, that the world of the remembered "acts as an underlying field of presentation for the specific content remembered, and in this respect it is more fully worldlike than the momentary mini-worlds of imagination" (p. 69). This proposition bears directly on the theory of fictional worldhood since the function of memory in reading narrative corresponds only tenuously to the momentary acts of imagination, of hallucination or daydream, and the "mini-worlds" that *they* create. Behind both Sartre and Casey (and thus behind Maitre and this discussion) lies Martin Heidegger's philosophy of worldhood ("*Weltlichkeit*"); see *Being and Time*, trans. John Macquarrie and Edward Robinson (New York: Harper & Row, 1962), pp. 200–212 (section 43).

44. Pynchon, *Gravity's Rainbow*, pp. 82–83.

45. Jerome Bruner, *Actual Minds, Possible Worlds* (Cambridge, Mass.: Harvard University Press, 1986), p. 22.

46. Bruner, *Actual Minds*, pp. 64–65.

47. Cervantes, *Don Quijote*, pp. 660–61; Cohen trans., pp. 641–42.

48. Ortega, *Meditations on the Quixote*, pp. 133–34.

49. The fascination with fiction as "second nature," or as a world in opposition to the real world, based on the human mind's power to imagine, has been brilliantly analyzed in Ronald Levao, *Renaissance Minds and Their Fictions: Cusanus, Sidney, Shakespeare* (Berkeley: University of California Press, 1985).

50. Cervantes, *Don Quijote*, pp. 957–58; Cohen trans., p. 924.

51. See Chapter 6 for a discussion of the ekphrases in Spenser. On the ekphrasis in Shakespeare's *Lucrece*, see R. R. Wilson, "Shakespearean Narrative: *The Rape of Lucrece* Reconsidered," *SEL* 28 (1988): 39–59.

52. Rodney Needham, *Exemplars* (Berkeley: University of California Press, 1985), p. 79.

53. Needham, *Exemplars*, p. 206.

54. Borges, *Ficciones*, p. 35; *Labyrinths*, pp. 17–18.

55. On the concept of dilation in fiction, and as a rhetorical term in the Renaissance, see Patricia Parker, *Literary Fat Ladies*, pp. 8–35.

56. Félix Martínez-Bonati, *Fictive Discourse*, p. 92

57. For a discussion of this genealogy, see Welsh, *Reflections*.

58. Robert Alter, *Partial Magic: The Novel as a Self-Conscious Genre* (Berkeley: University of California Press, 1975), p. 6.

59. Michel Foucault, *The Order of Things: An Archaeology of the Human Sciences* (New York: Pantheon Books, 1970), p. 46. For the original, see *Les Mots et les choses: Une archéologie des sciences humaines* (Paris: Editions Gallimard, 1966), p. 60.

60. Thomas S. Kuhn, *The Structure of Scientific Revolutions*, 2d ed. (Chicago: University of Chicago Press, 1970). In *Beyond Deconstruction*, Felperin accepts a simplified version of the Kuhnian notion of paradigm shift as immediately applicable to literature. It does seem, however, that, unlike the sciences which Kuhn discusses, "old" paradigms are never wholly replaced in literary studies.

61. Italo Calvino, *Invisible Cities*, trans. William Weaver (New York: Harcourt Brace Jovanovich, 1978).

62. Brian McHale, *Postmodernist Fiction* (London: Methuen, 1987), p. 44.

63. Ortega, *Meditations on the Quixote*, p. 163.

64. Robert Kroetsch, *What the Crow Said* (Toronto: General Publishing, 1978).

65. In her *Magical Realism*, Chanady discusses the history of the scholarly rubric "magic realism." See note 2 above.

CHAPTER 6

1. Culler, *Pursuit of Signs*, p. 106.

2. Michael Riffaterre, "Syllepsis," *Critical Inquiry* 6 (Summer 1980): 625–26.

3. Kristeva, *Séméiotikē*. For a bibliography on the problem of intertextuality, see Bruce, "Bibliographie annotée," pp. 217–58. The Bruce bibliography cites twenty-three entries by Michael Riffaterre on the problem of intertextuality.

4. Riffaterre, "Syllepsis," pp. 626–27. There is sharp disagreement among narrative theorists as to the definition of *intertext*. Gerald Prince cites three distinct uses of the term: (1) a text, or set of texts, that is "generally transformed" by another text; (2) a text "insofar as it absorbs and binds together a multiplicity of other texts" or, most generally, any text at all (since any text can be supposed to "bind" other texts in this manner); (3) a set of texts that "are intertextually linked" or between which intertextuality "obtains" (*A Dictionary of Narratology* [Lincoln: University of Nebraska Press, 1987], pp. 45–46).

5. Laurant Jenny, "The Strategy of Form," trans. R. Carter, in *French Literary Theory Today: A Reader*, ed. Tzetvan Todorov (Cambridge: Cambridge University Press, 1982), pp. 51–54.

6. Unnarrated only in the sense that they have not been told. Although such stories have not been textualized, they can be recognized as motifs that *might be told*. The use of this term in this chapter owes nothing to the practice of literary linguists who sometimes employ *unnarrated* or *nonnarrated* to signify narratives told in the simple preterite. Narratives told in

that tense, it is sometimes claimed, possess the authority of translucence, perhaps of windowness. See also Prince, *Dictionary of Narratology*; Chatman, *Story and Discourse.*

7. Culler, *Pursuit of Signs*, p. 118.

8. Linda Hutcheon, *A Theory of Parody: The Teachings of Twentieth-Century Art Forms* (London: Methuen, 1985), pp. 23, 2. See also Hutcheon, *Narcissistic Narrative*, pp. 24–25.

9. George Steiner, *Language and Silence: Essays on Language, Literature, and the Inhuman* (New York: Atheneum, 1967), p. 182.

10. Even the most complex narratives, *Don Quijote*, say, or *Gravity's Rainbow*, may be reduced, as a cognitive exercise, to a series of narrative incidents and indispensable narrative agents. In either case, this conceptual reduction would leave gaps that would be filled by a series of discrete incidents and narrative agents. The latter are the embedded, heterodiegetic narratives, such as "The Tale of Foolish Curiosity" in *Don Quijote* (I: 33–35), the presence of which indicates the necessary incompleteness of the exercise. The reductive process, which may seem rather like separating convexity from concavity (an exercise that, as Aristotle notes, is impossible though geometricians do it all the time), leads to an understanding of a narrative's necessary conditions. It also makes possible a distinction between these necessary conditions (that is, a number of essential incidents in chronological order plus the indispensable narrative agents) and all that is art: the elaboration, the dilation, the transformations that create discourse. The distinction between story and discourse seems basic to the formal analysis of literature and perhaps to common sense as well. It does not need to be defended, but, like any analytic concept, it can be clarified. Although it is implicit in Aristotle's *Poetics*, contemporary formulations derive from the work of the Russian formalists. Their distinction between *fabula* (story-stuff) and *sjužet* (plot), it has been said, moved the study of prose fiction "off dead center" and set the stage "for work on the history and theory of the novel" (see Chapter 2, note 12). The distinction has made available the analysis of narrative according to models of textual codes and grammars. Every use of the distinction as a methodological tool has assumed (1) that *story* is an empty concept or an analytic device to make certain kinds of critical explication possible and (2) that the time of story (or "story time") must be chronological, a natural order that narrative perturbs. Part of the argument in this chapter is intended to qualify those assumptions: the concept of story can have some positive content, and it does not necessarily postulate any specific time scheme, but merely the potential to have *some* time. When a story, evoked allusively, breaks into a narrative, erupting through a sudden fissure in the narrative order, it proclaims its own time but this does not need to be chronological. Spenser's ekphrases, for example, impose a potential for narrative time, something that *they* possess, not the narrative that contains them, but this is scarcely a "natural" or even a sequential time.

11. Chatman, *Story and Discourse.*

12. Culler, *Pursuit of Signs*, pp. 170–71.

13. Lodge, *Working with Structuralism*, p. 56.

14. Nothing in the argument of this chapter is intended to suggest that stories can be localized. The ordinary sense that stories can be recognized does not entail the proposition that there can be only one story, a classic or originary tale. A familiar story might not exist simply because no one had ever told it before or, if someone had, neither copies nor memories of a textualized version remained, could be found, or even imagined. The dangers of thinking too concretely about story are displayed in Barbara Herrnstein Smith's "Narrative Versions, Narrative Theories," *Critical Inquiry* 7 (Autumn 1980): 213–36. Seymour Chatman's response, "Reply to Barbara Herrnstein Smith" (*Critical Inquiry* 7 [Summer 1981]: 802–9), puts the fallacies of obsessive concreteness into sharp focus. In talking about stories, Chatman writes, no one especially wants to find the "real" version (p. 803).

15. Gilbert Murray, *The Classical Tradition in Poetry* (London: Oxford University Press, 1927), p. 236.

16. See Ross Chambers, *Story and Situation: Narrative Seduction and the Power of Fiction* (Minneapolis: University of Minnesota Press, 1984), p. 8. Anyone who has read Chambers's brilliant study will perceive that I have borrowed his phrase, and perhaps some of the import, but not the precise indices of his argument.

17. The concept of a colligatory motif derives from Tomashevsky's definition of *fabula* as an "aggregate of motifs" (*Russian Formalist Criticism: Four Essays*, trans. and ed. Lee T. Lemon and Marion J. Reis [Lincoln: University of Nebraska Press, 1965], p. 68). I have stressed the epithet *colligatory* because, in the argument of this chapter, the process of recognition entails being able to perceive motifs that belong together even if they are not all immediately copresent.

18. For a discussion of the concept of sufficiency, see Richard N. Bosley, *On Truth* (Washington, D.C.: University Press of America, 1982). The definition of *story* as a number of recognizable, colligatory motifs depends on the concept of sufficiency (and, conversely, deficiency) since there must be sufficient motifs both for a story (but not too many) and for the intuitive process of recognition to be possible.

19. In his *The Science in Science Fiction* (New York: Knopf, 1983), Peter Nicholls discusses a number of technological impossibilities. See especially "Elementary Errors in Physics," pp. 196–97.

20. Pavel, *Fictional Worlds*, p. 49. For the allusion to a "Kripkean theory of modality," see Pavel's bibliography under "Saul Kripke" (p. 164).

21. Many possible relationships between story and narrative can be imagined. Todorov indicates one in *The Poetics of Prose* when he discusses detective fiction. In such fiction, Todorov argues, there are two stories "of which one is absent but real, the other present but insignificant" (p. 46). Narrative that involves the search for a story that is not its story is probably common enough even outside of detective fiction. Something rather similar goes on in *Hamlet*.

22. Mikhail Bakhtin, *The Formal Method in Literary Scholarship: A Critical Introduction to Sociological Poetics*, trans. Albert J. Wehrle (Baltimore: Johns Hopkins University Press, 1978), p. 17.

23. Frank Kermode, "Secrets and Narrative Sequence," *Critical Inquiry* 7 (Autumn 1980): 85.

24. The exemplary instance of ekphrasis must be Homer's description, in Book XVIII of the *Iliad*, of the shield of Achilles, although the corresponding ekphrasis in Virgil's *Aeneid* (Book VIII, in which Virgil depicts the shield of proleptic devices that Vulcan has created for Aeneas) or the other instances of ekphrastic narrative in the *Aeneid* (such as the murals depicted in Book I) probably were better known to Renaissance writers such as Spenser. An important recent study of the rhetorical convention of ekphrasis is Page DuBois, *History, Rhetorical Description and the Epic: From Homer to Spenser* (Cambridge: D. S. Brewer, 1982). John B. Bender's study of pictorial imagery in Spenser, *Spenser and Literary Pictorialism* (Princeton: Princeton University Press, 1972), contains some discussion of ekphrasis, as does George Kurman's "Ecphrasis in Epic Poetry," *Comparative Literature* 26 (Winter 1974): 1–13. Anyone interested in the concept should read Pamela L. Royston's fine discussion, "Unraveling the Ecphrasis in Chapman's *Hero and Leander*," *South Atlantic Review* 49 (November 1984): 43–53. Ekphrasis seems to have taken on new importance in contemporary critical analyses. (*The Princeton Encyclopedia of Poetry and Poetics* does not even bother to define the term.) One reason is probably foreshadowed in Murray Krieger's essay "The Ekphrastic Principle and the Still Movement of Poetry; or *Laokoön* Revisited," in *Play and Place of Criticism* (Baltimore: Johns Hopkins University Press, 1967), pp. 105–28. Krieger extends the traditional signification of ekphrasis to mean the idea of a work of art in itself: an organic, whole, self-proclaiming object. Krieger's argument sketches a fundamental paradox: the convention of ekphrasis opens the text through narrative elaboration and dilation which interrupts the text's continuity (and, perhaps, unity), but it does so through the insertion of images that suggest the integrity and discrete wholeness of the artwork being depicted. Part of the current interest lies in the way ekphrasis constitutes a self-evident, but slightly oblique, instance of narrative embedding. An ekphrasis splits the text, follows a possibility of segmentation, and embeds another story, another cluster of motifs that itself suggests the potentiality for worldhood.

25. No single ekphrasis in Renaissance literature has attracted as much commentary as the "piece of skilful painting" in *The Rape of Lucrece*. See Ian Donaldson, *The Rapes of Lucretia: A Myth and Its Transformations* (Oxford: Clarendon Press, 1982), for a general introduction to the problem posed by the story. For commentary on the ekphrasis itself, see also D. C. Allen, "Some Observations on *The Rape of Lucrece*," *Shakespeare Survey* 15 (1962): 89–98; Richard A. Lanham, *The Motives of Eloquence: Literary Rhetoric in the Renaissance* (New Haven: Yale University Press, 1976), pp.

94–110, and "The Politics of *Lucrece*," *Hebrew University Studies in Literature* 8 (1980): 66–76; S. Clarke Hulse, "'A Piece of Skilful Painting' in Shakespeare's 'Lucrece,'" *Shakespeare Survey* 31 (1978): 13–22; David Rosand, "'Troyes Painted Woes': Shakespeare and the Pictorial Imagination," *Hebrew University Studies in Literature* 8 (1980): 77–97; Elizabeth Traux, "'Lucrece! What hath your conceited painter wrought?'" in *Shakespeare: Contemporary Critical Approaches*, ed. Harry R. Garvin (Lewisburg, Pa.: Bucknell University Press, 1980), pp. 13–30; Katherine Eisman Maus, "Taking Tropes Seriously: Language and Violence in Shakespeare's *Lucrece*," *Shakespeare Quarterly* 37 (Spring 1986): 66–82; Heather Dubrow, "The Rape of Clio: Attitudes to History in Shakespeare's *Lucrece*," *English Literary Renaissance* 16 (Autumn 1986): 425–41, rpt. in a revised and expanded version as chapter 2 in *Captive Victors: Shakespeare's Narrative Poems and Sonnets* (Ithaca: Cornell University Press, 1987), pp. 80–168; Wilson, "Shakespearean Narrative," pp. 39–59.

26. Lanham, in *Motives*, discusses the Renaissance conception of rhetoric as a sense of playfulness. *Copia*, one must suppose, translates, as purposeful objective, a drive toward playful expression. Patricia Parker has discussed the concept of dilation in four recent essays: "Anagogic Metaphor: Breaking down the Wall of Partition," in *Centre and Labyrinth: Essays in Honour of Northrop Frye*, ed. Eleanor Cook et al. (Toronto: University of Toronto Press, 1983), pp. 38–50; "Dilation and Delay: Renaissance Matrices," *Poetics Today* 5 (1984): 519–35; "Shakespeare and Rhetoric: 'Dilation' and 'Delation' in *Othello*," in *Shakespeare and the Question of Theory*, ed. Patricia Parker and Geoffrey Hartman (London: Methuen, 1985), pp. 54–74; "Deferral, Dilation, Différance: Shakespeare, Cervantes, Jonson," in *Literary Theory/Renaissance Texts*, ed. Patricia Parker and David Quint (Baltimore: Johns Hopkins Press, 1986), pp. 182–209. See also Parker, *Literary Fat Ladies*. On the concept of "split awareness" as an Ovidian convention of characterization (a strategy of maximalization), see Wilson, "Drawing New Lessons from Old Masters."

27. Bender, *Spenser and Literary Pictorialism*, p. 166.

28. No doubt, experienced Renaissance readers were more open to personification, as a mode of characterization, than are most contemporary readers. One recalls, for instance, the threats and terrors painfully endured by Beauty and Summer's Breath in Shakespeare's Sonnet 65. Time and again the embedded narratives of Shakespeare's plays turn inward toward a characterization that is a personification (e.g., *1 Henry IV*, 1.3.94–107, in which Hotspur's account of the battle between Mortimer and Glendower culminates in a witness running to hide his "crisp head in the hollow bank"; the witness is the river Severn). For a discussion of the theories of rhetoric and rhetorical education behind Renaissance characterization, including personifications, see Brian Vickers, "Epideictic and Epic in the Renaissance," *New Literary History* 14 (Spring 1983): 497–537.

29. Jenny, "Strategy of Form," p. 59.

30. Seymour Chatman, "What Novels Can Do That Films Can't (and Vice Versa)," *Critical Inquiry* 7 (Autumn 1980): 123.

31. An embedded narrative, placed within the linear segmentation of the text, at once breaking and dilating the text, can be said to be heterodiegetic if its incidents and narrative agents are disparate from, and outside of, the narrative line that it interrupts. Nonetheless, there can be a great deal of significant thematic congruence between diegetic line and an embedded heterodiegetic narrative. For example, in the *Quijote* the embedded narrative, "The Tale of Foolish Curiosity," may seem to have little to do with the main narrative line, but its thematic congruence, posing questions of illusion and reality, mistaken identity, false inference, and epistemological declarifications, obviously has much to do with the large thematic issues of the *Quijote*. To cite a further example: in *Hamlet* (1.1), Horatio tells two analeptic narratives; the first (lines 80–107) provides immediate background material and turns upon relationships between characters either figuring in the play or mentioned elsewhere, so it is homodiegetic; the second (lines 113–25) recounts the events that took place just before the assassination of Julius Caesar and is clearly heterodiegetic yet thematically congruent.

32. David Lodge, *Language of Fiction: Essays in Criticism and Verbal Analysis of the English Novel* (London: Routledge & Kegan Paul, 1966), pp. 159–63; Lodge, *Working with Structuralism*, pp. 37–45.

33. Lodge, *Working with Structuralism*, p. 45.

34. Cervantes, *Don Quijote*, p. 85; Cohen trans., p. 30.

35. Wilson, "Drawing New Lessons," pp. 130–33.

36. Félix Martínez-Bonati, "La Unidad del *Quijote*," *Disposito* 2 (Summer–Fall 1977): 127 (my translation).

37. Don Quijote exemplifies many Renaissance ideals of reading. He has read extensively. He has read high literature (chivalric romance and pastoral) both for content and for style. Above all, he has read characters as exemplifications of, or as lessons in, moral virtue. His reading has made him, if paradoxically, what Angus Fletcher calls a "Cyropaedic hero" (*The Prophetic Moment: An Essay on Spenser* [Chicago: University of Chicago Press, 1971]), a character who has been educated to be a hero. Moral idealism lies behind much Renaissance literature and is nowhere more evident than in the concept of character. The purpose of reading, Sidney makes plain in the *Defense*, is to become like the idealized characters of heroic poetry. Brian Vickers puts the problem of Renaissance reading succinctly: "The reader needs a split-level reading ability: one must be able to move diachronically, reading as an experience in time, yet one's 'intellect', as Tasso called it, must be working synchronically, assembling a unified picture of human, especially ethical, behavior" ("Epideictic and Epic," p. 528). Don Quijote reads in this "split" manner, at once absorbed in the diachronic experience of a text *and* assembling idealized models of ethical behavior.

38. Cervantes, *Don Quijote*, p. 515; Cohen trans., p. 440.

39. Cervantes, *Don Quijote*, p. 517; Cohen trans., p. 440.

40. Although I have cited Michael Riffaterre's essay "Syllepsis" for my definition of an intertext, I do not follow him in the definition of the term *syllepsis* itself. Riffaterre defines *syllepsis* (which George Puttenham, with happy Elizabethan acuity, names the figure of "the double supply") as a mode of paronomasia and carries through successive redefinitions until he reaches his final version: "Syllepsis is a word understood in two different ways at once, as meaning and as significance" (p. 638). In referring to the romance narratives that the Knight creates as sylleptic, I have followed Gérard Genette's usage. Syllepsis, in this sense, is a variety of iterative narrative: a singular instance that stands for plural instances. See Genette, *Narrative Discourse: An Essay in Method*, trans. Jane E. Lewin (Ithaca: Cornell University Press, 1980), p. 85n.

41. Cervantes, *Don Quijote*, p. 517; Cohen trans., p. 442.

42. Bakhtin, *Problems of Dostoevsky's Poetics*, p. 49.

43. Ortega, *Meditations on the Quixote*, p. 136. Pavel makes a similar point concerning the different "actualities" in the *Quijote* (*Fictional Worlds*, p. 63).

44. Ortega, *Meditations on the Quixote*, p. 137.

45. Joseph Conrad, Preface, *The Nigger of the "Narcissus,"* p. viii.

CHAPTER 7

1. A "Post-Lude" does conclude one recent collection of essays on play. See G. Guinness and A. Hurley, eds., *Auctor Ludens: Essays on Play in Literature* (Philadelphia: John Benjamins, 1986). For a discussion of this collection and the function of the "Post-Lude," see Brian Edwards's review in the *Canadian Review of Comparative Literature* 14 (June 1987): 274–77.

2. Gregory Bateson, *Mind and Nature: A Necessary Unity* (New York: Dutton, 1979), p. 125. In her *Metafiction*, Patricia Waugh follows Bateson, explicitly drawing the analogy between play and fiction since both, in her view, construct "an alternative reality by manipulating the relation between a set of signs (whether linguistic or non-linguistic) as 'message' and the context or frame of that message" (p. 35). Both play and fiction require a "meta" level to "explain the transition from one context to another and set up a hierarchy of contexts of meanings" (p. 36). Metafiction merely foregrounds what is elsewhere implicit. Kendall Walton (discussed in chapter 5) argues a similar position: a reader or viewer must be both within and outside a fiction, at once both actual and fictional, a spectator and a participant, to play its game of make-believe. The view that reading fiction involves a coded, or explicitly cued, shift in interpreting a set of signs, similar to the Batesonian shift in play situations, seems common in Anglo-American philosophy (as in speech act theory).

3. Lubomír Doležel, "Mimesis and Possible Worlds," *Poetics Today* 9 (Autumn 1988): 484–85.

4. Peter Farb, *Word Play: What Happens When People Talk* (New York: Bantam Books, 1981), p. 4.

5. Doležel, "Mimesis and Possible Worlds," pp. 488–89.

6. Michael Rawdon, "Paracursions," in *Green Eyes, Dukes and Kings* (Kingston, Ont.: Quarry Press, 1985), p. 49.

Bibliography

Abley, Mark. "Bugged." *Saturday Night* 102 (February 1987): 36–37.

Alexander, Peter. "Conventionalism." *The Encyclopedia of Philosophy,* 1:216–19. Ed. Paul Edwards. New York: Macmillan, 1972 [1967].

Allen, D. C. "Some Observations on *The Rape of Lucrece.*" *Shakespeare Survey* 15 (1962): 89–98.

Allman, Eileen Jorge. *Player-King and Adversary: Two Faces of Play in Shakespeare.* Baton Rouge: Louisiana State University Press, 1981.

Alpers, Paul. "Convening and Convention in Pastoral Poetry." *New Literary History* 14 (Winter 1983): 277–304.

Alter, Robert. *Motives for Fiction.* Cambridge, Mass.: Harvard University Press, 1984.

———. *Partial Magic: The Novel as a Self-Conscious Genre.* Berkeley: University of California Press, 1975.

Arac, Jonathan, ed. *Postmodernism and Politics.* Minneapolis: University of Minnesota Press, 1986.

Arnason, David. "Do Astronauts Have Sex Fantasies?" In *The Circus Performers' Bar,* 91–94. Vancouver: Talonbooks, 1984.

Austin, J. L. *How to Do Things with Words.* Ed. J. O. Urmson. New York: Oxford University Press, 1969.

———. *Sense and Sensibilia.* Oxford: Clarendon Press, 1962.

Ayrton, Michael. "On The Meaning of the Maze." *Labrys* 1 (February 1978): 12–23.

Bachelard, Gaston. *The Poetics of Space.* Trans. Maria Jolas. Boston: Beacon Press, 1969.

Bail, Murray. *Homesickness.* Melbourne: Penguin Books, 1981. [London: Macmillan, 1980.]

———. "Zoellner's Definition." In *Contemporary Portraits and Other Stories,* 65–74. St. Lucia, Qld.: University of Queensland Press, 1975.

Bakhtin, Mikhail M. *The Dialogic Imagination: Four Essays by M.M. Bakhtin.* Ed. Michael Holquist. Trans. Caryl Emerson. Austin: University of Texas Press, 1981.

———. *The Formal Method in Literary Scholarship: A Critical Introduction to Sociological Poetics.* Trans. Albert J. Wehrle. Baltimore: Johns Hopkins University Press, 1978.

———. *Problems of Dostoevsky's Poetics.* Trans. Caryl Emerson. Minneapolis: University of Minnesota Press, 1984.

———. *Rabelais and His World.* Trans. Hélène Iswolsky. Cambridge, Mass.: MIT Press, 1968.

Bembrough, Renford. "Universals and Family Resemblances." *Proceedings of the Aristotelian Society* 63 (1960–61): 207–22; reprinted in George Pitcher, ed., *Wittgenstein: The "Philosophical Investigations,"* 186–204. Garden City, N.Y.: Anchor Books, 1966.

Baroja, Julio Carlo. *El Carnaval: Analysis historico-cultural.* 2d ed. Madrid: Taurus, 1979.

Barrenechea, Ana Maria. *La Expression de las irrealidad en la obra de Borges.* Buenos Aires: Paidós, 1967.

Barth, John. *The Friday Book: Essays and Other Nonfiction.* New York: Putnam's, 1984.

Barthes, Roland. *The Grain of the Voice: Interviews 1962–1980.* Trans. Linda Coverdale. New York: Hill and Wang, 1986.

———. *The Pleasure of the Text.* Trans. Richard Miller. New York: Hill and Wang, 1975.

———. "The Reality Effect." In *French Literary Theory Today: A Reader,* 11–17. Ed. Tzetvan Todorov. Cambridge: Cambridge University Press, 1982.

———. *S/Z: Essai.* Paris: Editions du Seuil, 1970.

———. *S/Z: An Essay.* Trans. Richard Miller. New York: Hill and Wang, 1974.

———. "Theory of The Text." Trans. Ian McLeod. In *Untying the Text: A Post-Structuralist Reader.* Ed. Robert Young. Boston: Routledge & Kegan Paul, 1981.

Bateson, Gregory. *Mind and Nature: A Necessary Unity.* New York: Dutton, 1979.

Beazley, J. D. *Development of Attic Black-Figure.* Berkeley: University of California Press, 1951.

Bender, John B. *Spenser and Literary Pictorialism.* Princeton: Princeton University Press, 1972.

Berger, Harry, Jr. *Revisionary Play: Studies in the Spenserian Dynamics.* Berkeley: University of California Press, 1988.

Berne, Eric. *Games People Play: The Psychology of Human Relationships.* New York: Ballantine, 1973 [1964].

Blake, Kathleen. *Play, Games and Sport: The Literary Works of Lewis Carroll.* Ithaca: Cornell University Press, 1974.

Bloom, Harold, et al., eds. *Deconstruction and Criticism.* New York: Continuum, 1979.

Booth, Wayne. *The Company We Keep: An Ethics of Fiction.* Berkeley: University of California Press, 1988.

Bord, Janet. *Mazes and Labyrinths of the World.* London: Latimer New Directions, 1976.

Borges, Jorge Luis. "About *The Purple Land.*" Trans. Ruth L. C. Simms. In *Borges, A Reader: A Selection from the Writings of Jorge Luis Borges,* 136–39. Ed. Emir Rodriguez Monegal and Alastair Reid. New York: Dutton, 1981.

———. *The Aleph and Other Stories: 1933–1969.* Ed. and trans. Norman Thomas di Giovanni. New York: Dutton, 1978.

———. "Chess." In *Borges, A Reader: A Selection from the Writings of Jorge Luis Borges,* 280–81. Ed. Emir Rodriguez Monegal and Alastair Reid. Trans. Alastair Reid. New York: Dutton, 1981.

———. *Ficciones.* Madrid: Alianza, 1974.

———. *Labyrinths: Selected Stories and Other Writings.* Ed. Donald A. Yates and James E. Irby. New York: New Directions, 1962.

———. *Obras Completas.* 2d ed. 3 vols. Buenos Aires: Emecé Editores, 1974 [1966–68].

———. "Walt Whitman: Man and Myth." *Critical Inquiry* 1 (June 1975): 707–18.

Bosley, Richard N. *On Truth.* Washington, D.C.: University Press of America, 1982.

Bové, Paul. "The Ineluctability of Difference: Scientific Pluralism and the Critical Intelligence." In *Postmodernism and Politics,* 3–25. Ed. Jonathan Arac. Minneapolis: University of Minnesota Press, 1986.

Braithwaite, Richard B. *Theory of Games as a Tool for the Moral Philosopher.* Cambridge: Cambridge University Press, 1955.

Bremond, Claude. "La logique des possible narratifs." *Communications* 8 (1966): 60–76.

———. *Logique du récit.* Paris: Editions du Seuil, 1973.

Brooke-Rose, Christine. *A Rhetoric of the Unreal: Studies in Narrative and Structure, Especially of the Fantastic.* Cambridge: Cambridge University Press, 1981.

Bruce, Don. "Bibliographie annotée: Ecrits sur l'intertextualité." *Texte: Revue de critique et de théorie littéraire* 2 (1983): 217–58.

Bruner, Jerome. *Actual Minds, Possible Worlds.* Cambridge, Mass.: Harvard University Press, 1986.

Bruner, Jerome S., et al., eds. *Play: Its Role in Development and Evolution.* Harmondsworth: Penguin Books, 1978 [1976].

Bruss, Elizabeth. "The Game of Literature and Some Literary Games." *New Literary History* 9 (Autumn 1977): 153–72.

Caillois, Roger. *Les Jeux et les hommes: Le masque et le vertige.* Paris: Editions Gallimard, 1958.

———. *Man, Play and Games.* Trans. Meyer Burash. New York: Free Press, 1961.

Calderón de la Barca, Pedro. *La Vida es Sueño. Comedias.* Vol. 2. Ed. D. W. Cruikshank and J. E. Varey. London: Greggs International [in association with Tamesis Books], 1973.

Calvino, Italo. *Invisible Cities.* Trans. William Weaver. New York: Harcourt Brace Jovanovich, 1978.

Caramello, Charles. *Silverless Mirrors: Books, Self and Postmodern Fiction.* Tallahassee: Florida State University Press, 1983.

Casey, Edward S. *Imagining: A Phenomenological Study.* Bloomington: Indiana University Press, 1984.

———. *Remembering: A Phenomenological Study.* Bloomington: Indiana University Press, 1987.

Castiglione, Baldassare. *The Book of the Courtier.* Trans. Charles S. Singleton. Garden City, N.Y.: Anchor/Doubleday, 1959.

Cervantes, Miguel de. *The Adventures of Don Quixote.* Trans. J. M. Cohen. Harmondsworth: Penguin Books, 1984 [1950].

———. *El Ingenioso Hidalgo Don Quijote de La Mancha.* Madrid: Ediciones Castilla, 1963.

Chambers, Ross. *Story and Situation: Narrative Seduction and the Power of Fiction.* Minneapolis: University of Minnesota Press, 1984.

Chanady, Amaryll Beatrice. *Magical Realism and the Fantastic: Resolved versus Unresolved Antinomies.* New York: Garland, 1985.

———. "The Origins and Development of Magic Realism in Latin American Fiction." In *Magic Realism and Canadian Literature: Essays and Stories,* 49–60. Ed. Peter Hinchliffe and Ed Jewinski. Waterloo, Ont.: University of Waterloo Press, 1986.

Chatman, Seymour. "Reply to Barbara Herrnstein Smith." *Critical Inquiry* 7 (Summer 1981): 802–9.

———. *Story and Discourse: Narrative Structures in Fiction and Film.* Ithaca: Cornell University Press, 1978.

———. "What Novels Can Do That Films Can't (and Vice Versa)." *Critical Inquiry* 7 (Autumn 1980): 121–40.

Chatwin, Bruce. *Utz.* New York: Viking-Penguin, 1989.

Chicoine, Marie, et al., eds. *Lâches Lousses: Les fêtes populaires au Québec, en Acadie et en Louisiane.* Montreal: VLB Editeur, 1982.

Christensen, Inger. *The Meaning of Metafiction.* Bergen, Norway: Universitetsforlaget, 1981.

Clark, Katerina, and Michael Holquist. *Mikhail Bakhtin.* Cambridge, Mass.: Harvard University Press, 1984.

Conrad, Joseph. *The Mirror of the Sea.* London: J. M. Dent, 1946 [1923].

———. *Notes on Life and Letters.* London: J. M. Dent, 1949 [1923].

———. "Preface." In *Nigger of the "Narcissus,"* vii-xii. London: J. M. Dent, 1957 [1923].

———. "The Secret Sharer." In *'Twixt Land and Sea: Three Tales,* 91–143. London: J. M. Dent, 1947 [1923].

Coover, Robert. *Pricksongs & Descants: Fictions.* New York: New American Library, 1969.

Culler, Jonathan. "Convention and Meaning: Derrida and Austin." *New Literary History* 13 (Autumn 1981): 15–30.

———. *On Deconstruction: Theory and Criticism after Structuralism.* Ithaca: Cornell University Press, 1981.

———. *The Pursuit of Signs: Semiotics, Literature, Deconstruction.* Ithaca: Cornell University Press, 1981.

———. *Structuralist Poetics: Structuralism, Linguistics, and the Study of Literature.* Ithaca: Cornell University Press, 1975.

Dällenbach, Lucien. *Le Récit spéculaire.* Paris: Editions du Seuil, 1973.

Davenport, Guy. "The House That Jack Built." *Salmagundi* 43 (Winter 1979): 140–55.

Davis, Natalie Zemon. *Society and Culture in Early Modern France.* Palo Alto: Stanford University Press, 1975.

Derrida, Jacques. *La Dissémination.* Paris: Editions du Seuil, 1972.

———. *Dissemination.* Trans. Barbara Johnson. Chicago: University of Chicago Press, 1981.

———. *L' Ecriture et la différence.* Paris: Editions du Seuil, 1967.

———. *De la grammatologie.* Paris: Editions de Minuit, 1967.

———. *Of Grammatology.* Trans. Gayatri Chakravorty Spivak. Baltimore: Johns Hopkins University Press, 1974.

———. "The Law of Genre." Trans. Avital Ronell. In *On Narrative,* 51–77. Ed. W. J. T. Mitchell. Chicago: University of Chicago Press, 1981.

———. *Positions.* Paris: Editions de Minuit, 1972.

———. *Positions.* Trans. Alan Bass. Chicago: University of Chicago Press, 1981.

———. *Writing and Difference.* Trans. Alan Bass. Chicago: University of Chicago Press, 1978.

Diesing, Paul. *Patterns of Discovery in the Social Sciences.* Chicago: Aldine, 1971.

Dinshaw, Carolyn L. "Dice Games and Other Games in *Le Jeu de saint Nicolas.*" *PMLA* 95 (October 1980): 802–11.

Doležel, Lubomír. "Intensional Function, Invisible Worlds, and Franz Kafka." *Style* 17 (Spring 1983): 120–41.

———. "Kafka's Fictional World." *Canadian Review of Comparative Literature* 11 (March 1984): 61–83.

———. "Mimesis and Possible Worlds." *Poetics Today* 9 (Autumn 1988): 475–96.

———. "Towards a Typology of Fictional Worlds." *Tamking Review* 14 (1984–1985): 261–76.

———. "Truth and Authenticity in Narrative." *Poetics Today* 1 (Spring 1980): 7–25.

Donaldson, Ian. *The Rapes of Lucretia: A Myth and Its Transformations.* Oxford: Clarendon Press, 1982.

Donato, Eugenio. "The Museum's Furnace: Notes toward a Contextual Reading of *Bouvard and Pécuchet.*" In *Textual Strategies: Perspectives in Post-Structuralist Criticism,* 213–38. Ed. Josué V. Harari. Ithaca: Cornell University Press, 1979.

DuBois, Page. *History, Rhetorical Description and the Epic: From Homer to Spenser.* Cambridge: D. S. Brewer, 1982.

Dubrow, Heather. *Captive Victors: Shakespeare's Narrative Poems and Sonnets.* Ithaca: Cornell University Press, 1987.

———. "The Rape of Clio: Attitudes to History in Shakespeare's *Lucrece.*" *English Literary Renaissance* 16 (Autumn 1986): 425–41.

Eagleton, Terry. *Against the Grain: Essays 1975–1985.* London: Verso–New Left Books, 1986.

———. *The End of English: The Pratt Lecture, 1986.* St. John's: Memorial University of Newfoundland, 1986.

———. *Literary Theory: An Introduction.* Oxford: Basil Blackwell, 1986 [1983].

Eco, Umberto. "Metaphor, Dictionary and Encyclopedia." *New Literary History* 15 (Winter 1984): 255–71.

———. *The Role of the Reader: Explorations in The Semiotics of Texts.* Bloomington: Indiana University Press, 1976.

———. *A Theory of Semiotics.* Bloomington: Indiana University Press, 1976.

———. *Travels in Hyperreality: Essays.* Trans. William Weaver. London: Picador–Pan Books, 1987 [orig. *Faith in Fakes.* London: Secker & Warburg, 1986].

"Editorial." *Journal of Commonwealth Literature* 1 (September 1965): v–vii.

Edwards, Brian. "Deconstructing the Artist and the Art: Barth and Calvino at Play in the Funhouse of Language." *Canadian Review of Comparative Literature* 12 (June 1985): 264–86.

———. "Review of G. Guinness and A. Hurley, eds., *Auctor Ludens: Essays on Play in Literature.*" *Canadian Review of Comparative Literature* 14 (June 1987): 274–77.

Ehrmann, Jacques, ed. *Yale French Review* ["Game, Play, Literature]" 41 (1968).

Eigen, Manfred, and Ruthild Winkler. *Laws of The Game: How the Principles of Nature Govern Chance.* Trans. Robert Kimber and Rita Kimber. New York: Colophon–Harper & Row, 1983.

Emerson, Caryl. "Translating Bakhtin: Does His Theory of Discourse Contain a Theory of Translation?" *University of Ottawa Quarterly* 53 (January–March 1983): 23–33.

Erikson, Eric. *Childhood and Society.* Harmondsworth: Penguin Books, 1965.

———. *Toys and Reason: Stages in the Ritualization of Experience.* New York: Norton, 1977.

Erlich, Victor. *Russian Formalism: History-Doctrine.* New Haven: Yale University Press, 1981 [1965].

Evans, Maurice. *English Poetry in the Sixteenth Century.* London: Hutchinson Library, 1967.

Farb, Peter. *Word Play: What Happens When People Talk.* New York: Bantam Books, 1981 [Knopf, 1974].

Faure, Alain. *Paris Carême-prenant: Du carnival au XIX siècle, 1800–1914.* Paris: Hachette, 1978.

Felperin, Howard. *Beyond Deconstruction: The Uses and Abuses of Literary Theory.* Oxford: Clarendon Press, 1985.

———. "'Tongue-tied our queen?': The Deconstruction of Presence in *The Winter's Tale.*" In *Shakespeare and the Question of Theory,* 3–18. Ed. Patricia Parker and Geoffrey Hartman. New York: Methuen, 1985.

Fink, Eugen. "The Oasis of Happiness: Toward an Ontology of Play." Trans. Ute Saine and Thomas Saine. *Yale French Studies* 41 (1968): 19–30.

———. *Das Spiel als Weltsymbol.* Stuttgart: B. Umbreit, 1960.

Fletcher, Angus. *The Prophetic Moment: An Essay on Spenser.* Chicago: University of Chicago Press, 1971.

Foucault, Michel. *Les Mots et les choses: Une archéologie des sciences humaines.* Paris: Editions Gallimard, 1966.

———. *The Order of Things: An Archaeology of the Human Sciences.* New York: Pantheon Books, 1970.

———. *Power/Knowledge: Selected Interviews and Other Writings 1972–1977.* Ed. Colin Gordon. New York: Pantheon Books, 1980.

———. *Raymond Roussel.* Paris: Editions Gallimard, 1963.

Fowles, John. *The Aristos: A Self-Portrait in Ideas.* Boston: Little, Brown, 1970.

———. "Foreword." *The Magus,* 5–10. Rev. ed. Boston: Little, Brown, 1977.

Frank, Joseph. "Spatial Form: An Answer to Critics." *Critical Inquiry* 4 (Winter 1977): 231–52.

———. "Spatial Form in Modern Literature." *Sewanee Review* 53 (Spring, Summer, and Autumn 1945): 221–40, 433–56, 643–53.

———. *The Widening Gyre: Crisis and Mastery in Modern Literature.* New Brunswick, N.J.: Rutgers University Press, 1963.

Frenzel, Elisabeth. "Spieler." In *Motive der Weltliteratur,* 633–43. Stuttgart: Kroner, 1980 [1976].

Freud, Sigmund. *Introductory Lectures on Psychoanalysis.* Trans. James Strachey. Harmondsworth: Penguin Books, 1973.

Gadamer, Hans-Georg. *Truth and Method.* Trans. Garrett Barden and John Cumming. New York: Crossroad, 1988 [1975].

———. *Wahrheit und Methode: Grundzüge einer philosophischen Hermeneutik.* Tübingen: J. C. B. Mohr, 1960.

Gardner, Martin, ed. *The Annotated Alice.* New York: Bramhall, 1960.

Gass, William H. *Fiction and the Figures of Life.* New York: Knopf, 1970.

Gelley, Alexander. "Metonymy, Schematism, and the Space of Literature." *New Literary History* 11 (Spring 1980): 468–87.

Genette, Gérard. *Figures III*. Paris: Editions du Seuil, 1972.

———. *Narrative Discourse: An Essay in Method*. Trans. Jane E. Lewin. Ithaca: Cornell University Press, 1980.

Gilbert, Margaret. "Notes on the Concept of Social Convention." *New Literary History* 14 (Winter 1983): 225–51.

Graff, Gerald. *Literature against Itself: Literary Ideas in Modern Society*. Chicago: University of Chicago Press, 1979.

Grant, Mary, trans. *The Myths of Hyginus*. Lawrence: University of Kansas Press, 1960.

Greenblatt, Stephen. *Renaissance Self-Fashioning: From More to Shakespeare*. Chicago: University of Chicago Press, 1980.

Greg, Walter W. *Pastoral Poetry and Pastoral Drama*. London: A. H. Bullern, 1906.

Guillén, Claudio. *Literature as System: Essays toward the Theory of Literary History*. Princeton: Princeton University Press, 1971.

Guinness, G., and A. Hurley, eds. *Auctor Ludens: Essays on Play in Literature*. Philadelphia: John Benjamins, 1986.

Gullón, Ricardo. "On Space in the Novel." *Critical Inquiry* 2 (Autumn 1975): 11–28.

Hans, James S. "Derrida and Freeplay." *Modern Language Notes* 94 (1979): 809–26.

———. *The Play of the World*. Amherst: University of Massachusetts Press, 1981.

Hartman, Geoffrey. "Monsieur Texte: On Jacques Derrida, His *Glas*." *Georgia Review* 29 (Winter 1975): 759–97.

———. "Monsieur Texte II: Epiphony in Echoland." *Georgia Review* 30 (Spring 1976): 169–97.

Hassan, Ihab. "Pluralism in Postmodern Perspective." *Critical Inquiry* 12 (Spring 1986): 503–20.

———. *The Postmodern Turn: Essays in Postmodern Theory and Culture*. [Columbus]: Ohio State University Press, 1987.

Hawkes, Terence. *Structuralism and Semiotics*. Berkeley: University of California Press, 1977.

Heidegger, Martin. *Being and Time*. Trans. John Macquarrie and Edward Robinson. New York: Harper & Row, 1962.

Hein, Hilde. "Play as an Aesthetic Concept." *Journal of Aesthetics and Art Criticism* 27 (1968): 67–71.

Henke, Suzette A. *Joyce's Moraculous Sindbook: A Study of "Ulysses."* Columbus: Ohio State University Press, 1978.

Hintikka, Jaakko. *Logic: Language-Games and Information*. London: Oxford University Press, 1973.

Hintikka, Jaakko, and Jack Kulas. *The Games of Language: Studies in*

Game-Theoretical Semantics and Its Applications. Dordrecht, Holland: D. Reidel, 1983.

Hirsch, E. D., Jr. "Beyond Convention?" *New Literary History* 14 (Winter 1983): 389–97.

Hirst, R. J. "Illusions." In *The Encyclopedia of Philosophy,* 3–4: 130–33. Ed. Paul Edwards. New York: Macmillan, 1967.

Hofstadter, Douglas R. *Metamagical Themas: Questing for the Essence of Mind and Pattern.* New York: Basic Books, 1985.

Holland, Norman N. "Film, Metafilm, and Unfilm." *Hudson Review* 15 (Autumn 1962): 406–19.

Holland, William Jacob. "Museums of Science." In *The Encyclopaedia Britannica,* vol. 19, 64–69. 11th ed. Cambridge University Press, 1911.

Holquist, Michael. "Answering as Authoring." *Critical Inquiry* 10 (December 1983): 307–19. Reprinted in *Bakhtin: Essays and Dialogues on His Work,* 59–71. Ed. Gary Saul Morson. Chicago: University of Chicago Press, 1986.

———. "Bakhtin and Rabelais: Theory as Praxis." *boundary 2* 11 (Fall–Winter 1983): 5–14.

———. "The Carnival of Discourse: Bakhtin and Simultaneity." *Canadian Review of Comparative Literature* 12 (June 1985): 220–34.

———. "The Politics of Representation." In *Allegory and Representation: Selected Papers from the English Institute, 1979–80,* 163–83. Ed. Stephen J. Greenblatt. Baltimore: Johns Hopkins University Press, 1981.

Holquist, Michael, ed. *The Dialogic Imagination: Four Essays by M. M. Bakhtin.* Trans. Caryl Emerson. Austin: University of Texas Press, 1981.

Hooper, David, and Kenneth Whyld, eds. *The Oxford Companion to Chess.* Oxford: Oxford University Press, 1984.

Huizinga, Johan. *Homo Ludens: A Study of the Play-Element in Culture.* New York: Roy Publishers, 1950; reprint, Boston: Beacon Press, 1955.

Hulse, S. Clarke. "'A Piece of Skilful Painting' in Shakespeare's 'Lucrece.'" *Shakespeare Survey* 31 (1978): 13–22.

Hume, David. *A Treatise of Human Nature.* Ed. L. A. Selby-Bigge. Oxford: Clarendon Press, 1978.

Huston, Dennis J. *Shakespeare's Comedies of Play.* New York: Columbia University Press, 1981.

Hutcheon, Linda. "The Carnivalesque and Contemporary Narrative: Popular Culture and the Erotic." *University of Ottawa Review* 53 (January–March 1983): 85–92.

———. "Fringe Interference: Postmodern Border Tensions." *Style* 22 (Summer 1986): 299–323.

———. "Metafictional Implications for Novelistic Reference." In *On Referring in Literature,* 1–13. Ed. Anna Whiteside and Michael Issacharoff. Bloomington: Indiana University Press, 1987.

———. *Narcissistic Narrative: The Metafictional Paradox.* London: Methuen, 1984. [Wilfrid Laurier University Press, 1980.]

———. "The Postmodern Problematizing of History." *English Studies in Canada* 14 (December 1988): 365–82.

———. *A Theory of Parody: The Teachings of Twentieth-Century Art Forms.* London: Methuen, 1985.

Hutchinson, Peter. *Games Authors Play.* London: Methuen, 1983.

Irwin, W. R. *The Game of the Impossible: A Rhetoric of Fantasy.* Urbana: University of Illinois Press, 1976.

Iser, Wolfgang. "The Reality of Fiction: A Functionalist Approach to Literature." *New Literary History* 7 (Autumn 1975): 7–35.

Jacobson, Roman. "Closing Statement: Linguistics and Poetics." In *Style in Language,* 350–77. Ed. Thomas A. Sebeok. Cambridge, Mass.: MIT Press, 1960.

———. "Two Aspects of Language and Two Types of Aphasic Disturbances." In *Fundamentals of Language,* 55–82. Ed. Roman Jacobson and Morris Halle. The Hague: Mouton, 1956.

Jacobson, Roman, and Morris Halle. *Fundamentals of Language.* The Hague: Mouton, 1956.

Jameson, Fredric. "Postmodernism, or the Cultural Logic of Late Capitalism." *New Left Review* 146 (July–August 1984): 53–92.

———. "Regarding Postmodernism—A Conversation with Fredric Jameson." Ed. Anders Stephenson. *Social Text: Theory/Culture/Ideology* 17 (1987): 29–54.

Jenny, Laurant. "The Strategy of Form." Trans. R. Carter. In *French Literary Theory Today: A Reader,* 34–63. Ed. Tzetvan Todorov. Cambridge: Cambridge University Press, 1982.

Johnson, Samuel. *The Lives of the Most Eminent English Poets,* vol. 3. Chicago: Stone and Kimball, 1896.

Johnston, Martin. "Games with Infinity: The Fictions of Jorge Luis Borges." In *Cunning Exiles: Studies of Modern Prose Writers,* 36–61. Ed. Don Anderson and Stephen Knight. Sydney: Angus and Robertson, 1974.

Josipovici, Gabriel. *The Lessons of Modernism and Other Essays.* London: Macmillan, 1977.

———. *The World and the Book: A Study of Modern Fiction.* London: Macmillan, 1971.

Kafka, Franz. *Franz Kafka: The Complete Stories & Parables.* Ed. Nahum N. Glatzer. New York: Schocken Books, 1971 [1946].

Kellman, Steven. *The Self-Begetting Novel.* London: Macmillan, 1980.

Kelsey, R. Bruce. "The Actor's Representation: Gesture, Play, and Language." *Philosophy and Literature* 8 (April 1984): 67–74.

Kermode, Frank. *The Genesis of Secrecy.* Cambridge, Mass.: Harvard University Press, 1979.

———. "Secrets and Narrative Sequence." *Critical Inquiry* 7 (Autumn 1980): 79–97. Reprinted in *On Narrative,* 79–97. Ed. W. J. T. Mitchell. Chicago: University of Chicago Press, 1981.

Kern, Edith. *The Absolute Comic.* New York: Columbia University Press, 1980.

Klinkowitz, Jerome. *The Self-Apparent Word: Fiction as Language/Language as Fiction.* Carbondale: Southern Illinois University Press, 1984.

Koestler, Arthur. *The Act of Creation.* London: Pan Books, 1970.

Krieger, Murray. "The Ekphrastic Principle and the Still Movement of Poetry; or *Laokoön* Revisited." In *The Play and Place of Criticism,* 105–28. Baltimore: Johns Hopkins University Press, 1967.

Kristeva, Julia. *Séméiotikē: Recherches pour une sémanalyse.* Paris: Editions du Seuil, 1969.

Kroetsch, Robert. *Alibi.* Toronto: General Publishing, 1983.

———. *Labyrinths of Voice: Conversations with Robert Kroetsch.* Ed. Shirley Neuman and Robert Wilson. Edmonton, Alta.: NeWest Press, 1982.

———. *What the Crow Said.* Toronto: General Publishing, 1978.

Kuhn, Thomas S. *The Structure of Scientific Revolutions.* Chicago: University of Chicago Press, 1970 [1962].

Kundera, Milan. "Afterword: A Talk with the Author." *The Book of Laughter and Forgetting,* 229–37. Ed. Philip Roth. Trans. Michael Henry Heim. New York: Penguin Books, 1981.

———. "The Novel and Europe." Trans. David Bellos. *New York Review of Books* 31 (July 19, 1984): 15–19. Reprinted as "The Depreciated Legacy of Cervantes." In *The Art of the Novel,* 3–20. Trans. Linda Asher [revising Bello's original translation]. New York: Grove Press, 1986.

Kurman, George. "Ecphrasis in Epic Poetry." *Comparative Literature* 26 (Winter 1974): 1–13.

La Capra, Dominic. *Rethinking Intellectual History: Texts, Contexts, Language.* Ithaca: Cornell University Press, 1983.

Ladurie, Emmanuel Le Roy. *Le Carnaval de Romans: De la Chandeleur au mercredi de cendres, 1579–80.* Paris: Editions Gallimard, 1979.

Lanham, Richard A. *The Motives of Eloquence: Literary Rhetoric in the Renaissance.* New Haven: Yale University Press, 1976.

———. "The Politics of *Lucrece.*" *Hebrew University Studies in Literature* 8 (1980): 66–76.

———. *"Tristram Shandy": The Games of Pleasure.* Berkeley: University of California Press, 1973.

Lasch, Christopher. *The Culture of Narcissism: American Life in an Age of Diminishing Expectations.* New York: Norton, 1979.

———. "The Degradation of Work and the Apotheosis of Art." *Harper's* 268 (February 1984): 40–45.

Lem, Stanislaw. *A Perfect Vacuum: Perfect Reviews of Nonexistent Books.* Trans. Michael Kandel. New York: Harcourt Brace Jovanovich, 1979.

Lemon, Lee T., and Marion J. Reis, eds. and trans. *Russian Formalist Criticism: Four Essays.* Lincoln: University of Nebraska Press, 1965.

Lentricchia, Frank. *After the New Criticism.* Chicago: University of Chicago Press, 1980.

Levao, Ronald. *Renaissance Minds and Their Fictions: Cusanus, Sidney, Shakespeare.* Berkeley: University of California Press, 1985.

Levin, Harry. *Refractions: Essays in Comparative Literature.* New York: Oxford University Press, 1966.

Lewis, C. S. *Studies in Words.* Cambridge: Cambridge University Press, 1960.

Lewis, David. *Convention: A Philosophical Study.* Cambridge, Mass.: Harvard University Press, 1969.

———. *On the Plurality of Worlds.* Oxford: Basil Blackwell, 1986.

Leyerle, John. "The Game and Play of Hero." In *Concepts of the Hero in The Middle Ages and the Renaissance,* 49–82. Ed. Norman T. Burns and Christopher J. Reagan. Albany: State University of New York Press, 1975.

Livsay, J. Leon. "Shakespeare's 'Golden World.'" *Shakespeare Association Bulletin* 13 (1938): 77–81.

Lodge, David. *Language of Fiction: Essays in Criticism and Verbal Analysis of the English Novel.* London: Routledge & Kegan Paul, 1966.

———. "The Novelist at the Crossroads." In *The Novel Today: Contemporary Writers on Modern Fiction.* Ed. Malcolm Bradbury. Manchester: Manchester University Press, 1977 [Fontana 1977].

———. *Working with Structuralism: Essays and Reviews on Nineteenth- and Twentieth-Century Literature.* Boston: Routledge & Kegan Paul, 1981.

Lord, George de Forest. *Heroic Mockery: Variations on Epic Themes from Homer to Joyce.* Newark: University of Delaware Press, 1977.

Lyotard, Jean-François. *The Postmodern Condition: A Report on Knowledge.* Trans. Geoff Bennington and Brian Massumi. Minneapolis: University of Minnesota Press, 1984.

Lyotard, Jean-François, and Jean-Loup Thébaud. *Just Gaming.* Trans. Wlad Godzich. Minneapolis: University of Minnesota Press, 1985.

Macé, Marie-Anne. "Le Siècle des lumières ou les turbulences baroques." In *Quinze études autour de "El Siglo de las Luces" de Alejo Carpentier,* 187–204. Ed. Daniel-Henri Pageaux. Paris: Editions l'Harmattan, 1983.

Macksey, Richard, and Eugenio Donato, eds. *The Stucturalist Controversy: The Languages of Criticism and the Sciences of Man.* Baltimore: Johns Hopkins University Press, 1972.

Maitre, Doreen. *Literature and Possible Worlds.* London: Middlesex Polytechnic Press, 1983.

Malmgren, Carl Darryl. *Fictional Space in the Modernist and Postmodernist American Novel.* Lewisburg, Pa.: Bucknell University Press, 1985.

Manguel, Alberto, and Gianni Guadalupi, eds. *The Dictionary of Imaginary Places.* Toronto: Lester & Orpen Dennys, 1980.

Margolin, Uri. "Dealing with the Non-Actual: Conception, Reception, Description" [review of Maitre's *Literature and Possible Worlds* and Merrel's *Pararealities: The Nature of Our Fictions and How We Know Them*]. *Poetics Today* 9 (Winter 1988): 863–78.

———. "Narrative and Indexicality: A Tentative Framework." *Journal of Literary Semantics* 13 (October 1984): 181–204.

———. "On the 'Vagueness' of Critical Concepts." *Poetics* 10 (February 1981): 15–31.

Marino, James A. G. "An Annotated Bibliography of Play and Literature." *Canadian Review of Comparative Literature* 12 (June 1985): 306–58.

Martin, Wallace. *Recent Theories of Narrative.* Ithaca: Cornell University Press, 1986.

Martínez-Bonati, Félix. "El Acto de Escribir Ficciones." *Dispositio* 3 (Spring–Summer 1978): 137–44.

———. "The Act of Writing Fiction." *New Literary History* 11 (Spring 1980): 425–34.

———. *Fictive Discourse and the Structures of Literature: A Phenomenological Approach.* Ithaca: Cornell University Press, 1981.

———. "El *Quijote:* juego y significación." *Dispositio* 3 (Fall 1978): 315–36.

———. "Towards a Formal Ontology of Fictional Worlds." *Philosophy and Literature* 7 (October 1983): 182–95.

———. "La Unidad del *Quijote.*" *Dispositio* 2 (Summer–Fall 1977): 118–38.

Matejka, Ladislaw. "The Formal Method and Linguistics." In *Readings in Russian Poetics: Formalist and Structuralist Views,* 281–95. Ed. Ladislaw Matejka and Krystyna Pomorska. Cambridge, Mass.: MIT Press, 1971.

Matejka, Ladislaw, and Krystyna Pomorska, eds. *Readings in Russian Poetics: Formalist and Structuralist Views.* Cambridge, Mass.: MIT Press, 1971.

Maus, Katherine Eisman. "Taking Tropes Seriously: Language and Violence in Shakespeare's *Lucrece.*" *Shakespeare Quarterly* 37 (Spring 1986): 66–82.

Mazzotta, Giuseppe. *The World at Play in Boccaccio's "Decameron."* Princeton: Princeton University Press, 1986.

McAlindon, T[homas]. "Conrad's Organicist Philosophy of History." *Mosaic* 15 (September 1982): 27–41.

McHale, Brian. *Postmodernist Fiction.* London: Methuen, 1987.

———. "Telling Postmodern Stories." *Poetics Today* 9 (Autumn 1988): 545–71.

———. "'You Used to Know What These Words Mean': Misreading *Gravity's Rainbow.*" *Language and Style* 18 (Winter 1985): 93–118.

McKenna, Andrew. "After Bakhtin: On the Future of Laughter and Its History in France." *University of Ottawa Quarterly* 53 (January–March 1983): 67–82.

Merivale, Patricia. "Learning the Hard Way: Gothic Pedagogy in the Modern Romantic Quest." *Comparative Literature* 36 (Spring 1984): 146–61.

Merrel, Floyd. *Pararealities: The Nature of Our Fictions and How We Know Them.* Amsterdam: John Benjamins, 1983.

Miller, David L. "The Kingdom of Play: Some Old Theological Light from Recent Literature." *Union Seminary Quarterly* 25 (Spring 1970): 343–60.

Miller, J. Hillis. "Ariadne's Thread: Repetition and the Narrative Line." *Critical Inquiry* 3 (Autumn 1976): 57–77.

———. *Fiction and Repetition: Seven English Novels.* Cambridge, Mass.: Harvard University Press, 1982.

Miller, Stephen Nachmanovich. "The Playful, the Crazy, and the Nature of Pretense." *Rice University Studies* ["The Anthropological Study of Human Play," ed. Edward Norbeck] 60 (Summer 1974): 31–51.

Mistacco, Vicki. "The Theory and Practice of Reading Nouveaux Romans: Robbe-Grillet's *Topologie d'une cité fantôme.*" In *The Reader in the Text: Essays on Audience and Interpretation,* 371–400. Ed. Susan R. Suleiman and Inge Crosman. Princeton: Princeton University Press, 1980.

Mitchell, W. J. T. "Spatial Form in Literature: Toward a General Theory." *Critical Inquiry* 6 (Spring 1980): 539–67.

Moore, Brian. *The Great Victorian Collection.* Toronto: McClelland and Stewart, 1975.

Morgenstern, Oskar, and John von Neumann. *Theory of Games and Economic Behavior.* Princeton: Princeton University Press, 1944.

Morrison, Jim. *The Lords and the New Creatures: Poems.* New York: Simon and Schuster, 1987.

Morrissette, Bruce. *The Novels of Robbe-Grillet.* Ithaca: Cornell University Press, 1975.

Morson, Gary Saul. "The Heresiarch of *Meta.*" *PTL* 3 (October 1978): 407–27.

Morson, Gary Saul, ed. *Bakhtin: Essays and Dialogues on His Work.* Chicago: University of Chicago Press, 1986.

Motte, Warren F., Jr. *Oulipo: A Primer of Potential Literature.* Lincoln: University of Nebraska Press, 1986.

Murray, Gilbert. *The Classical Tradition in Poetry.* London: Oxford University Press, 1927.

Nabokov, Vladimir. *The Defense.* Trans. Michael Scammell. New York: Capricorn Books, 1970.

———. "The Visit to the Museum." In *Nabokov's Quartet,* 109–25. New York: Pyramid Books, 1966.

Nash, Christopher. *World-Games: The Tradition of Anti-Realist Revolt.* London: Methuen, 1987.

Needham, Rodney. *Exemplars.* Berkeley: University of California Press, 1985.

Neuwirth, Lee. "The Theory of Knots." *Scientific American* 240 (June 1979): 110–24.

Nicholls, Peter. *The Science in Science Fiction.* New York: Knopf, 1983.

Norbeck, Edward, ed. "The Anthropological Study of Human Play." *Rice University Studies* 60 (Summer 1974).

Olson, Elder. "On Value Judgments in the Arts." *Critical Inquiry* 1 (September 1974): 71–90.

Ortega y Gasset, José. *Meditations on the Quijote.* Trans. Evelyn Rugg and Diego Marín. New York: Norton, 1963.

Parker, Patricia. "Anagogic Metaphor: Breaking down the Wall of Partition." In *Centre and Labyrinth: Essays in Honour of Northrop Frye,* 38–50. Ed. Eleanor Cook et al. Toronto: University of Toronto Press, 1983.

———. "Deferral, Dilation, Différance: Shakespeare, Cervantes, Jonson." In *Literary Theory/Renaissance Texts,* 182–209. Ed. Patricia Parker and David Quint. Baltimore: Johns Hopkins University Press, 1986.

———. "Dilation and Delay: Renaissance Matrices." *Poetics Today* 5 (Autumn 1984): 519–35.

———. *Literary Fat Ladies: Rhetoric, Gender, Property.* London: Methuen, 1987.

———. "Shakespeare and Rhetoric: 'Dilation' and 'Delation' in *Othello.*" In *Shakespeare and the Question of Theory,* 54–74. Ed. Patricia Parker and Geoffrey Hartman. London: Methuen, 1985.

Pavel, Thomas G. *Fictional Worlds.* Cambridge, Mass.: Harvard University Press, 1986.

———. *The Poetics of Plot: The Case of English Renaissance Drama.* Minneapolis: University of Minnesota Press, 1985.

Pechter, Edward. "Of Ants and Grasshoppers: Two Ways (or More) to Link Texts and Power." *Poetics Today* 9 (Summer 1988): 291–306.

Petro, Peter. *Modern Satire: Four Studies.* Berlin: Mouton, 1982.

Piaget, Jean. *Six Psychological Studies.* Trans. Anita Tenzer. New York: Vintage Books, 1968.

Plato. *The Republic.* Trans. Benjamin Jowett. New York: Random House, 1937.

Poggioli, Renato. *The Oaten Flute: Essays on Pastoral Poetry and the Pastoral Ideal.* Cambridge, Mass.: Harvard University Press, 1975.

Poulet, Georges. *Proustian Space.* Trans. Elliott Coleman. Baltimore: Johns Hopkins University Press, 1977.

Pratt, Mary Louise. *Toward a Speech Act Theory of Literary Discourse.* Bloomington: Indiana University Press, 1977.

Prince, Gerald. *A Dictionary of Narratology.* Lincoln: University of Nebraska Press, 1987.

Propp, Vladimir. *Morphology of the Folktale.* Trans. Laurence Scott. Austin: University of Texas Press, 1975 [1968].

Putnam, Hilary. "Convention: A Theme in Philosophy." *New Literary History* 13 (Autumn 1981): 1–14.

Pynchon, Thomas. *The Crying of Lot 49.* New York: Bantam, 1967. [Philadelphia: Lippincott, 1966.]

———. *Gravity's Rainbow.* New York: Viking, 1973.

Quilligan, Maureen. *The Language of Allegory: Defining the Genre.* Ithaca: Cornell University Press, 1979.

Radar, Edmond. "A Genealogy: Play, Folklore, and Art." *Diogenes* 103 (Fall 1978): 78–99.

Radford, F. L., and R. R. Wilson. "Some Phases of the Jungian Moon: Jung's Influence on Modern Literature." *English Studies in Canada* 8 (September 1982): 311–32.

Rapoport, Anatol. *Fights, Games and Debates.* Ann Arbor: University of Michigan Press, 1960.

Rapoport, Anatol, ed. *Game Theory as a Theory of Conflict Resolution.* Dordrecht, Holland: D. Reidel, 1974.

Rath, Sura P. "Le Jeu et les jeux dans la fiction romanesque: Un nouveau paradigme de la critique." *Diogène* 136 (Oct.–Dec. 1986): 128–42.

Rath, Sura P., ed. "Game, Play, Literature" [special section]. *South Central Review* 3 (Winter 1986): 1–53.

Rawdon, Michael. "Ludopolites." *boundary 2* 15 (Fall 1986–Winter 1987): 323–42.

———. "Paracursions." In *Green Eyes, Dukes and Kings,* 41–53. Kingston, Ont.: Quarry Press, 1985.

Rawls, John. "Two Concepts of Rules." *Philosophical Review* 64 (1955): 3–32.

Ray, Satyajit. *The Chess Players* [*Shatranj Ke Khilari*]. Bombay: Devki Chitra, 1977. 133 minutes.

Redekop, Ernest H. "Labyrinths in Time and Space." *Mosaic* 13 (Spring–Summer 1980): 95–113.

Reeves, Charles Eric. "The Languages of Convention: Literature and Consensus." *Poetics Today* 7 (Spring 1986): 3–28.

Reynolds, Bonnie H., ed. "Games in Twentieth-Century Literature." *Perspectives on Contemporary Literature* 6 (1980): 3–142.

Riezler, Kurt. "Play and Seriousness." *Journal of Philosophy* 38 (September 1941): 505–17.

Riffaterre, Michael. "Syllepsis." *Critical Inquiry* 6 (Summer 1980): 625–38.

Robbe-Grillet, Alain. *L'Année dernière à Marienbad.* Paris: Editions de Minuit, 1961.

———. *Dans le labyrinth.* Paris: Editions de Minuit, 1959.

———. "Enigmes et tranparence chez Raymond Roussel." *Critique* 199 (December 1963): 1027–33.

———. *For a New Novel: Essays on Fiction.* Trans. Richard Howard. New York: Grove Press, 1965.

———. *Last Year at Marienbad.* Trans. Richard Howard. Picture ed. Robert Hughes. New York: Grove Press, 1962.

———. *Pour un nouveau roman.* Paris: Editions de Minuit, 1963.

———. *Two Novels by Robbe-Grillet: "Jealousy" and "In the Labyrinth."* Trans. Richard Howard. New York: Grove Press, 1965.

Rollin, Bernard E. "Nature, Convention, and Genre Theory." *Poetics* 10 (June 1981): 127–43.

Ronsand, David. "'Troyes Painted Woes': Shakespeare and the Pictorial Imagination." *Hebrew University Studies in Literature* 8 (1980): 77–97.

Rose, Margaret. *Parody/Metafiction: An Analysis of Parody as a Critical Mirror to the Writing and Reception of Fiction.* London: Croom Helm, 1979.

Royston, Pamela L. "Unraveling the Ecphrasis in Chapman's *Hero and Leander.*" *South Atlantic Review* 49 (November 1984): 43–53.

Santarcangeli, Paulo. "The Jester and the Madman, Heralds of Liberty and Truth." *Diogenes* 106 (Summer 1979): 28–40.

Santayana, George. "Carnival." In *Soliloquies in England and Later Soliloquies,* 139–44. New York: Charles Scribner's Sons, 1924.

Schiller, Friedrich. *On the Aesthetic Education of Man in a Series of Letters.* Trans. E. M. Wilkinson and L. A. Willoughby. Oxford: Clarendon Press, 1967.

Schleusener, Jay. "Convention and the Context of Reading." *Critical Inquiry* 6 (Summer 1980): 669–80.

Scholes, Robert. *Fabulation and Metafiction.* Urbana: University of Illinois Press, 1979.

Schulte, Hansgerd. *Spiele und Vorspiele: Spiel-elemente in Literatur, Wissenschaft und Philosophie.* Frankfurt: Suhrkamp, 1978.

Searle, John. *Expression and Meaning: Studies in the Theory of Speech Acts.* Cambridge: Cambridge University Press, 1979.

———. *Speech Acts: An Essay in the Philosophy of Language.* Cambridge: Cambridge University Press, 1969.

Sebeok, Thomas A., ed. *Style in Language.* Cambridge, Mass.: MIT Press, 1960.

Shaïtane. *Carnaval.* Paris: Editions Fernand Nathan, 1979.

Shakespeare, William. *The Riverside Shakespeare.* 6th ed. Ed. G. Blakemore Evans. Boston: Houghton Mifflin, n. d. [1974].

Sheridan, Alan. *Michel Foucault: The Will to Truth.* London: Tavistock, 1981 [1980].

Sicard, Alain. "*Homo Ludens:* L'Homme en jeu." *L'Arc* 80 (1980): 17–23.

Silverman, Hugh J., and Donn Welton, eds. *Postmodernism and Continental Philosophy.* Albany: State University of New York Press, 1988.

Singer, Alan. *A Metaphorics of Fiction: Discontinuity and Discourse in the Modern Novel.* Tallahassee: Florida State University Press, 1984.

Singer, Jerome L. *The Child's World of Make-Believe: Experimental Studies of Imaginative Play.* New York: Academic Press, 1973.

Skura, Meredith Anne. *The Literary Use of the Psychoanalytic Process.* New Haven: Yale University Press, 1981.

Smith, Barbara Herrnstein. "Narrative Versions, Narrative Theories." *Critical Inquiry* 7 (Autumn 1980): 213–36.

———. *On the Margins of Discourse.* Chicago: University of Chicago Press, 1978.

Smith, Hallett. *Elizabethan Poetry: A Study in Conventions, Meanings and Expressions.* Cambridge, Mass.: Harvard University Press, 1964.

Smithyman, Kendrick. "The Commonwealth Experience, the Common Response." *Journal of Commonwealth Literature* 6 (June 1971): 6–18.

Smitten, Jeffrey R. "Approaches to the Spatiality of Narrative." *Papers on Language and Literature* 14 (Summer 1978): 296–314.

Sontag, Susan. *Against Interpretation and Other Essays.* New York: Dell, 1961.

Spariosu, Mihai. *Literature, Mimesis and Play: Essays in Literary Theory.* Tübingen: Gunter Narr Verlag, 1982.

Spengler, Oswald. *The Decline of the West.* Trans. Charles Francis Atkinson. New York: Knopf, 1932.

Spenser, Edmund. *The Poetical Works of Edmund Spenser.* Ed. J. C. Smith and E. de Sélincourt. Oxford: Oxford University Press, 1966 [1912].

———. *The Works of Edmund Spenser: A Variorum Edition.* 10 vols. Ed. Edwin Greenlaw et al. Baltimore: Johns Hopkins University Press, 1932–1949.

Steele, Peter. *The Autobiographical Passion: Studies in the Self on Show.* Melbourne: Melbourne University Press, 1989.

———. *Jonathan Swift: Preacher and Jester.* Oxford: Clarendon Press, 1978.

Steiner, George. *Extraterritorial: Papers on Literature and the Language of Revolution.* New York: Atheneum, 1971.

———. "Introduction." In Johan Huizinga, *Homo Ludens: A Study of the Play Element in Culture.* London: Paladin-Granada, 1970.

———. *Language and Silence: Essays on Language, Literature, and the Inhuman.* New York: Atheneum, 1967.

———. *On Difficulty and Other Essays.* New York: Oxford University Press, 1978.

Stewart, Susan. *Nonsense: Aspects of Intertextuality in Folklore and Literature.* Baltimore: Johns Hopkins University Press, 1978.

———. *On Longing: Narratives of the Miniature, the Gigantic, the Souvenir, the Collection.* Baltimore: Johns Hopkins University Press, 1984.

———. "Shouts on the Street: Bakhtin's Anti-Linguistics." In *Bakhtin: Essays and Dialogues on His Work,* 41–57. Ed. Gary Saul Morson. Chicago: University of Chicago Press, 1986.

Strauss, Anselm, ed. *The Social Psychology of George Herbert Mead.* Chicago: University of Chicago Press, 1956.

Suits, Bernard. "The Detective Story: A Case Study of Games in Literature." *Canadian Review of Comparative Literature* 12 (June 1985): 200–219.

———. *The Grasshopper: Games, Life and Utopia.* Toronto: University of Toronto Press, 1978.

———. "What is a Game?" *Philosophy of Science* 34 (1969): 48–56.

Swinfen, Ann. *In Defence of Fantasy: A Study of the Genre in English and*

American Literature since 1945. London: Routledge & Kegan Paul, 1984.

Szabó, Istvan. *Square.* Budapest: Budapest Film Studios, 1963. 35mm, color, 5 minutes.

Thiher, Allen. *Words in Reflection: Modern Language Theory and Postmodern Fiction.* Chicago: University of Chicago Press, 1984.

Thompson, Clive, ed. "The Work of Mikhail Bakhtin (1895–1975)" [special issue]. *University of Ottawa Quarterly* 53 (January–March 1983): 5–131.

Todorov, Tzetvan. *The Fantastic: A Structural Approach to a Literary Genre.* Trans. Richard Howard. Ithaca: Cornell University Press, 1975.

———. *Mikail Bakhtine: Le principe dialogique.* Paris: Editions du Seuil, 1981.

———. *The Poetics of Prose.* Trans. Richard Howard. Ithaca: Cornell University Press, 1977.

Toliver, Harold. *Pastoral Forms and Attitudes.* Berkeley: University of California Press, 1971.

Traux, Elizabeth. "'Lucrece! What hath your conceited painter wrought?'" In *Shakespeare: Contemporary Critical Approaches,* 13–30. Ed. Harry R. Garvin. Lewisburg, Pa.: Bucknell University Press, 1980.

Valéry, Paul. *Oeuvres,* vol. I. Ed. Jean Hytier. Paris: Bibliothèque de la Pléiade–Editions Gallimard, 1957.

van Herk, Aritha. *A Frozen Tongue.* Aarhus, Denmark: Dangaroo Press, 1989.

Vickers, Brian. "Epideictic and Epic in the Renaissance." *New Literary History* 14 (Spring 1983): 497–537.

Vygotsky, L. S. *Mind in Society: The Development of Higher Psychological Processes.* Ed. and trans. Michael Cole et al. Cambridge, Mass.: Harvard University Press, 1978.

Walton, Kendall L. "Fearing Fictions." *Journal of Philosophy* 75 (January 1978): 5–27.

———. "How Remote are Fictional Worlds from the Real World?" *Journal of Aesthetics and Art Criticism* 37 (Fall 1978): 11–23.

———. "Pictures and Make-Believe." *Philosophical Review* 82 (July 1973): 283–319.

Waugh, Patricia. *Metafiction: The Theory and Practice of Self-Conscious Fiction.* London: Methuen, 1984.

Weinberg, Helen. *The New Novel in America: The Kafkan Mode in Contemporary Fiction.* Ithaca: Cornell University Press, 1970.

Weinsheimer, Joel C. *Gadamer's Hermeneutics: A Reading of "Truth and Method."* New Haven: Yale University Press, 1985.

———. "Theory of Character: *Emma.*" *Poetics Today* 1 (Autumn 1979): 185–211.

Welsh, Alexander. *Reflections on the Hero as Quixote.* Princeton: Princeton University Press, 1981.

Wheelock, Carter. *The Mythmaker: A Study of Motif and Symbol in the*

Short Stories of Jorge Luis Borges. Austin: University of Texas Press, 1969.

White, Hayden. *Tropics of Discourse.* Baltimore: Johns Hopkins University Press, 1978.

Whyte, Jon. *Open Spaces.* Banff, Alta.: Peter Whyte Gallery, 1977.

Wilson, R. R. "Drawing New Lessons from Old Masters: The Concept of Character in the *Quijote.*" *Modern Philology* 78 (November 1980): 117–38.

———. "Godgames and Labyrinths: The Logic of Entrapment." *Mosaic* 14 (December 1982): 1–22.

———. "Review of Alexander Welsh's *Reflections on the Hero as Quixote.*" *Modern Philology* 82 (August 1984): 120–24.

———. "Robert Kroetsch." In *Dictionary of Literary Biography,* vol. 53, 240–55. Ed. W. H. New. Detroit: Bruccoli Clark–Gale, 1986.

———. "Shakespearean Narrative: *The Rape of Lucrece* Reconsidered." *SEL* 28 (1988): 39–59.

———. "The *Struthiomimus*'s Tale: Discourse in the Tyrrell Museum." *Alberta: Studies in the Arts and Sciences* 1 (1988): 75–95.

———. "Three Prolusions: Toward a Game Model in Literary Theory." *Canadian Review of Comparative Literature* 8 (Winter 1981): 79–92.

Wilson, R. R., ed. "Game and the Theories of Game/*Jeu et théories des jeux*" [special issue]. *Canadian Review of Comparative Literature* 12 (June 1985): 177–370.

Wimsatt, W. K. "Belinda Ludens: Strife and Play in *The Rape of the Lock.*" *New Literary History* 4 (Winter 1973): 357–74.

———. "How to Compose Chess Problems and Why." *Yale French Studies* 41 (1968): 68–85.

Wittgenstein, Ludwig. *Philosophical Investigations.* Trans. G. E. M. Anscombe. Oxford: Basil Blackwell, 1953.

Yaeger, Patricia. *Honey-Mad Women: Emancipatory Strategies in Women's Writing.* New York: Columbia University Press, 1988.

Young, Robert, ed. *Untying the text: A Post-Structuralist Reader.* Boston: Routledge & Kegan Paul, 1981.

Zoran, Gabriel. "Towards a Theory of Space in Narrative." *Poetics Today* 5 (Summer 1984): 309–35.

Index